FILM

THE CRITICS' CHOICE

FILM
THE CRITICS' CHOICE

**150 masterpieces
of world cinema
selected and defined
by the experts**

Edited by Geoff Andrew

AURUM PRESS

First published in Great Britain in 2001 by

Aurum Press Ltd

25 Bedford Avenue

London WC1B 3AT

ISBN: 1 85410 798 4

10 9 8 7 6 5 4 3 2 1

2005 2004 2003 2002 2001

This book was conceived, designed and produced by

The Ivy Press Limited

The Old Candlemakers

West Street

Lewes

East Sussex

BN7 2NZ

Creative Director: Peter Bridgewater

Publisher: Sophie Collins

Editorial Director: Steve Luck

DTP Designer: Angela Neal

Designers: Alan Osbahr and Tony Seddon

Editors: Sarah Polden and Stephanie Driver

Project Editor: Rowan Davies

Picture Researcher: Vanessa Fletcher

This book is set in 10/15 Helvetica Light

Originated and printed by Hong Kong Graphics and Printing Ltd, in China

contents

Foreword   6
Bernardo Bertolucci

Introduction   14
Geoff Andrew

CHAPTER ONE   **The Silent Era**   20
                       David Bordwell

CHAPTER TWO   **America: The Studio Years**   52
                       David Thomson

CHAPTER THREE   **America: Years of Change**   84
                       Philip French

CHAPTER FOUR   **America: The Modern Era**   116
                       Amy Taubin and Kent Jones

CHAPTER FIVE   **Europe: The Golden Age**   148
                       Gilbert Adair

CHAPTER SIX   **Europe: New Waves**   180
                       Jonathan Rosenbaum

CHAPTER SEVEN   **Europe: A New Fin de siècle**   212
                       Jonathan Romney

CHAPTER EIGHT   **British Cinema**   244
                       Peter Wollen

CHAPTER NINE   **International Cinema**   276
                       Tony Rayns

CHAPTER TEN   **The Art of The Impossible**   308
                       Paul Wells

Glossary   340

Index   344

Acknowledgements   352

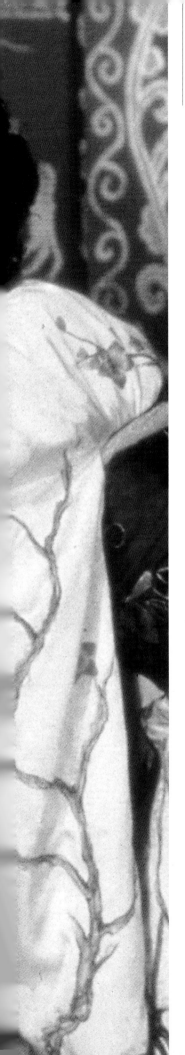

Bernardo Bertolucci

I wonder if Sir Ernst Gombrich's famous words about art, from his seminal book *The Story of Art*, can be applied to the cinema: *There really is no such thing as cinema. There are only filmmakers*.

In fact, my own point of view is quite the opposite: that cinema exists in and of itself. Richly nourished by every other language that preceded it – poetry, painting, music, literature, dance, photography, liturgy, architecture, theatre, sculpture, journalism, fashion and – later – television – it was cinema's productive, voracious belly that gave birth to filmmakers.

From this perspective, in *Film: The Critics' Choice* the cinephile will be able to celebrate the paradox that filmmakers can coexist so harmoniously despite the vast gulfs that separate them. And the book may inspire the reader to dream up strange and seemingly impossible connections between the likes of Renoir and John Woo, Dovzhenko and Hammer Films; Ozu and Lucio Fulci, Ophüls and Mike Leigh; John Ford and Jerry Lewis, Wong Kar-Wai and the Carry On films. It will become obvious to the reader that being a film director involves, in rather mysterious ways, a constant process of exchange, borrowing and giving back.

Topsy Turvy (Mike Leigh, 1999)

In the beginning, cinema, like any newborn baby, didn't know how to speak. Deprived of vocal cords, it expressed itself through visionary imagery, like a drunken oracle. A little later, cinema found its voice, not merely the modulation of *la voix humaine* but all the sounds of the world: the wind, the sea, sirens, trains. Then it discovered colour, the drug that brought film closer to real life, and cinema adopted the cruel, direct language of reality. Reality chose to express itself through film. At this point cinema began to look inwards at itself. We are now in the early sixties, and this is where my memories begin.

As a 20-year-old, the early films of Godard seemed to me the ultimate proof of the death of God and of the conventional *cinéma de papa*. This is it, I thought, experiencing almost a terrorist's satisfaction: cinema has finally become aware of itself. Throughout the sixties, which seemed to last forever, our films celebrated the marriage of an obsession with style with political passion (I am thinking here of works by auteurs of my generation such as Glauber Rocha, Straub-Huillet, Robert Kramer, Gianni Amico and Jean Eustache among many others). We don't make many films, we left-wing conspirators told ourselves, but to make up for it we made a lot of cinema. We were extremely sure of everything, we were the representatives of the parallel counterculture.

8

Les Vacances de Monsieur Hulot (Jacques Tati, 1953)

Here are two or three things I *knew* about cinema: *every camera movement is a moral statement; to prevent a film from being too literary, I never look at the script on set – instead I work using my memory of the script, like a blind man feeling his way around the furniture in his house; and, to me, the camera is like a musical instrument – one could, paradoxically, make a musical without music, relying only on the musical sensuousness of the camera's movements.* In other words, our films were high on theory but low on communication.

It wasn't until the seventies that I first engaged with the public. I was greatly inspired by Roland Barthes' *Le Plaisir du texte*. In those days, *pleasure* was not considered fashionable; indeed, we on the left saw it as a vaguely right-wing feeling. But I made Barthes' dream my own; I would like my films to say to each viewer, *'I love you, I desire you, I want to possess you and be possessed by you'*. Through this relationship between the film and the viewer, multiplied millions of times over, the positions of the camera become positions in an art of love which I call *Kamerasutra*. I discovered communication, and communication became ecstasy. And so the circle begins to close.

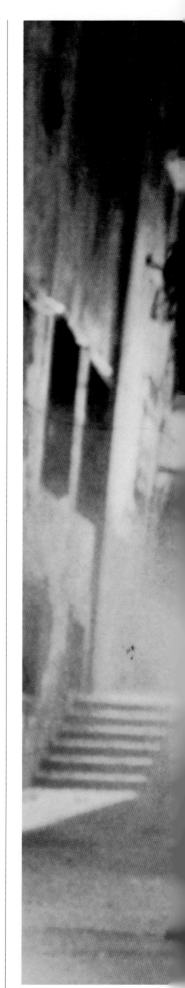

Recollections of the Yellow House (João César Monteiro, 1989)

The end of the millennium has triggered new changes in the world of cinema, a mutation more dramatic than any I've mentioned. Very soon film stock will disappear to be replaced by something revolutionary; perhaps it will be in digital format, or perhaps what we once called film will be contained in a microchip smaller than a pinhead. And the cinema, which we have raised onto a pedestal as if it meant everything, will again become simply one element in the larger scheme of things. Facing such a prospect, I can now confess that, whereas in recent years part of me had come to experience a secret dissatisfaction with the medium, I once again begin to feel a sense of hope.

Bernardo Bertolucci

Rome

November 2000

Toy Story (John Lasseter, 1995)

Geoff Andrew

Film, it is said, was *the* twentieth-century art form. But what is meant by this? That it was the most important, influential, rapidly maturing art-form of that era, but also that its history was virtually contemporaneous with the century. Moving pictures strung together to tell stories were first shown as entertainment to paying audiences in the mid-1890s; now, just over 100 years later, with digital technology set to affect not only the way films are made but how they are sold, sent around the globe, shown and (in the widest sense) seen, cinema is facing dramatic changes. At this stage, no-one can predict precisely what these changes will entail; few, however, would deny that we are on the brink of a seismic shift in the way movies are created and consumed.

The Awful Truth (Leo McCary, 1937)

It is timely, then, to look back over that brief but often brilliant history. Countless books already do this, of course, each with its own perspective, ideology or area of interest: chronological, national, political, biographical, technological, generic, auteurist, feminist, sociological, psychoanalytical, or simply gushing fan fare. Indeed, it sometimes seems there is now too much written about film – and far too little is good. Which is why this book exists. *Film: The Critics' Choice* looks at 150 of the finest achievements in cinema. At one stage or another, it draws upon most of the methodologies mentioned above, but it does so with admirable economy. The book also gathers together some of the very best writers on film. All know a great deal about cinema as a whole, but each also has a special enthusiasm for the area of film he or she is writing about. Moreover – and this, like a proper under-standing of film history, is increasingly rare – they can write.

In this rather special volume, then, some of the greatest films ever made – many well-known classics, others undeservedly obscure – are examined in a way that is informed, illuminating and unashamedly personal. The only instructions given about the selection of favourites were that each writer should keep to his or her particular territory, should not choose more than one film by any director, and that no film could feature in more than one chapter. That left leeway: Lang and Hitchcock appear in three chapters, Godard in two;

Psycho (Alfred Hitchcock, 1960)

although none of the contributors includes a documentary as such, several come close with films it would be inaccurate to describe as purely fictional; some include films about which their feelings are openly mixed; almost all chose at least one film which some readers may feel is 'off the wall'.

Finally, if there is a bias towards American and European cinema, that merely reflects what you are most likely to be able to see in the West. The chapters on non-Western cinema and animation derive from our recognition of their artistic value and cultural importance and of the difficulty of seeing such work in a world dominated, economically if not artistically, by Hollywood. Hopefully, this book will not only (re)introduce you to some truly glorious movies, but suggest precisely why you should become better acquainted with Portuguese cinema, Taiwanese film or the very earliest silents. All it needs is open eyes and an open mind: the riches of film await you.

Geoff Andrew

London

January 2001

A Touch of Zen (King Hu, 1969–71)

MAIN: *King Vidor's*
The Big Parade *(1925)*.
FAR LEFT: *V. I. Pudovkin's*
Mother *(1926)*.
MIDDLE LEFT: *William S.*
Porter's The Great Train
Robbery *(1903)*.
LEFT: *Abel Gance's*
Napoléon *(1927)*.

CHAPTER ONE

The Silent Era
David Bordwell

An amalgam of optics, chemistry and precision machining, cinema was a characteristically 19th-century invention. The illusory representation of movement through optical toys and magic-lantern shows had charmed audiences for decades; in the late 1880s, Emile Reynaud ran cartoon drawings on a ribbon of paper past a light source and bounced the images onto a screen, while, slightly earlier, rapid-exposure photography had appeared which enabled tinkerers like Jules-Etienne Marey and Eadweard Muybridge to dissect the movement of birds in flight or horses at a gallop. The sewing machine and the machine gun had shown how a strip of material could be shuttled past a fixed point, and after Marey and others had sliced up sheets of celluloid for their experiments, the photographic companies of Eastman and Lumière began producing standardized strips of flexible film stock. By 1895, cinema as we know it was technically feasible.

Just as characteristic of the 19th century was cinema's heady mix of domestic and urban imagery, and of high art and popular culture. In the movies, photographic and painterly traditions mingled, as did the conventions of opera and vaudeville, melodrama and the serialized novel. Cinema was employed to document daily life and historic events, to record striking performances and to tell stories on a scale hitherto unknown.

The 1910s and 1920s represented the golden age of the silent film. With technical developments now coming thick and fast, cinephiles could appreciate the way in which the medium was growing in sophistication. Editing, they felt, was what distinguished the cinema from all other media, particularly the theatre. After the primitive years of simply recording movement, directors like William S. Porter discovered how to tell a story through a string of shots, as in *The Great Train Robbery* (1903). Next came Griffith, who refined and extended Porter's discoveries with cross-cutting and close-ups. The 1920s played host to experimenters like Abel Gance, whose *La Roue* (1923) perfected rhythmic cutting, and the Soviet documentarist Dziga Vertov, whose *Man with a Movie Camera* (1928) was an eccentric display of everything editing could accomplish.

Neat as this story is, many critics and historians today are sceptical about it. They say that many 'classics' were simply lucky enough to be widely seen or to have been preserved. Sjöström's incandescent *Ingeborg Holm* (1913) was unknown to many critics who praised his internationally distributed *The Outlaw and His Wife* (1917). Robert Wiene's *The Cabinet of Dr Caligari* (1920) does not look so innovative alongside Robert Reinert's *Nerven*, released two months before, but *Nerven* was ignored for 80 years. Besides, researchers argue, cinema has no single essence that unfolds and is revealed with time: the rich tradition of deep-space staging dates from the first reels and shows that a film does not need florid editing to be captivating. Finally, historians now often trace the avenues not taken, the intriguing films that refuse to fit the standard story. Although 1920s theorists thought that 'pure film' should avoid language, Dekeukelaire's *Histoire du détective* (1929) is built around banal images and over-long intertitles.

The canon is always under reconstruction, so any list of silent classics (such as that included in this chapter) forms only one path into an era of explosive creativity. In these years filmmakers probed the expressive possibilities of moving images in fundamental and far-reaching ways.

Short Films Lumière company *1895–1905*

Although cinema-like contraptions were invented in several countries at the end of the 19th century, the work of only two entrepreneurs combined technical feasibility with practical show-business. In the United States Thomas Edison's Kinetoscope began as a peepshow in 1893, while in France Louis and Auguste Lumière devised a means of projecting moving images to several spectators. The Cinématographe had its premiere for a paying public at a café on 28 December 1895. Happily, the brothers' name means 'light'.

Under their father, the Lumière firm was Europe's leading manufacturer of photographic plates. Fascinated by the experiments in decomposed motion undertaken by Emile Reynaud and Jules-Etienne Marey, and asked to contrive something that would compete with the Kinetoscope, the brothers designed an apparatus that was far simpler and more portable than Edison's bulky camera. Their camera could also serve as a projector.

Their earliest films, which showed workers leaving the factory, Auguste and his family having a meal, and a train arriving at La Ciotat station near the family home, were evidently shot by Louis himself. When the demand for these brief moving snapshots swelled (they ran no longer than 40 seconds), the company hired cameramen to tour the world, introducing the product to new markets while photographing exotic scenes for future circulation. By 1898 the firm's catalogue boasted more than 1000 titles. Many countries, from Spain and Russia to Japan and Egypt, trace the origins of their national cinema back to Lumière shows.

From the start, the reels were a mix of fiction and documentary. There were *actualités*, records from life: cockfights, boxing matches, bathers in seascapes, international expositions and conferences, and – endlessly – people boarding and stepping off boats and trains. Some of the scenes are sheer home-movie material – flamingos in a fountain, a charming image of a Lumière daughter teasing her pet cat – while others were wholly contrived, such as episodes from the life of Christ or, most famously, the skit showing a mischievous boy stepping on a gardener's hose (*L'Arroseur arrosé*, originally *Arroseur and arrosé,* 1895). The Lumière films preserve the mundane events of turn-of-the-century life while also recording what the public thought was either grotesque or amusing.

Edison shot many of his films in his Black Maria, a dark, crude studio; but by plunging into life, the Lumière cameramen made visual discoveries. Their frames teem with action, opening onto vibrating patches of sunshine and an apparently infinite depth of field which gives an ordinary street or pier or lawn a gorgeous tangibility. Many operators instinctively chose expressive, energetic angles. Shot from an oblique position rather than a perpendicular one, the La Ciotat train comes looming towards us while passengers bustle through the frame in layer after layer. The refilmings of *L'Arroseur arrosé* themselves offer a suite of instructive variations for later film-makers on how to stage a simple action. The slow orthochromatic stock and the wire-sharp lenses yield images that do more than capture the mores of 100 years ago. Drenched in light, the Lumière moving pictures present a world at once crisp and fluid, solid and phantasmic, which would henceforth be the world of the cinema.

A record from life; L'Arrivee d'un train en gare de La Ciotat, *shot by Louis Lumière, 1895.*

A Trip to the Moon
Une Voyage dans la lune

Georges Méliès *1902*

Director and producer
Georges Méliès

In 1896, a stage conjuror named Georges Méliès decided to show films at his Parisian theatre. The Lumières refused to sell him a Cinématographe so he obtained a British projector and reverse-engineered his own camera. Soon his theatre was screening his own productions. He made films in all the genres of the time, including 'scenics' showing picturesque locations, tableaux of the life of Christ, and even reconstructed 'documentaries' showing the arrest of Dreyfus or the sinking of the *Maine*. He is best remembered, however, for his prodigious output of fantasy films, which combine traditions of stage magic and theatrical spectacle with captivating cinematic invention.

Méliès starts from a simple situation, an artist painting a model, an inn where no man can rest, or just a nondescript parlour set, and squeezes from it a torrent of tricks and stunts. Ghosts, devils, mermaids and Valkyries descend on hapless victims. Characters vanish or transmogrify into someone else. A face swells to fill a room. A compère takes off his head and tosses it up to a musical staff, where it hovers as a note and sings; then the compère does it again and again until a whole tune is laid out above him, each note a clone of his smiling face. Played at a breakneck pace, the bustle usually springs from Méliès himself, who glances towards us for approval, brazenly pointing at the chaos he has created and cackling in delight. The effect is of a benevolent sprite bent on twisting the world to his whim.

As a man of the magic theatre, Méliès made use of trap doors, trick sets and mirrors, but he also discovered some cinematic resources, most notably stop-motion. He became masterful in halting the action and stopping the camera and then replacing the performer or changing the set before starting to crank up again. To make the transformations smoother, he snipped out frames. When a clown leaps up and changes into a gentleman in mid-air, editing, carefully calculated to seem invisible, is doing its work.

A Trip to the Moon harvests the fruits of many years of trick work but also tells what was, for its day, an unusually complex story. A corps of scientists is packed into a space capsule and shot to the moon where they are captured by creatures living beneath the surface. Méliès had used editing to link shots into a complete story in previous films (notably *Cinderella* of 1899) but here he shows a richer understanding of plotting and pacing, as well as a wry sense of the absurdity of the whole enterprise: the capsule is fed into the cannon by a line of nautical showgirls staring into the camera, and the landing is presented as a punch in the moon's eye. Méliès' fortunes slowly declined until he went out of business in 1913, but what survives from the more than 500 films he made remains a treasure of fervid, unpretentious cinematic imagination.

Writer
Georges Méliès, from the
novel by Jules Verne

Cinematographers
Michaut and Lucien Tainguy

Production company
Star Films

Production designer
Georges Méliès

Cast
Victor André
Bleuette Bernon
Henri Delannoy
Depierre
Georges Méliès

Other films
★ *L'Affaire Dreyfus* (1899)
★ *Un Homme à la tête de caoutchouc* (1901)
★ *Faust en enfers* (1903)
★ *Les Aventures de Baron de Munchausen* (1911)

The chorines load the capsule into the cannon, in a typically absurd flight of fantasy from Méliès.

Ingeborg Holm
Victor Sjöström *1913*

Director
Victor Sjöström

Cinematographer
Henrik Jaenzon

A middle-class shopkeeper leads a happy life with his family, but when he dies his wife Ingeborg must struggle to support their children. She is forced to sell the shop and they are all sent to the poorhouse. Her son and daughter are given up for adoption, and although she escapes to try to see them, she is captured and returns in despair. Years later, her son arrives to discover that his mother has gone mad; only the sight of him briefly restores the memory of what she has lost.

Based on a play which Sjöström had staged some years before but with little success, the film was a triumph both commercially and critically, and many historians believe that it marked the moment at which the Swedish cinema came of age. The story of *Ingeborg Holm* might seem the epitome of melodrama, the kind of film that many viewers today associate with the crudeness of early cinema, yet the work, which is certainly overpowering in its emotional appeal, is a landmark in what was emerging as a distinctly European approach to film technique.

The performances, principally that of Hilda Borgström as the widowed protagonist, have none of the histrionics we expect from early theatrical adaptations. Sjöström, himself a successful stage actor, began directing for the Swedish company Svenska Biografteatern in 1912, and the surviving films from his early years display a delicacy of performance that still seems utterly fresh. Everything is conveyed through small gestures and slight glances. In one of *Ingeborg Holm*'s most affecting moments, Borgström must act entirely with her back. Standing in a courtyard, turned from the camera, she watches her son being taken away by a foster mother; as he pauses to look back, still turned from us, she dodges behind a wall to spare him the sight of her anguish.

At first glance, the lack of cutting – with most scenes played out in long takes and the actors seen nearly full-figure – looks old-fashioned. But as an alternative to the swift editing which was emerging in the American cinema, European filmmakers worked on developing meticulous compositions and choreography in depth. Each time we return to the family's shop, either the camera has been shifted or the props have been rearranged, so that early scenes emphasize the well-stocked shelves while later ones highlight the discarded cash register. When Ingeborg bids farewell to her children, her body blocks other performers, allowing us to concentrate on her face. But when a foster mother arrives, Ingeborg moves gently aside and buries her face in her daughter's shoulder, allowing the new character to catch our eye.

In the 1920s, European filmmakers would accept Hollywood's cutting-based approach; after several more striking films, notably *The Outlaw and His Wife* (1917) and *The Sons of Ingmar* (1918), Sjöström himself went to Hollywood and created such masterworks as *The Wind* (1928). Yet *Ingeborg Holm* remains a potent reminder of how nuances of feeling could arise and build in an unhurried, deeply absorbing rhythm. This subtle, supple theatricality proved a triumph for the art of cinema.

Writer
Victor Sjöström, from the
play by Nils Krook

Production company
Svenska Biografteatern

Cast
Hilda Borgström
Aron Lindgren
Erik Linhölm

Other films
★ *The Outlaw and his Wife* (1917)
★ *The Sons of Ingmar* (1918)
★ *The Scarlet Letter* (1926)
★ *The Wind* (1928)
★ *Under the Red Robe* (1937)

Hilda Borgström's luminous performance as the eponymous heroine marked the coming of age of Swedish cinema.

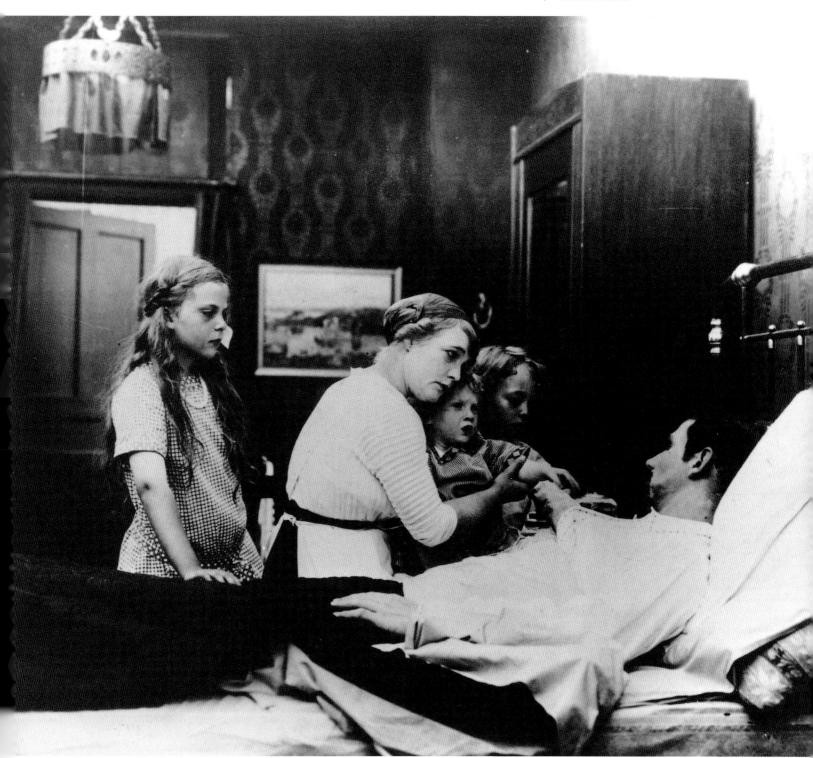

The Birth of a Nation D. W. Griffith *1915*

Director
D. W. Griffith

Producers
D. W. Griffith and Harry Aitken

Contrary to legend, Griffith did not invent close-ups, backlighting, tracking shots or cross-cutting. He did not father film language as we know it; his own style was somewhat idiosyncratic compared to work by younger directors. Yet in several of his Biograph short films (which ran for 15 minutes or so), such as *The Lonedale Operator* (1911), and *The Musketeers of Pig Alley* (1912), and above all in his monumental works later in the decade, he invented the modern movie. After *The Birth of a Nation* cinema was never the same.

The young Griffith barnstormed his way through stock companies before beginning to direct for the American Biograph company in 1908, just as longer and more complex films were becoming popular. Over the next five years he made over 400 one- and two-reelers (15 and 30 minutes in length). After leaving Biograph he wrote, directed and produced *The Birth of a Nation*, a three-hour epic about the American Civil War and its aftermath. The film's stupendous success – it remains, in relative terms, one of the highest-grossing films of all time – led to race riots, the revival of the Ku Klux Klan, and legitimacy for the young art of the motion picture.

A stalwart son of Kentucky, Griffith based his script on a virulently racist novel and play. The Cameron family live contentedly with their slaves, while in Washington the abolitionist Austin Stoneman keeps a mulatto mistress and befriends a power-hungry black man. Romances between the Cameron and Stoneman youngsters are blooming when war erupts. After the war, Congress launches a brutal reconstruction policy, and Colonel Cameron founds the Ku Klux Klan and takes back his town from freed slaves.

The film's bigotry remains all the more disturbing because Griffith gives us an engrossing, sometimes electrifying, piece of storytelling. He proved resolutely experimental, lending his action a novelistic scope and density. The plot assembles a remarkably large cast of characters, each individualized in a few strokes and swiftly woven into an intelligible historical fabric. The pace is deliberate at first but picks up commandingly when the Southern troops march off to war. The battle scenes have an unprecedented sweep, the assassination of Lincoln is a primer in suspense cutting, and the finale, with the Klan thundering to the rescue of besieged farmers, can still thrill an audience. Yet Griffith, also adept at pastoral lyricism, also provides many deeply poignant moments. A trip through the fields provides a chance for the Little Colonel to playfully take the cameo of Elsie from her brother. He will carry this into battle and then into the hospital where, miraculously, he will meet her. Returning home, he is reunited with his disillusioned sister, and the two stare into the distance, each locked in memories, before their mother's arms enfold them on the threshold.

Griffith's kinetic and lyrical gifts would later serve other melodramatic plots, especially in *Intolerance* (1916), *Broken Blossoms* (1919) and *Way Down East* (1920). Yet *The Birth of a Nation* remained the American cinema's benchmark of the naked power, for art and for social influence, of the new medium.

Writers
D. W. Griffith and Frank E.
Woods, from the novel by
Thomas F. Dixon

Production company
Epoch/D. W. Griffith
Corporation

Cinematographer
G. W. Bitzer

Cast
Henry B. Walthall
Mae Marsh
Lillian Gish
Ralph Lewis
Miriam Cooper
Mary Allen

Other films
★ *Intolerance* (1916)
★ *Broken Blossoms* (1919)
★ *Way Down East* (1920)
★ *Orphans of the Storm* (1921)
★ *Sally of the Sawdust* (1925)
★ *The Struggle* (1931)

The Ku Klux Klan ride into battle against Piedmont's black militia. Despite the racism of the piece, it is one of the acknowledged classics of the early cinema.

Les Vampires
Louis Feuillade *1915–16*

Director and writer
Louis Feuillade

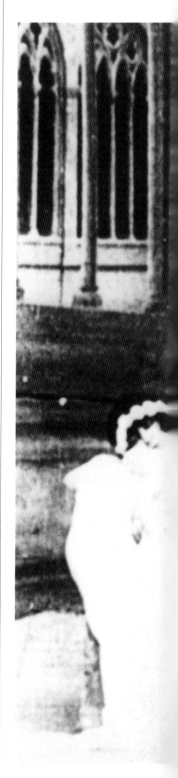

Like Griffith, Louis Feuillade began his career just when production companies were realizing that films could be longer and more intricately plotted. But instead of creating an independent firm as Griffith did, Feuillade remained steadfastly loyal to his first employer, Léon Gaumont, the only rival to the French film giant Charles Pathé. Working loyally for Gaumont, Feuillade proved to be a pioneer of unpretentious, engaging mass-market cinema.

Hired by Gaumont in 1906, Feuillade quickly rose from scenario writer to supervisor of his Paris studio. His position entailed purchased scripts, overseeing productions and directing at least 500 films. Through a combination of prodigality and natural talent, during these years he became the most popular filmmaker in France. In the last year of the First World War Feuillade moved to Nice, where he reigned over his troupe until his death in 1925.

His energy was boundless. Working with a cane clutched in both hands (handy for splintering in a fit of rage), Feuillade shot with a speed remarkable even for that era. Employees who could not keep up were sacked; a sick actor might return to find himself written out of the plot.

Feuillade cranked out films in every conceivable genre, including comedies, biblical pageants, melodramas and crime thrillers. Gaumont awarded him a bonus for every foot of film he finished (which was another spur to his rapid output), but Feuillade also felt compelled to satisfy the public. He believed that, for the ordinary moviegoer, 'the only thing that counts is to know if, in [a film's] 26 reels, there lies a sleeping princess whom a magician will awake with the beam of his marvellous lamp – I mean, a good story. That is the sole point: the story, the tale, the fiction, the dream …'

Feuillade is best known for his brilliant crime serials, the most legendary being the ten-part *Les Vampires*. A gleefully anarchistic gang is dedicated to robbing the bourgeoisie and flouting civic order. The journalist Philippe Guérande and his bumbling assistant Mazamette vow to bring them to justice. The gang loses and replaces its Grand Vampire with alarming frequency (chiefly because Feuillade's actors kept getting called to the front), but the driving force is the kohl-eyed, anagrammatically named Irma Vep, the silent cinema's most resourceful and unrepentant *femme fatale*.

Feuillade dreamed up each installment just before it was shot, creating a fantastical plotline that won the admiration of Surrealists, including the poet Apollinaire. A dancer performing a bat-ballet is poisoned before a mesmerized audience. A party of the *haut monde* is cut short by sleeping gas. A bishop checks into a hotel and calmly unpacks a cannon from his trunk, which he fires from his window at a ship in the harbour. The Vampires are captured while celebrating their victory with a frenzied dance; they have already sketched a rude caricature of Mazamette (going so far as to fill in his portrait's eyeball with a well-placed pistol shot). Filmed under wartime restrictions, when cameras were banned from the streets, the episodes lack the splendid cityscapes of *Fantômas* (1913) and the gorgeous Nice views of *Tih-Minh* (1918), but the nondescript hotel rooms and the overstuffed parlours nevertheless come alive through Feuillade's virtuosic staging in depth. *Les Vampires* remains a monument to the delirious zest of early cinematic storytelling.

Production company
Gaumont

Cinematographer
Manichoux

Cast
Musidora
Edouard Mathé
Marcel Lévesque
Jean Ayme
Fernand Herrmann
Stacia Napierkowska

Other films
★ *Fantômas* (1913)
★ *Judex* (1917)
★ *La Nouvelle mission de Judex* (1918)
★ *Tih-Minh* (1918)
★ *Barrabas* (1920)

One of the vampires' victims: A ballerina, performing as a bat, who will soon collapse after being poisoned by a ring.

The Cabinet of Dr Caligari
Das Cabinet des Dr Caligari

Robert Wiene *1920*

During the First World War, painters and poets began considering unorthodox ways of using the new medium of film. Many avant-garde schemes were hatched but only a few, such as Vsevelod Meyerhold's *Drama in Futurist Cabinet 13* (1914) and Abel Gance's *La Folie du Dr Tube* (1915), came to fruition, and those were known chiefly as curiosities. Far greater in its impact was *The Cabinet of Dr Caligari*, which became a commercial hit both in Germany and abroad. For many critics, Robert Wiene succeeded where Sjöström, Feuillade and Griffith had failed: he showed that cinema could be a fine art.

Surprisingly, *Caligari* was a thoroughly commercial project, overseen by the shrewd producer Erich Pommer. He accepted Carl Mayer and Hans Janowitz's script about a series of mysterious murders in Holstenwall, committed while a travelling mountebank is passing through. Francis the student discovers that Caligari's performing somnambulist Cesare is the murderer, and after Cesare has abducted Jane, Francis tracks the somnambulist to an asylum. There he discovers that Caligari is a therapist who has been experimenting on his patient. Francis unmasks Caligari before his colleagues.

In the original script, Francis told his tale years later, as a flashback, but someone came up with a new frame story that shows Francis beginning his tale in a garden. When Francis finishes his account we learn that he, like Jane and Cesare, is a patient in the asylum, and Caligari is the kindly doctor who is trying to cure them. Thus a script that began as an attack on authority, fuelled by Mayer and Janowitz's hatred of the warmongering German state, was filmed as a madman's fantasy.

Caligari was well received in Germany and it was in the vanguard of German film exports into France where it was acclaimed as a milestone of motion picture art. The film became the emblem of the Expressionist movement, which counted among its triumphs *Nosferatu* (1922), *Raskolnikow* (1923) and *Warning Shadows* (1923). Resolutely theatrical in many ways – it makes only minimal use of analytical editing and cross-cutting – *Caligari* also exemplifies what Jean Mitry has called 'graphic' Expressionism, with twisted cityscapes and jagged bursts of light painted directly onto the canvas sets. The skewed, heavily streaked alleys and houses are convulsed as if in a fairground mirror, and the distortion is matched by the stylized performances of Werner Krauss's waddling Caligari and Conrad Veidt's angular, haunted Cesare, a skeletal puppet in a black leotard.

As a prototype of deceptive narration, the film's frame story looks surprisingly subtle today. The spindly trees in the opening scene hint at the contortions of Francis' imaginary world. More subtly, faint outlines of the spidery dream-decor are visible in the 'normal' madhouse cell. The film's final image – Dr Caligari the therapist squinting out at the camera and remarking of Francis, 'I think I know how to cure him now' – is far from reassuring, raising fresh doubts about whether we have really left the hallucination behind.

Director
Robert Wiene

Producers
Erich Pommer and
Rudolf Meinert

Writers
Carl Mayer and
Hans Janowitz

Cinematographers
Willy Hameister and
Hermann Warm

Production company
Decla

Cast
Werner Krauss
Conrad Veidt
Lili Dagover
Friedrich Feher
Hans Heinz von Twardowski

Other films
★ *Genuine* (1920)
★ *Raskolnikow* (1923)
★ *Hands of Orlac* (1924)

Nosferatu, A Symphony of Horror
Nosferatu, Eine Symphonie des Grauens

F. W. Murnau *1922*

Director
F. W. Murnau

Writer
Henrik Galeen

The German silent cinema exploited several genres but it indisputably led the world in films of horror and the supernatural. *The Cabinet of Dr Caligari* (*see pages 32–33*) was one of a string of macabre fantasies, including *The Student of Prague* (1913) and *The Golem* (1914), both of which were remade in the 1920s under the influence of Expressionism. The finest director to work in this tradition was F. W. Murnau.

Murnau was trained in philology, literature and art history before joining Max Reinhardt's theatre troupe. After the war he founded his own film company and was soon making films for several other firms. Although many of his works appear to be lost, he created several classics of German cinema, notably *Der Letzte Mann* (*The Last Laugh*, 1924), the brilliant film-within-a-film *Tartuffe* (1925), and the spectacular *Faust* (1926). In Hollywood he made one of the last great American silents, *Sunrise: A Song of Two Humans* (1927). His masterpiece was *Nosferatu*.

Freely plagiarized from Bram Stoker's novel *Dracula* (1897), *Nosferatu* presents the familiar plot of the land agent Hutter being summoned from Bremen to distant Transylvania to arrange for a mysterious aristocrat, Count Orlok, to acquire property. Staying at the count's castle, Hutter becomes weak and delirious, unaware that the undead Orlok is draining his blood. Soon Orlok sets out for Bremen, where he will prey on the townspeople. Hutter rushes home as the plague strikes the town. Hutter's wife Nina sacrifices herself to Orlok, delaying him past dawn so that (in one of Murnau's eeriest shots) the sun's rays may strike him down.

Murnau freely incorporated American editing techniques, especially in a passage of eerie cross-cutting that makes a sleepwalking Nina in Bremen seem to halt Orlok in Transylvania as he stoops over Hutter. Murnau also extended the European depth-staging tradition of Feuillade and Sjöström. One of the most harrowing shots shows Nina at her window while Orlok (played by the uncannily named Max Schreck) watches from the house opposite. Another affecting scene has Nina fretting in the parlour while Hutter packs for his trip in the bedroom behind her. The image is echoed at the close: she dies in that bedroom, the chastened Hutter kneeling by her side as city elders grieve in the foreground. In contrast to the pasteboard look of *Caligari*, *Nosferatu* gives us a tangible, three-dimensional world.

For all its rich depth, the film is ruled by a grim geometry. In the opening sections, trees and bushes give Bremen a springtime luxuriance. Details in Orlok's castle introduce an arch motif seen most starkly in the torpedo-shaped door of Hutter's room, which creaks open like a coffin lid to reveal Orlok standing outside. And when Orlok's ship glides into Bremen, it becomes a city of blasted vegetation and sinister arches, concrete signs of the vampire's spiritual pollution. Yet the film is at pains to domesticate even this horrific figure. In intercut lectures, Dr Sievers explains that vampiric plants and animals are integral to nature – which makes the depredations of this creature all the more disturbing.

Producers
Albin Grau and Enrico
Dieckmann

Cinematographers
Fritz Arno Wagner and
Günther Krampf

Production company
Prana

Cast
Max Schreck
Gustav Botz
Gustav von Wangenheim
Alexander Granach
Greta Schröder
G. H. Schnell

Other films
★ *Der Letzte Mann* (1924)
★ *Tartuffe* (1925)
★ *Faust* (1926)
★ *Sunrise* (1927)
★ *City Girl* (1930)
★ *Tabu* (1931)

*Max Schreck (whose name means 'terror')
playing the vampire in* Nosferatu, *another twist
on the Dracula legend.*

The Battleship Potemkin
Bronenosets 'Potemkin'

Sergei Eisenstein *1925*

Director and writer
Sergei Eisenstein

The Battleship Potemkin lives today as an album of indelible images. Sailors are fed maggot-infested meat. A corrupt doctor is hurled overboard, his pince-nez dangling from the rigging. A skiff coasts serenely through the morning mist bearing a sailor's body. An armoured cruiser defies the imperial warships with a shout of 'Brothers!' from those on board. And, most searing of all, there is the massacre on the Odessa Steps: a mother carrying her wounded son into the rifles of the Cossacks; a pram bouncing down the staircase; a stone lion stirred to roaring life; a woman with smashed spectacles howling in close-up. The director, searching for the part that stands for the whole, created a film that has become a suite of set-pieces, a gallery of great moments.

Eisenstein's first film, *Strike* (1925), was a youthful extension of his theatrical experimentation, and mixed circus and vaudeville with dramatic agitprop. *The Battleship Potemkin* was more mature; the extravagant montages and clownish acrobatics were toned down, and Eisenstein aimed instead at a dramatic crescendo with an epic scope. The project began as one episode in a fresco about the abortive 1905 Revolution in Russia, but when Eisenstein saw the magnificent steps in the port of Odessa he realized that he could build an entire film around the mutiny aboard the armoured cruiser *Potemkin*. The plot presents an allegory of growing class solidarity. a crucial theme in Soviet Russia. The sailors unite to cast off their oppressive officers, then the people of Odessa support the mutiny. At the climax, the tsar's navy supports the mutineers and lets them pass into safe waters.

Painting in broad strokes, Eisenstein liked to cast his performers by physical type. Proletarian men are sturdy and stern, while the bourgeoisie pat their plump vests and wave their parasols. These political icons are brought to life by dynamic editing. Eisenstein carried what his Soviet colleagues called 'American montage' to a pulverizing limit, which in turn was to become known as 'Soviet montage'. *Potemkin* achieves a nervous, percussive rhythm by breaking every action into a hail of shots, cutting to minute details (the dangling pince-nez, blood oozing through a victim's belt buckle), stretching out time by flashing to the action elsewhere, juxtaposing contrasts of line or tonality.

Eisenstein also wanted his actors' gestures to arouse a physical–emotional state in the viewer. So the villainous captain watches the swaying, abandoned mess tables with tick-tock head movements that we involuntarily imitate, and the wounded Vakulinchuk lands on the rigging in the posture of a tired workman that makes us sag with fatigue too. The Odessa Steps sequence is a monumental thrust and counterthrust, the mechanical descent of the riflemen opposed by a series of women who confront them in varying attitudes: defiant, supplicating, but always stirring in our own bodies a sense of striving or recoil.

Although *The Battleship Potemkin* did not prove to be a commercial or critical success in Russia, it quickly became the paradigmatic silent film for interested intellectuals elsewhere. Everyone from Hollywood moguls to Joseph Goebbels, Hitler's future minister of propaganda, realized that at 27 the brash young director had burst open new avenues of expression within an art form that was only a little older than himself.

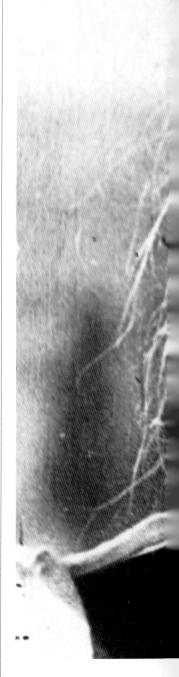

Cinematographer
Eduard Tissé

Production company
Goskino

Music
Nikolai Kryukov and
Edmund Meisel

Cast
Nikolai Antonov
Vladimir Barsky
Grigori Alexandrov
Mikhail Gomorov
Beatrice Vitoldi

Other films
★ *Strike* (1925)
★ *October: 10 Days that Shook the World* (1927)
★ *The General Line* (1929)
★ *Alexander Nevsky* (1938)
★ *Ivan the Terrible, Parts I and II* (1944–46)

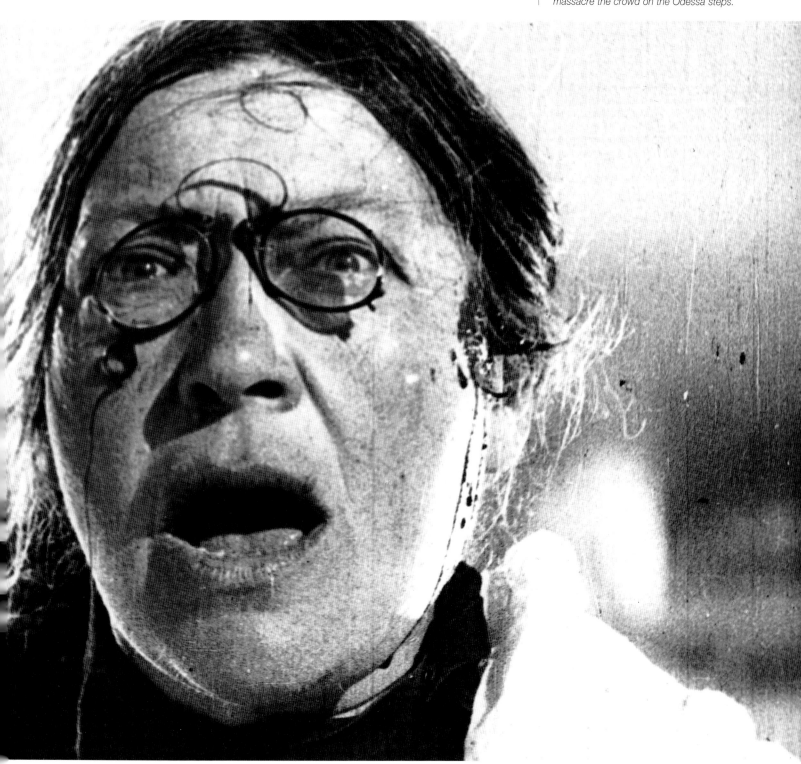

A characteristically telling Eisenstein close-up: The schoolmistress watches in horror as the cossacks massacre the crowd on the Odessa steps.

The Gold Rush
Charles Chaplin *1925*

If we find it difficult to imagine the excitement that stirred cinephiles during the 1920s, we should remember that virtually every month brought a revelation. The year 1925, for example, produced not only *Strike* and *Potemkin* (*see pages 36–37*) but also Murnau's *Tartuffe*, Dreyer's *The Master of the House*, and a dozen brilliant American films. At the time, however, no film overshadowed *The Gold Rush,* which quickly came to be considered Charlie Chaplin's masterpiece.

Chaplin led a scandal-strewn life, and eventually his peccadillos and his left-wing affinities would exile him from America. Yet onscreen he was the Little Tramp, and no one with any sense of humour or pathos could watch him unmoved. His arch elegance and balletic grace distinguished him from even the superb mimes of the Sennett troupe (Mack Sennett, a comic in the burlesque theatre, was the leading slapstick producer of the time). While executing routinely sadistic gags, Chaplin had a wry, detached resilience. His back was often his most expressive feature – wriggling, shrugging and often bursting into a back-kick that was at once resigned, defiant and obscurely joyous.

Soon he was the most popular comedian in the world, directing films which meticulously showcased his gifts. There seemed nothing he couldn't do. He proved a brilliant acrobat in *The Rink* (1916), a wistful romantic in *The Immigrant* (1916), and a genius at visual metaphor in *The Pawnshop* (1916), in which he transformed an alarm clock into a human heart and a tin of worms. He went on to make a string of hugely popular short features, among them *The Kid* (1921) and *The Pilgrim* (1923), in which he mimes the David and Goliath story. His visual technique seemed somewhat old-fashioned, but it was perfectly suited to his melodramatic, increasingly sentimental plots. *The Gold Rush* offers a perfect blend of sadness and laughter. Charlie has fallen in love with Georgina, the dancehall girl abused by her lover. The tramp is the romantic idealist, as ill-suited for a world driven by gold lust as his tight, shabby suit and bowler are for the Yukon snows. Chaplin misses no chance to tug at our heartstrings: Charlie thinking that Georgina is smiling at him in the bar, when she is looking at someone behind him; Charlie preparing a dinner which the guests have forgotten to attend; Charlie impaling two dinner rolls on forks so that they stand in for his big boots, and then putting them through a silly dance, his face floating sweetly above them.

What saves the film from bathos is the wild comedy of the tramp's bouts with prospector Big Jim McKay. Starving, Charlie boils his boot and Jim stares as Charlie deftly sucks the nails as if they were fishbones and twirls the laces like spaghetti. At the climax, when a windstorm blows their cabin towards a precipice, Chaplin squeezes giddy comedy out of the men scrambling to keep the building from teetering over the edge. For once, Charlie gets both the gold and the girl – a success that mirrors the rewards heaped upon the best-loved artist of silent cinema.

Director and producer
Charles Chaplin

Writer
Charles Chaplin

Cinematographers
Rollie Totheroh and
Jack Wilson

Production companies
Charles Chaplin Productions
and United Artists

Cast
Charles Chaplin
Mack Swain
Tom Murray
Georgia Hale
Henry Bergman

Other films
★ *The Kid* (1921)
★ *The Pilgrim* (1923)
★ *City Lights* (1931)
★ *Modern Times* (1936)
★ *The Great Dictator* (1940)
★ *Monsieur Verdoux* (1947)
★ *Limelight* (1952)

Lady Windermere's Fan

Ernst Lubitsch *1925*

Director
Ernst Lubitsch

By 1925, most filmmaking nations were losing momentum, but Hollywood was conquering the world. Los Angeles was drawing talent from all over Europe, and the first indisputably great director to emigrate was Ernst Lubitsch. In Germany, Lubitsch had begun in farcical comedy, as both performer and director, but he had made his reputation with splendid historical sagas like *Madame Dubarry* (1919), just the sort of thing, moguls reasoned, he could mount even better in Hollywood. The first result was *Rosita* (1923), a Mary Pickford vehicle that proved he could combine spectacle and light entertainment.

Soon, however, Lubitsch moved into romantic drama and social comedy. Probably inspired by Chaplin's cynical *A Woman of Paris* (1923), he turned out several satirical pieces on the upper class. These were quickly recognized as unparalleled in their clockwork plots, subtle performances and sly use of film language. *The Marriage Circle* (1924) and *So This Is Paris* (1926) are splendid, but neither has the adamantine brilliance of *Lady Windermere's Fan*.

Lubitsch's comedy depends upon each worldly, self-possessed character being quite deeply deluded. Lord Windermere fails to notice that Lord Darlington is trying to seduce his wife. Lady Windermere, unaware that her mother is alive and has returned to London as the notorious Mrs Erlynne, finds a cheque her husband has written to that lady; it was to buy her silence, but Lady Windermere believes her husband has found a mistress. And poor Lord Augustus, infatuated with Mrs Erlynne, is in the dark throughout.

Lubitsch plays out this comedy of errors in setpieces that exploit purely visual narration. Everything depends upon X looking at Y and thereby misunderstanding. Glimpsing Lord Windermere trying to hide a note, Lord Darlington assumes he is keeping a mistress. At the racecourse, gossips train their binoculars on Mrs Erlynne; when Lord Windermere objects to their backbiting (thus defending his wife's mother), Lady Windermere suspects his eye is roving. During a garden party, Lady Windermere sees her rival apparently wooed by Lord Windermere; the shrubbery conceals the real seducer, Lord Augustus. The climax comes when Lady Windermere decides to run off with Lord Darlington, only to find Mrs Erlynne prepared to shield her by sacrificing her own reputation. The crucial piece of evidence, once more woven into a pattern of glances which lead to false conclusions, is Lady Windermere's fan.

Part of the plot's intricacy is derived from from Oscar Wilde's 1892 play, but Lubitsch used virtually none of its dialogue. By 1925, the silent cinema was confident enough to turn witty repartee into suggestive props, misunderstood eyelines, understated reaction shots and carefully timed cuts. It was all the more remarkable, then, that Lubitsch would move effortlessly into sound cinema, creating some of the greatest comedies of the next two decades (*Trouble in Paradise*, 1932; *The Shop Around the Corner*, 1940, *see pages 62–63*). Having mined the resources of silence, he understood better than most exactly what sound could add to eloquent images.

Writer
Julien Josephson, from the
play by Oscar Wilde

Cinematographer
Charles van Enger

Production company
Warner Brothers

Cast
Ronald Colman
Wilson Bonge
Billie Bennett
Mrs Cowper-Cowper
Carrie Daumery
Helen Dunbar
Bert Lytell
May McAvoy
Irene Rich

Other films
★ *The Smiling Lieutenant* (1931)
★ *Trouble in Paradise* (1932)
★ *Design for Living* (1933)
★ *Desire* (1936)
★ *Ninotchka* (1939)
★ *The Shop Around the Corner* (1940)
★ *Heaven Can Wait* (1943)

*Ronald Colman (second from right, middle row)
and his co-stars participating in Lubitsch's take
on the famous Wilde comedy.*

The General Buster Keaton *1927*

In the 1920s, Buster Keaton was usually considered, along with Harold Lloyd and Harry Langdon, as gifted but distinctly inferior to the great Chaplin. As classics like *The General* and *Our Hospitality* (1923) became available again in the 1960s, tastes changed and critics and young audiences began to argue that Keaton was Chaplin's equal as a performer and one of the greatest directors in history.

Keaton adopted a resolutely unsentimental persona. He had a reflective air, cocking his head while thoughtfully considering why objects and nature conspired to assault him. He took comic catastrophe seriously. While Chaplin won hearts by flashing an embarrassed grin, Keaton never smiled. The body could spring into an exclamation mark of astonishment, but the face registered at best mild surprise.

He subjected himself to punishing stunts that would have broken anyone not trained in vaudeville knockabout. Keaton loved to take falls squarely on the base of his spine, embellished with a half-spin; he would then look around, slightly puzzled. In *Steamboat Bill, Jr* (1928), gales fling him about town like a rag doll. Time and again, what saves him is resilience and unflappable resourcefulness. If attacking natives use a palm tree as a ladder to board his ship in *The Navigator* (1924), he will study the situation before calmly yanking off coconuts to bop them. The unruffled demeanour comes from a dogged, irrational faith that the machinery of the world will not, finally, grind him up.

Keaton set his tiny hero against colossal forces – in *The General*, nothing less than the American Civil War. Johnnie is a loyal Southern engineer who gets embroiled in combat when his locomotive *The General* and his girlfriend Annabelle are abducted by bluecoats. He pursues the Unionist soldiers; after he rescues Annabelle and his engine, they pursue him. During the climactic battle at a river gorge, Keaton allows a real locomotive to plunge into the valley. There are also grim satirical swipes at Griffithian heroics, as when Johnnie's swordblade flies off and lands in the back of a sniper.

The plot has a pure architectonic beauty. Each scene in the first half has its counterpart in the second, and Keaton's gag-team spins hilarious variations on cowcatchers, water tanks, unhitched railway carriages and stray artillery. As usual, the hero's pluck has a physics-demonstration air (he uses one piece of timber to flip another piece off the tracks), but he needs luck too. At one point, Johnnie loads a rolling cannon but then becomes its target. The cannon fires just as his train rounds a bend and the strike lands near the Union train it's pursuing.

The General credits Clyde Bruckman as co-director, but almost all the elements display Keaton's clean-lined visual sensibility. His perpendicular long-shots typically set his hero against storms, battalions and mobs of policemen or brides with a kind of diagrammatic purity, using awesome contrasts of distance and scale. The unfussy rigour of Keaton's style matches his hero's sober adjustment to whatever the cosmos throws his way.

Directors
Buster Keaton and
Clyde Bruckman

Producer
Joseph M. Schenck

Writers
Buster Keaton, Clyde
Bruckman and Al Boasberg

Cinematographers
J. Devereux Jennings and
Bert Haines

Production companies
Buster Keaton Productions/
United Artists

Cast
Buster Keaton
Marion Mack
Glen Cavendar
Jim Farley
Frederick Vroom
Jim Keaton
Charles Smith

Other films
★ *Our Hospitality* (1923)
★ *The Navigator* (1924)
★ *Go West* (1925)
★ *Steamboat Bill, Jr* (1928)

Keaton displays his trademark facial impassivity as he strides down the locomotive tracks in search of his engine.

Metropolis Fritz Lang *1927*

Perhaps because it teeters constantly on the edge of kitsch, *Metropolis* is the silent film that haunts today's mass culture. The robot Maria, with her spasmodic movements and stylized breasts, the plodding lines of workers, and the streamlined cityscapes have all inspired music videos and commercials. What other 1920s movie could have been successfully re-released as *Metropolis* was in 1984, with a techno score by Giorgio Moroder and songs by Pat Benatar?

Metropolis verges on being a guilty pleasure, with its vision of a cyborg future and its near-parodic reconciliation of worker and planner by the man of conscience ('hands … head … heart'). Like other subjects treated by Fritz Lang – the master criminal in *Dr Mabuse* (1921–22), espionage in *Spies* (1928), space travel in *The Woman in the Moon* (1929), and the search for a serial killer in *M* (1931) – the premise of *Metropolis* verges on pulp. Yet Lang treats every implausibility with a crisp efficiency and not a trace of condescension. It was a skill that would stand him in good stead during his years in Hollywood, where equally unpromising material yielded *You Only Live Once* (1938), *The Ministry of Fear* (1944, *see pages 68–69*) and *The Big Heat* (1953).

Like Murnau, Lang had an education in the fine arts, but after the First World War he plunged into the realm of mass-market filmmaking dominated by Gaumont and Feuillade. He became a protégé of Joe May, working on serials and dramas. Soon he was at Decla, directing melodramas like *Hara-kiri* (1919) and the adventure saga *The Spiders* (1919–20). Trained as an architect and painter, he brought his love of massive spaces to *The Niebelungen* (1924).

Germany's largest movie firm, the Universumfilm Aktiengesellschaft (UFA), was already suffering financial difficulties when it began *Metropolis*, and the film's highly publicized budget overruns and delays in release almost bankrupted the company. The finished film ran so long that it was cut down for most foreign markets. As a result, it survives in several variants, and a complete version may never be reconstructed.

Nonetheless, all the footage we have displays mesmerizing inventiveness. From his wife Thea von Harbou's script, Lang created a larger-than-life world echoing the great themes of Expressionist theatre: the clash of labour and capital, the individual and the multitude, as well as the overweening pride of the man (here, Rotwang) who brings the machine to life. To these conceits the film gives unforgettable expression. The workers move in halting, robotic unison, the very image of capitalist oppression. When Freder ventures into the underworld to find what enables him to live in luxury, he spontaneously relieves a worker and takes up the absurd, ceaseless task of pinning the hands to the face of a clock, his outstretched arms foreshadowing his role as a Christ for the machine age. Despite the plot's optimistic conclusion, in its unsettling, vaguely perverse imagery the film created the tradition of dystopian science fiction that would produce *Blade Runner* (1982) and many other successors. *Metropolis* endures as one of Lang's precisely delineated parables of anxiety in the modern city.

Director
Fritz Lang

Producer
Erich Pommer

Writers
Thea von Harbou and Fritz Lang

Cinematographers
Karl Freund, Günther Rittau and Otto Hunte

Production company
UFA

Special effects
Ernst Kunstmann

Visual effects
Eugen Schüfftan

Cast
Brigitte Helm
Alfred Abel
Gustav Fröhlich
Rudolph Klein-Rogge
Fritz Rasp
Heinrich George
Theodore Loos

Other films
★ *Dr Mabuse* (1921–22)
★ *Spies* (1928)
★ *The Woman in the Moon* (1929)
★ *M* (1931)
★ *You Only Live Once* (1937)
★ *The Ministry of Fear* (1944)
★ *The Big Heat* (1953)

The End of St Petersburg

Konyets Sankt-Peterburga

Vsevelod Pudovkin *1927*

Directors
Vsevelod Pudovkin,
co-directed by Mikhail Doller

Once considered Eisenstein's peer, Pudovkin has wandered into the shadows. *Mother* (1926), a striking adaptation of Gorky's novel (1907), has largely been remembered for its textbook montage (the imprisoned son dreaming of freedom, coupled with shots of a river thawing and spring arriving). Adventurous experiments like *Storm over Asia* (1928), *A Simple Case* (1932) and *Deserter* (1933) have been largely forgotten. His later, more doctrinaire films have some meritorious moments, but he presented himself too often as a dutiful party hack, and historians have taken him at his word.

Trained in physics and chemistry, Pudovkin joined Lev Kuleshov's film workshop soon after the Bolshevik Revolution in Russia in 1917. He systematized the master's methods in the pamphlet *Film Technique* (1926), which ennobled editing as the alpha and omega of film art. Pudovkin also insisted that the filmmaker had to make every scene vivid through facial expression and those details of setting he called 'plastic material'. Although critics judged Eisenstein the deeper theorist, Pudovkin's doctrines became canonical for aspiring filmmakers everywhere.

By treating filmmaking as a matter of strict calculation, Pudovkin may have led critics to overlook his forceful storytelling and poetic imagination. *The End of St Petersburg* remains a powerful portrayal of the 1917 Revolution, seen from the bottom. A peasant, having come to St Petersburg looking for work, inadvertently reveals the underground work in which his city friend is involved. He redeems himself not only on the front during the First World War but also by taking wholehearted part in the coup that ends tsarist rule.

Pudovkin follows D. W. Griffith in contriving to balance historical sweep with personal drama in a way that *The Battleship Potemkin* never attempts. The police break in on the Communist's wife, who says her husband has not recently been there; but the officer notices a steaming cup of tea on the table and settles down for an ambush – a scene of pure Hitchcockian suspense. Even the metaphorical montages have nothing hyperintellectual about them. A factory supervisor learns of his promotion while riding in a lift with his boss, and Pudovkin intercuts the soaring lift with the man's dawning realization that he has risen into a new class. In the most famous sequence, Pudovkin cross-cuts the battlefield with the stock exchange not only to illustrate how war yields profits but also to stir our anger at the palpable contrast between frenziedly bidding brokers and dead soldiers frozen in the mud.

Throughout, the political lessons arise from emotional details. When the country youth arrives in the city, his host's wife does not offer him any of the potatoes she is peeling. After the Winter Palace has been seized, she finds the wounded boy and gives him some of the potatoes she is carrying. Making her way through the palace, she meets more weary heroes until, when she finds her husband, her empty hands tell him that she has given away all the potatoes intended for him. On his beaming face, not on any Bolshevik flags or speeches, this intimate epic ends.

Writer
Nathan Zarkhi

Cinematographer
Anatoli Golovnya

Production company
Mezhrabpom-Russ

Cast
Ivan Chuvelov
Vera Baranovskaya
A. P. Christiakov
V. Chuvelyov
V. Obolensky
Sergei Kumarov
Alexsei Davor

Other films
★ *Mother* (1926)
★ *Storm over Asia* (1928)
★ *A Simple Case* (1932)
★ *Deserter* (1933)

Framed in a dynamic angle typical of Soviet silent cinema, the factory owner tries to rally the workers.

La Passion de Jeanne d'Arc

Carl Theodor Dreyer *1928*

'A Dying Art Offers a Masterpiece' ran the headline for an American review of *La Passion de Jeanne d'Arc*. Released just when Hollywood was introducing all-talking pictures, the film seemed as anachronistic as its subject. Today, it looks anachronistic in a good sense, that is, timeless. Dreyer used the resources of silent-film technique to free the saint's life from verisimilitude and costume drama, and to thrust us into a no-man's-land between historical document and pictorial abstraction.

Dreyer does not depict Jeanne's childhood, her appeals to her king or her battles. He condenses the weeks of her trial into a single day – if any day ever stretched on for so long beneath an unchanging sky, bathed in a uniformly wan light. He fills the film with dialogue drawn from the transcript of Jeanne's arraignment, supplemented by a few lines which she exchanges with a sympathetic young priest. From *Caligari*'s set designer Hermann Warm, Dreyer ordered white walls, occasionally broken by a tilted arch or a squeezed battlement reminiscent of the style of medieval miniatures.

Above all, Dreyer decided to film each character in isolated shots, and often in close-ups. With no establishing shots with which to orientate the audience, only eyelines and posture suggest where the priests and their suspect are at any moment. The face, Dreyer declared, 'is a landscape one never tires of exploring'. No film had ever searched that landscape so hungrily. He fills the screen with moles and pockmarks: a girl's blink becomes an event, a bishop's frown a storm. As dialogues become duels between faces, Dreyer carries cutting to an elliptical extreme unseen even in the work of the Soviet masters. Now every eye-flick and flaring nostril is Pudovkin's 'plastic material'.

The full burden of the production therefore fell on the actors, many recruited from the Comédie Française. Dreyer's casting coup was Renée Falconetti, a stage actress known chiefly for light comedy. Stripping her of make-up, using lighting to enhance her freckled face and dusty eyebrows, Dreyer shoots her magnificent head from every conceivable angle. The camera records each indignity she suffers, from a wickerwork crown tossed on her head by her guards to the final moments in which her head is shaved, her tears and sweat mixing with snips of hair. The voluptuous tactility of Falconetti's face provides a literally skin-crawling performance.

The film traces Jeanne's movement from confused piety to fearful defiance, and finally to humble acceptance of her fate. When she is burned at the stake and birds scatter into the sky, the crowd that has watched her abjure her blasphemies rebelliously attacks the English soldiers. The people are driven back brutally, in splintered editing and somersaulting camerawork. Later Dreyer films like *Ordet* (1955) and *Gertrud* (1964) would achieve a calm translucence, but here the final outburst suits a film already pressed to hysterical limits.

While mobilizing everything that cinema had learned about cutting and set design, Dreyer's stylization never obliterates the sensuous feel of Jeanne's ordeal. Like Eisenstein and the other masters of the silent cinema, Dreyer shows that bold imagery need not arrest the palpable pulse of life. The result is a film which, though born of a dying art, remains audacious and inspiring.

Director
Carl Theodor Dreyer

Writers
Joseph Delteil and Carl Theodor Dreyer

Cinematographers
Rudolph Maté and Goestula Kottula

Production company
Société Générale de Films

Cast
Renée Falconetti
Eugene Silvain
Antonin Artaud
Michel Simon
Maurice Schutz
Jean d'Yd

Other films
★ *The President* (1919)
★ *Vampyr* (1932)
★ *Dies Irae* (1943)
★ *Ordet* or *The Word* (1955)
★ *Gertrud* (1964)

I Was Born, But ... Yasujiro Ozu *1932*

Not until the 1980s did Western cinephiles learn that Japan had a silent filmmaking tradition as prolific and excellent as those of Germany, France and the United States. It also became apparent that no country had finer filmmakers than Kenji Mizoguchi, the master of splendid camera movements and sorrowful stories of self-sacrificing women, or than Yasujiro Ozu, the director whom the Japanese most revered.

Ozu began directing in the late 1920s and learned his craft by studying American comedy, particularly the work of Lubitsch and Harold Lloyd. From 1927 to his death in 1963, Ozu worked almost exclusively for Shochiku, Japan's MGM. Shochiku films treated the lives of the urban masses with a mixture of everyday pathos and warm comedy. Although Ozu dabbled in student slapstick, romantic melodramas and gangster films, he found his métier in the film of quiet family life. Here he could present the conflict of generations, the problems of marriage, and the anxieties of lives lived on the edge of poverty with a warm lucidity that can only be called Chekhovian.

The situations are mundane. A clerk, or 'salaryman', is fired and must scrape together work carrying placards in Depression-era Tokyo (*Tokyo Chorus*, 1931). A mother who has struggled all her life to educate her son comes to Tokyo and finds him a penniless teacher, saddled with a wife and baby (*The Only Son*, 1936). Out of such commonplace situations Ozu coaxed humour, poignancy and a cinematic lyricism that marks him as a filmmaker of genius.

I Was Born, But ... is one of his finest accomplishments. Salaryman Yoshi has a new house in the suburbs, a kindly wife, two mischievous sons and an oafish boss. The boys quickly take over their school playground, leading their gang across the wastelands of expanding Tokyo and even bringing the boss's son, Taro, to heel. So the boys are puzzled by their father's kow-towing to his employer. The drama culminates in a screening of the boss's home movies, showing Yoshi clowning with a degrading silliness. After a late-night quarrel, the boys go on hunger strike – broken the next morning when Yoshi joins them to share his rice balls. The father pronounces his life a failure while the boys resign themselves to hierarchy, urging their father to bow to the boss and telling Taro that his father is the best.

The film is gently poised between a sympathy for the adults' passivity and a celebration of the instinctive ambitions of childhood. Just as captivating is Ozu's unique style: a consistently low camera position, angles that bring out sharply diagonal depth, cut-together close-ups of unerring precision, and a penchant for spatial jokes (as when Yoshi's morning exercise makes him look like a shirt fluttering on a washing line). In its delicate portrayal of ordinary life's compromises, *I Was Born, But ...* looks forward to Ozu's celebrated *Tokyo Story* (1953). One of that film's key lines – 'Life is disappointing, isn't it?' – could serve as the epigraph for the delightful and sobering *I Was Born, But ...*, one of the last masterpieces of international silent cinema.

Director
Yasujiro Ozu

Writers
Akira Fushimi and
Geibei Ibushiya

Cinematographers
Hideo Mohara and
Hideo Shigehara

Production company
Shochiku

Cast
Hideo Sugawara
Tomio Aoki
Tatsuo Saito
Mitsuko Yoshikawa
Takeshi Sahamoto
Seiichi Kojufita

Other films
★ *Tokyo Chorus* (1931)
★ *The Only Son* (1936)
★ *Tokyo Story* (1953)
★ *An Autumn Afternoon*
(1962)

Salaryman Yoshi takes his morning exercise alongside the family laundry in a wryly humorous composition.

MAIN: *Michael Curtiz's*
Casablanca *(1942).*
FAR LEFT: *John Ford's*
The Searchers *(1956).*
LEFT: *Billy Wilder's* Sunset
Boulevard *(1950).*

CHAPTER TWO

America: The Studio Years

David Thomson

I would not assert that the 15 films I have chosen for the period from the arrival of sound to the alleged demise of the studio system (broadly speaking, 1927–60) are indisputably the best made in the United States in those years. There are so many ways of defining 'best', from those that made the most money or won the most Oscars to those that have neither faded nor become camp. These are 15 films I like very much, and that I warmly recommend to those reading this book. They are some of the best Hollywood pictures by most observers' standards, a tribute to factory filmmaking when a few studios made and marketed film, and some even owned cinemas.

My choice is organized to show history in the making, and not always for the best. The history of movies has never known a more extensive or stable system than the one we call 'Hollywood' (unless it was the Soviet model in much the same years). Yet my 15 also illustrate the vitality of outsiders, from Josef von Sternberg to Orson Welles, and the steady value of players like James Stewart (here in four stages of his career), Cary Grant and even Ralph Bellamy, a supporting actor whose two most fabulous performances are included.

Much is omitted. Where is *Casablanca* (1942), one of the movies that did most deftly what Hollywood wanted and which gave such a helpful nudge to real history? And what of *Sunset Boulevard* (1950), epitomizing loss of confidence and backlash and truly deserving inclusion? Where is an example of John Ford's unsettled view of the West – and surely *The Searchers* (1956) is not just the best of the genre but the film that has the sharpest feeling for the close of an era? Well, now they have been mentioned, and there were many other close runners-up. But my selection is meant to trace two stories: the struggle

in Hollywood itself between the notion of film as entertainment (*Gone With the Wind*) and popular reassurance (*Meet Me in St Louis*), with intimations of art (*Citizen Kane*) and the realized fantasy of dream (*King Kong*); and the attempt to put personal, creative visions on film without necessarily losing sight of the larger audience.

Although the golden age of Hollywood is well past, along with the tidy Hollywood system, we are still not sure how America will answer a key question: whether film is a mass medium, inherently vulgar, trashy, sensationalist and depressing, or whether it can, under the various labels of 'independence', become a field for art and unique vision at least as valuable as the novel. Many elements of the old Hollywood movie have dated – the happy ending, the big musical number, the serene vision of Americana, the Western, and even the faith in stories with a beginning, middle and end. Yet *Titanic* (1998) is a movie from that golden era, made nearly 50 years later, and a testament to how far our understanding of the word 'movie' and our expectations of the medium were formed in those halcyon years.

Morocco Josef von Sternberg *1930*

By right of chronology, *Morocco* should be the most primitive of the films in this chapter, yet nearly the opposite case could be made. If that addresses the rare masochistic sensibility of Josef von Sternberg and the religious restraint of Dietrich, it also has something to do with the liberty of the medium around 1930. There was a moment, between the advent of sound and the onset of censorship in the Motion Picture Code, when movies straddled realism, poetry and suggestiveness, when talk was less information than a musical extension of light slipping off faces, when the latent surrealism in photography was like reflections in water.

So it is instructive to note how some original reviewers were offended by the fancifulness of *Morocco* – the idea and image of Amy Jolly kicking off fashionable shoes to follow her legionnaire, Tom Brown, into the desert, with her reduced to the status of the Arab whores who trail the legion. How ridiculous, critics said, how fantastic – they had a hard time tolerating the dream energy of film in those years. Had they really thought they were in *Morocco* (as opposed to a concoction of light and decor)? Did they believe they were watching a café singer and a foreign legionnaire, as opposed to the facets of desire? Were they unable to see stylization in the hushed way von Sternberg filmed human passions? Did they get no whiff of bourgeois obsolescence from the Adolphe Menjou character, common sense in a tuxedo, the mirror image of von Sternberg himself and the only absurd character on view?

Von Sternberg's cinema relied on the marvel of the intimate gesture, the ways people look at one another (or do not). Sound let him delay that sort of glance, making it so mannered that it takes on spiritual force. And because the continuum of sound was there – the rustling of clothes or movement, the felt heartbeat of

hesitation – so he could be more extreme in his visuals. I do not mean he was a German Expressionist or a Man Ray with movement – though there are hints of both. He loved supple, informal compositions in which we become more contemplative than investigative, and he meant to guide us into what needed to be seen – the nerve system of desire.

So *Morocco* observes the rite that moved von Sternberg most – the draining away of pride in lovers. But the film is unusual because it is the woman who gives up dignity and common sense. What that meant to Marlene and Jo in real life is better left open: they deserve that much kindness, just as they deserved each other (neither one was ever as powerful without the other). And von Sternberg was a director who aimed at the passion of misrule. Together, they made six of the most beautiful American films, and in the last, *The Devil Is a Woman* (1935), Sternberg touched hands with the Luis Buñuel of *That Obscure Object of Desire* (1977). What is remarkable, and sad, is that by the time of Buñuel's film, American film had been so taken over by commercial common sense that it could not have attempted (or conceived of?) that abandon.

Director
Josef von Sternberg

Writer
Jules Furthman, from the play *Amy Jolly* by Benno Vigny

Producer
Louis D. Lighton

Cinematographer
Lee Garmes

Production company
Paramount

Cast
Marlene Dietrich
Gary Cooper
Adolphe Menjou

Other films
★ *The Blue Angel* (1930)
★ *Shanghai Express* (1932)
★ *The Scarlet Empress* (1934)
★ *The Devil Is a Woman* (1935)

The nerve system of desire: von Sternberg's relationship with Dietrich imparted an emotional truth to their highly stylized collaborations.

King Kong
Merian C. Cooper and Ernest B. Schoedsack *1933*

Directors
Merian C. Cooper and
Ernest B. Schoedsack

If *Morocco* is the movie as a private, poetic novel, *King Kong* comes from the boisterous show-business world in which exploration and discovery have been eclipsed by the hunger for audience excitement. Thus, Carl Denham, the doubt-free moviemaker who goes to Skull Island to get his Kong, is more alarming and unstoppable than the mixed-up simian. Indeed, the ape acts like someone so affected by *Morocco* that he is enthralled by the idea of love.

Denham may be a tongue-in-cheek self-portrait of the directors Merian Cooper and Ernest Schoedsack, the intriguing couple drawn to the remote places of the earth who were yet mindful that their wildlife footage needed a punchy story. He could also be a sidelong nod to David O. Selznick (the original executive producer on the project and its early defender), a fellow who rarely put tongue in cheek when he could have been talking, and promoting, instead. It is Denham's driving ambition to get Anne Darrow to scream for real, and part of the fun of the film is that we become spectators at the rehearsals, watching her mouth grow larger.

Kong, meanwhile, can be whatever you want him to be. He is the largest known container of jungle juice, with a libido the size of the great bolt that locks the doors to the native compound (on Skull, the two parts of the brain are rigorously separated). He is the great lover whose hot breath will blow away Anne's flimsy clothes, as he holds her in his paw. If he is unable to get at her, no other living creature will.

Of course, Kong is also an amalgam of special effects, presided over by Willis O'Brien, but trusted by Cooper to be more potent than the best wildlife photography. He is the primal beast (though the filmmaking is sympathetic to most of his mayhem), and finally it is less with pathos than with a sense of release that he proceeds to trample on Manhattan itself. The Denhams of the world believe that the audience class deserves all it gets.

King Kong endures for all the primitive reasons wrapped up in its metaphor. But it has so many other virtues too: the lovely pluckiness of Fay Wray; the rapidity of its action; the comic energy of Armstrong's Denham; the sultry voodoo look of the 'natives'; Max Steiner's tom-tom music; and all the gorgeous flickering, trembly tricks O'Brien could command to make the ape stand up and lurch forwards.

Did these effects convince audiences in 1933, or was the film's charm always due to the ingenious attempt rather than the perfect illusion? O'Brien is the godfather of such effects and no doubt he would have luxuriated in today's cinema where the impossible is an everyday source of belief. But I wonder whether the real magic of Kong almost depends upon the way we can see and feel it trying to work. This contrivance is perfectly suited to Denham's childlike daydream of Beauty and the Beast and to the showman's rapture at making the beast breathe. The thunder of promotion rings in his ears, and merges with the roars of Kong.

FILM: THE CRITICS' CHOICE *America: The Studio Years*

Producer
Merian C. Cooper

Writers
James Creelman and
Ruth Rose, based on a
story by Edgar Wallace

Cinematographers
Edward Linden, Vernon
Walker and L. O. Taylor

Production company
RKO

Cast
Robert Armstrong
Fay Wray
Bruce Cabot

Other films
★ *Grass* (1925)
★ *Chang* (1927)
★ *The Four Feathers* (1933)

King Kong: *An amalgam of metaphor, sexuality and special effects.*

The Awful Truth Leo McCarey 1937

Leo McCarey

Anyone who loves *The Awful Truth* should have to come clean. To be so optimistic in 1937 required oblivion, madness or complete concentration on a great picture. That year had other things to offer: serious slippage in America's economic recovery, the Germans dining on Czechoslovakia, the fall of Nanking. There were even warning movies, like *Dead End* and *You Only Live Once*. Meanwhile, *The Awful Truth* is the flagrant depiction of a high society where no one has to work for a living and where nothing rivals marital status and the adventure of love. What is more, our lovers are spared any examination of the philandering and irresponsibility that has got them into trouble.

We must not let Hollywood off the hook for indulging these children, for preferring bright interiors and sunny futures (when many of the characters deserved to be locked up), or for endorsing a very English kind of upper class (Cary Grant was English, while Irene Dunne affected a drawl that would have passed in Belgravia). And if you doubt the movie's disdain for work and the American heartland, just remember the treatment of the Oklahoma oil man, Dan Leeson, who is Lucy's new suitor.

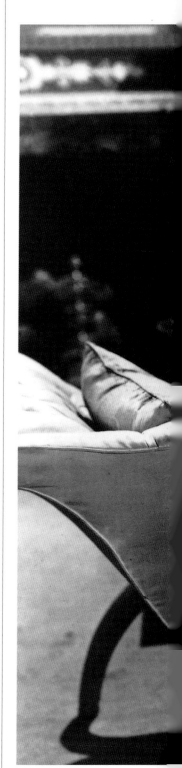

Jerry Warriner is vaguely cheating on his wife, Lucy. Mind you, we never see or smell adultery, just as we never witness her affair with Dan Leeson. The affairs didn't matter? Perhaps. The Warriners are children, too immature to have offspring of their own – so they have a dog, a fox terrier, Mr Smith. But once their marriage goes aground and the days are counting down until the decree absolute, they grow up. They suddenly start moving heaven and earth to make amends.

This takes the form of comedy, farce even, and sometimes slapstick (although the big fight between Jerry and Armand is heard, not seen), and the unfolding of a line of comic action and intrusion that is very well written (by Viña Delmar), gracefully directed (Leo McCarey received the Oscar for direction), but, above all, vitally played. We love Grant and Dunne, therefore they must love each other. It is a film of two-shots and group shots, with the couple looking sideways at each other, muttering and gesturing in a private language that would usually take years to learn. We are watching the casual acting-out of genius, and while *The Awful Truth* is great, it is not alone (I might have chosen Gregory La Cava's *My Man Godfrey*, 1936, Preston Sturges's *The Lady Eve*, 1941, Mitchell Leisen's *Midnight*, 1939, or George Cukor's *The Philadelphia Story*, 1940). We are talking about screwball comedy and, despite all the ugly holes in its concept and growth, this is the genre in which Hollywood did its best work.

This is not to say that Grant and Dunne were simply grand guys who rose above the limitations of their picture. They were great actors who had access to a free-flow comic exhilaration that is still enchanting. Why not look on the bright side? Why not accept that Hollywood was privileged, insecure and self-serving – and seeking to bring consolation? Over the decades, this has resulted in a few gems, and *The Awful Truth* does what gems do. It shines.

Writer	Production company	Other films
Viña Delmar	Columbia	★ *Duck Soup* (1933)
		★ *Ruggles of Red Gap* (1935)
Cinematographer	**Cast**	★ *Make Way for Tomorrow* (1937)
Joseph Walker	Cary Grant	★ *Love Affair* (1939)
	Irene Dunne	
	Ralph Bellamy	

Irene Dunne and Cary Grant, the film's stars, displayed the qualities of grace and comic timing that were the hallmarks of the era's best comedies.

Gone With the Wind
Victor Fleming *1939*

Gone With the Wind may be the ultimate proof that there was an American picture business – enormous, yet innocent; so unbusiness-like it often seemed to be masquerading as some passionately revered art form; and driven by producers, projects and publicity. Arguably, the film is at best a routine Technicolor epic romance of 3 hours and 40 minutes, but for sheer impact and continued romantic appeal it is an undisputed landmark in cinema history.

If the first half of Gone With the Wind is more vivid than the second, that is because producer David O. Selznick's rewriting process (or the restoration of Sidney Howard's original script) was only that far underway when shooting began, so the second part did not receive the tight scrutiny of the first. But promotion of the picture had begun with the purchase of the book, and it was so pure a scheme that Selznick had not read more than a fraction of the Margaret Mitchell novel when the deal was struck and, latterly, he became enthralled by the project rather than the detail.

He selected the story for the big Selznick International gamble, to prove the worth of the 'private' (Jock Whitney-financed) company he had founded on leaving his father-in-law and MGM in 1935. The selling points were not just scale and Technicolor (a new venture with Selznick International and Whitney as shareholders), but the spellbinding question, 'Who will play Rhett and Scarlett?' In answering the first, Selznick went back to MGM for Gable, ceding them a large part of the picture's future earnings. In dealing with the second, he made his play at the last moment, picking Vivien Leigh after he had run his eye over half the women in Creation. Leigh is the best thing in the film, and a key instance of Hollywood's sentimental affection for things English.

The first director, Selznick's friend George Cukor, had been worn out by rehearsing and testing for Scarlett – those central scenes had gone dead on him.

So Victor Fleming came on board, rediscovered the Howard script, and then dragged the film home – hating the story, Selznick and everyone except Clark Gable. He had help when he fell ill (for example, from Sam Wood), but he knew that Selznick was the overwhelming auteur on this project. The film opened just a few months after the Second World War began in Europe, and so America identified with this Civil War story of surviving at all costs – augmented by the fact that for three years they had been raised to want the movie (there is a funny lampoon of it in *The Awful Truth, see pages 58–59*).

Then it went on and on, so that for generations it was not just a classic but the epitome of that old marvel of going regularly to the movies. The picture has never stopped making money. But because Selznick, its exhilarated champion, was burnt out, he let the whole thing fall into MGM's hands. *Wind* kept Metro alive for years and decades when that studio was crumbling. For generations, its music and its look meant 'the movies'.

So there's no need to defend Gone With the Wind – but much reason for smiling at its eminence. It is proof that small stories about thwarted love and spoiled people have a better chance of making their mark than studies of race, the Civil War or women in the 19th century. So for many the war is still painted as Techicolor and Vivien Leigh's studious Southern accent, fire and Gable's slick grin, instead of an open wound and damage to so many ideas.

Director
Victor Fleming

Producer
David O. Selznick

Writer
Sidney Howard, from the novel by Margaret Mitchell

Cinematographers
Ernest Haller and
Ray Rennahan

Production company
Selznick International

Cast
Clark Gable
Vivien Leigh
Olivia de Havilland
Leslie Howard
Hattie McDaniel

Other films
★ *Red Dust* (1932)
★ *Bombshell* (1933)
★ *Captains Courageous* (1937)
★ *Test Pilot* (1938)
★ *The Wizard of Oz* (1939)

FILM: THE CRITICS' CHOICE America: The Studio Years

The Shop Around the Corner

Ernst Lubitsch *1940*

Everyday life in the United States in 1940 was under greater threat than in 1937. The US was not yet at war, and Hungary was still free from the worst Nazi domination, but the idea of Christmas at Matuschek's shop was already far-fetched. However, director Ernst Lubitsch's urge to recreate Budapest on the MGM soundstage was like a plea for the city's safe-keeping, the more touching in that there is no hint in the film of external or ideological threat.

The Budapest in *The Shop Around the Corner* is fixed on love and shopping, essential bourgeois habits. By 1942, Lubitsch's outrage was complete, and then he made *To Be or Not to Be*, a very American movie about Polish actors performing for Hitler, and the most vivid satire attempted during the Second World War. But do not be deceived by the precious delicacy – like a fine music box – of *The Shop Around the Corner*. Lubitsch knew the risks lovers ran. You can feel his crossed fingers.

This may be Hollywood's most poignant love story, set amid the fussy, heightened naturalism of a little shop where everyone is a character. At work, Alfred and Klara do not get on, no matter that they are James Stewart and Margaret Sullavan. They are vexed by misunderstandings and cross-purposes. But they share one thing: they are both writing heart-felt letters to an unknown correspondent, and through this epistolary communion they have fallen in love. Of course, a moment of discovery will come, and the great Felix Bressart makes it as tense as some moments in Hitchcock films. The real test is whether the two can learn from their secret truth, or whether vanity, pride and common sense will get in the way. It is a close-run thing, and American film has no more heartbreaking shot than that of Sullavan's face gazing into her empty letter-box.

Lubitsch had come so far – from German costume dramas and romantic comedies to Hollywood and Paramount, where he was put in charge of production. He enjoyed considerable acclaim for his silent pictures, including *Lady Windermere's Fan* (1925, *see pages 40–41*), and in the 1930s, with the advent of sound, created a further series of successes – *The Smiling Lieutenant*, *Trouble in Paradise*, *Design for Living*, *The Merry Widow*, *Angel*, and *Ninotchka*. He was the master of sophisticated comedy, whose light touch inspired people like Billy Wilder, who really got his break writing scripts for Lubitsch.

The Shop Around the Corner (written by Lubitsch's best writer, Samson Raphaelson) is something of a departure for the director in that its characters are poor and hard-working, and also because the film relies on the ambience of the shop, with Frank Morgan endearing as the grumpy yet lonely proprietor. It is also the picture in which Lubitsch himself seems most moved and anxious for his lovers. He could be cynical, he could see a heartless world passing by, whereas in *The Shop* there is a chance of real disaster. But it ends well – in one of romance's most tender part-nerships, that of Stewart and Sullavan, who were made for looking at each other. This may be the gravest and most lovely film of my 15, as well as a secure masterpiece.

Director and producer
Ernst Lubitsch

Writer
Samson Raphaelson

Cinematographer
William Daniels

Production company
MGM

Cast
James Stewart
Margaret Sullavan
Frank Morgan
Felix Bressart
Joseph Schildkraut

Other films
★ *Lady Windermere's Fan* (1925)
★ *The Smiling Lieutenant* (1931)
★ *Trouble in Paradise* (1932)
★ *Design for Living* (1933)
★ *The Merry Widow* (1934)
★ *Angel* (1937)
★ *Ninotchka* (1939)
★ *To Be or Not to Be* (1942)

Sullavan and Stewart recreate Budapest on a soundstage. The film was later re-made as You've Got Mail (1998).

His Girl Friday Howard Hawks *1940*

Director and producer
Howard Hawks

A year ahead of *Citizen Kane* (*see pages 66–67*), *His Girl Friday* spilled over with barely registered, overlapping dialogue. It was so assured and intricate that audiences fell back in stupefaction. Who ever said movies were going to be like this? *Kane* achieved a similar effect through brazen structure and so many new techniques, whereas *His Girl Friday* is a kind of remake, with the added force of the foot going down hard on the accelerator. It is recognizably akin to earlier movies – yet dauntingly fast, hard and intelligent. Indeed, this is a movie in which it really does seem to be fun to be in the newspaper business.

The Front Page (1931) had worked before; it would work again. The Hecht–MacArthur play is a fond satire on a raucous, cut-throat life that boys would never get out of their system. Then Howard Hawks supposed that in the loving duel of wits between editor and star reporter, the reporter could be a woman. Suppose, too, that they had been married once – and then divorced (because, honestly, it's no life for stay-at-home lovers). And suppose that Hildy kicks the game off by coming to the office to tell Walter that she is going to marry Ralph Bellamy – oh, sweet, obdurate Ralph Bellamy, as stiff as a wall, and who can play squash without a wall? (Never ask what Hildy ever saw in Ralph, just realize that the game has to be started somehow.)

So, *His Girl Friday* is the most frightening comedy of remarriage – those films (like *The Awful Truth*, *see pages 58–59*, and *The Philadelphia Story*, 1940) in which a marriage is renewed under threat of one of the freed partners marrying someone else. No wonder Hollywood loved that genre, for it had pioneered divorce, as well as the fearful/hopeful notion that you should try again. But Walter and Hildy are lovers only while they are at war, playing the game, a furiously adolescent attitude – or is it piercing wisdom: that people are only in love when they are at risk of losing one another? For within the frantic, exhilarating action, there is a bleak subtext: that to be in love requires not fine nature, just devilish cunning.

It is a matter of dismal fact that young audiences today cannot keep up with *His Girl Friday*. It talks too fast, it involves people who are charged with intelligence, and its mood shifts. So *Gone With the Wind* (*see pages 60–61*) and *Citizen Kane* are the eternally famous American pictures, monuments to box office and being arty. But here comes *His Girl Friday*, wriggling in between them, a big hit and a masterpiece of wit, a film as squeamish about family values and home truths as it is appalled by Bellamyism.

Yes, of course it is funny; and of course Cary Grant and Rosalind Russell have to be seen to be believed. But, more than 60 years on, this slight departure from a set genre is a timeless film, and one that cuts as deep into human nature as *Kane*. And it was made by Howard Hawks, a man who casually excelled in every genre his system could create, and who remains the most profound and American artist Hollywood ever had.

Writers

Charles Lederer and Ben
Hecht, from the play *The
Front Page* by Hecht and
Charles MacArthur

Cinematographer

Joseph Walker

Production company

Columbia

Cast

Rosalind Russell
Cary Grant
Ralph Bellamy

Other films

★ *Scarface* (1932)
★ *Twentieth Century* (1934)
★ *Bringing Up Baby* (1938)
★ *To Have and Have Not* (1945)
★ *The Big Sleep* (1946)
★ *Red River* (1948)

*Grant (in another timeless performance) and
Russell, swapping some of the fastest dialogue
in the history of film.*

Citizen Kane
Orson Welles 1941

Director and producer
Orson Welles

How does one convey a sense of *Citizen Kane* in a short essay? First of all, see it, then see it again. That is not facetiousness; *Kane* may be the first film made in the United States that needed to be seen more than once. That is a sign of ambition, grandeur, and worse. And it is a fatal error if you think – as most people did in 1941, as much as today – that you could take a movie in at one gulp. So *Citizen Kane* was made against the American grain.

Orson Welles was hired by RKO as no one had ever been before, in the hope that his boy-wonderism would spread from the theatre and radio to film. The story goes that he was given carte blanche by the studio, which is untrue, but he had liberty and final-cut enough to win him enemies forever in Hollywood. It was as if the system had said, 'Let's be artistic for a change', which was a way of snubbing all the 'easy' art of, say, Lubitsch, Sternberg and Hawks.

Then, in an act of self-destruction, Welles, his screenwriter Herman J. Mankiewicz, and his friend John Houseman took on the newspaper magnate William Randolph Hearst. This is also the first cloud of confusion for a movie that is really focused on George Orson Welles. It is a picture about a wonder boy – full of charm and empti-ness – and Welles could not resist the sly challenge of being that man on screen.

And so the story of a media tycoon actually circles the strange case of Orson Welles – genius, boy, master and invalid. So many contradic-tions and so much hope of grand meaning. With cameraman Gregg Toland, and with a fair knowledge of German Expressionism, Welles found a sumptuous Gothic studio style that was, incidentally, essential in the making of *film noir* and was ideally suited to Kane, a self-pitying gangster trapped in a large corner.

But Welles was an inveterate storyteller, brim full of excitement (another side of his personality, boredom, would ultimately prove to be his personal and creative enemy), and he was quite determined to make a picture that would both dominate and expose the mass of ordinary American films for what they were. It is, of course, no exaggeration to say that, by 1960, those aims had been met, but by then Welles was living out his own version of Kane's outcast existence – an *East of Eden* (see pages 70–71) in which no sentimental rescue works.

So, is it a great film? *The* great film? Of course it is, as well as a subtle curse on Welles himself and American film. He could not top it, but neither has the system. And so it continues to be voted the best film for ever and ever, which is enough to make you think the medium is dead. And why not? *Citizen Kane* is a film about death and posterity made by a young man already wistful about how he would be regarded after he was gone. And just as it has persuaded so many young people to go into film, so it has been the mocking observer of their relatively feeble efforts. If only we could forget it, or start again, but that is impossible. *Kane* is there, somehow, in nearly every good film made ever since. It is brilliant, it is moving, it is still new; it is surprising.

Writers
Herman J. Mankiewicz
and Orson Welles

Cinematographer
Gregg Toland

Production company
RKO

Cast
Orson Welles
Joseph Cotten
Dorothy Comingore
Everett Sloane

Other films
★ *The Magnificent Ambersons* (1942)
★ *The Lady from Shanghai* (1948)
★ *Othello* (1952)
★ *Mr Arkadin* (1955)
★ *Touch of Evil* (1958)

Welles (centre) with Everett Sloane (right) and Joseph Cotten (left). Cotten went on to work with Welles on The Magnificent Ambersons *(1942),* The Third Man *(1949) and* Touch of Evil *(1958).*

The Ministry of Fear Fritz Lang *1944*

Director
Fritz Lang

Neither Graham Greene, whose 1943 novel had inspired it, nor Fritz Lang, who directed it, liked the movie of *The Ministry of Fear*. It is easy to see why: although made in the midst of war, the film has a false English atmosphere. The plot and the acting have some of the artificiality associated with mystery stories of the Agatha Christie school. At face value, it is the story of Stephen Neale (Ray Milland), let out of an asylum for the criminally insane and plunged into a fanciful web of espionage. His love interest is played by Marjorie Reynolds, one of the flimsier actresses ever to take a lead role. Lang was also in a state of steady hostility with his producer and screenwriter Seton I. Miller.

And yet *The Ministry of Fear* is a masterpiece of film style, a living testament to the notion that material of the lowest sort and players of minimal interest could be elevated by a visionary director. As a matter of fact, the career of Lang – the Viennese-born would-be architect who became the maestro of German film after Murnau and Lubitsch had left Berlin, but who then followed them to the United States – is full of instances where trite material makes a better film than more respectable stories and ideas (see *Metropolis*, *pages 40–45*). For everything was coloured by Lang's way of seeing.

He used a strictly formal approach – the viewer of *The Ministry of Fear* would be well advised to count the doorways and thresholds that figure in the action. This is a way of fixing on what form meant to Lang. The threshold is a metaphor for the entrance to the unknown and the division between mysterious spaces. *The Ministry of Fear*, like most Lang films, is a study of claustrophobia and confinement; it is a maze in which we begin to wonder whether liberty or imprisonment is the more natural state.

This may sound far-fetched, or arty – almost as if film is only a pattern of geometric compositions – but Lang's art was stealthier than that: there is a clinging emotional charge in the constancy of the framing. The more intriguing question – especially in view of Lang's own earlier flight from Nazism – is how the fatalism really sinks in. Do we want the hero to survive, to break out of the trap, or does the implacable visual logic, and the beauty that expresses it, exult in the confinement? There is a happy ending to *The Ministry of Fear* that is both automatic and hollow. But the ending before the ending, which shows a policeman ascending a staircase and coming up to the doorway, is ambiguous in the extreme. Is the policeman a rescuer, or does he represent doom? Lang never fully made up his mind about such authority figures, because his way of seeing them was so full of foreboding and so much more persuasive than his intellectual attachment to virtue. In truth, Lang was too cold to see or feel virtue; his fear passes through his eyes and onto the screen, where it is sometimes paralysing to behold.

Producer
Seton I. Miller

Writer
Seton I. Miller, from the novel
by Graham Greene

Cinematographer
Henry Sharp

Production company
Paramount

Cast
Ray Milland
Marjorie Reynolds
Carl Esmond
Dan Duryea

Other films
★ *Dr Mabuse* (1921–22)
★ *Metropolis* (1927)
★ *Spies* (1928)
★ *The Woman in the Moon* (1929)
★ *M* (1931)
★ *You Only Live Once* (1938)
★ *The Big Heat* (1953)

Ray Milland (left), the focus of a paranoiac spy hunt. Graham Greene's famously cinematic writing provided the basis for other classics like Brighton Rock *(1947) and* The Third Man *(1949).*

Meet Me in St Louis
Vincente Minnelli *1944*

Director
Vincente Minnelli

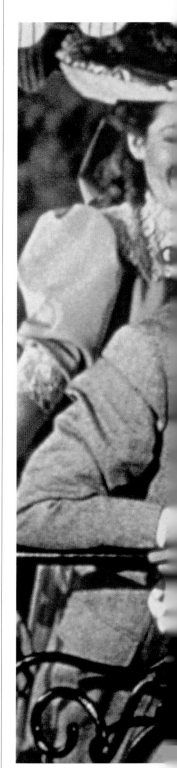

People usually pass over the stories that musicals are trying to tell; the appeal of the genre is in the song and dance. So it is enough for the plot to be some simple love story engaged in by wholesome but shallow kids. Not that Hollywood ever took that extra, logical step, and offered us a musical that had no story, where mood, song and atmosphere were everything. The more ambitious musicals – for example, *Lady in the Dark* (1944) – were flops on film. And the great modern musicals of Stephen Sondheim – melancholy dramas and interpretations of our culture – have never been attempted on screen.

So *Meet Me in St Louis* is one of the most daring and poignant movie musicals. There is convention: it moves along – like family life – from one season to another, and the plot seems nothing more than the way young people in a large provincial town fall in and out of love, and the rather remorseless way in which marriage closes in on them. It seems that Rose, the dullest girl in the family, will marry her beau, but Esther (Judy Garland) is going to do better than 'The Boy Next Door'. As for Tootie, her ship has not yet been built, let alone put to sea. But there is another plot motif. As the film begins, it is likely that the Smiths will be leaving St Louis. The father is good at his job, so New York beckons – and Judy Garland's eyes are as wide as Broadway. Moving is the American habit, or answer, far more so than in Europe. But these Smiths give it up. Why? Because St Louis, with its world's fair, is as good as anywhere? Because the children – those terrible conservatives – cannot bear to give up what they know? Because of some dread of change overshadowing the soul? Or is it simply 1944, with fighting men hoping that nothing will be altered in smaller towns than St Louis, or in the hearts of plainer girls than the Smiths?

So this is, in fact, a picture made by some smart, cosmopolitan people about the abiding charm of home, stasis and the lack of alteration, none of which is particularly or famously American. Yet the best songs in the film – like 'Have Yourself a Merry Little Christmas' – are poised on the edge of loss. The enchanted moments, like the front parlour cakewalk, are tributes to nostalgia and the undying light of memory that sustains it.

There are so many things to be enchanted by: the pretty tableaux that slide into life, the amber fall of Esther's hair, the songs, Judy, the vibrant colour, and Judy being gazed upon by Vincente Minnelli for the summer in which there was nothing wrong or awkward. Of course, none of that lasted: the marriage, Judy and the Technicolor all perished. Judy was so restless, she was looking to be someone in Sondheim. Re-made today, the story might start with Tootie, the last one left, selling the house, as in Welles's version of *The Magnificent Ambersons* (1942), where the Ambersons' mansion is sold and turned into a lodging house. But here, with the United States at war, the domestic kingdom of St Louis is safe and secure.

Producer
Arthur Freed

Writers
Irving Brecher and Fred F.
Finklehoffe, from the novel
by Sally Benson

Cinematographer
George Folsey

Production company
MGM

Cast
Judy Garland
Margaret O'Brien
Lucille Bremer
Mary Astor

Other films
★ *The Pirate* (1947)
★ *An American in Paris* (1950)
★ *The Bad and the Beautiful* (1952)
★ *Lust for Life* (1956)
★ *Gigi* (1958)
★ *Some Came Running* (1959)

*Judy Garland's performance, as vibrant as the
Technicolor, is at the centre of one of the all-time
great American musicals.*

It's a Wonderful Life Frank Capra *1946*

Director and producer
Frank Capra

Even without television and the American legislation that forced movie studios to sell off their cinemas, it is arguable that the audience of 1945 could never regain the mindset of the 1930s. So many ingredients in the American dream were now suspect – not least the happy ending. Thus, it is fascinating to see James Stewart and Frank Capra (both of whom had real personal wars in which they came close to breakdown) wrestling with the issue of the happy ending in *It's a Wonderful Life*.

An ordinary man, George Bailey has never taken great chances in life – in that sense, he is like the Smiths in *Meet Me in St Louis* (*see pages 70–71*). Rather than leave the small town of Bedford Falls for fame and fortune (and his own liberty), he has stayed. There have been compensations: he is married to Mary, his forever sweetheart; he runs a savings and loan bank that protects small people from the rapacious tycoon Potter; and he has the respect of his world.

But there is a mishap at the bank; vital money is believed to have been lost and George faces ruin and disgrace. At which point, as so often in Capra, the decent, stalwart man becomes hysterical. He plans suicide. But a trainee angel, Clarence, stops him by showing him what Bedford Falls would be like without George. It is a vision of *noir* and a threatening night-town thrown into the Christmas-card mix, and it is harrowingly convincing – over the years, we have seen this Pottersville come to life all over the United States.

So George is held back from self-destruction, and everything turns out all right in a wild haze of snow and tears that shows how close Capra was to break-down. Strangely, the film was not a huge success in 1946, yet over the following decades it became a landmark in America's sense of itself, and the obligatory Christmas movie (the film was partly inspired by Dickens' 1843 story, *A Christmas Carol*). Was the film's later success attributed to its rebuilding of personal confidence and its faith in common purpose? I think not – although there are great arguments about how to read this classic. It seems to me that *It's a Wonderful Life* is the annual rite of renewal in a culture that is no longer sure of confidence. The degree to which the ugliness of the night-town sequence was prophetic cannot be eliminated; it is a spur to the film's melancholy and George's anxiety. This is a picture about unease and vulnerability, and so it deserves to be seen as a crucial, if unconscious, *film noir*.

Historically, Capra never got his confidence back, and Stewart was always a more interesting actor afterwards because his hopeful eyes had grown guarded. The portrait of small-town America is an achievement rooted in the 1930s, replete with delicious supporting characters and a steadily white, mainstream cast. But no one, I would suggest, in modern times can see the film without adding after the given title the modernist coda, 'Isn't it?' And as the years pass, so we feel more and more in need of reassurance. Did Capra intend all that? I doubt it. Did it actually embody his postwar dismay? Yes, I think so. In which case – and this only adds to the poignancy – it is rather less his film than America's shared dream, or nightmare. In the immediate aftermath of a devastating war in which millions of Americans went 'back' to worlds they had left, this movie cherishes the shelter of an idyllic small town.

Writers

Frances Goodrich, Albert
Hackett and Frank Capra,
based on a story by Philip
Van Doren Stern

Cinematographers

Joseph Walker
and Joseph Biroc

Production companies

RKO/Liberty Films

Cast

James Stewart
Henry Travers
Donna Reed
Lionel Barrymore

Other films

★ *It Happened One Night* (1934)
★ *Mr Deeds Goes to Town* (1936)
★ *Mr Smith Goes to Washington* (1939)
★ *Meet John Doe* (1941)
★ *State of the Union* (1948)

Thomas Mitchell (left), Donna Reed and James Stewart in the film's seasonal finale. The Philip Van Doren Stern story on which the film was based had originally been written as a Christmas card.

In a Lonely Place Nicholas Ray 1950

Director
Nicholas Ray

Here is a portrait of Hollywood losing confidence in itself. Dixon Steele (Humphrey Bogart), a depressed screenwriter, comes under suspicion in a murder case. At the same time he meets Laurel Gray (Gloria Grahame) and feels the chance of a saving relationship. In the old formula, Laurel would help to prove his innocence, but now Dix is exonerated only after a prolonged ordeal that reveals to Laurel how easily he could have been a killer. In other words, his unhappiness (which includes the difficulty of doing good work) is murderous, and not even Laurel can save him from himself.

In a Lonely Place refers to Hollywood as much as to the recesses of personality, and it deserves to be seen in the context of several films around 1950 that suddenly regarded Hollywood, or show-business, with suspicion – *Sunset Boulevard*, *The Bad and the Beautiful*, *All About Eve*, *The Barefoot Contessa*. Yet *In a Lonely Place* is more sombre than these films because the corruption of Hollywood is viewed with less melodrama. Rather, the feeling is like that of a man preparing to do surgery on himself, estimating how far the infection has spread. Its director, Nicholas Ray, was one of the great hopes of the period – an idealist, a romantic and a stylist. *They Live by Night* (1949) was one of the most celebrated American debuts of the era, and ten years later, after *Rebel Without a Cause*, *Bigger Than Life* and *Bitter Victory*, Ray was a test case in the debate about what a good director should be doing. *In a Lonely Place* was highly relevant in that argument for it was made as the marriage between Ray and Grahame was corroding. Further, as Gloria Grahame went on to marry Ray's son by an earlier marriage, the chaos behind this ideal career was made painfully clear.

Shot in black-and-white and for a regular screen (it was made before CinemaScope became available), *In a Lonely Place* is not as desperately beautiful as some of Ray's later films, but its close-up photography brings out a wealth of psychological meanings. Ray was a leading figure in the last American generation to believe in the eloquence of camera style, and a fascinating figure in the line that reaches from D. W. Griffith to Martin Scorsese. But Ray's failure to sustain a career – because of his neurosis and instability as much as the system's hostility – is a warning to American film. He does not see the madness in the business and art of film as Wilder and Minnelli did. Instead, he feels the existential anxiety in all people, a feeling that is likely to block or interfere with sustained, profitable work. You can argue that Nick Ray was one of the first people who believed in (who longed for?) the death of film. If that seems perverse, remember that Steele is writing in a system he despises, and for a medium he doubts. He is so typical of the writer who gave up novels for a success that he hates.

Of course, Ray was a romantic, and was caught up in a self-destructive psychodrama. It would take Jean-Luc Godard's early work – especially *Contempt* (*Le Mépris*, 1963), a very Ray-like film – to show a romantic who could also analyse the pressures of business and media studies. Ray (like Dix Steele) was his own worst enemy. It was above all in the failure of love that Ray measured the tragic implications of life. Steele and Ray do not like themselves – and American cinema has not yet proved it can sustain that fissure.

Producer
Robert Lord

Writer
Andrew Solt, from the novel
by Dorothy B. Hughes

Cinematographer
Burnett Guffey

Production companies
Columbia/Santana

Cast
Humphrey Bogart
Gloria Grahame
Frank Lovejoy

Other films
★ *They Live by Night* (1949)
★ *Rebel Without a Cause* (1955)
★ *Bigger Than Life* (1956)
★ *Bitter Victory* (1957)
★ *55 Days at Peking* (1963)

*Humphrey Bogart and Gloria Grahame. Bogart's
character here is possibly the most fully realized
example of Ray's solitary, alienated protagonists.*

Rear Window Alfred Hitchcock *1954*

Director and producer
Alfred Hitchcock

Writer
John Michael Hayes, from a
story by Cornell Woolrich

Cinematographer
Robert Burks

Production company
Paramount

Cast
James Stewart
Grace Kelly
Thelma Ritter
Wendell Corey
Raymond Burr

Other films
★ *The 39 Steps* (1935)
★ *The Lady Vanishes* (1938)
★ *Rebecca* (1940)
★ *Notorious* (1946)
★ *Strangers on a Train*
 (1951)
★ *Dial M for Murder* (1954)
★ *Vertigo* (1958)
★ *North by Northwest*
 (1959)
★ *Psycho* (1960)
★ *The Birds* (1963)
★ *Marnie* (1964)

Why is *Rear Window* such fun? You can say that the teasing entertainer in Alfred Hitchcock was never better employed. You could point to the sweet transition from the humdrum – so many plain lives observed in one New York City courtyard – to magnificent melodrama: murder! You could throw in that the suggestiveness of Grace Kelly was never more fragrant. You can adore Thelma Ritter's grouchy masseuse, Wendell Corey's dry-starch cop, and Raymond Burr's ambivalent presence. Remember how much we identify with James Stewart, as the news photographer with a broken leg, so bored that he has nothing better to do than spy on his neighbours (though Stewart has a palpably chillier air than he had for Lubitsch or Capra).

But there is one larger thing: there is a cosiness in the set-up that reminds us how alike we are –. the audience and the Stewart character – sitting safe in the dark, watching and wondering. *Rear Window* whispers to us that we are all voyeurs now – and that it is OK.

The film comes from a Cornell Woolrich story, but it brightens it up. Woolrich was one of the most important, gloomy neurotics behind *film noir*. All Hitchcock and his writer John Michael Hayes had taken was the situation. They added the girl – and see how the panorama of lives on view is also a survey of marriage in the United States (from blinds-lowered honeymoon to murder): the one thing more imprisoning than a plaster cast that Lisa Fremont has in mind for L. B. Jeffries is marriage. It is this inner theme that permits those desperate moments in *Rear Window* when comedy and dread jostle together in tight situations (like Lisa flashing the lost wedding ring).

Hitch was in love with this project because it was an ideal sedentary model for the way he liked to treat the medium: all those movie-screen windows where he can control the information outlet meticulously, teaching us how to use our eyes and ears. For myself, I like the light touch he brings to the final question the murderer asks of Stewart – 'What do you want of me?' – because it keeps the metaphor for responsibility playful. There was another fellow in Hitchcock who could grow ponderous and sad, and *Vertigo* (1958) – much as I love it – strays into purely neurotic feelings. Hitch liked to be funny, and was always appreciative of smart, attractive characters that we like to look at. *Rear Window* is a great fantasy, as well as a gentle lesson: we want to be in that precious apartment, restless in the hot night, half awake, half asleep, not quite sure what we saw and when we saw it, but seduced by the mood.

So *Rear Window* has a level of pleasure that makes the meaning more palatable. Equally, I would take Hitch's *North by Northwest* (1959) over his *The Wrong Man* (1957) any time. It is a fascinating career in which a natural genius (though not the nicest of men) was always wondering how far he could go. At his best, and his worst, Hitchcock was such an enthusiast for the medium that he teaches us about it. That lesson could feel contrived, but Hitch is the best director for film studies.

East of Eden
Elia Kazan *1955*

Director and producer
Elia Kazan

Adapted from a John Steinbeck novel (1952), *East of Eden* is a version of the Cain and Abel story in which the maligned Cain becomes the hero. In the 1950s, the American film was actively rehabilitating former villains (with such engaging scoundrels or monsters as Robert Walker in *Strangers on a Train*, Kirk Douglas in *The Bad and the Beautiful*, Marlon Brando in *A Streetcar Named Desire*, Robert Mitchum in *The Night of the Hunter*). But in *East of Eden*, Cain's solitary and selfish nature is given over to the aching self-pity of James Dean.

The film is only a fraction of the novel. In the book, Steinbeck told the story of the parents when they were young. That is gone on screen, along with the character of Lee, a Chinese family retainer. What we get instead is a 1950s psychodrama about an un-appreciated boy, Cal, who persuades the receptive Abra and his father that he is more worthy of affection than dull brother Aaron.

Under the spell of Kazan's intense emotionalism, one accepts the stuffy Aaron as a way of seeing how much more mature and inquisitive Cal is. But deep down this is also Elia Kazan projecting his own story through the gestures of Method acting. Kazan only came to life as a director/artist once he had grasped his own unlikeability. In real life, he named names to the communist-hunting House Committee on Un-American Activities in 1952. *On the Waterfront* (1954) was his first 'liberated' film, and a thinly veiled validation of informing. *East of Eden* is a far better film and a more capacious metaphor in that the insidious magic of Cal depends not just on Dean's performance but on the powerful way in which the darkness subdues the wholesome, rural light.

The Method dated quickly: it was always open to charges of incoherence and self-indulgent hesitations. But Dean at the start was hungry and willing, and he needed a father figure as much as Kazan wanted to be seen as an outcast. The symbiotic relationship between director and actor has few richer examples. Further, Kazan was brilliant at pitching a favoured actor against other players – so Dean and Julie Harris were entirely empathetic, while Dean and Raymond Massey could scarcely co-exist.

For Kazan, this is a story about a son who is innately wiser than the father. That flattered the director's own life, and his decision to name others to the Committee. But it also delighted teen audiences in the 1950s. That Kazan was a great director of actors is beyond dispute – and *East of Eden* shows how far such command can go (just look at Jo Van Fleet's presentation of the mother in a few brief moments). But Kazan was more than that in the mid-1950s. He had fallen in love with screen space and composition, and he was one of several directors who saw a beautiful challenge in CinemaScope, a photographic and projection system with a sweeping range for a wide screen. So the emotions of this story are always being depicted in terms of physical *mise en scène* (the construction and composition of a scene), and the confines of space. In the end, though, the Method's inclination to turn films over to actors helps explain the worst examples of actor-power in Hollywood and the desolation of a Marlon Brando commanding a production but hardly knowing what to do with it. What is so rare about Kazan is that, while giving so much to actors, he remained so domineering a director. His greatest self-vindication was to leave Brando inept without him.

Writer
Paul Osborn, from the novel
by John Steinbeck

Cinematographer
Ted McCord

Production company
Warner Brothers

Cast
James Dean
Raymond Massey
Julie Harris
Dick Davalos
Jo Van Fleet

Other films
★ *Gentleman's Agreement* (1947)
★ *A Streetcar Named Desire* (1951)
★ *Viva Zapata!* (1952)
★ *On the Waterfront* (1954)
★ *Baby Doll* (1956)
★ *Wild River* (1960)
★ *Splendour in the Grass* (1961)

James Dean (left, with Julie Harris and Raymond Massey) benefited from Kazan's skill with actors, as had Brando before him.

Man of the West
Anthony Mann *1958*

The Western in *Man of the West* centres on a feud, long over but not forgotten. Link Jones (Gary Cooper, only three years away from death) is a reformed character, sent by his small town with the money to hire a schoolteacher. But his train is robbed and he is left travelling on foot, with two others as hindrances, to reclaim the money. Something about the sad, sunless country guides him back to an old house. At first it seems green and grey, sinking into the landscape, not just forgotten but abandoned. But his fears are proved correct, for outlawry and his own crooked family still live there.

One of the 'hindrances' Cooper picks up is a singer-whore, played by Julie London. Thus, in the house of the past he has to claim her as his woman, but still she is threatened with rape by his old associates, and even by his crazed father-figure, Dock Tobin (Lee J. Cobb). That accounts for the famous but ugly scene where London is forced to undress as Cooper is held at knife-point, and the scene where he strips one of the outlaws in revenge.

The film could be subtler without Julie London, who is unmistakably a 1950s singer trying to break into pictures. Suppose her character was a potential schoolteacher – suppose she was Cathy O'Donnell in Anthony Mann's *The Man from Laramie* (1955). And suppose she attracted Cooper, even as her correct language and academic knowledge let him know he was still wild. (Suppose he cannot read.) This is probably beyond the clearcut pathos of Gary Cooper in 1958; it is a role for a less secure actor, for Richard Widmark perhaps, a man who might slip back. The idea and reality of education need to occupy a stronger place in the film, and the Cooper character needs to feel some call of the wild. After all, we know now how long that lawless impulse for freedom lasted – as seen in the exultant self-destructiveness in Peckinpah's violent Western *The Wild Bunch* (1969; *see pp94–95*).

Still, Mann had no equal at putting a fable in its landscaped context, and *Man of the West* becomes sublime as the demented, ingrown gang plans to rob a large-town bank – their last hurrah. There is no way the shift from pasture to desert fits real country, but it is perfectly attuned to the Tobins' alienation that the vaunted Lassoo proves to be an abandoned ghost town. That is where the last confrontation takes place, and where Cooper proves that he is reformed by killing off his old family.

So, near enough, the classic Western genre ends with a beautiful film, yet one that misses the full historic complexity of what happened in the West from around 1860 until now. The Western was not made by movies alone – a rich written tradition inspired many screenplays – but all over the world it was brought to life on movie screens. This is a very good Western, nearly a great film, but it is most interesting now for how it falls short. The movies had failed American history: that is one of the most serious charges not yet settled.

Director
Anthony Mann

Producer
Walter M. Mirisch

Writer
Reginald Rose, from the novel *The Border Jumpers* by Will C. Brown

Cinematographer
Ernest Haller

Production companies
UA/Ashton

Cast
Gary Cooper
Lee J. Cobb
Julie London
Arthur O'Connell

Other films
★ *Reign of Terror* (1949)
★ *Winchester 73* (1950)
★ *The Naked Spur* (1953)
★ *The Far Country* (1954)
★ *The Man from Laramie* (1955)
★ *Men in War* (1956)
★ *El Cid* (1961)

Cooper standing guard over the 'singer-whore', played by Julie London.

Anatomy of a Murder Otto Preminger *1959*

Director and producer
Otto Preminger

Despite that alluring 'anatomy', we never see the murder or what prompted it in this film. Otto Preminger's favourite subject was what people thought of sensational events and how they then responded, with or without intelligence. So this is a courtroom movie that puts the audience in the position of the jury, but which never supposes a precious, single truth waiting to be trusted.

Jimmy Stewart is Paul Biegler, a bachelor and a lawyer, loyal to his old friends, to fishing and to jazz (the movie is enriched by Duke Ellington's witty and seductive score, while, by contrast, the Thunder Bay landscape remains plain and black-and-white). But Biegler is one mean lawyer: crafty, manipulative, playing the game, and just as good as George C. Scott's flamboyant prosecuting attorney, from the sophisticated city of Lansing. The film treats them as two expert practitioners, working in different styles (town and country), but both certain that a trial is an exercise in presentation, a play.

So, did the innkeeper rape Laura Manion (Lee Remick)? Was her husband, Lt Manion (Ben Gazzara), so demented that he responded to an irresistible impulse to kill? These questions are made doubly enthralling by the lazy insolence of Ben Gazzara, the flirty bounce of Lee Remick, and Preminger's interest in how irrational bias affects conscious action.

Anatomy of a Murder has many artful touches, not least the authenticity supplied by shrewdly chosen supporting players, including Eve Arden, Arthur O'Connell, Murray Hamilton and Joseph N. Welch – the honoured real-life lawyer who represented the army, accused by Senator McCarthy in 1952 of 'coddling communists'. It was said that Preminger was just being opportunist in casting Welch as the judge, but he was also extending the reach of ambivalence to test the sincerity and rhetoric in Welch's famous admonition of McCarthy, 'Have you no decency at last, sir?'

It is Welch in 1959 who helps us recognize how far Preminger had foreseen the America of televised courtroom dramas. The law is not made for fictional characters, for people we are sure of liking or disliking. Rather, it is an instrument through which society reaches decisions about people we can never know or stop wondering about. The O. J. Simpson trial was a fulfilment of Preminger's predictions.

So the law makes mistakes – like referees and umpires in other games – but the official documents and newspapers record the result. The value and efficacy of American justice depends on the shared understanding that the law must take its course and reach a decision. Yet, like Jean Renoir in *La Règle du jeu* (1939), Preminger believed not just that everyone has his reasons for acting in a specific way, but that everyone believes he is right – and so subjectivity comes into conflict with seemingly objective justice. This treatment of justice was the first step in a trilogy that also took on nationalism (*Exodus*, 1960) and religion (*The Cardinal*, 1963). But even in *Laura* (1944), Preminger's first real film, he was interested less in what had been done than in the mixed motives of Laura, Waldo and Mark.

Anatomy of a Murder is a timeless entertainment. We still need to be told by the judge to finish our giggling over the word 'panties', and then realize how much they mean in this case. So courts judge and wise people note the verdict while keeping their minds open. As in Preminger's best dramas, life is a story of the mistakes we make.

Writer
Wendell Mayes, from the
novel by Robert Traver

Cinematographer
Sam Leavitt

Production companies
Columbia/Carlyle/
Otto Preminger

Music
Duke Ellington

Cast
James Stewart
Ben Gazzara
Lee Remick
George C. Scott

Other films
★ *Laura* (1944)
★ *Daisy Kenyon* (1947)
★ *Angel Face* (1952)
★ *Carmen Jones* (1954)
★ *Bonjour Tristesse* (1957)
★ *Exodus* (1960)
★ *The Cardinal* (1963)

Lee Remick (left), James Stewart (centre), Eve Arden (second from right) and Ben Gazzara (right) in the courtroom.

MAIN: *A publicity still for Paul Morrisey's* Flesh *(1968, produced by Andy Warhol).*
BELOW TOP: *Sidney Poitier in Norman Jewison's* In the Heat of the Night *(1967).*
BOTTOM: *John Cassavetes'* Husbands *(1970).*

CHAPTER THREE

America: Years of Change

Philip French

In 1960, the one bright ray shining on Hollywood was the virtual ending of the black-list, which for 13 years had blighted the industry by forcing many left-wing artists out of business or compelling them to work under pseudonyms. Otherwise, the atmosphere was gloomy. The major studios – their chains of cinemas dispersed by federal trust-busting actions, their once grand rosters of contract artists and technicians reduced to skeleton staffs by television – were on the point of disappearing. Most established directors from Hollywood's golden age were approaching the end of their careers, although they were at last being acclaimed as old masters, as auteurs, by the influential writings of the critics-turned-directors who formed the French New Wave (*nouvelle vague*). The films of these young Frenchmen, along with innovatory work from elsewhere in Europe, made Hollywood appear dowdy, uninventive, moribund. Many gifted Americans moved to Europe.

But Hollywood fought back, beginning with the appointment in 1966 of President Johnson's chief aide Jack Valenti as head of the Motion Picture Association of America. His first act was to dispense with the stifling 36-year-old Production Code, which had set moral standards for films and had prevented American filmmakers from competing for adult audiences with foreign productions, but his chief project over the next three decades was to restore the American industry's worldwide pre-eminence.

The big Hollywood studios survived through mergers with multinational corporations, but their new bosses were sober executives who lacked the showbiz flair of the immigrant entrepreneurs. Following the examples of prewar maverick moguls Sam Goldwyn and David O. Selznick and of the mini-studios known collectively as Poverty Row, independent companies and producers entered the fray. Most produced mainstream pictures, others exploited niche markets. Individualists like Andy Warhol and John Cassavetes, working outside the industry, made films radically different in style and theme. Hollywood was becoming the commercial world cinema; the independent sector was creating an indigenous American cinema.

Fast film and lightweight equipment ushered in a less formal style, influenced by the French New Wave and the documentary movement dubbed *cinéma vérité*. As film schools sprang up across the United States, a new generation of cine-literate moviemakers laid siege to Hollywood, and these 'movie brats' took over from the old masters who had begun their careers during the silent era. They dominated the 1970s, one of the great decades of American cinematic creativity. There was also a major change in the nature of the male stars. Black actors at last had central roles in mainstream cinema (Sidney Poitier emerged in the mid-1960s as the first black superstar) and statuesque all-Americans gave way to physically slighter, less obviously heroic performers, whose names – Pacino, De Niro, Keitel, Hoffman – proclaimed their ethnic hyphenated-American status.

As the 1970s progressed, it also proved to be a dangerous, ill-disciplined time of drugs, egotism, over-reaching conceit and gross financial irresponsibility. By 1980, producers and businessmen were running Hollywood once more. The lunatics who had taken over the asylum (as Chaplin, Griffith, Pickford and Fairbanks had tried to do 60 years before) were restrained again, straitjacketed in their plushly padded cells.

Psycho Alfred Hitchcock *1960*

The 1960s began with one of the most influential movies ever made, a masterpiece of audience manipulation by Alfred Hitchcock, the only movie director immediately recognizable to the general public. Shot in black-and-white for a paltry $800,000, *Psycho* stunned audiences by killing off heroine Marion Crane less than a third of the way through. First seen in white underwear enjoying a guilty tryst, Marion heads off wearing black lingerie and carrying $40,000 stolen from her employer, a Phoenix real-estate agent, to buy happiness with her impoverished lover.

Taking a wrong turning in the rain, Marion is forced to put up at a remote empty motel, where she has a snack with its nervous proprietor, Norman Bates, who lives in a gothic house nearby with his unseen, overbearing mother. In the shower that night, Marion is stabbed to death, apparently by old Mrs Bates. A distraught Norman disposes of her, her car, and the stolen money in a swamp. After this jolt to the system, the viewers are unsure where to place their sympathies – with Marion's sister, Marion's surly boyfriend, the private detective Arbogast sent from Phoenix to recover the money, or with the lonely, fragile Norman who only wants to keep the world at bay and get on with his taxidermy.

From the opening scene, where the camera comes through a hotel bedroom window to intrude on the lovers, Hitchcock creates a sense of unease, which is compounded by Bernard Herrmann's tingling score, performed entirely by stringed instruments. There are only two murders: those of Marion in the shower (a sequence as shocking and as brilliantly edited as the Odessa Steps massacre in Eisenstein's *Battleship Potemkin, see pages 36–37*) and of the private eye on the staircase of the Bates mansion. But a feeling of menace hangs over every foot of the film,

as well as a dark humour, some of which (for example, Norman's line 'Mother – what's the phrase? – isn't quite herself today') is not apparent at a first viewing.

The movie is often cited as an example of pure cinema, where the essential relationship is that between the director and the audience he is toying with and terrifying. But it is also Hitchcock's most wholly American movie. Based on a pulp novel by Robert Bloch (1959), the story is concerned with respectable, lower-middle-class people, and is one of the few Hitchcock movies without a European authority figure. The final scene satirizes the glib, simplistic conclusions of psychoanalysis, but, on a broader canvas, the film is essentially a fable about the corrupting effects of money. Norman Bates, the man who has withdrawn into a backwater of life, is the only character not obsessed with the status–cash nexus. *Psycho* was a great popular success from the start, partly due to a clever publicity campaign, but most critics hated it. 'The film is a reflection of a mean, sly, sadistic little mind', Dwight Macdonald wrote in *Esquire*. 'All in all, a nasty little film'. But critical opinion gradually changed and Hitchcock became the most discussed, analysed and revered filmmaker in cinema history.

Director and producer
Alfred Hitchcock

Writer
Joseph Stefano, from an original novel by Robert Bloch

Cinematographer
John L. Russell

Production company
Shamley Productions

Music
Bernard Herrmann

Cast
Anthony Perkins
Janet Leigh
Vera Miles

Other films
★ *The 39 Steps* (1935)
★ *The Lady Vanishes* (1938)
★ *Rebecca* (1940)
★ *Notorious* (1946)
★ *Strangers on a Train* (1951)
★ *Dial M for Murder* (1954)
★ *Rear Window* (1954)
★ *Vertigo* (1958)
★ *North by Northwest* (1959)
★ *The Birds* (1963)
★ *Marnie* (1964)

The Hustler Robert Rossen 1961

Director and producer
Robert Rossen

Born in New York in 1908, Robert Rossen was the son of poor Jewish immigrants and became a professional boxer to pay his way through college. He established himself as a hard-hitting screenwriter in the late 1930s, was briefly a member of the Communist Party, and became a writer-director in the postwar years, winning an Oscar for *All the King's Men* (1949). He was then black-listed for refusing to discuss his political allegiances, but recanted two years later, named 50 former communist associates and was reinstated. The experience was morally shattering and his subsequent films are about cowardly, self-hating people. The masterpiece that emerged from this dark night of the American soul is *The Hustler*, the finest example of the low-life movie.

The film takes place in a stylized underground inhabited by people who have chosen to live there because they like its smoke-filled atmosphere and existential values, not because they are victims of society. The names of the leading pool players – young contender Fast Eddie Felson (Paul Newman) and reigning champion Minnesota Fats (Jackie Gleason) – are out of Damon Runyon. But there is nothing comic about them. The movie brings the world of *Guys and Dolls* into sharp conjunction with the hard-boiled pulp fiction of Jim Thompson, under the aegis of the satanic gambler Bert Gordon (George C. Scott). The result is a poetic fable about winning and losing, character and self-respect, loyalty and betrayal. It is about people who seek grace but reject social graces.

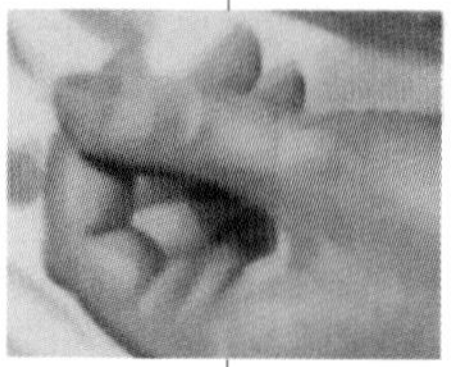

Eddie has come to town with his rather tired middle-aged partner (Myron McCormick), who is a collaborator in Eddie's small-scale hustling and trickery. On the brink of entering the big time, they have a legendary exchange in the New York pool-hall. 'It's like a church, the church of the good hustler,' Fast Eddie says. 'More like a morgue, these tables are like the slabs they lay corpses on,' says his partner. Eddie drops this weak father figure and, after his ignominious defeat by Minnesota Fats, embarks on a healing relationship with a disabled woman (Piper Laurie). She comforts him, feeds off him, and is then destroyed when Eddie finally fulfils the Faustian bargain that he has made with Bert Gordon to re-enter the big time.

There are flaws in this picture (the speeding hands on the poolroom clocks, for example), but they are minor. Scott established himself, in his third screen appearance, as a complex presence; the television comic Gleason took on a tragic aura; and Newman emerged from the twin shadows of Marlon Brando and James Dean to become a bruised, vulnerable star in his own right. Piper Laurie, after a decade of demeaning roles, did justice to a part as resonant as anything Davis or Garbo tackled. Rossen's designer, Harry Horner, went on to work with Walter Hill on *The Driver* (1978), while his assistant, Ulu Grosbard, directed Mamet's *American Buffalo* on Broadway and the low-life movie *Straight Time* (1977). The editor, Dede Allen, cut *Bonnie and Clyde* (1967, *see pages 92–93*), *Dog Day Afternoon* (1975) and *Reds* (1981). The atmospheric images, in black-and-white Cinema-Scope, are the work of Eugen Schüfftan, the innovative veteran German cinematographer who won an Oscar for the film. Oscar-nominee Newman eventually got his award reprising Fast Eddie in Martin Scorsese's *The Color of Money* (1986), which is a film of some quality but inferior to *The Hustler*.

' *... maybe for both of to leave each other alone* "

A 20th CENTURY-FOX
CINEMASCOPE
PICTURE

PAUL

CO STARRING

PIPER LA

MYR

WITH

Writer
Robert Rossen
and Sidney Carroll

Cinematographer
Eugen Schüfftan

Production company
20th Century Fox

Cast
Paul Newman
Jackie Gleason
Piper Laurie
George C. Scott

Other films
★ *All the King's Men* (1949)
★ *Lilith* (1964)

Academy Awards
Oscars for Eugen Schüfftan (Cinematography) and Art Direction (Harry Horner); nominations for Best Picture, Paul Newman as Best Actor, Piper Laurie as Best Actress and Robert Rossen as Best Director, 1962

Paul Newman and Piper Laurie in the original poster for the film. Newman, along with Scott, was nominated for an Oscar.

The Manchurian Candidate

John Frankenheimer *1962*

Director and producer
John Frankenheimer

The Broadway playwright George Axelrod adapted Richard Condon's 1959 novel for John Frankenheimer, a prolific director of live television drama who was establishing himself as one of Hollywood's leading talents. *The Manchurian Candidate* and its successor, *Seven Days in May* (1963), subtly shifted Hollywood's political agenda and created a new kind of conspiracy thriller. President Kennedy helped persuade United Artists to finance the film and later provided White House locations for *Seven Days in May*, the story of an attempted right-wing military coup.

The Manchurian Candidate is laced with black humour in a style reminiscent of Alfred Hitchcock, casting Janet Leigh from *Psycho* (*see pages 86–87*) as the sympathetic heroine and Reggie Nalder, the assassin from *The Man Who Knew Too Much* (1956), as a Soviet villain. Angela Lansbury is a monstrous Hitchcockian mother, while Laurence Harvey, at his most coldly charming, plays her son, the dislikeable upper-class journalist Raymond Shaw.

Shaw, as a national-service soldier, is abducted with the other members of a patrol led by Major Bennett Marco (Frank Sinatra) during the Korean War. During three days captivity he is turned into a brainwashed assassin by scientists from the Pavlov Institute. His comrades (except for two the Russians make him kill) have been conditioned to believe that he has saved their lives, and Raymond returns to the United States a hero. Back home, Major Marco and another soldier have nightmares that spring from their experiences at the Manchurian hospital, and Marco begins to suspect that Raymond is not all he seems. Meanwhile the Russians are preparing to use this zombie-like killer to further the career of his stepfather, Senator Iselin (James Gregory), a communist-baiting McCarthy figure who is being manipulated by his wife, Raymond's hated mother. 'If Iselin were a paid Communist agent he couldn't do more damage than he's doing,' an angry opponent observes.

The movie captures with documentary realism the tense nature of the political world of its time and the emerging role of television in public affairs. However, there is also a strong surrealist element both in the depiction of the brainwashing sessions and in the portrayal of the process through which Raymond is controlled by playing solitaire, as well as in the amusing dialogues between the disturbed Marco and the considerate heroine. Memorable jokes include the cut from a bottle of Heinz ketchup to the dim-witted Iselin declaring to the Senate that there are '57 card-carrying members of the Communist Party' in the State Department; and the shot of milk pouring from the hole in a carton through which a bullet has passed to kill a sanctimonious lily-white liberal. The movie attacks the destructive vindictiveness of the reactionary right without losing sight of the dangers represented by international communism. It uses jokes about paranoia to attack conspiracy thinking (the leading Russian scientist urges his subordinate to develop a sense of humour), but anticipates the national obsession with conspiracy theories following the assassination of Jack Kennedy a year later. In 1968, Bobby Kennedy stayed at Frankenheimer's Californian home the night before he too was assassinated. George Axelrod was later heard to remark – somewhat ruefully – that the film 'went from flop to classic without passing through a period of profitability'.

Co-producers
George Axelrod and
Howard W. Koch

Cinematographer
Lionel Lindon

Writer
George Axelrod, from the
novel by Richard Condon

Production companies
United Artists and
M. C. Productions

Cast
Frank Sinatra
Laurence Harvey
Janet Leigh
Angela Lansbury
Henry Silva

Other films
★ *Birdman of Alcatraz* (1962)
★ *French Connection II* (1975)

Academy Awards
Nominations for Angela Lansbury
(Best Supporting Actress) and Ferris
Webster (Best Film Editor), 1963

*Frank Sinatra (left), Laurence Harvey (centre)
and Tom Lowell (right). The film was one of
Sinatra's best non-musicals, revealing him to
be an actor of distinction.*

Bonnie and Clyde Arthur Penn *1967*

Director
Arthur Penn

Few films of the 1960s made the double impact of this movie, which was first excoriated by leading critics and shortly afterwards celebrated for brilliantly capturing the zeitgeist. *Time* magazine's anonymous review denounced it for glamorizing the lives of its eponymous gangsters, who (like earlier family outlaw bands after the American Civil War) cut a bloody swathe across the southwest in the first years of the Depression before going to early graves. Three months later *Time* made the picture the subject of a laudatory cover story.

The screenplay was written by two fashion-conscious movie buffs, Robert Benton and David Newman, both editors at *Esquire*, who set out to bring the French New Wave together with the Warner Brothers gangster flick of the 1930s. Actor–producer Warren Beatty brought the project to Warners, and in the final sequence he wears a pair of dark glasses with a missing lens in homage to Jean-Paul Belmondo in *A Bout de souffle* (*Breathless,* 1960). The film was offered to François Truffaut and Jean-Luc Godard before Arthur Penn, a stage director with four uneven movies behind him, was given the chance to make his first masterpiece. Beatty also brought in Robert Towne (a key writer of the 1970s) as special consultant, and gave production designer Dean Tavoularis (who designed *The Godfather* trilogy) and costume designer Theadora Van Runkle (*The Godfather Part II*, 1974, *New York, New York*, 1977) their first major assignments. Flatt and Scruggs' jaunty 'Foggy Mountain Breakdown' on the soundtrack introduced country music to mainstream movies. The adventurous nature of the production continued with the casting of the unknown Gene Hackman and Estelle Parsons as the ebullient Buck Barrow and his neurotic wife Blanche, the odd juvenile character actor Michael J. Pollard as the simple-minded getaway driver C. W. Moss, and above all the beautiful newcomer Faye Dunaway playing a frustrated and plausibly working-class Bonnie Parker.

From the opening scene when the dapper Clyde Barrow picks up Bonnie in Depression-haunted West Dallas, the picture explicitly links sex and violence through Clyde's impotence and the pair's love of guns. It also shows the gang as a parodic family, clinging together in the face of a hostile world. They are romantic psychopaths, not sadistic professional criminals, and like the outlaws of the Old West they are in thrall to their own myth, posing for pictures, writing poems to celebrate their deeds, seeing themselves as latterday Robin Hoods, who win the sympathy of the rural dispossessed. The writers see them as more anti-authoritarian than antisocial. They are, of course, doomed, and intimations of imminent death are constant. The movie works by contrasts: the characters' wild energy set against the paralysed society, their sense of community against the general moral breakdown, terrible violence in idyllic surroundings, tender feelings discovered in squalid motels. Beatty's ideal model for a shoot-out was Jack Palance killing Elisha Cook outside the saloon in *Shane* (1953). Repeating this exponentially, *Bonnie and Clyde* upped the stakes on screen violence overnight.

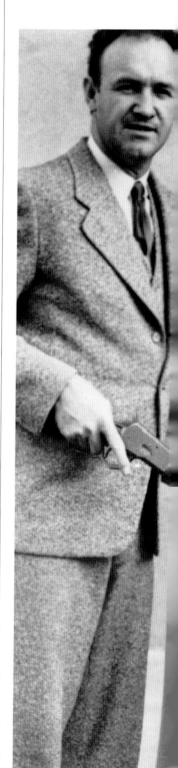

Producer
Warren Beatty

Writers
Robert Benton and David
Newman

Cinematographer
Burnett Guffey

Production company
Tatira-Miller

Cast
Faye Dunaway
Warren Beatty
Gene Hackman
Estelle Parsons
Michael J. Pollard
Gene Wilder

Other films
★ *Alice's Restaurant* (1969)
★ *Four Friends* (1981)

Academy Awards
Oscars for Estelle Parsons
(Best Supporting Actress)
and Burnett Guffey
(Cinematography), 1967

(l–r) Gene Hackman, Estelle Parsons, Warren Beatty, Faye Dunaway and Michael J. Pollard.

The Wild Bunch Sam Peckinpah *1969*

Director
Sam Peckinpah

Sam Peckinpah, whose pioneering grandfather had a Californian mountain named after him, was Hollywood's most troublesome maverick since Erich von Stroheim. After some success as a television writer and director and a period assisting Don Siegel, he made three widescreen Westerns in quick succession – the little-seen *The Deadly Companions* (1961), the masterly *Ride the High Country* (1962) and the flawed *Major Dundee* (1965) – before dropping out of feature films following a row with the producer of *The Cincinnati Kid* (1965). He returned in triumph four years later with this, his greatest movie.

Like all Peckinpah's work, *The Wild Bunch* is a violent, macho, elegiac tale of men at odds with society in changing times, unaccommodated loners choosing the conditions of their deaths. The film is set in 1916 and the central characters belong to an ageing outlaw band led by Pike Bishop (William Holden), reduced in a ferocious opening sequence to a mere half-dozen men following a failed raid on a bank in a Texan border town. They subsequently hire themselves out to steal guns for a vindictive Mexican warlord who is suppressing Zapatista rebels with the aid of German advisers. Too late they realize that they are helping the wrong side and turn on their sadistic employer in the biggest scene of climactic blood-shedding since Shakespeare's *Titus Andronicus*.

Peckinpah's characters do not attempt to ingratiate themselves. They are ruthless – 'If they move, kill 'em,' says Bishop, telling an underling how to treat hostages. They can associate happily only with whores, preferably Mexican. They live by a private code of honour, and they eventually die by it as they expect to. 'I want to enter my house justified,' (a quotation from Luke 14:18) says Joel McCrea as the upright ex-marshal on his last assignment in *Ride the High Country* (called *Guns in the Afternoon* in Britain), and most of Peckinpah's heroes are preparing for their quietus. Bishop's closest friend (Robert Ryan), trapped by a railway company into leading a posse of degen-

erates in pursuit of Bishop and his gang, says, 'They're men, and I wish to God I was riding with them.' Bishop's 'wild bunch' are an unidealized version of Kurosawa's *Seven Samurai* (1954; a movie Peckinpah revered); they are another group of lost Americans down Mexico way, like the gold seekers in John Huston's *The Treasure of the Sierra Madre* (1948; another Peckinpah favourite), whose laughter in the face of a malign fate they consciously echo. They are also an embodiment of contemporary America itself, committed to a mad, self-destructive expedition in Vietnam. The film involves us with its apparently antisocial characters, and disarms and entrances with the astonishing beauty of its lyrical violence. Taking just a few hints from *The Seven Samurai*, Peckinpah uses slow motion to turn a succession of cinematic bloodbaths into elegantly orchestrated dances of death, reaching new heights of poetic cinema that evoke memories of the Jacobean theatre. This masterful movie has been much imitated, by Peckinpah himself among others, especially in his *Bring Me the Head of Alfredo Garcia* (1974), but he was never to equal it. For all his rebarbative and quarrelsome nature, he created – as the best directors do – an informal repertory company, and more than half-a-dozen actors and a similar number of technicians on *The Wild Bunch* made three or more movies with him.

Producers
Phil Feldman and
Roy N. Sichner

Writers
Walon Green, Roy N. Sichner
and Sam Peckinpah

Cinematographer
Lucien Ballard

Production company
Warner Seven Arts

Cast
William Holden
Ernest Borgnine
Robert Ryan
Ben Johnson
Edmond O'Brien
Warren Oates
Jaime Sanchez

Other films
★ *Ride the High Country* (1962)
★ *Pat Garrett and Billy the Kid* (1973)

Academy Awards
Nominations for Best Screenplay (*see*
Writers, left) and Best Music (Jerry Fielding)

*(l–r) Ben Johnson, Warren Oates, William Holden
and Ernest Borgnine; outlaws embracing their fate.*

Five Easy Pieces Bob Rafelson *1970*

Bob Rafelson created the television pop group the Monkees and directed them in the surrealistic movie spin-off *Head* (1968), which he scripted with his friend, the actor Jack Nicholson. With Bert Schneider and Steve Blauner, Rafelson created the counter-cultural production company BBS which had a big hit with *Easy Rider* (1969, Dennis Hopper) before going on to make some of the most adventurous Hollywood films of the early 1970s, including *The Last Picture Show* (*see pages 98–99*), *Five Easy Pieces* and Nicholson's directorial debut, *Drive He Said* (1970). *Easy Rider* took the 32-year-old Nicholson from the Corman exploitation stable and brought him close to star status. *Five Easy Pieces* made him a star, giving him a defining role as the middle-class drop-out Bobby Dupea, a combination of irresistible charm and fearsome anger.

A classical pianist who works as an oil-rigger, Bobby despises the pretentious, over-cultivated world of his artistic family, and has attempted to sink into the hard-hat world of bowling alleys and trailer parks inhabited by his lover Rayette (Karen Black), a cheerful, uneducated waitress.

The two worlds he inhabits are quite brilliantly contrasted through the production designs of Tobe Rafelson (the director's wife) and in the film's music. Tammy Wynette's country songs are the musical leit-motif for the blue-collar ambience Bobby has embraced; piano pieces by Bach, Mozart and Chopin represent the culti-vated background he has deserted. These irreconcilable sides of American life are brought into conflict when Bobby returns home with a pregnant Rayette in tow to visit his paralysed father at the family's island home in Washington State and is drawn to his brother's fiancée (Susan Anspach), a fellow classical pianist. But he ends up rejecting both worlds, and in one of the most devas-tating endings to a picture of its time, he deserts Rayette for a self-mortifying journey north to the frozen wilds of Alaska.

At the time, Nicholson's complex performance seemed principally to embody the rebellion and alien-ation of the 1960s social revolution and the anger of the Vietnam era. It now seems a brilliant portrait of the American malcontent, a man incapable of finding satisfaction, settling down, accepting compromise. Characteristic of its time, the film is more generously disposed to the blue-collar workers than to the artistic middle-class intellectuals, who are crudely caricatured. But the representatives of the counter-culture – an aggressive lesbian (brilliantly played by Helena Kallianiotes) and her passive lover – are cruelly mocked. Their scenes remind us that this is one of the seminal road movies (the two lesbians derive from the bickering couple whose car has crashed in Bergman's *Wild Strawberries* of 1957), and that *Five Easy Pieces* is hilariously funny. The exem-plary 'No substitutions' encounter between Bobby and the by-the-rules waitress is among the iconic sequences of its decade. The screenwriter Adrien Joyce based this scene on a routine she once observed at a diner involving an angry young actor whom she later met. He was Jack Nicholson.

Director and producer
Bob Rafelson

Co-producers
Bert and Harold Schneider and Richard Wechsler

Writer
Adrien Joyce [also known as Carole Eastman]

Cinematographer
László Kovács

Production companies
Columbia, BBS and Raybert Productions

Cast
Jack Nicholson
Karen Black
Fannie Flagg
Billy 'Green' Bush
Susan Anspach

Other films
★ *Head* (1968)
★ *The King of Marvin Gardens* (1972)
★ *Stay Hungry* (1976)
★ *The Postman Always Rings Twice* (1981)
★ *Blood and Wine* (1997)

Academy Awards
Nominations for Best Picture, Jack Nicholson (Best Actor), Karen Black (Best Actress), Adrien Joyce (Best Screenplay), 1970

The Last Picture Show

Peter Bogdanovich *1971*

As critic and author of monographs on Hitchcock, Lang, Hawks, Dwan and Ford, Peter Bogdanovich helped make audiences aware of the classic American stylists. When he became the first established film critic to become a Hollywood writer–director, he consciously made pictures in the manner of his revered mentors. His low-budget debut *Targets* (1969), produced by Roger Corman, who brought him into movies, contrasts different forms of violence by interweaving the stories of a dignified old-style horror star (Boris Karloff), who is about to retire, with the meaningless shooting spree of a deranged young middle-class sniper. Included in the movie is a clip of Karloff in Hawks's *The Criminal Code* (1930). The more expensive and expansive *The Last Picture Show* also uses cinema as a metaphor for social change.

Based on a 1966 novel by Larry McMurtry, *The Last Picture Show* is one of a number of teenage rites-of-passage pictures of the early 1970s (other examples are Robert Mulligan's 1971 *Summer of 42,* and George Lucas's 1973 *American Graffiti*) that look back to a recent, pre-permissive past, in this case to a small town on the plains of northern Texas in the early 1950s. Two boys from blue-collar families, Duane (Jeff Bridges) and Sonny (Timothy Bottoms), are in their final year at high school, playing on a losing football team and seeking to lose their virginity. The swaggering Duane eventually has sex with the town beauty Jacy (Cybill Shepherd), an oil tycoon's coquettish daughter who plays the friends off against each other. Sonny becomes the lover of the frustrated 40-ish wife (Cloris Leachman) of the high-school sports coach, and the movie takes a frank look at the repressed lives of small-town America without the phoney moralizing tone of a *Peyton Place*.

The picture's moral centre is Sam the Lion (an Oscar-winning performance from John Ford veteran Ben Johnson), the loved and respected owner of the local cinema, pool saloon and diner, a man of old-fashioned probity rather like the old-timer played by Melvyn Douglas in *Hud* (1963, also taken from a McMurtry novel). Sam represents the traditional values, and when he dies the cinema closes down to be replaced by television. This deeply moving, elegiac picture is shot in grainy monochrome and includes two visits to Sam's Royal cinema. In the first, Sonny and his coy girlfriend see Minnelli's idealized portrait of American family life, *Father of the Bride* (1950); in the second, the night before Duane leaves for the Korean War, he and Sonny are reunited at the cinema's closing performance, a screening of Howard Hawks's *Red River* (1948), in which the cattle drive, a symbol of shared endeavour, begins in the same area of Texas. The music, all heard from radios and jukeboxes, is made up of country songs and pop hits of the time; during the painful final sequence where Sonny goes to apologize to the coach's bereft wife, a comic record of the day, Johnny Standley's 'It's in the Book', plays in the background.

Bogdanovich's career went into a sad decline from the mid-1970s on, and *Texasville* (1990), a sequel to *The Last Picture Show*, was a dismal failure.

Director
Peter Bogdanovich

Producers
Stephen J. Friedman and Bert and Harold Schneider

Writers
Peter Bogdanovich and James Lee Barrett, from the novel by Larry McMurtry

Cinematographer
Robert Surtees

Production companies
BBS and Columbia

Cast
Cybill Shepherd
Jeff Bridges
Timothy Bottoms
Ben Johnson
Cloris Leachman
Ellen Burstyn

Other films
★ *What's Up Doc?* (1972)
★ *Paper Moon* (1973)
★ *Daisy Miller* (1974)
★ *Mask* (1985)
★ *Texasville* (1990)

Academy Awards
Oscars for Ben Johnson (Best Supporting Actor) and Cloris Leachman (Best Supporting Actress); nominations for Best Picture, Best Director and Best Screenplay, 1971

Cybill Shepherd as Jacy, the object of desire among the young men in The Last Picture Show.

The Godfather
Francis Ford Coppola *1972*

Director
Francis Ford Coppola

Two Italian-Americans seeking commercial success came together to make this milestone movie. 'Movie brat' Francis Coppola, having directed a succession of flops and won an Oscar for scripting *Patton* (1970, *Patton – Lust for Glory* in Britain), needed a box-office hit. Mario Puzo, after a series of well-received books that had not sold, wrote a blockbuster novel about the Corleones, a leading New York Mafia family founded by Vito Corleone, a turn-of-the-century Sicilian immigrant. The result of their collaboration (a troubled production from which Coppola was nearly fired twice) was a three-hour movie that attracted critical and popular acclaim and breathed new life and adult confidence into a moribund industry. It revived the career of Marlon Brando as Vito, the ageing patriarch, and made a star of Al Pacino as his youngest son Michael.

The first and best film in what became *The Godfather Trilogy* (1972, 1974 and 1990) takes place over the postwar decade, beginning in 1945 when Michael Corleone returns from wartime service as a US Marine Corps officer and attempts to break away from the family business of organized crime. The attempted assassination of his father brings him back into the family, first to exact violent revenge, which leads to a period in Sicilian exile. He then takes over from his father when the oldest brother (James Caan) is murdered and the weak second brother (John Cazale) proves unfit to lead. Like *Little Caesar* and *Scarface* in the early 1930s, this is a portrait of what Robert Warshow called 'the gangster as tragic hero'. But, thanks to the disappearance of the Hollywood Production Code, it is not a story of necessary retribution. In *The Asphalt Jungle* (1950), a philosophical crook remarks that 'crime is a left-handed form of human endeavour', and *The Godfather* is a story of crime pursued by self-styled honourable men, seekers of the American Dream who have been excluded by social prejudice from more apparently honest pursuits. It is also a story of a man trapped in a web of fatal family obligations in a world where euphemism conceals the true brutality of life. The film introduced into the language the phrase 'I made him an offer he couldn't refuse'.

The Godfather revived the ailing American movie industry which, during the 1960s, had been artistically and commercially outstripped by the cinema of Europe and Asia. A romantic saga with the majestic sweep of *Gone With the Wind* (*see pages 60–61*), it drew on the imaginative boldness of the European arthouse movie and elevated Hollywood genre cinema to epic heights. The long opening sequence of the wedding of Michael's sister Connie, where all the main characters are introduced and the principal themes announced, is clearly inspired by the great ball that concludes Visconti's *The Leopard* (1963). The cinematographer Gordon Willis, who lit all three *Godfather* pictures, also worked on Alan Pakula's neo-*noir* conspiracy thrillers (*Klute*, 1971, *The Parallax View*, 1974, and *All the President's Men*, 1976) as well as numerous Woody Allen films and contributed to the sombre tone of 1970s cinema.

Producers
Albert S. Ruddy and
Gray Frederickson

Writers
Francis Ford Coppola
and Mario Puzo

Cinematographer
Gordon Willis

Production company
Paramount Pictures

Cast
Marlon Brando
Al Pacino
Diane Keaton
Robert Duvall
James Caan
Sterling Hayden

Other films
★ *Godfather Parts II* and *III* (1974 and 1990)
★ *Apocalypse Now* (1979)

Academy Awards
Oscars for Best Picture, Best Actor
(Marlon Brando) and Best Screenplay,
plus other nominations

(l–r) James Caan, Marlon Brando, Al Pacino and John Cazale in a scene from The Godfather, *one of the most influential movies of the 1970s.*

Mean Streets Martin Scorsese *1973*

Director
Martin Scorsese

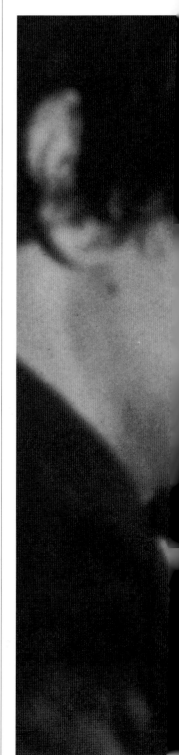

One of the greatest directors to emerge in the last quarter of the 20th century, Martin Scorsese at the age of 31 brought so much together in *Mean Streets* that a confluence became a spring. The enigmatic short movies he made as a student allied him to the New York experimental underground. As chief editor of Michael Wadleigh's documentary *Woodstock* (1970), he was part of the canny counter-culture.

Scorsese had just received many good reviews for directing the Roger Corman exploitation picture *Boxcar Bertha* (1972), his first commercial film, when his professional mentor John Cassavetes advised him to get out of Hollywood and make a personal work. So he brushed up a semi-autobiographical script about a quartet of young Italian-Americans in Manhattan's violent, mob-run Little Italy and, drawing on Raymond Chandler's phrase 'down these mean streets a man must go' (used to describe the urban terrain of the knight-errant private eye), he called it *Mean Streets*.

The budget was a mere $300,000, Corman undertook the distribution, and most of the interiors and the final crash scene were shot in Los Angeles with eight days of location work in New York. If the most revered independent film-maker, Cassavetes, encouraged Scorsese to make it, the notion of using classic rock music throughout on the soundtrack came from *Scorpio Rising* (1964), which had been directed by the most notorious underground moviemaker, Kenneth Anger. In choosing to make *Mean Streets* character-driven rather than tightly plotted, Scorsese created a film that would influence the future course of independent cinema. Subsequently alternating between commercial movies and personal projects, he helped create a new kind of career.

Mean Streets opens with a statement that might be the epigraph to Scorsese's work: 'You don't make up for your sins in church, you do it in the streets, you do it at home. The rest is bullshit and you know it.' The words are heard over a blank screen as Scorsese's alter ego, Charlie (Harvey Keitel), wakes from a nightmare. But they are spoken by Scorsese, whose voice on the soundtrack acts as the super-ego of Charlie, the guilt-ridden Catholic working as an errand boy for his mobster uncle. Troubled by his heavily carnal relationship with his epileptic girlfriend Teresa, Charlie seeks redemption by looking out for his reckless, psychopathic friend Johnny Boy (Robert De Niro). Much of the action takes place in and around a garish, red-lit nightclub and bar owned by another friend, Tony, and the plot turns upon Johnny Boy's refusal to repay a loan from the minor mafioso and loan shark Michael. The brooding intensity of Charlie, as revealed in the opening scene in church, and the dangerous volatility of Johnny Boy, first seen dropping a bomb into a mailbox, established Keitel and De Niro as major actors, icons of a new American cinema. The film's rich texture, moral power, complex characterization, unflinching, unglamorous violence, dramatic tracking shots, and imperceptible use of slow motion combined to confirm the arrival of a cineaste of rare depth and authority.

Producers
E. Lee Perry and
Jonathan Taplin

Writers
Martin Scorsese and
Mardick Martin

Cinematographer
Kent L. Wakeford

Production companies
Taplin-Perry and Scorsese
Productions

Cast
Robert De Niro
Harvey Keitel
David Proval
Amy Robinson
Richard Romanus

Other films
★ *Taxi Driver* (1976)
★ *New York, New York* (1977)
★ *Raging Bull* (1980)
★ *The King of Comedy* (1982)
★ *Goodfellas* (1990)
★ *Casino* (1995)
★ *Kundun* (1997)
★ *Bringing Out the Dead* (1999)

Robert De Niro (left) and Harvey Keitel in Mean Streets, *the first of many collaborations between De Niro and Scorsese.*

Jaws
Steven Spielberg *1975*

Director
Steven Spielberg

This thriller is many things: a high point in the 1970s group-jeopardy cycle; a Hitchcockian horror picture for the carriage trade; the massive box-office hit that established the reputation of Steven Spielberg (who had made only one theatrical movie before, 1974's *The Sugarland Express*, although an extended version of his television film *Duel*, 1971, had been a major success in European cinemas); and the movie that created a new fashion for releasing films nationally with several thousand prints.

Jaws was also a canny conflation on the part of novelist Peter Benchley of two 19th-century classics, Ibsen's *An Enemy of the People* (1882: idealistic whistle-blower challenges the mayor of a resort town who is concealing an ecological danger from the public) and Melville's *Moby-Dick* (1851: band of determined men led by Captain Ahab take to the sea in pursuit of a dangerous leviathan).

Television had taught Spielberg to grab the audience in the opening sequence (a naked girl, taking a midnight swim on a New England beach, is dragged under by some terrible force), but *Duel* had shown him that our fear of the unseen dictates that our direct confrontation with the giant shark should be delayed.

Spielberg's brilliantly edited and scored film unfolds in three classically conceived acts. In the first, tension builds as the ironically named island of Amity (it should have been called Gnashville) appreciates that its livelihood as a tourist attraction is threatened by the presence of a man-eating shark. Only the troubled police chief Brody (Roy Scheider), who has a pathological fear of the sea, and hippie ichthyologist Hooper (Richard Dreyfuss) take it seriously. In the second act, the slimy mayor keeps the beaches open for the Independence Day holiday, resulting in further deaths and the narrow escape of Brody's own son. In the third act, Brody and Hooper accompany salty old fisherman Quint (Robert Shaw), the film's obsessed Ahab figure, to confront the great white shark in his own element. The film carefully balances suspense and humour, provides the police chief with a believable home life, creates credible characters in Brody and Hooper, and something controversially legendary in Quint, whose very name has the ring of a sailor on Ahab's *Pequod*.

Several things give the movie an extra dimension. First, the picture came out in the immediate aftermath of the Watergate scandal, the biggest cover-up and public deception in American political history, and playing the craven Mayor of Amity is Murray Hamilton, an actor associated with devious authority figures, most famously Mr Robinson in *The Graduate* (1967). The second is the teaming of a uniformed policeman and a bearded hippie as the principled opponents of a dishonest community. The third factor, the one that gives true depth to *Jaws*, is the revelation that Quint was a survivor of the *Indianapolis*, the American warship torpedoed in July 1945 after delivering the A-bomb to be dropped on Hiroshima. As he eloquently recalls, nearly 800 sailors out of a crew of 1100 perished while clinging to the wreckage, most killed by sharks. *Jaws* was the second collaboration between Spielberg and composer John Williams, who won his first Oscar for the score, and also with the legendary editor Verna Fields, who won an Oscar for her virtuoso work here, and earlier edited Bogdanovich's *Targets* (1967).

Producers
David Brown and
Richard D. Zanuck

Writers
Peter Benchley and
Carl Gottlieb

Cinematographer
Bill Butler

Production companies
Universal Pictures and
Zanuck/Brown Productions

Cast
Roy Scheider
Richard Dreyfuss
Robert Shaw
Lorraine Gray
Murray Hamilton

Other films
★ *ET* (1982)
★ *Schindler's List* (1993)
★ *Saving Private Ryan* (1998)

Academy Awards
Oscars for Verna Fields (Best Editor)
and John Williams (Original Music);
nominated for Best Picture, 1976

Roy Scheider gets to grips with the enemy in Jaws,
one of the highest-grossing films of the 1970s.

Nashville Robert Altman *1975*

Director and producer
Robert Altman

Robert Altman was an unknown 45-year-old director of television series and occasional feature films when he made *M*A*S*H* (1970), a black comedy set in a Mobile Army Surgical Hospital during the Korean War, but really about the madness of Vietnam. Its anarchic irreverence, dark humour, large ensemble cast, multi-layered soundtrack and busy widescreen images captured the mood of those rebellious, druggy times. The film was a critical and box-office success and over the next eight years Altman made a succession of similar but much less popular movies, before retreating into low-budget filmed plays for a decade. He returned to his influential earlier style in the 1990s. The peak of his maverick career is *Nashville*, which was nearly aborted when United Artists backed out at the last minute, but Altman found independent financing.

A succession of movies (*Bonnie and Clyde*, see pages 92–93, *Five Easy Pieces*, see pages 96–97, *I Walk the Line*, 1970, *Payday*, 1972) had given country-and-western songs a peculiar resonance for movie audiences. They prepared the way for a film that used Nashville, Tennessee, the capital of country music, as a metaphor for a confused America, reeling from the Vietnam War and Watergate yet about to celebrate its bicentenary. *Nashville*, a birthday card edged with barbed wire, takes place over four or five days as Hal Phillip Walker, a dubious populist candidate representing the Replacement Party, is running for the American Presidency with the slogan 'New Roots for the Nation'. Walker is never seen but his suave manager (Michael Murphy) is recruiting entertainers to perform at a televised rally at the Parthenon. This quasi-classical building was erected in 1876 for the first centenary of the United States when Nashville was called 'The Athens of the South', and is as dubious a symbol of democracy as Walker's party. There are some 20 characters, most connected with the music business or aspiring to be in it, and their paths cross or collide before they all end up in the crowd or on stage at the Parthenon rally. One of them is a would-be assassin, the murder weapon inevitably concealed in an instrument case.

The movie is a complex mosaic, an ever shifting kaleidoscope about the hopes, frustrations, dreams, deceptions, venality, decency and dishonesty of the United States. Most of the incidents and characters ring true, although a false thread runs through it in the form of a tiresome Englishwoman (Geraldine Chaplin), claiming to represent the BBC. Several characters are based on legendary country stars, and Altman's performers entered into the spirit of the film so much that they wrote their own songs. One of these – Keith Carradine's 'I'm Easy' – won an Oscar, and Henry Gibson's bicentennial song has the poignant refrain 'We must be doing something right to last 200 years'. When the movie explodes into violence at the end and panic ensues, it is the singers who rally round. Gibson as Haven Hamilton, Nashville's king of country music, attempting to calm the croud at the Parthenon, shouts out: 'This isn't Dallas, this is Nashville. You show them what we're made of … Just sing!'

Writer
Joan Tewkesbury

Cinematographer
Paul Lohmann

Production companies
Paramount and ABC

Cast
Geraldine Chaplin
Lily Tomlinson
Scott Glenn
Jeff Goldblum
Shelley Duvall
Ned Beatty
Karen Black
Michael Murphy
Keith Carradine

Other films
★ *M*A*S*H* (1970)
★ *The Player* (1992)
★ *Short Cuts* (1993)

Academy Awards
Oscar for Keith Carradine
(Best Song); nominations for
Best Picture, Best Director
and others, 1975

An on-stage assassination provides the dramatic climax to Nashville, a typically accomplished ensemble piece from director Robert Altman. At centre stage (in white) is Henry Gibson, playing Haven Hamilton.

The Outlaw Josey Wales

Clint Eastwood *1976*

Director
Clint Eastwood

In the mid-1960s, Clint Eastwood went to Italy as a lightweight lead in *Rawhide*, a long-running television series, and was transformed into a star by Sergio Leone's 'Dollars Trilogy' of baroque Spaghetti Westerns. In 1968, with *Coogan's Bluff*, he embarked on the first of a succession of impressive collaborations with one of Hollywood's most accomplished directors of no-nonsense action movies, Don Siegel. This proved the springboard for a major career as producer–actor–director that has continued for some 30 years and reached its grandest professional peak with *Unforgiven*, Eastwood's 1992 Western, with its dedication 'For Sergio and Don', which won Oscars for best movie and best direction.

The Outlaw Josey Wales is arguably Eastwood's finest achievement to date, although it began unhappily when after a week's shooting he took over the direction from its highly gifted co-screenwriter Phil Kaufman. The budget-conscious Eastwood thought Kaufman was indecisive. Made three years after the end of the Vietnam War (and shortly after the ignominious American withdrawal from Saigon), it was an informal contribution to the 1976 bicentennial celebrations. This picaresque Western, which takes place during and after the Civil War, centres on Josey Wales, a simple farmer from Missouri who has thrown in his lot with a band of Confederate irregulars after his wife and child have been murdered by Unionist guerrillas. Refusing to be reconciled after the armistice and bent on killing the northerner who murdered his wife, Wales heads south for Texas, with a price on his head and an ever-growing reputation as a gunfighter as he kills bounty hunters and military trackers. Along the way he is joined by other outsiders and eventually they settle on a ranch which had been left to one of them, an elderly grandmother-figure, by her late son.

The movie uses the varied landscape (forests, deserts, plains, mountains) and weather (pouring rain, scorching sun) to dramatic effect. In various ways it echoes John Ford's *The Searchers* (1956), another fable of a healing journey in post-Civil War Texas undertaken by a vengeful veteran whose family has been brutally killed. In this case, however, the US cavalry and the Texas Rangers are the enemy, while Wales's closest friend is a dignified, dryly humorous Cherokee played by Chief Dan George. Wales also makes a personal peace pact with the Comanches, who are led by Will Sampson, another Native-American actor. Instead of ending with the death of an Indian, the film's last act of violence sees Redleg, the villainous Union officer who has pursued Wales since the Civil War, being impaled on his own sword. Following Eastwood's first Western as director, the cynical, Italianate *High Plains Drifter* (1973), *The Outlaw Josey Wales* is an altogether more affirmative affair, emphasizing the rewards of community and the consolations of forgiveness. Wales's final line – 'I guess we all died a little in that damn war' – applies as much to Vietnam as to the Civil War.

Producer
Robert Daley

Writers
Phil Kaufman and
Sonia Chernus

Cinematographer
Bruce Surtees

Production companies
Warner and Malpaso

Cast
Clint Eastwood
Chief Dan George
Sandra Locke
Bill McKinney
Will Sampson
John Vernon

Other films
★ *Play Misty for Me* (1971)
★ *High Plains Drifter* (1973)
★ *Bronco Billy* (1980)
★ *Bird* (1988)
★ *Unforgiven* (1992)

Will Sampson (left) and Clint Eastwood in The Outlaw Josey Wales, *a film that encompassed contemporary concerns about the Vietnam War.*

Annie Hall Woody Allen *1977*

Director
Woody Allen

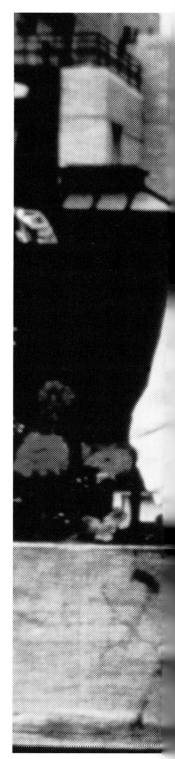

Between 1969 and 1975, Woody Allen directed himself in five movies, all parodies of familiar genres. They come across like a series of comic sketches, a form that is actually taken by *Everything You Always Wanted to Know About Sex* (1972). With the semi-autobiographical *Annie Hall*, in which he, his ex-lover Diane Keaton and his best friend Tony Roberts play versions of themselves, Allen found his own distinctive voice and style.

The central character, Alvy Singer, is a successful but depressed stand-up comic, a self-conscious Jew, a classic malcontent. He talks straight to camera (in the manner of several Ingmar Bergman films of the 1960s), reflecting on his life as, like Allen himself, he turns 40. In flashbacks and flashforwards, Alvy recalls his Brooklyn childhood, his two failed marriages to humourless Jewish intellectuals, and most especially his extended affair with the eccentric ('kooky' as they said back then) middle-class WASP from Wisconsin, Annie Hall (Keaton), whom he meets at a Manhattan tennis club.

Annie is a cheerful unemployed photographer and would-be club singer, and Alvy, Pygmalion-like, attempts to turn her into a tortured, self-questioning, death-obsessed New York Jew like himself. 'You're incapable of enjoying life', Annie tells him after she finishes the relationship and moves to Los Angeles, a place Alvy despises. Long after their affair has ended they meet briefly in New York with new partners. This sad, bittersweet film says that nothing lasts, that love inevitably fades.

Annie Hall is verbally and visually witty, and stylistically one of Allen's most elaborate pictures. There is a cartoon pastiche of *Snow White* (1937); Alvy's childhood home is placed directly under the Coney Island rollercoaster; he is transformed into a bearded Hasidic Jew while dining with Annie's anti-Semitic family; in a cinema foyer he suddenly produces the real Marshall McLuhan from behind a placard to settle a row with a pretentious intellectual queuing behind him. The movie proved to be Allen's greatest box-office success. It brought Diane Keaton an Academy Award for best actress as well as winning Oscars for best film, script and direction, although Allen did not attend the Hollywood ceremony, preferring to play clarinet with his New Orleans band in his regular session at Manhattan's Michael's Pub.

According to Ralph Rosenblum, who had edited four earlier Allen movies, the first cut of 140 minutes was an ill-disciplined enterprise of which Allen's co-author Marshall Brickman despaired. It only came to centre on Annie and Alvy when Rosenblum (as he recounts in his 1979 book *When The Shooting Starts … The Cutting Begins*) pared it down to 95 minutes. Moreover, Allen's working title was *Anhedonia*, a clinical term for the inability to experience pleasure. He was talked out of this and a variety of alternatives (such as *A Roller Coaster Named Desire*, *Me and My Goy*, *It Had to be Jew*) before settling on *Annie Hall*. The film created a new movie genre, the freewheeling 'relationship movie', a natural successor to what the philosopher Stanley Cavell dubbed 'the comedy of remarriage' (*The Awful Truth*, see pages 58–59, *The Philadelphia Story*, 1940), a rewarding form forced on filmmakers by the Production Code. The most flattering imitation of Annie Hall, perhaps, is Rob Reiner's *When Harry Met Sally* (1989), scripted by Nora Ephron, which was nearly a carbon copy.

110

Producers
Robert Greenhut, Jack Rollins, Charles H. Joffe and Fred Gallo

Writers
Woody Allen and Marshall Brickman

Cinematographer
Gordon Willis

Production company
Rollins-Joffe Productions

Cast
Woody Allen
Diane Keaton
Tony Roberts
Carol Kane
Shelley Duvall
Paul SImon

Other films
★ *Manhattan* (1979)
★ *Hannah and Her Sisters* (1986)
★ *Radio Days* (1987)

Academy Awards
Oscars for Best Picture, Best Screenplay, Best Director and Best Actress (Diane Keaton), 1977

Diane Keaton (left) and Woody Allen in Annie Hall, *a breakthrough film for Allen and his most successful movie to date.*

Star Wars George Lucas *1977*

Director and writer
George Lucas

Producer
Gary Kurtz

After making the dystopian science-fiction film *THX 1138* (1971) and the rites-of-passage movie *American Graffiti* (1973), writer–director George Lucas spent four years developing and working on this galactic fantasy. Inspired by the Flash Gordon cartoon strip and film series, it cost $8 million and was made in Britain with a trio of little-known Americans in the leading roles, supported by British actors.

Star Wars begins with the legendary opening phrase – 'A long time ago, in a galaxy far far away'. This is followed by the simple adventure yarn of three young people – Luke Skywalker (Mark Hamill), an idealistic youth of apparently humble birth, Princess Leia (Carrie Fisher), and cynical space pilot Han Solo (Harrison Ford) – taking on the Evil Empire with the help of the benevolent old warrior Obi-Wan Kenobi (Alec Guinness). Assisted by jokey robots and *Sesame Street*-style animals, they restore the peace-loving Republic.

The dogfights are based on a close study of Second World War films while, in addition to Flash Gordon, Lucas draws on samurai films, Westerns and every kind of myth, ancient and modern, with specific references to, among other pictures, Ford's *The Searchers* (1956), Kubrick's *2001: A Space Odyssey* (1968), Fleming's *The Wizard of Oz* (1939), and Riefenstahl's *Triumph of the Will* (1936). 'It's not just like one kind of ice cream', said Lucas, explaining the multiplicity of sources and allusions, 'but rather a very big sundae'. His target audience for *American Graffiti* had been 16- to 18-year-olds; 'I set this one at 14 and maybe younger than that', he said at the time.

The result was immediate success, a film that became one of the great phenomena of cinematic history. Before *Star Wars* had reached Great Britain, it had become the most commercially successful film ever made. Spawning to date two sequels and one prequel (1980, 1983, 1999) and endless imitators, it generated billions of dollars' worth of ancillary merchandising and created a demand for spectacular blockbusters that has not yet ended. Lucas was able to build the special effects unit that serviced the film, Industrial Light and Magic, into a multi-billion-dollar organization based in Marin County, north of San Francisco, and he became and has remained one of Hollywood's most powerful figures.

The eclectic *Star Wars*, which drew on so many sources, became itself a legendary work with the slogan of the Republic's Jedi Knights – 'May the Force be with you' – entering the language. Subtitled 'A New Hope', the film struck a nerve in an America recovering from the humiliations of the Vietnam War. President Reagan, elected three years after the film was made, spoke of the Soviet Union as 'the Evil Empire' and gave his proposed space-defence system the title Star Wars. The original *Star Wars* trilogy contributed to the worldwide renewal of the moviegoing habit, but in creating an appetite for childlike blockbusters that depend on special effects rather than on character and subtle narrative, the movie played a key role in what was to be called 'the dumbing down' of America and of popular culture.

Cinematographer
Gilbert Taylor

Production companies
TCF/LucasFilm

Special effects
John Dykstra and
David Lester

Cast
Mark Hamill
Carrie Fisher
Harrison Ford
Alec Guinness
David Prowse

Other films
★ *THX 1138* (1971)
★ *American Graffiti* (1973)

Academy Awards
Oscars for Art Direction, Costume
Design, Sound, Editing and Visual
Effects, plus other nominations, 1978

*Peter Mayhew (as Chewbacca), Mark Hamill, Alec
Guinness and Harrison Ford at the controls of the
Millennium Falcon.*

The Deer Hunter Michael Cimino *1978*

There was a number of allegorical Westerns and pictures about returning veterans, but John Wayne's gung-ho *The Green Berets* (1968) was the only big-budget Hollywood feature made about the Vietnam War while the conflict raged. Then the floodgates opened and a succession of films appeared, all angry and critical of the American involvement. Most controversial, as well as being a worldwide success, was *The Deer Hunter*, the second movie of writer–director Michael Cimino, which was nominated for nine Oscars and received five – for best picture, director, supporting actor (Christopher Walken), sound and editing.

The film opens with an articulated lorry thundering through a grimy industrial town at dawn. This juggernaut is an emblem for the overwhelming emotional experience the audience will share with the film's characters over the next three hours.

The Deer Hunter unfolds in three acts from 1968 to 1975. In the first act, six friends from a tight-knit Russian-American community live in the shadow of a Pennsylvania steel mill. One runs a bar, the other five work in the mill's hellish inferno that prefigures the Vietnam War (the film's French title is *Voyage au bout de l'enfer*, 'journey to the depths of hell') for which three of them – Mike (Robert De Niro), Nick (Christopher Walken) and Steven (John Savage) – have volunteered to serve with the airborne forces. Steven marries his pregnant fiancée, and during the wedding reception they meet a Vietnam veteran incapable of discussing the war. After a hunting expedition to the mountains, where their leader Mike is revealed as a one-shot control freak, the scene shifts to Vietnam two years later. Mike, Nick and Steven are taken prisoner and are forced by their Viet Cong captors to play Russian roulette, Cimino's central metaphor for the absurdity of war. In the third act, Steven is back in the United States, a cripple in a veterans' hospital, Mike is a much-decorated sergeant who is unable to discuss his war experiences, and Nick, who has gone out of his mind, is in Saigon, constantly playing Russian roulette in casinos. Mike has become the lover of Nick's girlfriend (Meryl Streep), and as the United States government makes its ignominious withdrawal from Vietnam, he returns to Saigon in a vain attempt to rescue his old friend.

The Deer Hunter, as its title suggests, goes back to the novels of Fenimore Cooper and his taciturn frontier heroes, and comes up to the present through the psychologically wounded, war-weary protagonists of Hemingway's stories and novels who sought solace in shooting and fishing. It is about the effects of war on people who have been drawn into the conflict for romance, patriotism, social solidarity or to test their manhood. A universal story, in fact. This superbly acted film is a blue-collar *War and Peace* that does not patronize the inarticulate. Inevitably Cimino was attacked for refusing to be either political or polemical.

Cimino went on to make the liberal Western *Heaven's Gate* (1980), a great movie destroyed by a hostile press and insensitive critics, some of whom were apologizing to the outspoken Jane Fonda for having initially enthused about *The Deer Hunter*, a film she considered racist, reactionary and pro-American. When Fonda first made these charges (at a time when her own Vietnam film, *Coming Home* (1978) was competing with The Deer Hunter in the 1978 Oscars) she had yet to see the film.

Director, producer and writer
Michael Cimino

Co-producers
Barry Spikings, Michael Deeley and John Peverall

Writer
Deric Washburn

Cinematographer
Vilmos Zsigmond

Production companies
EMI Films and Universal Pictures

Cast
Robert De Niro
Christopher Walken
John Cazale
John Savage
Meryl Streep

Other films
★ *Thunderbolt and Lightfoot* (1974)
★ *Heaven's Gate* (1980)
★ *Year of the Dragon* (1985)

Academy Awards
Oscars for Best Picture, Best Director, Best Sound, Best Editor and Best Supporting Actor (Christopher Walken); nominations for Best Actor (Robert De Niro), Best Supporting Actress (Meryl Streep), Best Screenplay and Cinematography in 1978.

MAIN: James Cameron's Terminator 2 *(1991).*

FAR LEFT: Spike Jonze's Being John Malkovich *(1999).*

MIDDLE LEFT: Charles Burnett's To Sleep with Anger *(1990).*

LEFT: Clint Eastwood's Unforgiven *(1992).*

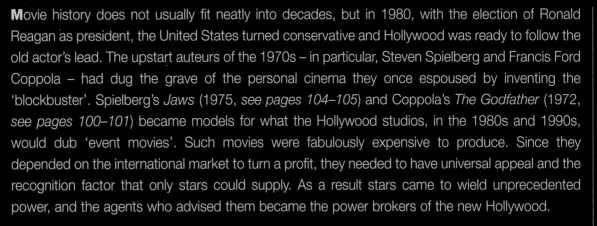

CHAPTER FOUR

America: The Modern Era

Amy Taubin and Kent Jones

Movie history does not usually fit neatly into decades, but in 1980, with the election of Ronald Reagan as president, the United States turned conservative and Hollywood was ready to follow the old actor's lead. The upstart auteurs of the 1970s – in particular, Steven Spielberg and Francis Ford Coppola – had dug the grave of the personal cinema they once espoused by inventing the 'blockbuster'. Spielberg's *Jaws* (1975, *see pages 104–105*) and Coppola's *The Godfather* (1972, *see pages 100–101*) became models for what the Hollywood studios, in the 1980s and 1990s, would dub 'event movies'. Such movies were fabulously expensive to produce. Since they depended on the international market to turn a profit, they needed to have universal appeal and the recognition factor that only stars could supply. As a result stars came to wield unprecedented power, and the agents who advised them became the power brokers of the new Hollywood.

Although most event movies were good for nothing more than drawing a crowd, there were exceptions. With its allegory of the industrial age (in other words, the age of the movies) making its last stand against a dehumanized and unknowable technological future, James Cameron's *Terminator 2* (1991) powerfully captured the prevailing anxiety of the 1990s. In such films as *Thelma and Louise* (1991), *The Silence of the Lambs* (1990) and the *Alien* trilogy (1979, 1986 and 1992), Hollywood finally caught up with a new feminist consciousness. But in general, the movies that mattered – as art, entertainment or social commentary – were being made not in Hollywood but in the precarious independent film sector, where the concept of auteurism still held sway.

Once a subcultural fantasy, the amorphous notion of independent film has turned into a minor media obsession. However subversive it seemed when compared with Hollywood's standardized product, independent film is as American as apple pie – what could be more American than the marriage of self-expression and entrepreneurship? Indies achieved a higher public profile in the mid-1980s with films fuelled by identity politics and the oppositional dialogue around race and gender. Jim Jarmusch's elegant, post-punk *Stranger than Paradise* (1984) put indie film on the international map when it won the Camera d'Or at Cannes in 1984. Two years later Spike Lee created almost as big a stir with *She's Gotta Have It* (1986). Soon the indie scene was a hotbed of African-American filmmaking (Lee, Charles Burnett, Julie Dash) and gay filmmaking (Gus Van Sant, Todd Haynes.) It was, however, a film about white southern Yuppies – Steven Soderbergh's *sex, lies and videotape* – that in 1989 captured the attention of the financially bloated and creatively sluggish Hollywood industry.

Scenting fresh blood, the studios went on a feeding frenzy, swallowing up entire indie production and distribution companies as well as individual talents. The marriage of the studios and the indies was consummated when Disney acquired Miramax, Harvey and Bob Weinstein's savvy and aggressive distribution company. Today, every studio has an indie film division to churn out lower-budget versions of Hollywood pap. But that does not mean that there are not filmmakers out there who want to fill up the screen with dreams that money cannot buy. You will just have to look harder to find them.

Raging Bull   Martin Scorsese *1980*

Director
Martin Scorsese

An anomaly among modern American directors, Martin Scorsese has, for roughly 30 years, made highly personal, formally sophisticated films inside the Hollywood industry. Of his 17 features, *Taxi Driver* (1976) has had the most profound effect on our collective cultural unconscious. However, *Raging Bull* (1980) is Scorsese's greatest film, and the greatest American film of the 1980s and 1990s.

Based on the autobiography of the middleweight champion boxer Jake La Motta, *Raging Bull* is the second film in Scorsese's Italian-American trilogy, coming between *Mean Streets* (1974) and *Goodfellas* (1990). Where *Mean Streets* dealt with Scorsese's peers and his own experience as a young man on the Mafia-friendly streets of New York City's Little Italy, *Raging Bull*, which is set largely in the 1940s, focuses on his parents' generation. In that sense, it is a deeply Oedipal drama. Scorsese, as fetishistic a director as Hitchcock, even borrowed the cross from his parents' apartment to hang above the troubled marital bed of Jake (played by Robert De Niro) and his gorgeous, long-suffering wife Vickie (played by Cathy Moriarty).

Raging Bull is a film about a man who legally brutalizes people for a living. As unsparing of its audience as La Motta was of his opponents, the film is structured as a relentless series of fights. Jake's battles in the ring mirror his tumultuous home life; both are projections of a psyche that eroticizes violence. Scorsese's great talent is to be able to show the dynamics between basic human drives and the culture that shapes them. Jake's destructive impulses – targeted as much against himself as the outside world – make us uncomfortable because they are not completely foreign to our own experience. His behaviour, however, is utterly specific to his first-generation, Italian-American subculture. He may be an extreme case, but what distinguishes him from the neigh-bourhood gangsters who want a piece of him is only a matter of degree. They deride him as 'an animal', but the only animals that behave like Jake are human.

Scorsese's devastating critique of the very codes of masculinity that shaped him as a filmmaker is made flesh through Robert De Niro's performance (for which he won an Academy Award). Jake's struggle towards a championship is a metaphor for Scorsese's own experience trying to become a major Hollywood director. The gangsters who will give Jake a chance at a title fight only if he agrees to throw a preliminary match – thus making them some easy money and proving that he is under their control – are stand-ins for the studio bosses, who demand artistic compromise to ensure big box-office grosses.

But from the first shot of Jake, alone in the ring, jogging in slow motion, his face obscured by the hood of his robe, like a monk in Roberto Rossellini's film about St Francis of Assisi (*Francesco, Giullare di Dio*, 1950), we know that for Scorsese this is the title fight and it is only art that is at stake. A fusion of Hollywood melodrama and personal psychodrama, couched in images and sounds that are kinetic and visceral, and closer to poetry than pulp, *Raging Bull* is a perfect match of form and content. In the 20 years that followed, Scorsese would make many great films, but none of them as complicated a meditation on the relations between spectacle, entertainment and art.

Producers
Robert Chartoff
and Irwin Winkler

Writers
Paul Schrader and
Mardik Martin

Cinematographer
Michael Chapman

Cast
Robert De Niro
Cathy Moriarty
Joe Pesci
Frank Vincent

Other films
★ *Mean Streets* (1973)
★ *Taxi Driver* (1976)
★ *New York, New York* (1977)

★ *The King of Comedy* (1982)
★ *Goodfellas* (1990)
★ *The Age of Innocence* (1993)
★ *Casino* (1995)
★ *Kundun* (1997)
★ *Bringing Out the Dead* (1999)

Academy Awards
Oscar for Robert De Niro as Best Actor, 1981

A glimpse of Robert De Niro's famously Method-inspired, Oscar-winning performance.

Fast Times at Ridgemont High

Amy Heckerling *1982*

Director
Amy Heckerling

Producers
Art Linson and Irving Azoff

The curious thing about Amy Heckerling's film version of Cameron Crowe's high-school 'exposé' is that it feels so unassuming. Just like the director's terrific *Clueless* (1995; two perfect teenage movies in an otherwise nowheresville career), nothing about *Fast Times* feels weighty or self-important. There is never a sense that you are about to see a Very Important Film that finally tells the true story of life in an American high school – which is precisely what it does. The fact that it does so with such a light touch makes it all the more remarkable.

There is no plot to speak of, just the kaleidoscopic drama of adolescence presented as frankly as any American movie has managed. Stacy (a pudgy Jennifer Jason Leigh in her first substantial role) loses her virginity in a pitch-perfect, brutally matter-of-fact scene, and gets a blow-job lesson with a carrot from her more 'worldly' friend, Linda (Phoebe Cates). Stacy's slightly off-kilter brother, Brad (Judge Reinhold), gets caught by Linda doing what adolescent boys do whenever they are alone with a little time to kill. Mark Ratner (Brian Backer) is the shy kid who takes Stacy out on a date and is counselled by his 'suave' friend, Mike (Robert Romanus), to 'play side three of *Led Zeppelin IV* ' if he wants to make out. But the greatest gift that *Fast Times* gave us was Sean Penn's immortal Spicoli, the unapologetic stoner.

Ebullient yet shambling, fully committed to his own special brand of inattentiveness, Spicoli is quite a creation. He is brilliantly conceived on paper, but unthinkable without Penn. His goofy, winning smile, shoulder-length dirty blond hair and open-mouthed surprise (with his eyelids at half-mast) are redolent of a bygone era. Between Spicoli, his romantic outcast in *Bad Boys* (1983) and his pipsqueak drug entrepreneur in *The Falcon and the Snowman* (1985), Penn explored every corner of adolescence in the United States in the 1970s and early 1980s.

Fast Times moves like no other teenage movie: it bounds from one scene to the next with a buoyant energy that seems perfectly in tune with its subject, with the backdrop of a modish pop score that fits the Southern Californian ambience nicely. The considerable talents of its youthful cast helps to imbue it with a genuine teenage sensibility. In fact, *Fast Times* kept Hollywood stockpiled with talented young actors for years to come. In addition to Leigh, Cates, Reinhold and Penn (sadly, the careers of Backer and Romanus, brother of *Mean Streets*' Richard Romanus, never took off), also tucked away in the cast are Forest Whitaker, Eric Stoltz, James Russo, Nicolas Cage and Anthony Edwards. The film also paved the way for John Hughes' empire of teenage angst and helped to establish Crowe, who has since become a very talented director himself.

Writer
Cameron Crowe

Production companies
Refugee Films and
Universal Pictures

Cinematographer
Matthew F Leonetti

Cast
Sean Penn
Jennifer Jason Leigh
Judge Reinhold
Phoebe Cates
Brian Backer
Ray Walston

Other films
★ *Look Who's Talking* (1989)
★ *Clueless* (1995)

*Rocking out: the painful ignominy of teenage
social events is pitilessly explored.*

Videodrome David Cronenberg *1982*

Director and writer
David Cronenberg

David Cronenberg is the Baudelaire of contemporary cinema, the poet of body-horror. All his films are meditations on sex and death. They make you aware (to borrow Freud's terms) of Eros and Thanatos fighting it out in every cell of your body.

A Canadian who lives and works in Toronto, David Cronenberg is something of an outsider to both Hollywood and the American independent sector. His early horror films found an international cult audience, but it was not until the release of *Videodrome* (1982) that Hollywood took notice. *The Fly*, produced four years later by 20th Century Fox, is as close as he has come to making a blockbuster. Since then, his work has become increasingly austere. Leaving the blatant imagery of the horror film behind, he has become North America's most subversive art-film director. *Videodrome* (1982), which marks the end of Cronenberg's splatter-shock period, is not as great a film as his elegiac *Dead Ringers* (1988) or his millennial *Crash* (1997). But thanks to its subject – the power of television to transform not only society but human biology, right down to the DNA – it is the most influential.

Having been put through the censorship wringer because of the extremely visceral imagery of his earlier films, Cronenberg played devil's advocate in *Videodrome*. The film proposes that a man exposed to violent images might begin to hallucinate such violence and to act on his hallucinations. Max Renn (James Woods), a producer at a small cable television station specializing in soft-core porn, comes across a mysterious programme called Videodrome, in which women are tortured and killed on camera.

Max's exposure to Videodrome coincides with his sexual involvement with a talk-radio celebrity (punk-rock singer Deborah Harry) who takes pleasure in pain.

Initially, the film seems like a sci-fi thriller about a conspiracy to take over the world by using TV as mind control. But unlike most thrillers, *Videodrome* is couched entirely in the first person. The film puts the viewer inside the experience of an extremely unreliable narrator. After one dose of the Videodrome signal, Max begins to suffer paranoid delusions. The talking heads on his television address him by name. A bloody, vagina-like slit opens in Max's belly; while probing it with his gun – as if it were a foreign body – his arm becomes trapped in the wound up to the elbow. Intermittent at first, these hallucinations eventually become the entirety of his consciousness. Does Max shoot his colleagues and then blow his brains out, or is what we see on screen the projection of a fantasy? Absolutely self-reflexive, *Videodrome* derives its meaning and power from the ambiguity. Initially conceived as a mordant satire about censorship, the film evolved into a more complicated expression of Cronenberg's belief that 'technology is us; it is our will made physical.' 'Long live the new flesh' proclaims Max, as he blows himself to smithereens. More than a special effect, *Videodrome*'s new flesh lingers in the mind as a distinct possibility.

Producers
Pierre David, Victor Solnicki
and Claude Héroux

Cinematographer
Mark Irwin

Editor
Ron Sanders

Production companies
Famous Players, Filmplan,
Guardian Trust, Canadian Film
Development Corporation,
Universal Pictures

Cast
James Woods
Sonja Smits
Deborah Harry
Peter Dvorsky

Other films
★ *Shivers* (1975)
★ *Scanners* (1981)
★ *The Fly* (1986)
★ *Dead Ringers* (1988)
★ *Naked Lunch* (1991)
★ *Crash* (1997)
★ *eXistenZ* (1999)

*A dramatic composition from the most subversive
art-film director in North America.*

Stranger Than Paradise Jim Jarmusch *1984*

Director and writer
Jim Jarmusch

Producer
Sara Driver

The theme song of Jim Jarmusch's *Stranger than Paradise* is Screaming Jay Hawkins' recording of 'I Put a Spell on You.' Perhaps it is the power of suggestion, but that is exactly what this fragile, diffident film seems to have done to its audiences. What other explanation could there be for the way it instantly transformed the image of the American independent filmmaking from idealistic but artistically naïve to subversive and ultra-hip?

Made on a miniscule budget and with grainy black-and-white film stock left over from a Wim Wenders film, *Stranger than Paradise* is rooted in the less-is-more aesthetic that defined punk rock (Jarmusch was a member of the post-punk group, the Del Byzantines) and New York's underground film and theatre scene in the 1970s and early 1980s. The film's major influences were the photography and films of Swiss-born Robert Frank and the work of Squat, an experimental theatre company made up of Hungarian émigrés. Jarmusch found a visual correlative to his own alienated perspective in Frank's melancholy photographic album, 'The Americans', and in *Pull My Daisy* (1959), his avant-garde film portrait of a bunch of beat-generation luminaries hanging out in a Bowery loft. The Squat connection provided Jarmusch with his central comic conceit – that from New York's East Village bohemia to the industrialized midwest to the beaches of Florida, the landscape of the United States is every bit as bleak as anything in an Eastern European movie.

But *Stranger Than Paradise* is less about a place than a state of mind. Its governing consciousness is Willie (John Lurie), a permanently depressed, two-bit gambler, who spends most of his time hanging out in his tiny, sparsely furnished apartment, either on his own or with his sad-sack friend Eddie (Richard Edson). Out of the blue, Willie's teenage cousin Eva (Eszter Balint) arrives from Hungary to visit for a few days before going on to Cleveland to live with their aunt. Eva's presence stirs some faint memory of familial warmth in Willie and, for a few seconds after she leaves, he feels his loneliness more acutely.

A year later, Willie and Eddie make some fast money cheating at poker and, to be safe, they decide to get out of town for a while. They drive to Cleveland to visit Eva, more out of default than desire – she is the only person they know. In the film's emblematic scene, Eva takes them sightseeing to the shore of Lake Erie. But because the snow is falling hard, there is nothing to look at except a vast indeterminate field of grey – no water, no horizon line, just greyness everywhere. When Eva asks to go somewhere warm, they head for Florida, the Sunshine State. But even there it is always cloudy, the beach is as grey as Lake Erie and their motel room is as bleak as Willie's New York apartment. A film that is figuratively and literally about missed connections, *Stranger than Paradise* closes with Willie, Eddie and Eva headed, by accident, in separate directions. For someone as shut down as Willie, there is no more apt fate than an open ending.

Cinematographer
Tom DiCillo

Editors
Jim Jarmusch and
Melody London

Production companies
Cinesthesia Productions and
Grokenberger Film

Cast
John Lurie
Eszter Balint
Richard Edson
Cecilia Stark
Danny Rosen

Other films
★ *Down By Law* (1986)
★ *Mystery Train* (1989)
★ *Night On Earth* (1991)
★ *Dead Man* (1996)
★ *Ghost Dog: The Way of the Samurai* (1999)

Richard Edson as Eddie, contemplating the bleakness of contemporary Florida.

Aliens James Cameron *1986*

Director and writer
James Cameron

The *Alien* series was a response to the rapidly changing status of women at the end of the 20th century. James Cameron's *Aliens*, the second film in one of Hollywood's most profitable franchises, is not as disturbing or complicated as the first, Ridley Scott's *Alien* (1979) or the third, David Fincher's *Alien³* (1992), which was so laden with millennial anxiety that it killed off Ripley (Sigourney Weaver), the series' wildly popular heroine. Ripley rose from the grave in *Alien Resurrection* (1997), a confused and unnecessary addendum to what in retrospect seemed like a fully resolved trilogy.

Viewed outside the context of the series, *Aliens* is merely an extremely exciting, well-crafted action movie, one which would seem formulaic except for the fact that it has a female protagonist. But if we compare it to the original *Alien*, we see how brilliantly it reflects a shift in the cultural and political climate of the United States from the relative liberalism of the late 1970s to the resurgent Cold War militarism and conservative social policies of the Reagan era.

Released at the end of the 1970s, Scott's *Alien* played on the fears set loose by a decade of feminist and gay activism. It showcased a great female action hero, the cool, resourceful, tomboyish Lieutenant Ellen Ripley. But it also created a monster – the alien – that had no respect for gender. In the film's most horrifying scene, a baby alien bursts out from the chest of a male crew member (John Hurt). *Alien* spoke to both female empowerment and male anxiety; that a man could be impregnated was its ultimate outrage.

Cameron's sequel, on the other hand, fetishized military hardware and the nuclear family. In this sci-fi/war movie hybrid, Ripley is a member of a Marine squadron sent to rescue a colony of families who may have fallen victim to the aliens. In *Alien*, Ripley was the archetype of the independent, single woman; her only emotional bond was with the ship's cat. In *Aliens*, however, not only does she subscribe to the belief that families come first, but she is also painted as a maternal figure through her protection of Newt, the little girl who is the colony's sole survivor.

Like Ripley, the alien has also been reconfigured as a mother, pure and simple. Gone is the terrifying hermaphroditic creature that H. R. Giger designed for the first film, with its phallic head and its toothy, slavering mouth that resembled the mythic *vagina dentata*. Cameron's alien is depicted as a giant womb, the guardian of hundreds of embryos. When Ripley finally goes one-on-one with this monster, the implication is that the good mother is fighting the bad. And if Ripley is the emblem of the privileged white woman, then the alien suggests the favourite scapegoat of the Reagan/Bush era – the black mother on state benefit, that supposed parasite on the economy whose reproductive drive was driving the United States into bankruptcy. As in all great sci-fi movies, the thing from outer space is a projection of psyche and ideology.

Gale Anne Hurd

Cinematographer
Adrian Biddle

Production companies
20th Century Fox and
Brandywine Productions

Editor
Ray Lovejoy

Cast
Sigourney Weaver
Carrie Henn
Michael Biehn
Paul Reiser
Lance Henriksen
Bill Paxton

Other films
★ *Terminator* (1984)
★ *The Abyss* (1989)
★ *Terminator 2* (1991)
★ *True Lies* (1994)
★ *Titanic* (1997)

Sigourney Weaver as Ripley, one of modern cinema's most iconic female characters.

Blue Velvet David Lynch *1986*

*B*lue Velvet was quite an object to land in first-run American movie-houses at the end of the Reagan era – less for its psycho-sexual content, which was hair-raising yet in keeping with the spirit of the times, than for its extraordinary formal potency. With *The Elephant Man* (1980) and *Dune* (1984), Lynch had found popular material suitable for his then unique talents (nightmarish logic; a sense of mounting dread; an all-consuming visual sensibility, at once attractive and repulsive). *Blue Velvet* reversed the equation. The narrative is skimpy. A small-town boy (Kyle MacLachlan) stumbles into a horrible intrigue between a brutalized woman (Isabella Rossellini) and a deranged monster of a man (Dennis Hopper) who has kidnapped her child, and gets a quick, vivid education in the basest human instincts. In fact, the plot material is nothing more than a vessel in which Lynch – the artist, the man and the sexual being – can sail off to the horizon. There are few filmmakers who have worked so hard to give form and voice to their fears and desires.

Of the film's several (in)famous set-pieces, the apartment encounter between MacLachlan, Rossellini and Hopper remains the most stunning: the sequence is carefully gradated, to the point where it seems to have reached the limits of dread and sexual aberrance, and every detail is perfectly realized, from the dingy colour to the shocking turns in behaviour (Rossellini ordering MacLachlan to strip at knifepoint, Hopper's infantile sexual desires). While *Blue Velvet* is every inch a director's film, it is also inconceivable without MacLachlan and Hopper. The two actors obviously represent two sides of Lynch's psyche (innocence and experience? or is it just light and darkness?) but they both put plenty of flesh on the bones of their potentially schematic characters. As he proved in *Dune*, MacLachlan is one of the rare actors capable of making virtue and normalcy compelling (probably because he always looks like he is quietly fighting to maintain his hold on them). And this was the most nuanced, modulated piece of acting that Hopper had done in years.

As startling as *Blue Velvet* undoubtedly seemed at the time, nevertheless it did not exactly feel liberating. There is an odd sense, expressed in the film, that sexuality is a dangerous force that is in need of containment, in order that the world might be made safe for a typically 1950s-era gentility. As much as Lynch climbed out to the extreme edge of narrative cinema, he also seemed to find himself in accordance with an essentially conservative cultural stance. Perhaps this explains why he was able to parlay his 'undergrowth of genteel America' idea into a franchise three years later with the hugely successful television series *Twin Peaks* (1989). Perhaps it is also why his breakthrough spawned so much garbage from lesser talents about introverted psychopaths living alone in sumptuously decaying environments. As for Lynch himself, he has stayed true to his buttoned-down yet unbridled self, creating his most breathtaking work with the opening 40 minutes and closing 10 minutes of *Lost Highway* (1998).

Director and writer
David Lynch

Producer
Richard Roth

Cinematographer
Frederick Elmes

Editor
Duwayne Dunham

Production company
De Laurentis

Production design
Patricia Norris

Cast
Kyle MacLachlan
Isabella Rossellini
Dennis Hopper
Laura Dern
Hope Lange
Dean Stockwell
George Dickerson

Other films
★ *Eraserhead* (1977)
★ *The Elephant Man* (1980)
★ *Wild At Heart* (1990)
★ *Lost Highway* (1997)
★ *The Straight Story* (1999)

Kyle MacLachlan and Isabella Rossellini acting out Lynch's bizarre but essentially conservative fantasies.

Do The Right Thing   Spike Lee *1989*

Director, producer and writer
Spike Lee

Cinematographer
Ernest K. Dickerson

Spike Lee introduced himself to us with *She's Gotta Have It* (1986). This delightful film hit a welcome note: breezy urbanity crossed with sexual frankness. It also had the added benefit of Lee's hilariously deadpan, incantatory speech in the role of Miles. *She's Gotta Have It* was a modest film, but it also felt spontaneous, at times lighter than air, less than exciting formally yet open to the idea of formal excitement. Lee followed this up with a misstep, *School Daze* (1988). However, he then jumped into the breach with the thrilling *Do the Right Thing*. Lee and his cinematographer Ernest K. Dickerson worked up a visual style that felt perfectly in tune with the Public Enemy songs on the soundtrack – vibrant primary colours, canted angles that suggested comic-book frames, and visceral, zapping editing rhythms. Few films have ever looked or felt so completely urban.

Do the Right Thing spans a day in the life of a block in New York City's Bed-Stuy neighbourhood, on the hottest day of the summer. The residents are predominantly African-American, and are served by white and Korean business owners. Everyone speaks his or her piece: the 'mayor' of the block (Ossie Davis), looking to live the rest of his days in peace with Mother Sister (Ruby Dee); the white pizzeria proprietor (Danny Aiello) and his two sons, one tolerant (Richard Edson), the other a racist (John Turturro); the 'militant' (Giancarlo Esposito) who wants to force the pizza man out of the neighbourhood; the silent Radio Raheem (Bill Nunn) who speaks through the rap music that blares from his ever-present 'ghetto blaster'; Mookie (Lee), the non-committal delivery boy; and his loud, rude, luscious, pregnant girlfriend (Rosie Perez). Lee manages to create a multiplicity of different viewpoints which hum across the movie like warring electrical currents. He also creates a rather wonderful push–pull tension; everyone is forever competing with each other to be heard above the din and through the heat – essentially, competing to command the colourful, mobile soapbox that is the movie. When the tension finally explodes with the death of Radio Raheem in a police chokehold (a scenario that is based on a true incident, the death of Michael Stewart while in police custody, which received a lot of press at the time that it occurred), the impact is shattering – as is the ominous summertime quiet before Mookie gets up and throws a garbage can through the window of the pizza parlour, inciting a riot.

When *Do the Right Thing* lost the Palme d'Or at the 1989 Cannes Film Festival to the Coen Brothers' *Barton Fink* (prompting this memorable New York tabloid headline: 'Spike Lee Gets the Back d'Or'), Wim Wenders famously commented that he thought Mookie 'wasn't enough of a hero.' A remarkably obtuse statement.

Production companies
40 Acres and
Mule Filmworks

Editor
Barry Alexander Brown

Music
Bill Lee

Cast
Danny Aiello
Ossie Davis
Spike Lee
John Turturro
Rosie Perez
Giancarlo Esposito
Ruby Dee
Bill Nunn

Samuel L. Jackson
John Savage

Other films
★ *She's Gotta Have It* (1986)
★ *Mo' Better Blues* (1990)
★ *Jungle Fever* (1991)
★ *Malcolm X* (1992)
★ *Get On The Bus* (1996)
★ *Summer of Sam* (1999)

A moment of tension between Jon Savage and Giancarlo Esposito on a hot day in Bed-Stuy.

sex, lies and videotape Steven Soderbergh *1989*

For better or worse, Steven Soderbergh's *sex, lies and videotape* made the Hollywood film industry aware that something was happening in the tiny world of American independent film. Soderbergh's smartly written, sensuously photographed, deliciously acted four-hander premiered in 1989 at Sundance; the next day what had been a sleepy little festival, inconveniently located in a Utah ski resort, was overrun with Hollywood representatives who had heard the buzz.

Both a critical and a commercial success, *sex, lies and videotape* won, among many other prizes, the Palme d'Or at the Cannes Film Festival. Its writer-director spent the next decade dodging expectations and displaying his versatility in a number of films. The most accomplished of them are the pulp-thriller *Out Of Sight* and the ingenious hit-man fable *The Limey*, which tenderly sideswipes the 1960s. In 2000, he achieved a place on Hollywood's A-list with the back-to-back, multiple Oscar-winning successes of *Erin Brockovich* and *Traffic*. But none of these films capture a cultural moment as sharply as *sex, lies and videotape*.

The title itself seemed to have siphoned the essential elements from the guilty fantasies of just about everyone in the United States at the end of the 1980s. It made you feel as if you had been found out even before you entered the cinema. And it is no slight on the movie to say it does not live up to the title. There's no way it could.

sex, lies and videotape is, in Hollywood's terminology, a character-driven film, but, more accurately, it is a film about relationships. The setting is New Orleans. Ann (Andie MacDowell in her first major screen role) is married to John (Peter Gallagher), a yuppie lawyer and dedicated womanizer who's having an affair with her sister, Cynthia (Laura San Giacomo). Into this potentially explosive situation comes Graham (James Spader), who is as different from John, his former high-school buddy, as Ann and Cynthia are from each other. Silky-smooth on the surface, the film is driven by an anger and wounded narcissism that the characters express in different ways. John and Cynthia are openly hostile, aggressive and competitive. Ann and the mysterious Graham turn out to be kindred spirits in that they both internalize their anger and refuse to admit their sexual desires, even to themselves. If the film poses Ann as its object of desire, it makes Graham its point of identification. Graham, who describes himself as once having been as much of a 'macho man' as John, is impotent. Withdrawing from the terrors of physical intimacy, he has discovered the pleasure and power in voyeurism. Graham videotapes women talking about their sex lives, which, for both Ann and Cynthia, turns out to be a liberating experience.

Implicit in the film is a comparison between Graham's videotaping and, on the one hand, psychoanalysis (when we first encounter Ann, she is talking to her therapist) and, on the other, the act of filmmaking itself. Soderbergh turns the heat on himself, implying that there is something perverse in the power of the director and also in the society that celebrates its auteurs and envies the licence the camera bestows on them.

Director, writer and editor
Steven Soderbergh

Producers
Robert Newmyer and John Hardy

Cinematographer
Walt Lloyd

Production companies
Outlaw Productions and Virgin

Music
Cliff Martinez

Production Design
Joanne Schmidt

Cast
James Spader
Andie MacDowell
Peter Gallagher
Laura San Giacomo
Ron Vawter
Steven Brill

Other films
★ *Kafka* (1991)
★ *King of the Hill* (1993)
★ *The Underneath* (1995)
★ *Schizopolis* (1996)
★ *Out Of Sight* (1998)
★ *The Limey* (1999)
★ *Erin Brockovich* (2000)
★ *Traffic* (2000)

My Own Private Idaho
Gus Van Sant *1991*

With its jazzy, improvisational rhythms, its freewheeling, on-the-road narrative, and its passion for both 'America, the beautiful' and the most dispossessed of her inhabitants, Gus Van Sant's *My Own Private Idaho* is the last great work of art inspired by the beat aesthetic. It's also a film of ambitious intertextuality that draws on such diverse sources as the avant-garde trance-film genre and Shakespeare's *Henry IV*.

The film's governing consciousness is Mike (River Phoenix), a narcoleptic, teenage hustler who is hopelessly in love with Scott Favor (Keanu Reeves), a slumming preppie prince. Mike's narcolepsy is a defence against the agony of his childhood abandonment. Anything that reminds him of his long-lost mother triggers a violent psychosomatic reaction. Without warning, he can fall into a stupor while alone on a highway or turning a trick. Mike's snoozing subjectivity gives *Idaho* its dream-like structure; it anchors the heterogeneous visual associations, the dense layering of spoken word and music and the split-second shifts between the burlesque and the heartfelt.

Mike and Scott are part of a loose-knit crew of young street prostitutes who live as squatters in a derelict Portland hotel. Their leader is Bob Pigeon (William Reichert), a beer-guzzling chicken hawk, who is besotted with the narcissistic Scott. Bob and Scott act out their relationship as Shakespeare's Falstaff and Prince Hal, challenging each other to ever greater heights of bowdlerized verse. Scott also protects the vulnerable Mike, a situation which is bound to end in heartbreak since Scott, the son of the mayor, is merely sowing his wild oats while Mike has no option but the street. As a final fling, Scott goes on a trip with Mike, who is in search of his mother. Huddled beside a camp fire, Mike risks, or perhaps courts, a repetition of his primal loss by confessing his love to Scott. 'I just want to kiss you, man,' he says softly, hugging his arms around his chest. Phoenix fills the moment with an absolute, naked need that blasts through the conventional categories of sexual orientation. Tapping into the liminal state between identification and desire, and giving expression to the repressed yearning in countless westerns where 'real' men bed down next to each other in the wild, Phoenix and Van Sant created one of the most moving love scenes in the history of cinema. Throughout the film, one can sense the trust between the actor and the director, the shared sense that they are involved in a project that will define both of their careers.

My Own Private Idaho climaxes with a double funeral. Scott Favor's real father and his adoptive father, Bob Pigeon, are being buried on opposite sides of the same cemetery. The stiff-necked Favor clan, now led by Scott and his new bride, are desperately trying to ignore the carnivalesque spectacle of Mike and his fellow outcasts dancing on Bob's grave. The scene speaks volumes about the polarization of haves and have-nots in the United States and adds a political dimension to a film of rapturous beauty and wild invention.

Director and writer
Gus Van Sant

Producer
Laurie Parker

Cinematographers
Eric Alan Edwards
and John Campbell

Production company
New Line Cinema

Editor
Curtiss Clayton

Music
Bill Stafford

Cast
River Phoenix
Keanu Reeves
James Russo
Udo Kier
William Reichert
Rodney Harvey
Chiara Caselli
Grace Zabriskie
Tom Troupe

Other films
★ *Mala Noche* (1985)
★ *Drugstore Cowboy* (1989)
★ *Even Cowgirls Get the Blues* (1993)
★ *To Die For* (1995)
★ *Good Will Hunting* (1997)
★ *Psycho* (1998)

Thelma and Louise
Ridley Scott *1991*

The most radically feminist movie Hollywood ever produced, *Thelma and Louise* claims the mythic landscape of the American southwest for two women on the run. Its high spirits and dazzlingly good looks notwithstanding, this female-driven road movie shows that the situation of women in a society ostensibly founded on the principal of 'liberty and justice for all' is dire indeed. When Louise (Susan Sarandon) comes to the rescue of her best friend Thelma (Geena Davis) by putting a bullet in the heart of the man who had been trying to rape her, few in the audience feel that the killing is unjustified. And when Louise rejects Thelma's suggestion that they go to the police and explain what happened with a despairing, 'A hundred people saw you dancing cheek to cheek. Who's going to believe us?' we know she's probably right about that, too.

Opening in the summer of 1991 with little support from its studio, MGM (fighting off bankruptcy at the time), the film nevertheless generated such passionate debate that its two stars made it on to the cover of *Time* magazine, under the headline, 'Why *Thelma and Louise* Strikes a Nerve'. Those who were outraged by the film claimed it promoted 'kamikaze' feminism and tried to seduce women into abandoning the moral high ground, a lofty metaphor that is no substitute for real power. Implicit in this argument is the acceptance of a double standard for men and women. Had Louise been a man defending his girlfriend, his action would have been viewed as a sign of courage and character. Moreover, male heroes were allowed to kill with impunity the women who got in their way. In *Total Recall* (1990), the big movie of the previous summer, Arnold Schwarzenegger, *Übermensch* of the Reagan/Bush era, casually shoots a woman to death, while quipping, 'Consider that a divorce'. Indeed, it is that very double standard that is exposed by the film's revision of traditionally male-oriented genres.

Thelma and Louise opens as a classic buddy comedy, except that the buddies are women. Louise, an overworked, tough-talking waitress with a soft heart and boyfriend who will not commit, and her friend Thelma, an infantilized housewife with a loutish husband whose only way of relating to her is to put her down, take off for a fishing trip in Louise's cherished 1960s turquoise convertible. Their plans for a relaxing weekend are turned upside down when Thelma is violently assaulted by a local Lothario and Louise stops him with a bullet from the gun that Thelma had brought along for protection when they were alone in the woods. In a panic, the pair speed away and wake up the next day to find themselves outlaws. As they head for Mexico with the FBI in pursuit, *Thelma and Louise* turns into a western and road movie rolled into one. Scott's wide-screen visuals give the film its mythic scale, but it is his collaboration with screenwriter Callie Khouri as well as the two stars that makes *Thelma and Louise* not only symbols of female empowerment but sisters of the heart.

Director
Ridley Scott

Producers
Ridley Scott and
Mimi Polk

Writer
Callie Khouri

Cinematographer
Adrian Biddle

Music
Hans Zimmer

Production companies
MGM, Pathé Entertainment and United International

Cast
Geena Davis
Susan Sarandon
Harvey Keitel
Michael Madsen
Christopher MacDonald
Brad Pitt

Other films
★ *Alien* (1979)
★ *Blade Runner* (1982)
★ *Legend* (1985)
★ *Black Rain* (1989)
★ *Gladiator* (2000)
★ *Hannibal* (2001)

Academy Awards
Oscar for Callie Khouri for Best Screenplay, 1992

137

Clerks Kevin Smith *1993*

*C*lerks (1993) makes the absence of style a virtue in its depiction of working-class depression and desire. Kevin Smith's first feature is confined to a single day in the life of Dante (Brian O'Halloran), a New Jersey convenience-store clerk and college drop-out, who is procrastinating over some big decisions about his future.

Made for a penurious US$27,000 (and this in the days before digital video made the $1000 feature a possibility), *Clerks* was legendary even before it was released. The 22-year-old Smith quit film school after four months, borrowed to the limit on 10 credit cards, sold his comic book collection, turned to his family for money, added his own savings from working at the two strip-mall stores that became the film's primary locations, and went into production. *Clerks* was shot in grainy 16mm black-and-white; few members of the cast and crew had any prior filmmaking experience.

Luckily, the writer-director had a vision, and *Clerks* reveals a world of young working-class guys that had never been shown on screen before. The 'average Joe' may be a Hollywood staple, but with rare exceptions, Hollywood neutralizes and glamorizes him. *Clerks*, on the other hand, is an inside job. It is not so much a film about a guy desperate to get out of, but also paralyzed by, a dead-end, boring job: it is the film that guy would have made – and, in fact, did.

Raising the sense of being trapped – in a job, in a relationship, in one's body – to an existential condition, *Clerks* opens an avenue of escape through humour. Smith's great talent is for writing dialogue that is outrageously and hilariously ribald and scatological. Dante, his buddy Randal, his ex-girlfriend Caitlin, his current girlfriend Veronica and the two omnipresent observers, Jay and Silent Bob (the latter played by Smith himself), are the contemporary equivalents of Shakespeare's low-lifes. From Dante and Veronica arguing about whether blow-jobs count as sex (a prescient scene in the light of the Clinton/Lewinsky follies) to Randal discoursing about the callous disregard for the working class in George Lucas' *Return of the Jedi* (1983), *Clerks* roots its humour in moral dilemmas which are as pressing for the characters as their sexual desires.

With the exception of two brief scenes, *Clerks* is entirely located in and around the Quick Stop convenience store. The film takes a standard romantic comedy conceit – a man trying to choose between two women – and transforms it by showing us that although Dante is obsessed with finding a mate, he spends most of his time working. The economic constraints on Dante's life dovetail with those Smith faced in making a self-financed first feature. What is most ingenious about *Clerks* is the way it exploits its limited production resources. The fact that it looks as if it were made with a surveillance camera only adds to its sense of authenticity. As few films do, *Clerks* creates a world, one which Smith has extended not only in subsequent features but with his idiosyncratic and wildly popular website, viewaskew.com.

Director and writer
Kevin Smith

Producers and editors
Kevin Smith and
Scott Mosier

Cinematographer
David Klein

Production company
Miramax and View Askew

Music
Scott Angley

Cast
Brian O'Halloran
Jeff Anderson
Marilyn Ghigliotti
Lisa Spoonauer
Jason Mewes
Kevin Smith

Other films
★ *Mallrats* (1995)
★ *Chasing Amy* (1997)
★ *Dogma* (1999)

Brian O'Halloran (left) and Jeff Anderson, in a film that is less a glamorized version of ordinary slacker lifestyles than an 'inside job'.

Hoop Dreams Steve James *1994*

Director
Steve James

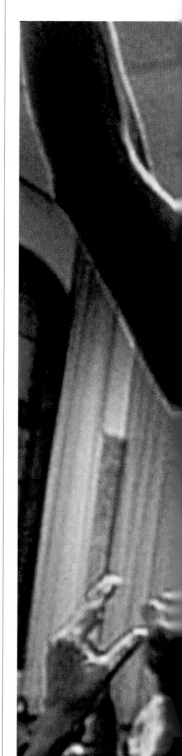

The most critically celebrated documentary of the past two decades, *Hoop Dreams* follows two teenage African-American basketball players as they are channelled by families, coaches and their own passionate ambition towards the almost impossible goal of playing in the NBA, the professional league. The filmmakers, Steve James, Frederick Marx and Peter Gilbert, started out in 1990 to make a short about playground basketball in Chicago, then the hometown of megastar Michael Jordan. The NBA was at its height of popularity: every kid in America wanted to 'be like Mike'. Focusing on two talented 14-year-olds, William Gates and Arthur Agee, the filmmakers became so intrigued by the boys and their families that they continued to follow them for five years, accumulating 250 hours of videotape, which they edited into a rapid-fire, elliptical three-hour narrative.

Gates and Agee are both recruited by St Joseph's, a suburban private school famed for having nurtured the talent of NBA superstar Isaiah Thomas. Although they have to travel three hours every day to get to and from school, and their families must bear the financial burden of the expenses not covered by their scholarships, no one ever considers turning down this supposedly golden opportunity. The St Joseph's basketball coach pins his hopes for a championship on Gates, and when his parents cannot meet their financial obligations, the school finds a wealthy sponsor to cover his costs. Less secure and not as physically developed, Agee gets an indifferent reception from the coach and no help is offered when his parents fall behind in their payments. Not only does St Joseph's expel him but the school also refuses to forward his records to his neighbourhood high school until his parents pay the outstanding balance.

But real life provides more reversals than any screenwriter would dare. Gates fulfils his promise for two years. Then he suffers a severe knee injury, tries to come back too soon (the coach, who should know more than his young player about the risk he is taking, makes no effort to stop him) and injures his knee again. His body, confidence and love of the game are irreparably damaged. Agee, on the other hand, thrives at his new school, where the African-American coach treats his players as human beings rather than as potentially profitable pieces of meat. While Gates is missing his clutch shots, Agee leads his team to the finals of the all-state championship.

More than a basketball story, *Hoop Dreams* is an intimate depiction of family life in the inner city, where money is in short supply but love and determination are not. Its most remarkable character is Arthur's mother, Sheila Agee, who at one point, inquires angrily of the filmmakers: 'Do you ever ask how I keep this house and feed these children on $268 a month?' Despite having to chose between food and electricity (at one point the family lives by candlelight), she finishes a nursing-assistant training programme with the highest grades in her class. It is hard to decide whether her success or Arthur's is more thrilling, but one thing is certain: he would be nowhere without her.

Writers and producers
Fred Marx, Steve James
and Peter Gilbert

Cinematographer
Peter Gilbert

Editors
Fred Marx, Steve James
and Bill Haugse

Production companies
KTCV-TV and Kartemquin Films

Cast
William Gates
Arthur Agee
Emma Gates
Ken Curtis
Sheila Agee
Arthur 'Bo' Agee

Other films
★ *Grassroots Chicago* (1991)
★ *Higher Goals* (1993)
★ *Prefontaine* (1997)

A moment of exhilaration is captured on video in one of the most acclaimed documentaries of recent years.

Pulp Fiction Quentin Tarantino *1994*

Director and writer
Quentin Tarantino

Producer
Lawrence Bender

Quentin Tarantino's experience as a video-store clerk is often cited as the key to his aesthetic. For his fans, it signifies the triumph of geeky connoisseurship – this was the guy who made nerdiness truly hip. For his traditionalist enemies, Tarantino's behind-the-counter experience is an all-too-apt symbol of a new, disturbingly acquisitive form of cinephilia. His films do not feel like the work of someone who has spent hours in the dark, soaking up images as they unfold in linear time. To enter Tarantino's universe is to experience the discontinuous time of the obsessive collector, sitting in the privacy of his home and endlessly replaying favourite moments until they become part of his DNA. His films appear to be extending the emotional tone of the films he grew up with in the 1970s: the sombre, low-key imagery; the lengthy stretches of screen time devoted to behavioural byplay between laid-back guys; the bright, full-frontal physicality of 'blaxploitation'. Just like a master DJ with his albums, the emotion is in the devotional sensitivity to every aspect of those memorized – and memorialized – images, and the exquisite manner in which they are manipulated into a whole new object.

If Tarantino had made only *Reservoir Dogs* (1991), he would merit nothing more than a footnote in movie history. As ingenious and soulful as that film is, it still feels like nothing more than a new wrinkle on an old genre. *Pulp Fiction* was something else, a whole new kind of movie-toy to play with. Garlanded with a string of lovable actors adored by their director, the film dips and soars from one emotional extreme to the next: John Travolta's drug rush; Uma Thurman's needle-in-the-heart resurrection; Christopher Walken's hilarious vaudeville turn; Ving Rhames' revenge on his hillbilly rapists; the head-splatter in the car. *Pulp Fiction* is guiltlessly dedicated to the pursuit of satisfaction. Its spectacularly confident leaps and reversals in time and complete freedom from social responsibility move the film through its purely filler moments, to a realm of fullness and delight that is almost primal. (On the other hand, it is important to remember that the movie's key elements of irresponsibility and artful satisfaction do not speak to everyone – some members of the African-American community wondered who all this fun was for.)

If there has not been anything like it since, it is not for lack of trying. In the United States, the film spawned many second-rate imitations that drained all the fun out of its narrative complexities and standardized its anti-social traits, while lacking the redeeming virtue of its infectious exuberance. As for Tarantino himself, he understood better than anyone that his breakthrough was one-of-a-kind, and followed up three years later with the less spectacular but more soulful *Jackie Brown*. In that film's lovely relationship between Robert Forster's bail bondsman and Pam Grier's ex-con, Tarantino extended and sustained the graceful lilt of *Pulp Fiction*'s one truly magical moment, John Travolta and Uma Thurman gracefully segueing into a junked-out twist. Our *wunderkind* turned out to be the poet of depletion and enervation.

Cinematographer
Andrzej Sekula

Production company
A Band Apart, Jersey Films
and Miramax

Editor
Sally Menke

Cast
John Travolta
Uma Thurman
Samuel L. Jackson
Bruce Willis
Harvey Keitel
Tim Roth
Steve Buscemi
Rosanna Arquette

Other films
★ *Reservoir Dogs* (1991)
★ *Jackie Brown* (1997)

Academy Awards
Best Screenplay Oscar for
Quentin Tarantino, 1995

John Travolta (sprayed with gore after accidentally shooting someone) and Samuel L. Jackson as the fabulously violent hit-men.

[Safe] Todd Haynes *1995*

Director and writer
Todd Haynes

Set in a wealthy Southern California suburb in 1987, Todd Haynes' *[Safe]* tells the story of Carol White (Julianne Moore), a not-quite Stepford wife, saved from banality by her inchoate sense that something is not right in her seemingly perfect world. Carol is afflicted with environmental illness (also known as multiple chemical sensitivity). It is a syndrome which many in the medical establishment refuse to recognize; those who do consider its sufferers, most of them women, to be the canaries of the 21st century. Carol's immune system is being destroyed by just about everything with which she comes into contact – from auto exhaust fumes to her husband's deodorant to the stain-resistant fabric on her new sofa. During the course of the film, she wastes away before our eyes.

Made with the kind of analytic intelligence that was the signature of Stanley Kubrick, but also with a tenderness that Kubrick seldom permitted, *[Safe]* is an intellectual horror film. For the first 45 minutes, we follow Carol as she goes about her daily routine. A drive on the freeway behind a smoke-spewing truck causes a coughing fit of epic proportions. At the hairdressers, she is happily examining her new perm in the mirror when blood begins to drip from her

nose. As in standard horror films, the heroine of *[Safe]* knows that the plague has descended, but no one believes her. Carol's husband, doctors and friends think that her problem is in her head. In order to survive, Carol must leave her protected, passive existence behind. She attempts to investigate and take charge of her illness. But unfortunately, her investigations lead her to Wrenwood, a New Age retreat where she is as isolated as in her suburban cocoon.

Keeping Carol at a distance – a fragile, almost paralysed figure in a chill, repressive environment – Haynes nevertheless locates the film within her subjectivity. Rather than alienating us from her, the measured, wide-angle, hyper-real *mise-en-scène* becomes an expression of the alienation she experiences. As her health deteriorates, we realize that everything in her environment – which is not very different from our own – is potentially lethal. The tension between identification and remove gives the film great gravity. Every frame seems charged with the push–pull of desire and loathing.

'It's scary,' Haynes once remarked, 'how much I identify with Carol White.' *[Safe]* is Haynes' second feature, sandwiched between the defiantly homoerotic *Poison* and the glam-rock musical *Velvet Goldmine* (1998), but thematically it is closest to *Superstar: The Karen Carpenter Story*, his 43-minute biopic of the anorexic 1970s popstar, which was shot on miniature sets with a cast of Barbie dolls. *[Safe]* has the most conventional surface of all Haynes' films, but it makes the greatest demand on viewers. It would be wrong to look for the film's meaning in the words of the affable guru of Wrenwood. Nothing could be further from Haynes' position than the New Age prescriptions. 'Do you smell the fumes?' is the inscription on a flyer that catches Carol's eye. *[Safe]* suggests that we are all vulnerable to the fumes; the rest is up to us.

Producers
Christine Vachon
and Lauren Zalaznick

Cinematographer
Alex Nepomniaschy

Production companies
American Playhouse,
Channel 4, Chemical Films,
Good Machine and Kardana

Production design
David Bomba

Editor
James Lyons

Cast
Julianne Moore
Xander Berkeley
Dean Norris
Julie Burgess

Peter Friedman
Susan Norman

Other films
★ *Superstar: The Karen Carpenter Story* (1987)
★ *Poison* (1991)
★ *Velvet Goldmine* (1988)

Carol (Julianne Moore, centre) flanked by her affluent LA friends in this modern alienation fable.

Eyes Wide Shut Stanley Kubrick *1999*

Director and producer
Stanley Kubrick

He may have lived in England for the last 35 years of his life, and he may have been a towering artist, but Stanley Kubrick was also the last of the great American showmen. He knew how to deliver a total experience, in which everything in and around the movie itself played a part – the legendary cloak of secrecy; the long gaps between films, during which the occasional press item would appear; the dead-end projects, abandoned for mysterious reasons; the big announcements, followed by lengthy, carefully guarded shoots; the stories that inevitably leaked out, about endless retakes and obsessive details; the trailers (over which he had total control), the first sign of a real movie.

Kubrick's detractors used his showmanship as a criticism of his films, claiming that they were only simple stories writ portentously and pompously large, all form and no substance. And these detractors were never so merciless – or so numerous – as they were with his final film, *Eyes Wide Shut*, which was released posthumously in the summer of 1999. The minute Kubrick's long-awaited adaptation of Arthur Schnitzler's turn-of-the-century novella, *Dream Story*, appeared, the invective came fast and furious. The film was too slow. Its vision of New York was hopelessly out of touch (Kubrick recreated a few blocks of Manhattan in Pinewood, a British studio). It was misogynist. It was ugly. Its notion of sexuality was old-fashioned. It was unfinished. The rumours were dished out to a public that finally had no use for this most intimate and nakedly emotional of Kubrick's films.

Eyes Wide Shut is the story of a young Manhattan doctor (Cruise) who uses his wife's spontaneous confession of past unrequited desire for another man as license to explore his own desires, only to encounter an endless series of prohibitions and frustrations. Cruise's character embarks on a nocturnal journey from a lavish Christmas party hosted by his wealthiest patient (Sydney Pollack) where he must tend to a model (Julienne Davis) who has overdosed on drugs, to his apartment for a tortured interaction with his wife (Nicole Kidman), to the deathbed of his mentor, over which the man's daughter (Marie Richardson) confesses her undying love for him, to an encounter with a beautiful hooker (Vinessa Shaw), to a costume rental shop where the owner (Rade Serbedzija) prostitutes his daughter (Leelee Sobieski), to an exclusive, high-toned, Long Island orgy. He spends the following evening trying to retrace his steps, and is faced with his own limitations as a human being.

For those who could not, or would not, see *Eyes Wide Shut* on its own terms, it appears a deeply silly movie by a reclusive, out-of-touch director. For those who went to Kubrick's movie with their eyes wide open, it is one of his greatest films, composed and enacted in dream logic, set in the ravishing tones of fin-de-siècle Viennese painting. Martin Scorsese has suggested that *Eyes Wide Shut* is Kubrick's *Viaggio in Italia* (1953, *Voyage to Italy*), and this is an astute assessment. Like Roberto Rossellini in the earlier film, Kubrick uses his two devoted superstars to dig deep into uncomfortable emotional issues. Both movies recount tortuous journeys that end with tentative, touching affirmations.

Like most of Kubrick's work, *Eyes Wide Shut* will make the shift to classic status in about ten years' time. For some of us, it already feels like a moving, triumphant farewell from one of the greatest artists who ever worked in the cinema.

Writers
Stanley Kubrick and
Frederick Raphael, from
Dream Story by Arthur
Schnitzler

Cinematographer
Larry Smith

Editor
Larry Galt

Cast
Tom Cruise
Nicole Kidman
Sydney Pollack
Marie Richardson
Rade Sherbedgia
Todd Field
Vinessa Shaw
Alan Cumming

Other films
★ *Lolita* (1962)
★ *Dr Strangelove* (1964)
★ *2001: A Space Odyssey* (1968)
★ *A Clockwork Orange* (1971)
★ *The Shining* (1980)
★ *Full Metal Jacket* (1988)

*Tom Cruise and Nicole Kidman share an unusually
intimate moment in Kubrick's final film.*

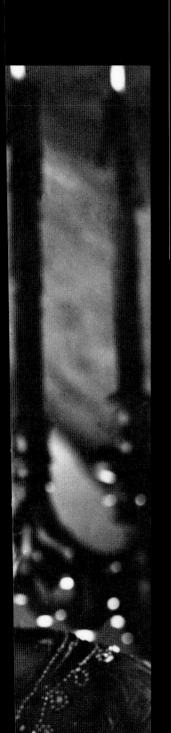

MAIN: *Pavel Kadochnikov (right) and Nikolai Cherkassov (left) in Sergei Eisenstein's* Ivan the Terrible *(1942–46).*

FAR LEFT: *Jacques Becker's* Rendez-vous de juillet *(1949).*

LEFT: *Jacques Tati in his own* Les Vacances de Monsieur Hulot *(1953).*

CHAPTER FIVE

Europe: The Golden Age

Gilbert Adair

Since, nowadays, 'art films' tend to be regarded by the cinema industry as little more than what department stores call loss-leaders, luxury items not themselves expected to turn a profit but prominently displayed nevertheless in order to attract the public's attention to what is really for sale, it is easy to forget that such was not always the case. In the 1930s, 40s and 50s there already existed, to be sure, a number of maverick masterpieces destined to receive only posthumous appreciation. One might cite Sergei Eisenstein's two *Ivan the Terrible* films (made between 1942 and 1946) from Soviet Russia, Roberto Rossellini's *Viaggio in Italia* (1954) from Italy and Max Ophüls's *Lola Montès* (1955) from France. Yet these same artists also enjoyed genuine public success with films that, hindsight being a great leveller, strike us now as not notably different from their failures and fiascos: respectively, *Alexander Nevsky* (1938), *Paisà* (1946) and *La Ronde* (1950). Because Hollywood, if ubiquitous and tentacular even then, enjoyed no totalitarian monopoly of audience tastes and affections, the European cinema was more generous, more eclectic, more inclusive, than it can currently afford to be.

The films I have chosen to write about in this section belong to both of the above categories, the margin and the mainstream, from Mañoel de Oliveira's *Aniki-Bobó*, one of the cinema's still too numerous *clandestine* classics, and Abel Gance's *La Vénus aveugle*, a wonderful, terrible melodrama, to Marcel Carné's *Les Enfants du paradis* and Federico Fellini's *La Dolce Vita*, neither of which needs, as they say, any introduction.

That there is a French bias to my selection is undeniable: eight films out of fifteen, even if two of these, Carl Dreyer's *Vampyr* and Ophüls's *Madame de*, were made by non-French directors. This bias reflects not only my own, equally undeniable Francophilia but the fact that, until the advent of Italian neorealism (location shooting, non-professional actors, socially conscious themes) in the immediate wake of the Second World War, with its revelation of films by Rossellini (*Roma, città aperta,* 1945), Luchino Visconti (*La Terra Trema*, 1948) and Vittorio de Sica (*Umberto D*, 1952), the French cinema was by far Europe's healthiest, wealthiest and most prestigious. The first half of the 1930s, after all, produced Jean Vigo's

L'Atalante (1934), arguably the greatest film ever made, and the second half produced Jean Renoir's *La Règle du jeu* (1939), arguably the greatest film ever made, and both of these greatest-films-ever-made were French.

Inevitably, omissions abound: of favourites for which, alas, no room could be made (Jacques Tati's universally adored *Les Vacances de Monsieur Hulot*, 1953; *Monsieur Hulot's Holiday*); of unjustly, incomprehensibly neglected little marvels (Jacques Becker's *Antoine et Antoinette*,1947, and *Rendez-vous de juillet*, 1949); of works which it would be meaningless to single out from their context (the trilogy of Andrez Wajda consisting of *A Generation*, 1954; *Kanal*, 1957; and *Ashes and Diamonds*, 1958); and, finally, of irrefutably major achievements of which I, personally, would be capable of offering only a dutiful and hence less than plausible defence (pretty much anything, for example, by Ingmar Bergman, a great director but never a passion of mine).

And those works I *have* written about? Have they anything in common? Only this, perhaps: that their creators made films as they breathed and seemed to *know* that they were living through a golden age.

149

M

Fritz Lang *1931*

Here is a curiosity: the sinister prominence with which the letter 'M', one tailor-made for the branding iron, figures in Fritz Lang's filmography. His best known, although far from finest, film was *Metropolis* (1927, *see pages 44–45*), whose heroine's name was Maria. His most celebrated creation, the protagonist of two silents and one late sound feature, was the verminously arachnoid mastermind Dr Mabuse. Three of his most memorable Hollywood productions were *Man Hunt* (1941), *The Ministry of Fear* (1944, *see pages 68–69*) and, long the favourite of cultishly minded Langians, *Moonfleet* (1955). (A whimsical case can even be made that the title of another work from the American period, *The Woman in the Window*, 1944, contained two inverted Ms.) Lang himself made a moving valedictory appearance in 1963 in Jean-Luc Godard's *Le Mépris*.

And, of course, there is his masterpiece, a still unmatched portrait of a child molester and murderer, titled baldly *M*. Lang's *M* is arguably the first film in the history of the cinema *for which absolutely no excuses need be made*, one completely emancipated from the naivety, whether formal, stylistic or psychological, that marred even the greatest works preceding it. Although, throughout what would turn out to be a prolific career, half-German and half-American, Lang retained a penchant for the eye-popping props of pulp – omniscient evil geniuses, castrating vamps, eleventh-hour reversals of fortune, cliffhanging climaxes, vengeful leper colonies, secret documents encoded in invisible ink and the unlikely like – for this film he jettisoned all such gaudy, moth-eaten trappings. Paring his visual style to the bone and drawing from his leading actor, Peter Lorre, one of the finest of all screen performances, comparable to that of Anthony Perkins in Hitchcock's *Psycho* (1960, *see pages 86–87*) almost 30 years later, he descended into (with this director one seemingly cannot escape the letter 'M') the maelstrom of a monster's mindset.

Lang had two strokes of genius. The first was to choose for his protagonist a mousy little individual, ordinary in everything save his psychosis (the character was based on a notorious infanticide, the so-called 'Vampire of Düsseldorf'). The second was to attribute his downfall not to the forces of order but to the loathing of 'normal' villains for anyone who goes, by their standards, too far. There is a near-Brechtian lucidity to the scenes in which the local criminal community organizes its ruthless pursuit of a pariah whose offences, to which it remains morally indifferent, have begun to strain its complaisant relationship with the police.

Even now, *M* is a film that operates on us without anaesthetic, obliging us, as few works of art have done, to confront our conflicting sympathies (or antipathies): on the one hand, a hapless, friendless child-killer; on the other, a vicious mob (one, moreover, with its own opportunistic agenda), determined to track him down like a terrified beast. Lang refuses to make it easy for us. And we have only to recall certain paedophile witch-hunts of late to realize that rarely has a film been so relevant for so long.

Director
Fritz Lang

Writers
Paul Falkenberg, Fritz Lang and Thea von Harbou

Producer
Seymour Nebenzal

Cinematographer
Fritz Arno Wagner

Production company
Nero Film

Cast
Peter Lorre
Gustaf Gründgrens
Ellen Widmann
Inge Landgut
Otto Wernicke
Franz Stein
Theodore Loos

Other films
★ *Dr Mabuse* (1921–22)
★ *Metropolis* (1927)
★ *Spies* (1928)
★ *The Woman in the Moon* (1929)
★ *You Only Live Once* (1938)
★ *The Ministry of Fear* (1944)
★ *The Big Heat* (1953)

Peter Lorre, mesmerizing as the serial killer: 'one of the finest of all screen performances'.

Vampyr

Carl Theodor Dreyer *1932*

Director
Carl Dreyer

Just as there are *films noirs*, so Carl Dreyer's *Vampyr* is a *film blanc*; a film, moreover, which has come to acquire the autonomous texture, one might almost say the patina, of a great painting. Its director's first sound feature, based on Sheridan Le Fanu's story *In a Glass Darkly* (1872) and privately financed by a wealthy Dutch aristocrat, *Vampyr* was a hopeless commercial failure on its original release, in spite (or because?) of the fact that it was, and remains to this day, one of the very few real masterpieces of cinematic horror.

Equally, perhaps, the film flopped because (or in spite?) of the fact that, like Hitchcock spurning the wearily clichéd setting of a shadowy, rain-swept dark alley when he exposed Cary Grant to mortal danger in the celebrated crop-dusting sequence of *North by Northwest* (1959), Dreyer (with the aid of his superlative cinematographer, Rudolph Maté) repudiated the genre's stereotypically gee-isn't-this-scary! darkness in order to invest his film with what might be described as a *complexion* of deathly pallor.

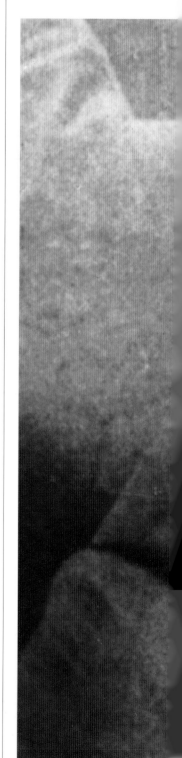

The ethereal Dreyer, not an artist much associated with genre films (his four best-known works, all of them among the cinema's greatest, were *La Passion de Jeanne d'Arc*, 1928, *see pages 48–49*, *Dies Irae*, 1943, *Ordet*, 1955, and *Gertrud*, 1964), adopted an unexpectedly audience-friendly attitude towards the effect he sought to achieve in *Vampyr*. 'Imagine', he said, 'that we are sitting in an ordinary room. Suddenly we are told there is a corpse behind the door. In an instant, the room is completely altered; the light, the atmosphere have changed, though they are physically the same. This is because *we* have changed, and the objects are as *we* perceive them.' It might be Hitchcock speaking.

The film's premise is simplicity itself. A bizarre, faintly dandified young man, David Gray, played by Baron Nicholas de Gunsberg, the industrialist mentioned above (though he is credited as 'Julian West'), arrives in a remote inn in an unspecified country and slowly, insidiously comes to the realization that he is surrounded by vampires. On a certain level it scarcely matters whether they are vampires or not. In *Vampyr* the supernatural is not, as numerous students of the film have proposed over the years, merely the other, latent side of the natural; it is, rather, the same side. It is almost as if, for Dreyer, the cinema itself were fundamentally supernatural, as if it were, in both senses of the word, a *médium*.

As in no other horror films – although an exception might be such Val Lewton productions, directed by Jacques Tourneur in the 1940s, as *Cat People*, *I Walked With a Zombie* and *The Leopard Man* – the natural and the supernatural bleed into one. And this convergence is crystallized in the famous scene in which David Gray dreams of his own death, and Dreyer films his vision as a first-person tracking shot from within his coffin. Given the conventional function of such a point-of-view shot in the codified grammar of filmmaking, it would seem to be inviting the spectator to identify with a cadaver.

Writers
Carl Dreyer and Christen Jul,
from the novel by Sheridan
Le Fanu

Producers
Carl Dreyer and Julian West

Cinematographers
Rudolph Maté and
Louis Née

Production companies
Athos Films, Chaumiane
and Filmstudio

Cast
Julian West
Maurice Schultz
Rena Mandel
Sybille Schmitz
Jan Hieronimko

Other films
★ *La Passion de Jeanne d'Arc* (1928)
★ *Dies Irae* (1943)
★ *Ordet* or *The Word* (1955)
★ *Gertrud* (1964)

An apparition hovers above David Gray (Baron Nicholas de Gunsberg, aka Julian West), epitomizing the film's eerie quality.

La Nuit du carrefour
Night at the Crossroads

Jean Renoir *1932*

Director and producer
Jean Renoir

Of the baker's dozen of films that were made by Jean Renoir between the end of the silent period and the eruption of the Second World War, practically any one could be singled out as the most representative of his genius. *La Chienne*, *Boudu sauvé des eaux* (*Boudu Saved from Drowning*), *Toni*, *Le Crime de Monsieur Lange* (*The Crime of Monsieur Lange*), *Partie de campagne* (*A Day in the Country*), *La Grande illusion*, *La Bête humaine* (*The Human Beast*) and, inevitably, *La Règle du jeu* (*The Rules of the Game*) – there is no other instance in the history of the cinema of a filmmaker who, for so long, could do no wrong. It seemed, for the Renoir of the interwar years, that the masterpiece was simply his speciality, his preferred genre, just as the thriller was for Hitchcock.

Although Renoir (who was, of course, the son of the quintessentially Impressionist painter Auguste) was the least formal, the least pompous, of great directors, the works cited above, all of them enshrined in the hallowed film-historical pantheon, have, over the years, become 'official' masterpieces. *La Nuit du carrefour* is another matter altogether. The cinema's very first of umpteen adaptations of Simenon (the director's brother, Pierre Renoir, plays Inspector Maigret), it is, by every conventional criterion, a shambolic mess.

Its impenetrable plot – involving several murders, a cache of stolen gems and a dilapidated cottage inhabited by a weirdly accented, morphinomaniac siren (the English actress Winna Winfried) – resembles a piece of cheese that is nothing but holes. A lot of its soundtrack (it was filmed in natural sound, an uncommon practice for the period) is close to inaudible. And if its imagery, which is not only nocturnal but continuously swathed in mist, already makes for a frustrating experience in the cinema, it has rendered it absolutely impossible to watch on television.

On top of which, there is a mystery at the heart of the film, a mystery which derives not from the whodunit conventions of Simenon's narrative but from the fact (or legend? Even now the question remains a vexed one) that two (or three, as Jean-Luc Godard has claimed?) reels of the original and irreplaceable negative were unaccountably lost by Renoir's friend and collaborator, the future film critic and historian Jean Mitry.

True perfection is a subtle cocktail of virtues and flaws and it matters not at all whether Mitry was in reality guilty of so monumental a blunder (the film's unusually and uncommercially brief running time of 73 minutes suggests, however, that he might have been). Having been liberated, for whatever reason, from the mechanics of the traditional thriller, *La Nuit du carrefour* is an astounding exercise in pure cinema, cherished by connoisseurs of the surreal for its potent atmospherics – a black car speeding through a silent, shuttered hamlet, the curdled odour of rain-sodden fields (for this is a film which, if one has difficulties seeing and hearing it, one can certainly *smell*), the squalid garage, the mystifying, sometimes even downright incomprehensible drama played out in the tumbledown house near the crossroads.

Some films are called sleepers. *La Nuit du carrefour* is a dreamer.

Writer
Jean Renoir, from a novel by
Georges Simenon

Cinematographer
Marcel Lucien

Editor
Marguerite Renoir

Art director
William Agnet

Cast
Michael Duran
Georges Koudria
Jane Pierson
Pierre Renoir
Winna Winfried

Other films
★ *La Chienne* (1931)
★ *Boudu sauvé des eaux* (1932)
★ *Toni* (1935)
★ *Le Crime de Monsieur Lange* (1935)
★ *Partie de campagne* (1936)
★ *La Règle du jeu* (1939)

A shot of the garage, one of the stock settings employed in the film.

Le Roman d'un tricheur
The Story of a Cheat

Sacha Guitry *1936*

Director and writer
Sacha Guitry

Were artists to be 'twinned' as cities are, then Noël Coward might have found himself bracketed with the comparably versatile French actor, wit, playwright and filmmaker Sacha Guitry, with whom he shared a flamboyant urbanity, a sentimental jingoism and, not least, a partiality to garish silk dressing gowns. Sacha – as with Noël, Oscar (Wilde) and Jean (Cocteau), the familiar form of address seems apposite – was born in 1885 and died, a national institution, in 1957.

During 60 of the intervening years, he wrote, directed and starred in a lengthy series of mostly drawing-room comedies (seldom has the triangle of Husband, Wife and Lover been more literally 'eternal' than in Guitry's filmography) enlivened by his actorish aplomb and indelibly nasal whinny. *Le Roman d'un tricheur*, which he based on his own novel, is his masterpiece, as airy and insubstantial as a bubble, perhaps, but a lovingly chiselled one.

In it Guitry plays a suavely amoral adventurer who, finding his good deeds systematically punished and his bad ones systematically rewarded, finally accepts what would appear to be his fate and becomes a professional con man. So laconic a précis, though, fails to do justice to the irresistible, almost toe-tapping rhythm of the film; to the ebullition of its narrative; to its generous quota of quotable *mots*; to its ironic commentary on the hypocrisy of social hierarchies; and, above all, to the vertiginous virtuosity of its central conceit. I mean the fact that the plot is narrated from start to finish by Guitry himself, who 'dubs' the dialogue of virtually every single character on the screen, including that played by his wife, Jacqueline Delubac, and who would therefore have written that dialogue with his own incomparable delivery in mind, exactly as a musician might compose for a specific vocal timbre.

It was for such ingenuities that he was adulated by the New Wave, one French critic even going so far as to describe him as 'the father of modern cinema'. Going so far or going too far? How, one wonders, could so frivolous, so determinedly bijou, an artist be considered a precursor?

Guitry's modernity derives, paradoxically, from his often-expressed *contempt* for the cinema, a medium that he exploited almost exclusively as a means of granting wider currency, by an adaptive process sometimes as casual as stencilling, to works originally conceived for the stage – or, as was the case with *Le Roman d'un tricheur*, the page. Disdaining film as he claimed he did, he consequently ignored (as would an avant-gardist, if of course for very different reasons) many of its long-established codes and practices. Which would explain, in *Le Roman d'un tricheur*, the voice-over dialogue, the speedy, uncumbersome shooting style, the assumption of total, indeed imperious, control over his material several decades before the formulation of the *auteur* theory, and, above all, the apotheosis of the director as the film's true author.

In one sense at least, then, he was what is called 'ahead of his time'. 'I believe the cinema to be past its peak' is, these days, an unexceptionable statement. It was made by Sacha Guitry in 1912.

Producer
Serge Sandberg

Cinematographer
Marcel Lucien

Production company
Cinéas

Music
Adolphe Borchard

Cast
Sacha Guitry
Marguerite Moreno
Jacqueline Delubac
Roger Duchesne
Rosine Deréan
Elmire Vautier

Other films
★ *Bonne chance* (1935)
★ *Mon père avait raison* (1936)
★ *Désiré* (1937)
★ *La Malibran* (1943)
★ *Toâ* (1949)
★ *La Poison* (1951)

Left to right: Jacqueline Delubac (Guitry's wife), Sacha Guitry and Rosine Deréan. Guitry voiced the parts of all the characters in the film.

By the Bluest of Seas
Ou samovo sinevo moria

Boris Barnet *1936*

Director
Boris Barnet

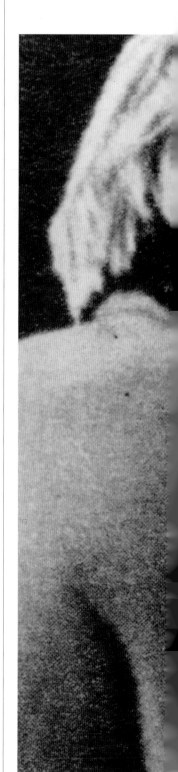

Who is the greatest of all Russian filmmakers? There would appear to be an *embarras de richesses*. Eisenstein? Dovzhenko? Dziga Vertov? Pudovkin? Donskoi? Heretically, one might counterpropose the much less familiar name of Boris Barnet, whose continuing neglect offers conclusive proof that, even a century after their inception, film history and criticism remain in a constant state of revision and reinvention.

Barnet, the director of *By the Bluest of Seas*, has never quite made it to the captain's table of 20th-century cinema. Although he is dutifully listed in, as they say, all good film dictionaries, even the best-informed of cinephiles would probably be hard-pressed to cite a single title from his filmography: the silent, Keatonesque farce *Devuska s korobkoj (The Girl with the Hat Box,* 1927) and *Okraina* (1933), a harsh and still harrowing First World War drama, are the most plausible candidates for whatever degree of immortality can currently be claimed for him. Nor has the cause of his posterity been advanced by the fact that he ended his career, like many of his terminally demoralized compatriots, cranking out the social-realist comedies and melodramas that passed for escapism in the gruesome heyday of Soviet Russia.

Yet *By the Bluest of Seas* is a miracle. It is a dissident film, to be sure, yet also one so serene, sparkling and good-humoured, not to mention luminously shot and acted, that it is difficult for a Western spectator to credit that it could ever have been a target of bureaucratic censure. Except, of course, that it happens to be one of the most erotic films ever made (of an eroticism, all the more pungent for its relative discretion, comparable to that of Frank Borzage's *The River*, 1929, and Giuseppe De Santis's *Riso Amaro,* or *Bitter Rice*, 1949), and the Soviet cinema, if one of the world's most prestigious, has never been notorious for its sexiness.

As is true of many supremely great films, a brief recap of its plot – in a collective farm on a remote island, a dot in a glittering, highlight-sequinned ocean, two rivals squabble over the love of a woman who in turn loves a third – would make it seem pretty infantile, destined exclusively for the Soviet equivalent of those gum-chewing stenographers and switchboard operators who flocked to Hollywood's perennial 'women's pictures'. Barnet, however, transforms it into what one of its champions, the Georgian filmmaker Otar Iosseliani, has described as a hymn to 'desire and fidelity', imbuing its every scene with that profoundly unfashionable sentiment, then (in 1936) as now, the love of life.

As Iosseliani also wrote, 'Anything is possible at any moment of this film.' And that, its director's genius apart, is what distinguishes it above all from even one of the American cinema's superior romances. The irony is that, while Barnet was still capable in Stalin's Soviet Union of creating a work as intoxicatingly personal and refreshingly ideology-free as *By the Bluest of Seas*, the contemporaneous Hollywood of the studio system had become the centre of collectivist filmmaking.

Writer
Klimenti Mints

Cinematographer
Mikhail Kirillov

Music
Sergei Pototsky

Production designer
Viktor Aden

Cast
Nikolai Kryuchkov
Yelena Kuzmina
Lyalya Sateyeva
Semyon Svashenko
Lev Sverdlin

Other films
★ *The Girl with the Hat Box* (1927)
★ *Okraina* (1933)
★ *Courage* (1941)
★ *A Priceless Head* (1942)
★ *The Poet* (1956)

Nikolai Kryuchkov and Yelena Kuzmina, two angles of the love quadrangle featured in By the Bluest of Seas.

Aniki-Bobó Mañoel de Oliveira *1942*

Director
Mañoel de Oliveira

Writers
Mañoel de Oliveira, from the
novel by Rodrigues de
Freitas

Producer
Antonio Lopes Ribeiro

Cinematographer
Antonio Mendes

Production company
Produçöes Antonio
Lopes Ribeiro

Cast
Feliciano David
Nascimento Fernandes
Fernanda Matos
Antonio Palma
Armando Pedro
Antonio Santos
Horacio Silva
Antonio Soaves

Other films
★ *Douro, Faina Fluvial*
 (1931)
★ *The Satin Slipper* (1985)
★ *No, or the Vainglory of
 Command* (1990)
★ *Vale Abraão* (1993)
★ *Journey to the Beginning
 of the World* (1997)
★ *La Lettre* (1999)

There was a time, not all that long ago, when, even for the most fanatical cinephile, referring airily to having seen 'the latest Oliveira', as one might say 'the latest Scorsese' or 'the latest Rohmer', would have constituted an outlandishly rarefied form of snobbery. It was not simply that the films of Mañoel de Oliveira, Portugal's greatest director, were difficult to see; nor indeed that there were few enough of them anyway. His long neglect was due supremely to the fact that anyone who had admired his first feature, *Aniki-Bobó*, made in 1942, would then have been forced to wait all of *two decades* for *Passion of Jesus*, its successor in the canon, followed, a full nine years later, by the third, *Past and Present*, and so (as it must have felt) on.

In fact, not so. Over the decades, Oliveira has speeded up rather than slowed down, contriving in his ever-expanding filmography to encompass almost the entire history of cinematic forms, from Eisensteinian montage to Buñuelian absurdism, from Mizoguchian fluidity to the guillotine framing of Dreyer and Bresson. He has reversed what one has always assumed to be the 'natural' course of an artistic career by starting as one of the least prolific of filmmakers and ending up by making practically a feature a year. Nowadays, after such absolute masterpieces as *Francisca* (1981), *The Satin Slipper* (1985), *No, or the Vainglory of Command* (1990; *see pp228–229*) and *Abraham's Valley* (1993), no cinephile need feel elitist when referring to 'the latest Oliveira'.

As for *Aniki-Bobó*, the very earliest Oliveira, whose mystifying title is a Portuguese variant on 'eeny-meeny-meiny-mo', it is a film about, and to some degree for, children. Set in Oporto, the director's native city, its slight plot centres upon the rivalry – for the affection of the local stunner – of a pair of matching mop-haired tots, one of whom, a blond cherub who might have stepped down from a Tiepolo altarpiece, is unjustly accused of having shoved the other onto a railway line. The film, one of the finest of all with a cast composed predominantly of infants, is often sentimental, sometimes downright corny and, ultimately, a pure enchantment.

In the cinema, to be sure, such ostensibly contradictory epithets have never been mutually exclusive. What, though, makes *Aniki-Bobó* unique is its blatant *theatricality*, a word scarcely ever used to describe children's films. As witness the endearingly actorish performances which Oliveira coaxes from his diminutive performers, his film is unequivocally a melodrama. And even if its loose and deceptively artless shooting style (it was filmed wholly on location) seems to anticipate the revolutionary strategies of neorealism, the result is reminiscent less of De Sica's work, say, than of Pagnol's Marseillais trilogy, *Marius*, *Fanny* and *César* (1931, 1932, 1936), by virtue of both the dockside setting and the tiny if nevertheless eternal triangle so solemnly, so touchingly, played out before it. Like Pagnol's own films, what *Aniki-Bobó* offers is a persuasive illustration and defence of cinema as *open-air theatre*.

A classroom scene from Aniki-Bobó, one of
the few truly great films whose cast is
composed primarily of children.

La Vénus aveugle
Blind Venus

Abel Gance *1943*

In 1927, in a war cry of characteristically grandiloquent lyricism, whose every single word, even 'of', 'than' and 'and', one feels should be followed by an exclamation mark, Abel Gance articulated his vision of the cinema's future thus: as 'a mad and tumultuous upheaval of artistic values, a sudden and magnificent blossoming of dreams greater than all that went before'. Abel Gance, Abel Extravagance!

Outside his native France, Gance, who lived from 1889 to 1981, is known almost exclusively for one film, *Napoléon*, shot in 1926, restored and triumphantly revived in 1981. Such was the ecstatic reception given to this revival, it has overshadowed not just the fact that its director's filmography was in reality a lengthy one (he was still active in the 1960s), but that almost none of the post-*Napoléon* works listed in it could honestly be described as a 'tumultuous upheaval of artistic values'. Although, as he aged, Gance's carefully cultivated mane of snow-white hair and heaven-rolling eyes made one think of a 19th-century Romantic poet, he was a 20th-century filmmaker like any other, capable of the great, the good and the downright awful, the sublime and the ridiculous alike, often co-existing in the same film.

La Vénus aveugle is a case in point. The French word *navet* means literally 'turnip' and figuratively, in the context of film criticism, 'dud', and *La Vénus aveugle* is the cinema's most grandiose dud, a turnip as monstrously outsized as one of those obscene marrows that win first prizes at country fairs. Its narrative defies summarization. Suffice to say that the film is set in and around a smoky dockside café, whose resident singer, fast losing her sight, heroically elects to break with her sea-captain lover whose unborn and all-too-soon-to-die infant she is carrying. Having begun as a 'sublime tragedy', to quote Gance's own, parodically exalted phrase (nowhere, curiously, does he use the word 'melodrama'), it ends on a note of no less 'sublime' comedy, as the captain, assuring the now blind Venus that he intends to take her on a voyage around the world, just as he always promised he would, has his dumpy little ship simply traverse the local harbour, back, forth and back again, while indiscriminately exotic sounds and smells (African tom-tom drums, Oriental bazaar aromas and so on) are craftily wafted across its bow. To cap it all, the film was brazenly dedicated to Marshal Pétain, Hitler's compliant puppet in wartime France, and, when it first opened, was dismissed by critics for what was widely perceived as its pro-collaborationist incitement to servile self-sacrifice.

A dud, undoubtedly. If it were a novel, it would be an embarrassment pure and simple. But the cinema is a river that is never more mysteriously beautiful than when it overflows its banks. And, because of its own delirious excess, because of the sheer force of Gance's faith in his disreputable material, hokum not merely squared but cubed, and above all because one genuinely does find oneself moved, sometimes even moved to tears, *La Vénus aveugle* is one of the medium's crazy masterworks.

Director
Abel Gance

Writers
Abel Gance and
Stève Passeur

Producer
J. J. Mecatti

Cinematographers
Henri Alekan and
Léonce-Henri Burel

Production company
Société France Nouvelle

Cast
Viviane Romance
Jean Aquistapace
Georges Flamant
Philippe Grey
Henri Guisol
Gérard Landry
Lucienne Le Marchand
Géo Lecomte

Other films
★ *J'Accuse!* (1919)
★ *La Roue* (1922)
★ *Napoléon* (1927)
★ *La Fin du monde* (1934)
★ *Lucrezia Borgia* (1935)
★ *Beethoven* (1936)

Rome, Open City
Roma, città aperta

Roberto Rossellini *1945*

Although Roberto Rossellini was indisputably one of the most influential of European directors, the fact that his influence was founded upon a philosophical or conceptual attitude towards the medium rather than upon the imitation of stylistic devices or thematic preoccupations has meant that Anglo-American film historians in particular tend to pay little more than lip service to his achievement, when not ignoring it altogether. Yet such indifference constitutes a major injustice not merely to a director who redefined the very parameters of the cinema but to one of the supreme 'documenters', in any art form, of the latter half of the 20th century.

Documenter, not documentarist. Rossellini's films were documents, not documentaries – documents of the Second World War, for example, as in the trilogy of *Rome, Open City*, *Paisà* (1946) and *Germania Anno Zero* (1947: *Germany, Year Zero*). *Rome, Open City* is not just about the last months of the German occupation of Italy, it was actually part of the experience. It was made in 1945, under horrendous conditions, only weeks after the Germans had finally quit the capital. The material privations that it depicts – the power cuts, the food shortages, the problems of transport – it itself suffered from. If its images have a grainy newsreel feel, this was not due to any desire on Rossellini's part to mimic the embattled realities of the occupation years but simply because his often less than impeccable film stock had been purchased in ordinary photography shops. And if it was shot mostly in exteriors, that was because the Roman studios had been appropriated by the occupiers as military barracks. For students of contemporary Italian history, *Rome, Open City,* the portrait of a whole populace under siege, is not a secondary but a primary text.

Out of such externally imposed difficulties, however, there arose an entirely new conception of the cinema, a movement to which the name 'neorealism' was given. It was Rossellini himself who offered the most radical and limpid statement of its ideology. 'Things are there,' he said. 'Why manipulate them?' As a war film for which, uniquely, nothing had to be reconstructed, *Rome, Open City* can therefore be regarded as a manifesto of neorealism.

For a minor but striking instance of the film's honesty, consider the sequence in which a lorry-load of prisoners is ambushed by a group of partisans. During the attack, a little dog trots placidly out into the road before suddenly making a terrified U-turn. It was just one of those pesky accidents which occur during the making of a film. A Hollywood director would have bawled out his assistant and had the dog unceremoniously ejected from the location. Or else, deciding that its presence would after all add a certain piquancy to the action, he would have built the whole scene around it, albeit employing *another* dog, one which had been specially trained for the purpose. Rossellini did neither. He sought neither to correct nor enhance the reality of the image. He simply filmed the event, exactly as it happened in front of his camera.

Director
Roberto Rossellini

Writers
Sergio Amidei, Federico Fellini and Roberto Rossellini

Producers
Ferruccio de Martin and Roberto Rossellini

Cinematographer
Ubaldo Arata

Production companies
Excelsa Film and Minerva Film

Cast
Aldo Fabrizi
Marcello Pagliero
Maria Michi
Henry Feist
Anna Magnani
Uito Annichiarico

Other films
★ *Paisà* (1946)
★ *Germania Anno Zero* (1947)
★ *Stromboli* (1949)

Academy Awards
Nominated for Best Screenplay in 1946

'The portrait of a whole populace under siege'; a German soldier in occupied Rome.

Les Enfants du paradis

Marcel Carné *1945*

It is virtually an article of faith with the film-critical establishment that any defiant, subversive or seditious intention in a movie must necessarily go hand-in-hand with visual, even budgetary, austerity. Lavish sets, ostentatious costumes and a cast of thousands are (so received wisdom would contend) the preserve of escapist blockbusters whose sole ambition is to entertain. By contrast, those higher-minded works that set out to undermine the status quo, social, political or aesthetic, are expected to be sober, modestly budgeted and often unrelievedly glum affairs too busy edifying the public ever to find the time to amuse it.

Marcel Carné's *Les Enfants du paradis*, a baroque tale of interlinked liaisons set predominantly in a theatrical milieu, is one of the most dazzling exceptions to that rule. It is, to be sure, an 'escapist' film – except that the word should be read more literally than usual. Carné started shooting in the late summer of 1943, and it was from the rigours and horrors of occupied France that he intended the film's audiences to escape – he intended them, in short, like certain Allied POWs, *to escape from the Germans*. Consequently, its gigantic budget (58 million francs, an unheard-of sum for the 1940s), its starry cast (Arletty, Jean-Louis Barrault, Pierre Brasseur, Marcel Herrand, Maria Casarès et al), its spectacular reconstruction of the 19th-century Boulevard du Crime and, above all, its celebration of Paris as the world's epicentre of wit, fantasy, charm and chic were paradoxically subversive attributes. France is not dead, was the message. Its fabled vivacity has not been snuffed out by four terrible years of corruption, torture and death. Paris *is* burning – with all its former fiery passion.

Although, because of its unprecedentedly protracted shoot, *Les Enfants du paradis* was released only in 1945, it proved just as much of a bombshell in the immediate wake of the scarcely less austere period of liberation as it would have been in wartime. Over the years, indeed, valiant attempts have been made to interpret the film as an allegory: Arletty's Garance (a name which, probably coincidentally, rhymes with 'France') besieged by would-be invaders, and so on. These interpretations are simply not plausible and it is François Truffaut's sensible view – 'I cannot accept the sometimes espoused patriotic theory that the historical or fantasy films made during the Occupation delivered a courageous message encoded in favour of the Resistance' – which has prevailed. Yet there is more than one way of raising a subversive fist in the air and we should not be surprised that the stratagem adopted by Carné and his scenarist, Jacques Prévert, the poet of populist Surrealism – to fabricate a luxury item in an epoch when luxury items were only a memory, to make a movie *as though the war did not exist* – would turn out to be so quintessentially Parisian.

Not for the first time in the history of the cinema, from chaos an authentic masterpiece was born. *Les Enfants du paradis* is a sumptuously romantic melodrama which needs no special pleading. A rival to *Gone With the Wind* (*see pages 60–61*), perhaps. But with subtitles – and subtleties.

Director
Marcel Carné

Writer
Jacques Prévert

Producers
Raymond Borderie
and Fred Orain

Cinematographers
Marc Fossard and
Roger Hubert

Production company
Pathé Pictures

Cast
Arletty
Jean-Louis Barrault
Gaston Modot
Pierre Brasseur
Marcel Herrand
Maria Casarès
Pierre Renoir
Louis Salon

Other films
★ *Drôle de drame* (1936)
★ *Quai des brumes* (1938)
★ *Le Jour se lève* (1939)
★ *Les Tricheurs* (1958)
★ *Trois chambres à
  Manhattan* (1965)

Gaston Modot and Jean-Louis Barrault in the studio-reconstructed 19th-century Paris of Les Enfants du paradis.

Madame de Max Ophüls 1953

Director
Max Ophüls

Producer
Ralph Baum

Cinematographer
Christian Matras

Music
Oscar Straus and
George van Parys

Cast
Danielle Darrieux
Charles Boyer
Vittorio de Sica
Jean Debucourt

Other films
★ *The Exile* (1947)
★ *Letter From an Unknown
Woman* (1948)
★ *The Reckless Moment*
(1949)

Strangely for a film of which frivolity is not merely the theme but the style, *Madame de* was once the symbol of a polemical quarrel between two implacably opposed critical camps. On the left were the humanists, who subscribed to the doctrine that a film's significance was proportional to the socio-ideological relevance of its subject-matter; and on the right were the auteurists, for whom the primary (and sometimes sole) focus of attention was the filmmaker's personality, as indelibly imprinted on the screen as a set of fingerprints. In short, the high-minded melodramas of Vittorio de Sica versus the frivolous melodramas of Max Ophüls. Or, to put it even more succinctly, *Umberto D* (1952) versus *Madame de*.

In the most celebrated of De Sica's neorealist films, *Bicycle Thieves* (1948: *Ladri di biciclette*), the protagonist is rendered unemployable by the theft of his bicycle and risks destitution unless he recovers it. In *Madame de*, to pay off her personal debts, the titular countess (Danielle Darrieux) sells a pair of diamond earrings given to her by her husband (Charles Boyer); pretends to have lost them; then, ermined and determined, finds herself obliged to recover them if she is not in turn to lose her lover, a suave Italian diplomat (played, interestingly enough, by Vittorio de Sica). Is either one of these dilemmas more of a tragedy than the other? To answer such a question is surely to play God. Madame de suffers no less than the unnamed hero of *Bicycle Thieves* (but then, she herself is only half-named). Indeed, she dies of her suffering where he does not.

If *Madame de* is as poignant as any film in the history of the cinema, of whatever movement, school or genre, it is because no director was more sensitive than Ophüls to the elusive volatility of love, the fragility and transience of desire. How else can we explain his career-long predilection for sinuous camera movements and heart-stopping dolly shots, for mirrors so beautiful that they themselves become vain, for imagery so mercurially elegant and graceful that the cinema screen seems to be made of watered silk? Until its heroine's climactic death, there is scarcely a single static shot in *Madame de*, as though there were a direct correlation for Ophüls between movement and life, stillness and death, as though, like nature, he too abhorred a vacuum.

Like Ravel, Ophüls was a supreme orchestrator (he alone would have been capable of filming the composer's eerily haunting homage to the Viennese waltz, *La Valse*), and he was one of the few directors capable of rendering the past *present* – as he does, precisely, in *Madame de* – without making his performers resemble guests at a fancy-dress ball. This, though, is not the essential point. In a sense, *Madame de* was ahead of its time and is maybe better appreciated now than when it was originally released. For its heroine, her husband and her lover destroy themselves out of loyalty to a code of honour that, just a half-century later, audiences are likely to find absurd. Is that not the real tragedy?

Danielle Darrieux as the titular countess,
contemplating the diamond earrings around
which the plot revolves.

Bob le flambeur
Jean-Pierre Melville *1956*

The French New Wave radically updated what would now be termed the cinema's 'interface'. Of the three principal candidates for the Film Most Likely To Have Paved The Way For Such A Change, Agnès Varda's *La Pointe courte* (1954), Roger Vadim's *Et Dieu créa la femme* (*And God Created Woman*, 1956) and Jean-Pierre Melville's *Bob le flambeur* (1956), it is for the last that by far the most convincing case can be made.

Varda's film, although innovatory in its freewheeling approach to location shooting, remains a transitional hybrid, stilted and rather theatrical. Vadim, it soon became clear, was no more than the froth that precedes every wave. But *Bob le flambeur* (a *flambeur*, in Parisian slang, is an addicted gambler) can now be perceived as having so uncannily anticipated the methods and even the themes of the New Wave, of early Godard in particular, that *A Bout de souffle*, a landmark film as it was and continues to be, must strike anyone familiar with Melville's earlier work as crucially less new and revolutionary than when it was first screened to an astonished public in 1960.

Not very much happens in *Bob le flambeur* (as was also true of the pioneering New Wave films). The impecunious Bob (Roger Duchesne), a fiftyish loner, if something of a dandy, lives in Montmartre, half in, half out of criminality, frequenting racecourses by day, propping up the local bars by night. Seriously on his uppers – gambling debts, naturally – he prepares to pull off the job of a lifetime, holding up the Deauville casino, and spends much of the film's running time gathering together, then training, a gang of trusted accomplices. It all goes awry, as these things invariably do in the cinema, but not too calamitously for Bob himself, who, having been strategically located for the needs of the heist at one of the casino's gaming tables, finds himself winning a fortune nearly as great as any he could ever have hoped to steal.

The film might have been entitled *Bob le flâneur*, or *Bob the Idler*. As much as a thriller (it is not, to be absolutely honest, all that thrilling), it is a documentary on the genre's bleary, woozily neon-lit nightscapes, through which Bob, resplendent in his eternal trenchcoat and nonchalantly angled fedora, imperturbably wanders, *un vrai gentleman*, as the French affect to put it. Nothing appears to matter too much to him, except the enjoyment to be taken in Paris's nocturnal sounds, sights and smells. Unlike the steely protagonist of Melville's subsequent, self-consciously abstract *Le Samouraï* (*The Samurai*, 1967), a poker-faced hoodlum for whom being caught in the act of actually, visibly *enjoying* the fruits of his crimes would cause his iconic purity to be fatally compromised, Bob likes nothing better than money, girls, gambling and the virile solidarity of the underworld.

Thus, despite ending with Bob's arrest and potential incarceration, the film is *almost* a comedy, and it is that 'almost' that makes it so modern (Godard's films were *almost* thrillers, Truffaut's *almost* melodramas, Demy's *almost* musicals) and so affecting.

Director
Jean-Pierre Melville

Writers
Auguste le Breton and
Jean-Pierre Melville

Cinematographer
Henri Decaë

Production companies
Organisation Générale
Cinematographique, Play Art
and Productions Cyme

Cast
Roger Duchesne
Isabelle Corey
Daniel Cauchy
André Garrot
Claude Cerval
Howard Vernon

Other films
★ *Les Enfants terribles*
   (1950)
★ *Le Deuxième souffle*
   (1966)
★ *Le Samouraï* (1967)

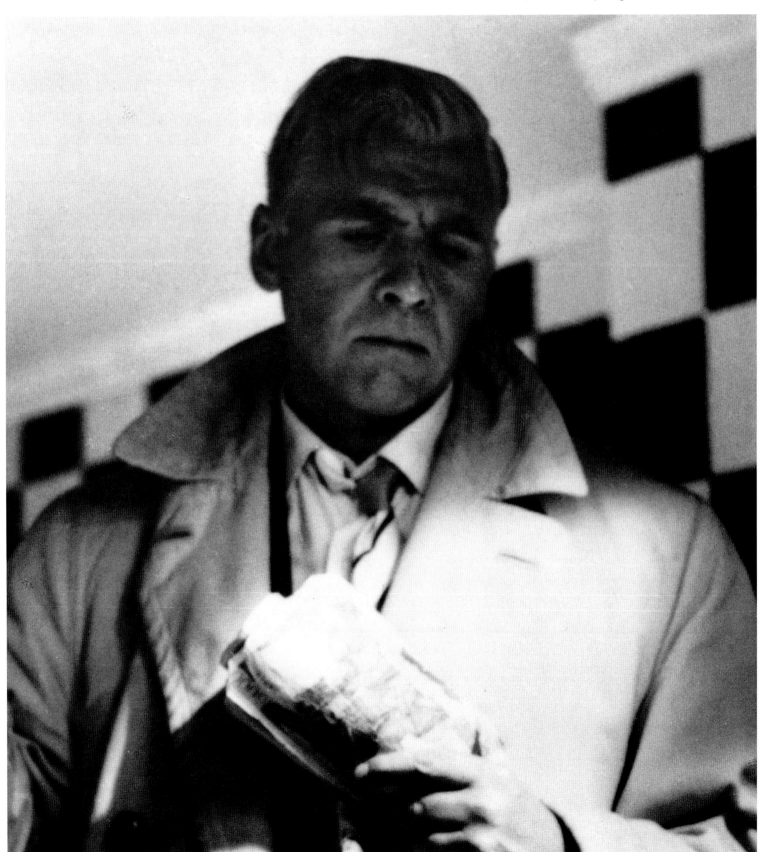

Roger Duchesne as Bob Montagné,
compulsive gambler and underworld legend,
in the act of placing a bet.

Pickpocket Robert Bresson *1959*

Perfection is where artists eventually arrive – if they can. For Robert Bresson it was a point of departure. From his first feature, *Les Anges du péché* (1943), to his last, *L'Argent* (1983), four decades later, he was responsible for an almost unbroken sequence of masterpieces. During the closing titles of numerous current American movies, the spectator is diverted by a montage of mildly hilarious out-takes; with Bresson's work such a conceit would be utterly unthinkable.

As befits a practising Christian, his themes were primarily of a religious nature, focusing essentially on the classic Catholic trinity of transgression, redemption and grace. Yet, even if of an unprecedented formal and thematic rigour, his cinema was by no means bloodlessly minimalist. A rich brew, it included both contemporary and period narratives, original screenplays and literary adaptations, mute, enigmatic epiphanies and even a cluster of unexpectedly spectacular set-pieces. Only he could have made the spiritual cohabit so intensely with the sensual.

Never more intensely, perhaps, than in *Pickpocket*, the story of a young Parisian moocher for whom criminality becomes a vocation into which he enters as one might enter a religious order. *Pickpocket* is a paradox: an austere diamond. Made three years after Alfred Hitchcock's *The Wrong Man*, it is Bresson's most Hitchcockian film, just as *The Wrong Man* is Hitch's most Bressonian . (Bresson's haunting and haunted hero, played, as usual, by a non-professional, Martin Lassalle, even bears an uncanny resemblance to the youthful Henry Fonda, star of *The Wrong Man*.) The ultimate reference for each of them, moreover, was the work of Dostoevsky: *Crime and Punishment* was patently the original inspiration for *Pickpocket*.

As always with Bresson, sin is the one ineluctable station on the path to salvation. So outmoded and potentially rebarbative a theme is, however, revitalized, reinvented, by the near-erotic pleasure which he takes in filming the pickpocket's art, in choreographing (there is no other word) the swift evisceration of a wallet before it is returned to its none-the-wiser owner. The film's repeated shots of its hero's hands insinuating themselves into the intimate orifices of his victims' pockets transform the legerdemain of petty theft into a jubilantly sensual, almost sexual practice.

The mystery of *Pickpocket* is that, although it is an overwhelmingly beautiful film, pure, pared-down and to the point, it would be difficult to extract from its imagery what is conventionally regarded as a beautiful shot, with the hint of the postcard inevitably implied by such a phrase. It was the director himself who wrote of his methodology, in *Notes on the Cinematographer*, a rather chilly anthology of aphorisms first published in English in 1986, 'Each shot is like a word, meaning nothing by itself. It is lent meaning by its context.' Which means that the appropriate term, here, is not 'beauty' but, in both its spiritual and aesthetic senses, 'grace', that miraculous grace which *contaminates* both *Pickpocket*'s protagonist and the film itself.

Director and writer
Robert Bresson

Producer
Agnès Delahaie

Cinematographer
Léonce-Henri Burel

Production companies
Lux and Conpagnie
Cinématographique de
France

Cast
Martin Lassalle
Marika Green
Jean Pélégri
Dolly Scal
Pierre Leymarie
Kassagi

Other films
★ *Les Anges du péché*
(1943)
★ *Les Dames du bois du Boulogne* (1945)
★ *Un Condamné à mort s'est échappé* (1956)
★ *Au Hasard Balthazar* (1966)
★ *Quatre nuits d'un rêveur* (1983)
★ *L'Argent* (1983)

Martin Lassalle as the obsessive pickpocket. The critic Dilys Powell has noted that silent, tense facial close-ups are one of this film's visual motifs.

La Dolce Vita
Federico Fellini *1960*

It was Federico Fellini's *La Dolce Vita*, released in 1960, which launched the soon-to-be-ubiquitous cult of the paparazzi, a neologism coined by the director himself. (Paparazzo is actually the name of the photographer who figures most prominently in the narrative.) 'Soon-to-be-ubiquitous' is putting it mildly. Watching the film today, more than 40 years later, it is impossible not to be amazed by the prescience with which, treating these paparazzi as only the most visible signifiers of an entire culture in thrall to ephemera, it foreshadows the tinselly textures and trappings of the new millennium.

La Dolce Vita, a picaresque trawl through a squalid, glitzy netherworld of journalists, movie stars, prostitutes and perennial hangers-on, is set in what was, in the late 1950s (rather than dreary, stuffy and still far from swinging London), the coolest city on the planet – Rome. (Woody Allen's Manhattan-set *Celebrity* of 1998 can be regarded as an unacknowledged remake). The Italian film industry was booming. When not housing some monstrous Hollywood superproduction like *Ben Hur* (1959), Cinecittà, the huge local studio complex, was churning out peplums, those cheaply budgeted, so-called epics in which brawny Macistes and Hercules rippled obscene biceps beneath dainty mini-togas. Starlets were the supermodels of the period, Camparis the cappuccinos, and the centre court of this gangrenously hot, steamy and cosmopolitan metropolis was the Via Veneto, a gaudy neon necklace of cafés, restaurants, nightclubs and cinemas.

The paparazzi, crawling over the screen like flies over a carcass, are everywhere. They swarm around Anita Ekberg, the film's female lead, gawking at her cleavage, snapping (in both senses of the word) at her heels. They worm their way into a fashionable restaurant to ambush a playboy prince at supper with his mistress, bribing the head waiter to inform them on what has been consumed. They pounce on a drunken and semi-comatose has-been of an American actor, one of them propping up his lolling head to obtain a still more sensational shot. They callously zoom in on a woman whose husband, unknown to her, has just killed their two children and put a bullet into his own brain. And they haggle over residual rights to this last scoop with Marcello (Mastroianni), Fellini's gossip-columnist protagonist. ('We'll sell it worldwide – I'll give you 50 per cent of the fee!') Almost the only differences between then and now are that their camera equipment has come to seem clunkily antiquated and they ride Vespas instead of motorcycles.

From the very first sequence of this episodically structured fresco, in which a mammoth, helicopter-borne statue of Christ casts its shadow over the city, to the infamous (if by now risibly tame) climactic orgy, from the hysteria surrounding the supposed Marian visitation (uncannily reminiscent of Britain's own more recent bout of Dianolatry) to the scathing dissection of a raffishly hedonistic aristocracy that might have stepped straight off the pages of *Hello!*, *La Dolce Vita* is an extraordinarily ambitious satire. (It is comparable only, in contemporary literature, to Tom Wolfe's 1988 novel *The Bonfire of the Vanities*.) And perhaps its enduring fascination derives from the fact that it now strikes us less as an indictment than as a celebration of the vulgarity it presumably set out to debunk.

Director
Federico Fellini

Writers
Federico Fellini, Ennio Flaiano, Tullio Pinelli and Brunello Rondi

Producers
Giuseppe Amato and Angelo Rizzoli

Cinematographer
Otello Martelli

Cast
Marcello Mastroianni
Yvonne Furneaux
Anouk Aimée
Anita Ekberg
Alain Cuny
Annibale Ninchi
Magali Noël
Lex Barker
Walter Santesso

Other films
★ *8½* (1963)
★ *Fellini's Roma* (1972)
★ *Casanova* (1976)

Academy Awards
Nominated for Best Director, Best Screenplay and Best Art Direction, 1962

Viridiana Luis Buñuel *1961*

Director
Luis Buñuel

In view of Luis Buñuel's currently uncontested status as one of the cinema's giants – in view of the fact, more specifically, that the now ubiquitous qualifier 'Buñuelian' tends to be bandied about by journalists exclusively with reference to his late, glossy French period – it is easy to forget the meanderings of his long, prolific, peripatetic career. Easy to forget, for example, that, following his two Surrealist masterpieces *Un Chien andalou* and *L'Age d'or* (1928 and 1930, both of them conceived in collaboration with Salvador Dali), he spent three decades in the wilderness. Or rather, in the wilderness's cinematic equivalent, Mexico, where he was put out to premature graze on a series of lurid (though by no means negligible) melodramas.

Viridiana, which he filmed at the age of 60, signalled his belated return to Europe, to Spain, to form and to fame. It was at least a return to form and fame as far as his much diminished notoriety was concerned. Here again, after so many years, was the sulphuric, all-but-forgotten Buñuel of old, attacked on the left for his willingness to work in Franco's Spain, on the right for his unrepentant anticlericalism. Here, intact, was the Buñuel who had been responsible for the literally *unwatchable* image (the very first that he ever committed to celluloid and one still unsurpassed in horror) of an eye being sliced in the opening scene of *Un Chien andalou*.

Viridiana also contains an image that was destined to go around the world. Inspired, if Buñuel's own account is to be credited, by a dream in which he raped the Queen of Spain, the film relates the tale of a virginally pure young woman (Silvia Pinal) who, having almost suffered the same fate at the hands, so to speak, of her uncle (Fernando Rey), resolves to turn his house over to the homeless. This being a Buñuel film, the dishevelled tramps, vagrants, wastrels and winos who gleefully abuse her hospitality hold a wild orgy, at the anarchic height of which the director freezes them all in a blasphemous parody of Leonardo's 'Last Supper'.

As a filmmaker, Buñuel was stylistically unostentatious, on occasion even downright amateurish. He had no truck with spectacular set-pieces, ingenious camera movements or the type of modishly protracted sequence-shots that make one think of swimmers holding their breath for as long as they can underwater.

That one unforgettable image, however, resounded like a pistol shot. It announced the return not merely of Buñuel himself but, for the cinema, of a long-buried liberty and licence of expression. After the stagnant 1950s, it felt as if almost anything might be possible again.

There exist several candidates for the first authentically modern film – Alain Resnais's *Hiroshima mon amour* (1959), Jean-Luc Godard's *A Bout de souffle* (1960), Michelangelo Antonioni's *L'avventura* (also 1960) – but all cinephiles who are old enough to remember know, even if they may be incapable of precisely articulating why, that something fundamental changed after *Viridiana*.

Writers	Cast	Other films
Luis Buñuel and	Silvia Pinal	★ *Un Chien andalou* (1928)
Julio Alejandro	Francisco Rabal	★ *L'Age d'or* (1930)
	Fernando Rey	★ *Los Olvidados* (1950)
Producer	José Calvo	★ *El* (1952)
Ricardo Muñoz Suay	Margarita Lazano	★ *Belle de jour* (1967)
	Victoria Zinny	★ *The Discreet Charm of the Bourgeoisie* (1972)
Cinematographer	Teresa Rabal	★ *That Obscure Object of Desire* (1977)
José F. Aguayo		

The anarchic vagrants, whose antics provided
Buñuel with one of cinema's most famous images.

Zacharovannaya Desna
The Enchanted Desna

Julia Solntseva *1970*

Director
Julia Solntseva

'**I**f Dovzhenko had lived, I would never have become a director', claimed Julia Solntseva, the creator of *The Enchanted Desna*. 'All I do I consider as "propaganda, defence and illustration" of Dovzhenko.' The lady protests too much. Solntseva was the widow of Alexander Dovzhenko, a great Russian filmmaker and a matchless celebrant of the Soviet Eden, whose loyal helpmate she had been throughout his life. When he died in 1956, she proceeded to film, one after the other, his handful of unrealized scripts almost as if they had been bequeathed to her, as if she were executing his deathbed request; and when there were no more left to film, she simply downed tools and retired.

It has to be said, in addition, that the films themselves, somewhat more so than Dovzhenko's own, are unabashedly, inflexibly Stalinist in ideology: Solntseva was very much a pillar of the Soviet Establishment. Yet, notwithstanding these drawbacks (which make writing about her especially problematic for both auteurists and feminists), it can be argued that she remains the greatest of all women filmmakers, possibly even a greater artist than her husband (although Solntseva herself, who died in 1989, would indignantly have rejected such a compliment as heretical and near-blasphemous).

If ever a film were a poem, it is *The Enchanted Desna*. A pantheistically phosphorescent hymn to nature as equally to the gleaming tractors and ploughs which were destined to transform it (and a personal favourite, intriguingly, of Jean-Luc Godard), it must be, at just 81 minutes, the briefest of cinematic works ever to have been shot in the 70mm wide-screen process. Adapted by Dovzhenko from his own virtually plotless autobiographical novel, and relating a series of loosely connected episodes from his charmed infancy in the Ukraine, it offers moments of unparalleled visual splendour – most notably, a magical lakeside nocturne – imbued with the preternatural vividness of perception we traditionally ascribe to those aware of their own impending death. Again and again, Solntseva succeeds in investing the most insignificant of the planet's nervous tics – an apple dropping from a tree, for example, or the first beadlet of rain on a window-sill or the gliding of a shadow over grass – with the incomparability and unrepeatability of a miracle.

The visual motifs that we have come to associate with Dovzhenko's cinema – the skies so low-hung we feel the characters will have to hunker down on all fours to crawl beneath them, the cornfields waving goodbye in unison (Dovzhenko himself once said that his was 'a cinema of farewells') – are just as present in *The Enchanted Desna*. But his wife's own personal genius was to have understood that, for a filmmaker possessed of epic ambitions, there exists a direct correlation between the aesthetics of the silent cinema and the aesthetics of the contemporary widescreen spectacle. Certainly, her pyrotechnical panning and tracking shots, aligned to a surreal deployment of Sovcolor, attain a lyrical intensity irresistibly reminiscent of the earliest Soviet masterpieces. And, confronted with the Ukraine's massive forests, rivers, valleys and endlessly vast expanses of fertile soil, traversed by Solntseva's camera as by a combine harvester of images, one is seized by what can only be described as horizontal vertigo – or 'horizontigo'.

Writer
Alexander Dovzhenko

Cinematographer
Alexei Temerin

Music
Gavriil Popov

Production design
Alexander Borisov

Cast
Boris Andreyev
Vladimir Goncharov
Zinaida Kiriyenko
Yevgeni Samojlov

Other films
★ *Shors* (1939)
★ *Liberation* (1940)
★ *Soviet Earth* (1945)
★ *Inspectors Against their Will* (1955)
★ *Poem of the Sea* (1959)
★ *Unforgettable* (1967)
★ *Such High Mountains* (1974)

Flanked by his playmates, little 'Alexander Dovzhenko' listens to tales of Ukrainian folklore.

MAIN: *Roman Polanski's*
Cul-de-sac *(1966).*
FAR LEFT: *Polanski's*
Repulsion *(1965).*
MIDDLE LEFT: *Chris Marker's*
La Jetée *(1962).*
LEFT: *Michelangelo Antonioni's*
L'avventura *(1960).*

Europe: New Waves

Jonathan Rosenbaum

When the term *nouvelle vague* (New Wave) first appeared in the French press in the autumn of 1957, it simply referred to French youth. But by the time the first features of Claude Chabrol, Jean-Luc Godard, Alain Resnais, Jacques Rivette, Eric Rohmer and François Truffaut appeared a few years later, it meant a particular generation of (mainly) young adults: film freaks turned directors. Most of them were eccentric film critics writing for the cultish monthly journal *Cahiers du cinéma*, and where they differed most crucially from their predecessors was in their acquaintance with film history – most of it gathered and dispersed by the equally eccentric film archivist Henri Langlois, co-founder of the Cinémathèque Française. Many of the directors' similarities can be traced back to this interest; and it is no surprise that most New Wave films take place in big cities, for you generally had to live in a metropolis to study film history in any kind of depth.

Although the older critic and theorist André Bazin – who died the day after shooting began on Truffaut's first feature, *The Four Hundred Blows* (*Les Quatre cents coups*, 1959) – is thought of as the father of the French New Wave, Langlois was at the very least the whimsical Wizard of Oz figure for the Young Turks, the guru who mixed and matched much of what they saw and so helped to hatch their strange medleys. Radically international, scornful of subtitles and intertitles, Langlois viewed the Tower of Babel as a utopian edifice that really made it all the way up to heaven through the medium of film, enabling Kenji Mizoguchi and Otto Preminger, or Jean Renoir and Fritz Lang, to converse, at least figuratively and stylistically.

Individuality and innovation lie at the heart of New Wave cinema, but there are certain common characteristics often found in the films: loose, unpredictable plotlines coloured by an existential sense of absurdity, sometimes culminating in the gratuitous deaths of one or more of the leading characters (as in *A Bout de souffle*, *Shoot the Pianist*, *Jules et Jim* and *Les Bonnes femmes*); a preference for open-air settings; fresh, spontaneous filming facilitated by lightweight cameras, coupled with elliptical cutting to create striking juxtapositions; allusions to earlier films to pay homage, mark or break continuity, or as a self-reflexive hint that this is, after all, a movie.

Although short-lived in its purest form, the New Wave nevertheless enjoyed international influence. Yet, while the 1960s was a decade when youth was becoming increasingly politicized, especially in Italy and the United States, most of the French New Wave filmmakers were slower to make it to the barricades than many of their contemporaries; and a few, like Chabrol and Rohmer, tended to stay away altogether, due to either temperament or ideology.

In hindsight, many of the most radical New Wave films of this period, formally as well as politically, came from Communist Eastern Europe, where the very notion of history had been subject to various kinds of Stalinist deep-freeze until radical re-evaluations of the past and present began to create bold new configurations. Alas, these efforts were not sustained, generally leading to either exile or retrenchment. The same could be said for the more radicalized French directors, notably Godard and Rivette, after the anti-Gaullist demonstrations and student occupations of May 1968: while the former spent much of the next decade re-inventing his identity for both film and television, the latter made his most radical film in the early 1970s – the nearly 13-hour-long *Out 1* – only to find it suppressed after state-run French television refused to show it. When in was finally screened in the 1990s, its historical moment had passed.

Popiół i Diament
Ashes and Diamonds

Andrzej Wajda *1958*

Set in a small provincial town in Poland the day after the country's liberation in the spring of 1945, *Ashes and Diamonds*, Andrzej Wajda's third film, may still be the most influential of his career. Yet, curiously, its impact both today and some 40 years ago seems predicated in part on the slightly anachronistic effect produced by superimposing the mid-fifties over the mid-forties – specifically, existentialist angst laid over a gloomy sense of exhaustion at the end of the war.

Above all, the black-leather-jacketed figure of Zbigniew Cybulski as Maciek, an uncertain resistance assassin – clearly derived from the Marlon Brando of *The Wild One* (1954) even more than the Brando of *On the Waterfront* from the same year, or the James Dean of *East of Eden* (*see pages 78–79*) and *Rebel Without a Cause* from the following year – reinvented postwar Poland in hipster terms. And the resulting image of the actor (who died prematurely in a railway accident less than a decade later) was fixed in the popular imagination for good. Indeed, the 19th-century Romanticism that is said to infuse much of Polish literature – not only the 1940s novel of the same title by Jerzy Andrzejewski that *Ashes and Diamonds* is based on, but the poetry of Cyprian Norwid (the source of the title) and the plays of Juliusz Slowacki and Stanislaw Wyspiański – received a kind of updating from Cybulski's definitive performance as Maciek.

Told to assassinate an arriving Communist secretary named Szczuka (Wacław Zastrzezynski), Maciek and another gunman ambush a jeep in the film's opening moments, only to discover that they have shot the wrong men. After Maciek is ordered to make another attempt, he and Szczuka take separate rooms at the same seedy hotel, where an extended, drunken celebration is underway, and most of the remainder of the film is devoted to crosscutting ironically between assassin, victim, and banquet-in-progress over that night and the following morning, during which time both characters end up dying.

Rather like Hamlet, Maciek keeps putting things off, experiencing enough doubts about his mission to make him an existential prevaricator of the first order. He has a brief, touching fling with a barmaid (Ewa Krzyżewska) over the long night, and finally shoots Szczuka in the street only after the party has broken up at dawn. Szczuka, meanwhile, has a son who is in the same anti-communist underground as Maciek, so the degree to which the relationship between killer and victim is Oedipal is emphasized.

A baroque director, Wajda frequently recalls Orson Welles in his use of low angles and deep focus, as well as in his fancy sense of dramatic detail and counterpoint: a Christ-like figure hanging upside down from the rafters of a bombed-out building, an explosion of fireworks occurring at the same moment that Szczuka dies in the arms of Maciek's murderous embrace.

Director
Andrzej Wajda

Writers
Andrzej Wajda and Jerzy Andrzejewski, from the novel by the latter

Cinematographer
Jerzy Wójcik

Editor
Halina Nawrocka

Production designer
Roman Mann

Production companies
Film Polski, Film Agency and ZAF Kadr

Cast
Zbigniew Cybulski
Waclaw Zastrzezynski
Ewa Krzyżewska
Adam Pawlikowski
Bogumil Kobiela

Other films
★ *A Generation* (1954)
★ *Kanal* (1956)
★ *L'Amour à vingt ans* (1962)
★ *Everything for Sale* (1968)
★ *Promised Land* (1974)
★ *Man of Marble* (1976)
★ *Man of Iron* (1981)
★ *Danton* (1982)
★ *Pan Tadeusz* (1999)

The last moments of the hero, Maciek (Zbigniew Cybulski), after he has been shot and is staggering towards his death.

Chronique d'un été
Chronicle of a Summer

Jean Rouch and Edgar Morin *1961*

Directors and writers
Jean Rouch and
Edgar Morin

Producers
Anatole Dauman and
Philippe Lifchitz

Cinematographers
Jean Rouch, Roger Morillière
and Jean-Jacques Tarbès

Editors
Jean Ravel, Néna Barabier
and Françoise Colin

Production company
Argos

Other films: Rouch
★ *Les Maîtres fous* (1955)
★ *La Pyramide humaine*
  (1959)
★ *Jaguar* (1967)
★ *Petit à petit* (1970)

A collaboration between the French ethnographer-filmmaker Jean Rouch and the sociologist Edgar Morin (author of *The Stars*, 1960) resulted in this remarkable documentary investigation into what Parisians – regarded as a 'strange tribe' – were thinking and feeling during the summer of 1960. This was when the war in Algeria (1954–62, fought for independence from French colonial rule) was still a live issue, although many other topics are discussed, private as well as public. At first, everyone is simply asked, 'Are you happy?' As a whole, the film brilliantly catches the shifting emotional tenor of a few lives over a brief, specific period.

The filmmakers treat their interviewees with a great deal of respect and sensitivity. Among them are Marilou, an Italian émigré working as a secretary on the magazine *Cahiers du cinéma*; a French student called Jean-Pierre; Angelo, a factory worker; an African student named Landry; Henri and Maddie, a painter and his wife; and a pollster named Marceline who is assisting with some of the interviews.

Not only do we see these individuals in diverse groupings and circumstances, even on holiday in St Tropez; we also see many of them becoming friends over the course of the film. Finally, Rouch and Morin screen a rough cut for the participants and film their contrasting responses, and then shoot their own auto-critique as they stroll together through the Musée de l'homme.

The biggest surprise about this seminal work is that, even though it is made by two eminent social scientists, its value ultimately has relatively little to do with either anthropology or sociology. Rouch as a filmmaker had already discovered in his innovative African documentaries that you best catch people 'being themselves' if you film them 'playing themselves', and this film is actually a kind of home-movie about life being self-consciously lived. We soon learn that Marceline – who years later would become the personal and professional partner of Joris Ivens, the great Dutch documentarist – actually selected Jean-Pierre as an interview subject because he is a former boyfriend, and her feelings about their failed relationship become part of the ongoing discussion. The first time Marilou speaks to Morin, she is lonely and on the verge of tears; the second time she is much happier and we briefly glimpse her with her boyfriend when they go out for a walk (Jacques Rivette, as it happens, with whom she would later write scripts). Rouch asks Landry if he understands the meaning of the tattoo on Marceline's arm, and Marceline goes on to explain that she is a Jewish concentration-camp survivor. Even more than his ethnographic works about Africans, *Chronicle* makes it clear in its graceful spontaneity why Rouch was a key influence on the French New Wave, so it is no surprise to discover in the closing credits that Raoul Coutard – the key cinematographer of that movement, who shot most of the first features of Godard, Truffaut and Demy – worked on this film as well.

Two carefree interviewees in the summer of 1960.

Tirez sur le pianiste
Shoot the Pianist

François Truffaut *1960*

Director
François Truffaut

Considering how romantic it is, how sad and funny and charming, it is a sobering fact that François Truffaut's second feature – and the first that qualifies as a quintessential New Wave expression – was a disaster at the box office. Indeed, if this eccentric adaptation of David Goodis's 1956 crime novel *Down There* illustrated any general commercial principle, this may have been that one subverts overall genre expectations at one's peril. For *Tirez sur le pianiste* is a *film noir* that literally turns white (through such images as piano keys or a snowy hillside) when the plot is at its darkest, and one that sometimes interrupts the viewer's laughter with a disquieting catch in the throat.

The opening sequence already sends out bewildering crossed signals. A man fleeing in panic through dark city streets at night collides with a streetlamp, then finds himself talking quite calmly with a sympathetic stranger – a character who exits the movie immediately thereafter – about the latter's love for his wife. Moreover, while the fluid and flexible black-and-white cinematography (by Raoul Coutard) is in the anamorphic process Dyaliscope, the ambience is cramped and cosy in the best low-budget tradition. It turns out that the man, named Chico Saroyan (Albert Rémy), is looking for his long-lost brother Edouard (Charles Aznavour), a former concert pianist now playing folksy ragtime in a dive under an alias, Charlie Kohler – although it takes us a while to discover why, in an extended flashback. (Aznavour, a crooner who became famous after this film was made, does not sing a note, although as Edouard he periodically delivers a kind of stream-of-consciousness voiceover.)

The film recounts at least two tragic love stories that result in Edouard's retreat, and the camera participates in the action almost as fully as the characters. It circles the bedroom of a barmaid (Marie Dubois) while she and Edouard make love in superimposition, follows a mysterious young woman with a violin case out of a rehearsal room while his piano thunders offscreen, and later carries us in stages all the way from city to country and into snowy weather from the front seat of a car.

A study of a shy man who periodically hides behind his music, this film was a shift for Truffaut after his autobiographical *The Four Hundred Blows* (*Les Quatre cents coups*, 1959), but was arguably just as personal. Although the earlier film's treatment of children is often said to bear the influence of Jean Vigo's *Zéro de conduite* (1933), *Tirez sur le pianiste* has a comic sequence with a gangster in a car boasting about his possessions to a kidnapped boy – another of Edouard's brothers – that seems inspired directly by *Zéro*'s opening sequence on a train. And when the hood swears his mother will drop dead if he isn't telling the truth, Truffaut cuts abruptly to a silent-movie image of the mother doing precisely that – a characteristic signal that this picture might do anything if it takes the director's fancy. We experience this less as indulgence than as Truffaut generously sharing his delight in making movies.

Writers
Marcel Moussy and
François Truffaut

Producer
Pierre Braunberger

Cinematographer
Raoul Coutard

Production company
Films de Pléiade

Cast
Albert Rémy
Charles Aznavour
Marie Dubois
Nicole Berger
Claude Mansard
Daniel Boulanger

Other films
★ *Les Quatre cents coups* (1959)
★ *Jules et Jim* (1961)
★ *L'Enfant sauvage* (1969)
★ *La Chambre verte* (1978)
★ *Vivement dimanche!* (1983)

Charles Aznavour, before his career as a singer took off, playing the former concert pianist who has fallen on hard times.

Les Bonnes femmes

Claude Chabrol *1960*

Director
Claude Chabrol

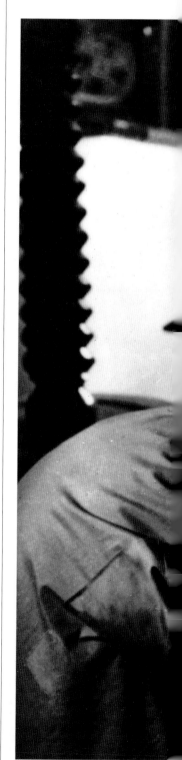

There is something approaching a consensus, shared by the filmmaker himself, that the best of Claude Chabrol's early films is *Les Bonnes femmes*, his fourth feature. Yet the film was a box-office flop when it first appeared, widely attacked in France and elsewhere for being ugly, misanthropic and cynical. And it might be fair to say that this response was not so much superseded as reinterpreted in the years that followed. For *Les Bonnes femmes* is probably Chabrol's most pessimistic work, harping relentlessly on vulgarity, boorishness and cruelty.

Focusing on four young woman who work from nine to seven at an electrical appliance shop in Paris, the film offers a definitive look at what they want from life and how poorly they fare in their aspirations – culminating in a remarkable, ambiguous final sequence set in a dancehall, leaving everything up to the audience's troubled imagination, about another young woman who isn't identified at all dancing with an equally unidentified stranger.

Jane (Bernadette Lafont), the shopgirl who visibly expects the least from life, goes out carousing with a couple of men in an early sequence and is virtually raped. Rita (Lucille Saint-Simon) looks forward to marrying her doltish fiancé who mercilessly coaches her to speak about Michelangelo when she meets his parents for lunch. Ginette (Stéphane Audran) sneaks off nightly to sing sentimental songs in a black wig at a music hall, until her colleagues turn up one night and recognize her, shattering her private identity. And Jacqueline (Clotilde Joano), the most self-contained and idealistic of them all, secretly in love with a stranger named André (Mario David) who silently follows her, finally meets him and goes off with him to the country on his motorbike, where he promptly strangles her to death.

If all that interested Chabrol and his screenwriter Paul Gégauff was harrowing the viewer with grimness about the human condition, then this movie might have been the horror-show its detractors claimed. Admittedly, Jacqueline's fate is only the last of a string of deflating narrative stripteases that echo a literal striptease seen in a nightclub early in the film. (Another grisly storyline reveals that the personal fetish of an older woman in the shop is a handkerchief soaked with the blood of a guillotined sex murderer, treasured since her girlhood.) Yet it is significant that Jacqueline meets André only after he saves her from the 'prank' of being pushed underwater repeatedly at an indoor swimming pool by the same two men who picked up Jane at the beginning – a sequence showing that the difference between joking and killing, or between banal horror and ultimate horror, is sometimes only one of degree.

It is worth adding that the creepy-lyrical sequence of Jacqueline's murder in the woods was in effect reprised as the grand climax of Rainer Werner Fassbinder's 13-part miniseries *Berlin Alexanderplatz* (1980) – not as a facile piece of Hitchcockian irony but as a piece of tragic fatalism, more relevant to the detached viewpoint of a Fritz Lang.

Writers
Claude Chabrol and
Paul Gégauff

Producers
Robert Hakim and
Raymond Hakim

Cinematographer
Henri Decaë

Production companies
Hakim Panitalia
and Paris Film

Cast
Bernadette Lafont
Lucille Saint-Simon
Stéphane Audran
Clotilde Joano
Mario David

Other films
★ *Le Beau serge* (1959)
★ *Ophélia* (1962)
★ *Le Scandale* (1966)
★ *Les Biches* (1968)
★ *Le Boucher* (1969)
★ *Nada* (1974)

Stéphane Audran (left) and Bernadette Lafont
contemplating life's disappointments.

L'Année dernière à Marienbad
Last Year in Marienbad

Alain Resnais *1961*

Director
Alain Resnais

Director Alain Resnais and screenwriter Alain Robbe-Grillet's radical experiment in film form remains the most controversial feature of the French New Wave, a provocation that has probably started as many arguments as all the films of Godard and Rivette combined. A highly seductive (albeit frightening) parable about seduction, couched in the atmosphere of a hypnotic fairytale – set in and around a baroque château-cum-hotel, where the nameless hero (played rather awkwardly by Giorgio Albertazzi) tries to persuade the nameless heroine (the wonderful Delphine Seyrig) that they met there the previous year and vowed to go away together – it was a surprising commercial success when it came out.

This success was due in part to the fact that nothing like it had been seen before, but also because the sumptuous visuals and startling sound editing held the attention in spite of manifold uncertainties about the storyline. As Penelope Houston wrote tellingly of the ending, 'The film's last shot is of the great chateau; and, with its few lighted windows, it no longer looks like a prison but like a place of refuge.' A primal master-piece, it left everything up for grabs, including critical interpretation.

Last Year in Marienbad was just Resnais' second feature film – made on the heels of his similarly groundbreaking *Hiroshima, mon amour* (1959), written by Marguerite Duras – and his only feature to date in 'Scope, shot by Sacha Vierny in otherworldly black-and-white. It oscillates ambiguously between past, present and various conditional tenses, mixing memory and fantasy, fear and desire. And although Resnais had become a master of editing and camera movement while making innovative short documentaries during the 1950s, *Marienbad* put a new spin on those experiments by suggesting a precise study of the labyrinthine journeys and fluctuating moods of an erotically crazed, fantasy-ridden mind.

In fact, the overall tone is a poker-faced parody of Hollywood lushness and melodrama: one entire scene from Vidor's *Gilda* (1946) – a dialogue in a bedroom – is restaged shot by shot; a life-size blow-up figure of Alfred Hitchcock is glimpsed in a corridor; Seyrig's poses in Chanel dresses are as flamboyant as Josef von Sternberg's shots of Marlene Dietrich; and a recurring game using matches played by the hero and his slippery romantic rival (Sacha Pitoeff) – which thanks to the movie became a favourite party pastime in the early 1960s – is as mordantly ritualistic as a Western showdown. Yet the film's dream-like cadences, frozen tableaux and distilled Surrealist poetry are too eerie and even too terrifying to shake off simply as camp. Even Francis Seyrig's dirge-like score, performed on the organ, is too solemn and obsessional to garner any obvious laughs. Far funnier were the paranoid and pretentious Rorschach-test interpretations – ranging from charges of communist propaganda to intricate Freudian readings – which eventually led to a backlash of attacks once it became clear that the film was blissfully and triumphantly critic-proof. Today it remains as beautiful and scary as ever.

Writers
Alain Resnais and Alain
Robbe-Grillet

Producers
Pierre Courau and
Raymond Froment

Cinematographer
Sacha Vierny

Music
Francis Seyrig

Cast
Giorgio Albertazzi
Delphine Seyrig
Sacha Pitoeff
Françoise Bertin
Pierre Barbaud
Luce Garcia-Ville

Other films
★ *Hiroshima, mon amour* (1959)
★ *Muriel* (1963)
★ *Je t'aime, je t'aime* (1968)
★ *L'Amour à mort* (1984)

'As flamboyant as Josef von Sternberg's shots of Marlene Dietrich': Delphine Seyrig with Georgio Albertazzi.

L'Eclisse
The Eclipse

Michelangelo Antonioni *1962*

The concluding part of Michelangelo Antonioni's loose trilogy about the contemporary world at mid-century – preceded by *L'avventura* (1960) and *La notte* (1961) – this 1962 feature is in many ways his greatest. He made it when his popularity was close to its height, peaking four years later with *Blow Up*. And yet *The Eclipse* has the least plot in the ordinary sense of any of his films, and part of the marvel is how much Antonioni manages to do with so little, and how much resonance he brings to this haunting work.

Vittoria (Monica Vitti), a translator living in Rome – still recovering from an unhappy love affair that is ending, after a depressing all-night vigil, in the opening sequence – briefly links up with an energetic stock-broker, Piero (Alain Delon), whom she encounters at the stock exchange, where she has gone to meet her mother, during a frenzy of buying and selling. Many of her desultory and aimless activities have been charted before they meet, and the same sort of narrative progression might be said to continue afterwards, albeit in a more stylized, poetic manner.

It is a slow and tentative courtship. Vittoria and Piero go to her mother's flat, and Piero tries to kiss her in her old bedroom. Some time later, after many further casual encounters and some exchanged flirtations, passion flares in Piero's apartment one afternoon, and they very nearly have sex. By now their relationship seems to have developed distinct romantic possibilities, and they agree to meet again at their favourite rendezvous spot – a building site – that evening, at 8 o'clock. The camera eagerly arrives at the designated spot ahead of them, but neither turns up as the late afternoon gradually drifts into night. Throughout the film's stunning final montage sequence – perhaps the most powerful thing Antonioni has ever done – we see and hear all sorts of prosaic, everyday events and comments, but neither of the leads. Astonishingly, the film ends with the camera zooming into the glare of a solitary streetlamp.

Alternately an essay and a prose poem about the modern world in which the 'love story' actually occurs as one of many interweaving motifs, *The Eclipse* is remarkable both for its visual/atmospheric richness and its polyphonic/polyrhythmic *mise en scène*. Antonioni's choreographic handling of crowds and individual details at the Roman stock exchange, juggling foreground and background activities with a dexterity recalling the early work of Orson Welles, is never less than amazing. And even though Welles was one of Antonioni's harshest detractors – largely, it seems, because of their diametrically opposed attitudes towards actors – it could be argued that Vitti and Delon both actually give their finest as well as their most animated performances in this film. In fact, it is in part thanks to their charisma that *The Eclipse* gets by with so little in the way of a story; the absence of both actors in the final sequence would be far less disturbing if they were not so memorable.

Writers
Michelangelo Antonioni,
Elio Burtolini, Tonino Guerra,
Ottiero Ottiori

Producers
Robert Hakim and
Raymond Hakim

Cinematographer
Gianni di Venanzo

Production companies
Cineriz, Interopa Film and
Paris Film

Cast
Monica Vitti
Alain Delon
Francisco Rabal
Lilly Brignone
Louis Seigner

Other films
★ *L'avventura* (1960)
★ *La notte* (1961)
★ *Blow Up* (1966)
★ *Professione: reporter* (1975)

Monica Vitti and Alain Delon, giving the most charismatic performances of their careers.

Prima della Rivoluzione
Before the Revolution

Bernardo Bertolucci *1964*

Director
Bernardo Bertolucci

It is not surprising that Bernardo Bertolucci's second feature film – made when he was only 22 and released a year later in 1964 – has never been as fashionable as *The Conformist* (*Il conformista*, 1969) or as popular as *Last Tango in Paris* (1972). But even though it is sometimes ragged and choppy as storytelling, *Before the Revolution* is still possibly the most impressive thing he has done to date.

In 1962, when he was asked to adapt a story by Pier Paolo Pasolini into a screenplay and then to direct it (*The Grim Reaper*, or *La commare secca*), thereby paying tribute to his main Italian mentor, he also published his first collection of poetry, *In Search of Mystery*. And *Before the Revolution*, which pays homage to his primary French inspiration, Jean-Luc Godard, is in some ways closer to a poetry collection than it is to a novel – despite the fact that the characters are named after those in Stendhal's *The Charterhouse of Parma* (1839), Bertolucci's favourite novel at the time, and Parma is the central setting.

Indeed, the movie's eclectic set-pieces are as flamboyant and almost as fleeting and disconnected (in their Godardian jump cuts) as a set of precocious lyrical poems. There probably isn't another Bertolucci film, at least until the recent *Besieged* (*L'assedio*, 1998), that is constructed so closely around individual pieces of music, pop, jazz and classical, culminating in a climactic première of a Verdi opera, *Macbeth*, heard off-camera but never seen. And like John Cassavetes's *Shadows* (1960) – evoked directly in one love scene between the callow young hero Fabrizio (Francesco Barilli) and his slightly older and neurotic aunt Gina (Adriana Asti), played out to the accompaniment of a tenor saxophone solo – *Before the Revolution* has all the vibrant emotional intensity of youth giving its all. Moreover, the bisexuality that features more directly in many subsequent Bertolucci films is already present here in embryo form, in Fabrizio's attachment to his friend Agostino (played by Bertolucci regular Allen Midgette, an American actor) who commits suicide just before Fabrizio begins his affair with Gina.

Like almost all of Bertolucci's films, this story struggles to reconcile Marx and Freud, played out in this case through Fabrizio's battle to reconcile his 'nostalgia for the present' with his Marxism, and his idealism with his class ('My bourgeois future is in my bourgeois past', he declares sorrowfully to a favourite teacher during a workers' rally). But this time the essential matter is triumphantly and movingly the stuff of everyday life: Gina and Fabrizio shopping one afternoon to the strains of a heartbreaking Italian pop tune, or visiting a member of the landed gentry about to lose his property (whose lament becomes an offscreen oratorio). It is even seen in such ephemera as Agostino repeatedly crashing his bike while clowning for Fabrizio, performed to the contrasting lilt of a sad circus tune, or an altar boy trying to hold back an unwanted giggle during Fabrizio's eventual marriage to a conventional bourgeois debutante.

194

Writers
Bernardo Bertolucci and
Gianni Amico

Cinematographer
Aldo Scavarda

Production company
Cineriz Iride Cinematografica

Editor
Roberto Perpignani

Cast
Francesco Barilli
Adriana Asti
Allen Midgette
Morando Morandini
Domenico Alpi
Giuseppe Maghenzani

Other films
★ *The Conformist* (1969)
★ *Last Tango in Paris* (1972)
★ *La luna* (1979)
★ *The Last Emperor* (1987)
★ *Little Buddha* (1993)
★ *Stealing Beauty* (1996)
★ *Besieged* (1998)

Francesco Barilli (left) and Morando Morandini in one of the film's set-pieces.

Alphaville Jean-Luc Godard *1965*

By general agreement, *A Bout de souffle* (*Breathless*, 1959), Godard's first feature, is felt to be his most important, in part because of its highly charismatic leads (Jean-Paul Belmondo and Jean Seberg) and its famous jump cuts. Not counting the many American independent spin-offs of *Bande à part* (*Band of Outsiders*, 1964), it is the only Godard movie to date to have prompted a Hollywood remake. Why, then, opt for his brilliant, creepy and beautiful ninth film?

For one thing, *Alphaville* (1965) more successfully shows the strength of Godard's cinema as film criticism, as an extension of his writing. As he acknowledged decades later in his magnum opus on video, *Histoire(s) du cinéma* (1998), the specific critique offered in the film – through the quirky adventures of special agent Lemmy Caution (Eddie Constantine), supposedly arriving via his Ford Galaxy at the remote city/planet of *Alphaville*, run by a computer and ravishingly filmed in high-contrast black-and-white – is of the silent German cinema and its many derivatives. Thus the revolving doors and elevator of the hotel in *The Last Laugh* (1924), diverse images and lighting patterns from *Destiny* (1921) and *Faust* (1926), some of the poetics of *Orphée* (1950), and the metaphysics of both *Metropolis* (1927, *see pages 44–45*) and *Kiss Me, Deadly* (1955), are all marshalled together – not simply as 'tributes' but more pointedly as ways of testing various facets of present-day Paris against the ideas suggested by these precedents. Even the beautiful, redemptive fairytale princess (Anna Karina) who Lemmy rescues from the murderous computer is linked to these cold, haunted images.

This is the only film in my selection qualifying as science fiction – offering a low-budget, low-tech alternative to Stanley Kubrick's *2001: A Space Odyssey* (1968), the other key science-fiction film of the decade – and one that would ultimately prove even more influential as it ushered in an era of futuristic thrillers using contemporary locations. (George Lucas's 1971 *THX 1138* was one of the first.) Godard was the pioneer to prove plastically, without resort to sets or special effects, that the dark future had already arrived and was fully installed in the modern city. And so the complex irony of *Alphaville*, initially misread in some quarters as camp, was in fact one of Godard's first in-depth reflections on the organization of modern urban life and the pathos of the consumer culture.

Kubrick's notion of science fiction also had something Germanic about its tone and sources, but it was Godard's example that ultimately paved the way for everything from modernist 1960s thrillers like *Point Blank* (1967) to *fin-de-siècle* notions of Wagnerian spectacle such as Tim Burton's *Batman* (1989). This was mainly because of Godard's taste for pop art iconography, which often pitted primitive man against technology: an early discarded title of *Alphaville*, *Tarzan vs. IBM*, could have served for almost any early John Boorman picture, including *Point Blank* or *Zardoz* (1974). What this meant in practical terms was that you didn't have to command a huge budget in order to make a SF epic; sometimes mere action and attitude sufficed.

Director
Jean-Luc Godard

Writers
Jean-Luc Godard, from the novel by Paul Elnard

Producer
André Michelin

Cinematographer
Raoul Coutard

Editor
Angès Guillemot

Music
Paul Misraki

Production companies
Athos Films, Chaumiane and Filmstudio

Cast
Eddie Constantine
Anna Karina
Akim Tamiroff
Michel Delahaye
Howard Vernon
Laszlo Szabo

Other films
★ *A Bout de souffle* (1960)
★ *Les Carabiniers* (1963)
★ *Le Mépris* (1963)
★ *Pierrot le fou* (1963)
★ *Bande à part* (1964)
★ *Weekend* (1967)
★ *Tout va bien* (1972)
★ *Sauve qui peut* (1980)
★ *Passion* (1982)
★ *Histoire(s) du cinéma* (1998)

Les Demoiselles de Rochefort
The Young Girls of Rochefort

Jacques Demy *1967*

Director and writer
Jacques Demy

In selecting Jacques Demy's greatest feature, one could make strong arguments for *Lola* (1960), *The Umbrellas of Cherbourg* (*Les Parapluies de Cherbourg*, 1964), or the lesser-known *Une Chambre en ville* (1982). But Demy's most ambitious effort is this 1967 big-budget musical – a tale of various dreamers searching for and generally missing their ideal mates, who are usually located only a few streets away. It is the only film in which Catherine Deneuve and her older sister, the late Françoise Dorléac, both star, playing twins no less – and forming the hub of a musical-comedy plot that is all but Shakespearean in its complexities.

Others in the cast include a wonderful mix of American dancers (Gene Kelly, George Chakiris, Grover Dale) and inspiring French actors (including Danièle Darrieux as the twins' mother, Michel Piccoli as her former lover, and Demy standby Jacques Perrin as a sailor-artist). It is also the only Demy film shot in separate French and English versions – although the latter is much harder to come by today and, ironically, has never received much exposure in English-speaking countries. (With few exceptions, the actors are dubbed by others in both versions when they sing.)

As in Jacques Tati's *Playtime* (1967) – another highly populated, comic, festive, multilingual French epic being shot at the same time – near-misses are as important to this movie's intricate plot choreography as eventual get-togethers. The score is arguably Michel Legrand's finest to date, with various jazz elements, lyrics in Alexandrines by Demy, and intricately structured reprises that match the poetic, crisscrossing plot. Demy's grand, colourful and unorthodox approach to the material pays tribute to the American musical, yet adds all the essential accoutrements of French poetic realism: dreams and reality coexist more strangely and stubbornly than in most other musicals, so that dancers on the street are sometimes glimpsed only peripherally. While the film was shot on location in Rochefort, with not a set in sight, a large portion of the city was brightly repainted for the occasion. And the gigantic town square – where a commercial fair selling motorbikes comes to town and the characters meet or miss one another over a single crowded weekend – could have been built expressly for the movie's purposes.

Though Norman Maen's choreography has been criticized for being lacklustre next to its more stream-lined Hollywood equivalents, it could be argued that Demy's mode of musical-comedy bliss is more French and therefore more Cartesian – that is, structured around the imagination rather than feats of physical expertise or tech-nological perfection – than the American classics which inspire him. By the same token, we may remember all the film's tragic near-misses a bit longer than the symmetrical and over-determined happy endings that are provided by all the subsequent meetings and reconciliations, because the latter are more fleeting; and the last of these even takes place off-screen.

Producers
Mag Bodard and
Gilbert de Goldschmidt

Cinematographer
Ghislain Cloquet

Production companies
Madeleine Films and
Parc Film

Editor
Jean Hamon

Cast
Catherine Deneuve
Françoise Dorléac
Gene Kelly
Danièle Darrieux
George Chakiris
Grover Dale

Other films
★ *Lola* (1960)
★ *La Baie des anges* (1962)
★ *The Umbrellas of Cherbourg* (1964)
★ *Model Shop* (1968)
★ *Une Chambre en ville* (1982)

Gene Kelly (centre) adds US know-how to this unusual European musical.

Sedmikrásky
Daisies

Vera Chytilová *1966*

Director
Vera Chytilová

My favourite Czech film, one of the most exhilarating stylistic and psychedelic explosions of the 1960s, is Vera Chytilová's highly aggressive feminist farce *Daisies,* which erupts in all directions. At any given moment, shots can switch from luscious colour to black-and-white to sepia to a rainbow succession of colour filters, shatter into shards like broken glass, rattle through rapid-fire montages like machine-gun volleys, and leap freely between time frames and locations. While many American and Western European filmmakers during this period prided themselves on their subversiveness, it is quite possible that the most radical film of the decade, ideologically as well as formally, came from the East – from the liberating ferment building towards the short-lived political reforms of 1968's Prague Spring.

Featuring two giggling, nihilistic 17-year-olds, both named Marie – a brunette (Ivana Karbanova) and a redhead (Jitká Cerhova) – *Daisies* does not have a narrative or even characters in the ordinary sense: just a good deal of provocation that typically garners more laughter from the women in the audience than the men. (As a gender statement, it is many years in advance of the French New Wave and only *Celine and Julie Go Boating, see pages 208–209*, would learn from its example.) Chytilová, working collaboratively with cinematographer Jaroslav Kučera (her husband) and co-writer and art director Ester Krumbachová, underlines her feminist impulse by having her heroines indulge in several anti-phallic gags, such as slicing up pickled cucumbers and bananas. (Food and/or drink appear in almost every scene.)

The film mainly intercuts between segments showing the girls in bikinis near a swimming pool, in their bedroom, in restaurants (usually wolfing down food with dirty old men in exchange for promised sexual favours that are never delivered – with the men in each case summarily and hurriedly sent home on trains), and in the country. The escalating sense of outrage culminates in a protracted free-for-all of the girls set loose in an enormous banquet hall containing the fanciest food imaginable. Constructed musically, the sequence develops from tentative samplings of dishes to sinking hands into salads and sauces to wielding chickens, guzzling whisky, pigging out on pastries and then slinging them at one another like Laurel and Hardy – the girls finally dancing on the table, smashing plates and glasses, and swinging gaily from a chandelier. (Some of this is suggestively played out to the Austrian national anthem.) Even more transgressive is a speculative epilogue with the girls dressed in costumes made of newspaper tied with string returning to the scene of the crime and pretending to clean up all the carnage: scraping food off the floor and heaping it back onto trays, and partially reassembling plates like jigsaw puzzles. Then the film ends, over newsreel shots of aerial bombardment, with a stinging title to suggest its moral: 'This film is dedicated to all those who are horrified only by the sight of stomped-on lettuce.'

Writers
Vera Chytilová and
Ester Krumbáchová

Producers
Bohumil Smida and
Ladislav Fikar

Cinematographer
Jaroslav Kucera

Production company
Filmove Studio Barrandov

Cast
Ivana Karbanova
Jitká Cerhova
Julius Albert
Marie Cesková
Jan Klusák

Other films
★ *Green Street* (1960)
★ *A Bagful of Fleas* (1962)
★ *Pearls of the Deep* (1965)
★ *Prefab Story* (1979)
★ *Prague* (1985)
★ *The Fuckoffguysgoodbye* (1993)
★ *Flights and Falls* (2000)

Jitká Cerhova (left) and Ivana Karbarova looking for mischief in Daisies.

Teorema
Theorem

Pier Paolo Pasolini *1968*

Director and writer
Pier Paolo Pasolini

Apart from his scandalous *Salò, or the 120 Days of Sodom*, 1975 – another film with spiritually-induced levitation – this shocking 1968 feature, Pier Paolo Pasolini's last film with a contemporary setting, may be his most controversial work, displaying the kind of audacity and excesses that send some audiences into gales of derisive, self-protective laughter. (For a contemporary near-equivalent, think of Bruno Dumont's 1999 film *L'Humanité*, 1999.)

The 'theorem' of the title is a mythological figure whose arrival is heralded by Pasolini's favourite fetish-actor, Ninetto Davoli, bringing a telegram to the home of a Milanese industrialist (Massimo Girotti). An attractive young man in tight-fitting trousers (Terence Stamp) then pays an extended visit, proceeding with solicitous devotion to seduce every member of the household – father, mother (Silvana Mangano), teenage daughter (Anne Wiazemsky), somewhat older son (Andrès José Crux), and maid (Laura Betti) – to the recurring strains of Mozart's Requiem Mass and a modernist score by Ennio Morricone.

Then the stranger leaves as mysteriously as he came, and everyone in the household undergoes cataclysmic and traumatic changes. The provincial maid, whom he saved from suicide, returns to her village, meditates and eventually levitates. The daughter goes into a catatonic trance, the mother begins to pick up young men on the street, and the son retreats to his room and paints in a wild,  chaotic fashion that includes urinating on one of his canvases. The father not only gives away his factory to its workers but takes off all his clothes in the middle of Milan's Central Station and is later seen trekking across a desert, howling like a wounded animal. Pasolini may have been as much in conflict with his own divided nature as any of his characters.

Almost everyone rejected *Teorema* in 1968, and it has not necessarily grown any more acceptable in the intervening years – even if Pasolini's status as one of the key Italian poets of the 20th century remains intact. If anything, what Stuart Hood (who translated Pasolini's novel) suggests may be 'Pauline misogyny that informs Pasolini's attitude towards his women characters' and what film theorist Richard Dyer describes as 'the association of gay sex with humiliation' make *Teorema* even more politically unacceptable today than it was over three decades ago.

While he was making this film, Pasolini wrote a parallel novel of the same title, part of it in verse; neither work is strictly speaking an adaptation of the other but a recasting of the same elements, and the stark, utterly sincere poetry of both is like a triple-distilled version of Pasolini's personal view of the world – a view in which Marxism (as opposed to communism), Christianity (as opposed to the Catholic church), and homosexuality are forced into mutual and scandalous confrontations. The style is eclectic but never dilettantish. To emphasize the importance of Stamp's arrival – seen in Old rather than New Testament terms, with a citation from the book of Exodus – the film begins silently and in black-and-white, moving to sound when Davoli appears, then to colour with the entrance of Stamp.

Producers
Franco Rossellini and
Manolo Bolognini

Cinematographer
Giuseppe Ruzzolini

Production company
Aetos Films

Editor
Nino Baragli

Cast
Ninetto Davoli
Massimo Girotti
Terence Stamp
Silvana Mangano
Anne Wiazemsky
Andrès José Crux

Other films
★ *Accattone* (1961)
★ *The Gospel According to Matthew* (1964)
★ *Oedipus Rex* (1967)
★ *Pigsty* (1969)
★ *Medea* (1970)
★ *Arabian Nights* (1974)
★ *Salò, or the 120 Days of Sodom* (1975)

The maid, played by Laura Betti, is buried.

W.R. Misterije Organizma
WR – Mysteries of the Organism

Dušan Makavejev *1971*

It is surprising how much radical cinema in the late sixties and early seventies was concentrated in Eastern European Communist countries. The English, French and American cinemas may have prided themselves on their countercultural fervour, but the Czech *Daisies* went further in matters of gender and non-narrative experiment (*see pages 200–201*), while the Hungarian *Red Psalm* (1971, *see pages 206–207*) was singular in marrying radical form to radical politics. No less revolutionary was *WR – Mysteries of the Organism*, made by Serbian filmmaker Dušan Makavejev.

Makavejev made the film in English and Serbo-Croat, mixing 16-mm footage shot in the United States with 35-mm material shot in Yugoslavia. *WR* explores the interface between sex and politics while deconstructing the very form of the feature film. The director succeeded so well in this endeavour that he was forced into semi-permanent exile while the Yugoslav censors banned the movie for the next 15 years.

What captured Makavejev's attention was not so much the politics of sexuality as the sexuality of politics – the marriage of Marx and Freud represented by Wilhelm Reich, the Austrian psychoanalyst who began as both a Freudian and a Marxist, proposed the importance of regular orgasms for mental health, and ended as a martyr to both sides of the Cold War. Beginning as a documentary about Reich's sexual theories, the film veers off into such varied yet related topics as the transvestite Jackie Curtis; the hippie poet Tuli Kupferberg dressed as an armed US marine and singing The Fugs' contemporary protest hit 'Kill for Peace'; several archival black-and-white film representations of Joseph Stalin that highlight his role as an erotic and phallic figure; the editor-in-chief of the American counterculture tabloid *Screw* having a plaster cast made of his erect penis by a woman sculptor; and an extended story about a Yugoslav beautician (Milena Dravić) preaching communist free-love while her randy flatmate (Jagoda Kaloper) continuously has sex. The beautician eventually takes up with a champion Russian ice skater (Ivaca Vidović) who, after a bit of dalliance, slices off her head with one of his skate blades – an allegorical/political act if ever there was one. But her severed head continues to speak and dream.

WR represents the apotheosis of radical juxtaposition through editing that can be traced back to Eisenstein – a global trend predicated on cutting between seemingly autonomous blocks of fictional and non-fictional material that was revived during this period in such films as Godard's English *1+1/Sympathy for the Devil* (1969), Edgardo Cozarinsky's Argentinean *Dot Dot Dot* (1971), and Mark Rappaport's American *Casual Relations* (1973). As the critic Raymond Durgnat recently put it in a definitive monograph about *WR* (BFI Modern Classics, 1999), 'The film alternates between the Yugoslavian and the American scene, pursuing each in its own terms, as befitting "opposite" societies. The USA has more freedom than Socialism, Yugoslavia has more Socialism than freedom ... [and] the Socialist tragedy ... is closest to the film's heart.'

Director, writer and producer
Dušan Makavejev

Cinematographers
Aleksander Petkovic
and Pega Petkovic

Music
Bojana Marijan

Editor
Ivanka Vukasovic

Production design
Dragoljub Lukov

Cast
Milena Dravić
Jagoda Koloper
Zoran Radmilovic
Tuli Kupferberg
Jackie Curtis
Betty Dodson
Jim Buckley
Nancy Godfrey

Other films
★ *The Switchboard Operator* (1967)
★ *Manifesto* (1988)
★ *Danske Piger Viser Alt* (1996)

Milena Dravić strikes a pose.

Még Kér a Nép

Red Psalm

Miklós Jancsó *1971*

Director
Miklós Jancsó

A recent documentary about communist musicals called *East Side Story* (*Dana Ranga*, 1997) assumes that Communist-bloc directors were just itching to make Hollywood extravaganzas and invariably ended up looking strained, square and ill-equipped. But *Red Psalm* (1971), Miklós Jancsó's dazzling, open-air revolutionary pageant, is a highly sensual communist musical that employs occasional nudity as lyrically as the singing, dancing and nature. That is to say, within its own specially and exuberantly defined idioms, it swings as well as wails.

Set towards the end of the 19th century, when a group of peasants demand basic rights from a landowner and soldiers arrive to quell the rising, *Red Psalm* is composed of only 26 shots. (With a running time of 84 minutes, this adds up to an average of three minutes per shot. Jancsó's earlier feature from 1969, *Winter Sirocco*, is said to consist of only 13 shots.) Each long take is an intricate choreography of panning camerawork, landscape and clustered bodies that constantly traverse, join and/or divide the separate groups. The music, ranging from revolutionary folk songs to 'Charlie Is My Darling', is highly infectious, and the colours are ravishing. The picture won Jancsó the prize for best director at Cannes, and it may well be the greatest Hungarian film of the sixties and seventies, summing up an entire strain in his work that lamentably has been forgotten in more recent years.

The film's original Hungarian title, *Még Kér a Nép*, is said to translate into English as 'and the people still ask'. This suggests that the charge of formalism frequently levelled against Jancsó may stem in part from an inability to fully comprehend his historical and political meanings – combined with an understandable temptation to become intoxicated by the stylistic virtuosity of the extended takes and intricately plotted camera movements, thereby overlooking what the film's images actually mean. According to Hungarian film theorist Yvette Biró, who used to write scripts for Jancsó, 'bleeding white doves, a white shirt pierced through with a dagger, a long lingering shot of a gun tied with a red ribbon' are all 'taken from the folklore of our collective memory … Symbols here are elements of a folk community's language. Through a dance, Jancsó brings back to life this community, whose fate, in the fairy tale we are presented, is determined by ancient, biblical and folkloristic ritual; hence, the recurring presence of these rites is an organic and justified part of the story.'

Jancsó's awesome fusion of form with content and politics with poetry seems fully contemporary with the innovations of the French New Wave during the same period. And as the Hungarian title suggests, one of Jancsó's characteristic achievements is to create a striking continuum between past and present – a sense of immediacy about history that can be found in few other period films.

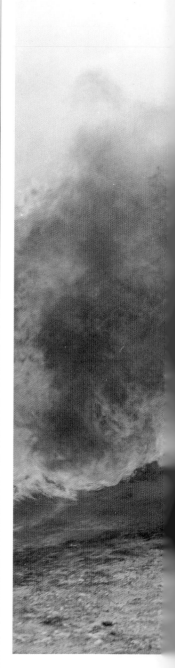

Writer
Gyula Hernadi

Producer
Ottó Föld

Cinematographer
János Kende

Production company
Mafilm

Editor
Tomás Csek

Cast
Lajos Balázsovits
András Bálint
Gyöngyi Bürös
Andrea Drahota
József Madaras

Other films
★ *The Round-Up* (1965)
★ *The Red and the White* (1967)
★ *The Confrontation* (1968)
★ *Elektreia* (1975)
★ *Private Vices, Public Virtues* (1975)

The peasants dance around a fire.

Céline et Julie vont en bateau
Céline and Julie Go Boating

Jacques Rivette *1974*

Jacques Rivette's 193-minute comic extravaganza *Céline and Julie Go Boating* – which can be read as the final, irreverent flowering of the French New Wave, many years after it officially ended – is as frightening and unsettling in its narrative high jinks as it is hilarious and exhilarating in its uninhibited slapstick. Arguably, its feminism already places it in quite a different category from its machocentric predecessors (apart from a few Agnes Varda films, such as *Cléo de 5 à 7*, 1961; *Cléo from 5 to 7*), although the fact that it was shot in 16mm (subsequently blown up to 35mm) gives it a footloose spirit that is closer to the New Wave's origins.

Like the numerous and varied neighbourhood cats putting in impromptu cameo appearances, the film emerges from a particular time and setting – Paris's Montmartre during a lazy summer – and the overall mood of fantasy growing out of daydreams smacks of Lewis Carroll.

The slow, sensual beginning stages a mysterious, semi-flirtatious encounter between Céline (Juliet Berto), flamboyant nightclub magician, and Julie (Dominique Labourier), shy librarian. Eventually they meet, swap tall tales and end up sharing a flat. They occasionally even swap identities: on different days, Céline disposes of Julie's childish boyfriend from the sticks and Julie trashes Céline's nightclub act by insulting the male patrons. Finally, a plot-within-a-plot entitled 'Phantom Ladies Over Paris' magically takes shape – a Jamesian, Victorian and hilariously sexist melodrama featuring Bulle Ogier, Marie-France Pisier, Barbet Schroeder (the film's producer) and a little girl – as, on successive days, Céline and then Julie visit a dark old house in which the same events take place, like a movie in repeat showings, with each heroine acting as a nurse attending to the little girl.

Both plots in *Céline and Julie* are outlandish, and the remarkable thing about Rivette's intricate balancing act is that each firmly holds the other in place. The elaborate doublings of characters and even shots – influenced by the 1950s criticism of Hitchcock thrillers like *Shadow of a Doubt* (1943) and *Strangers on a Train* (1951) by Rivette and his friends, which delighted in discovering as well as tracing such patterns – are so beautifully worked out that this film steadily grows in resonance and power, and the final payoff is well worth waiting for.

Rivette's grandest experiment, made just before – the completely improvised *Out 1*, edited first into a 13-hour serial (1971), then into a substantially different four-hour feature subtitled *Spectre* (1972) – also had many comic and fanciful elements, but neither film was seen widely. *Céline and Julie* was conceived as a shorter, semi-improvised comedy designed to get into cinemas. The four main actresses scripted their own dialogue with Eduardo de Gregorio and Rivette, and the film derives many of its most euphoric effects from a wholesale ransacking of the cinema of pleasure: cartoons, musicals, thrillers and serials are evoked at various junctures.

Director
Jacques Rivette

Writers
Juliet Berto, Dominique Labourier, Bulle Ogier, Marie-France Pisier and Jacques Rivette

Producer
Barbet Schroeder

Editor
Nicole Lubtchansky

Music
Jean-Marie Sénia

Cinematographer
Jacques Renard

Production companies
Action Films, Films Christian Fechner, Les Films 7, Les Films du Losange

Cast
Juliet Berto
Dominique Labourier
Bulle Ogier
Marie-France Pisier
Barbet Schroeder

Other films
★ *Paris nous appartient* (1961)
★ *L'Amour fou* (1968)
★ *Out 1* (1971)
★ *Le Pont du nord* (1981)
★ *La Belle noiseuse* (1991)
★ *Jeanne la pucelle* (1994)

Dominique Labourier, playing Julie, prepares for a
spot of roller-skating.

Perceval le Gallois
Perceval

Eric Rohmer *1979*

Eric Rohmer's least typical film, *Perceval* might also be his best: a wonderful version of Chrétien de Troyes' 12th-century epic poem, set to music, about the adventures of a callow and innocent knight (Fabrice Luchini). Deliberately contrived and theatrical in style and setting – the perspectives are as flat as in medieval tapestries, the colours bright and vivid – the film is as faithful to its source as possible, given the limited material available about the period.

Luchini, who would later play Octave in Rohmer's much more characteristic *Les Nuits de la pleine lune* (*Full Moon in Paris*, 1984), called *Perceval* 'a scholarly project, touched with insanity'. That is both its charm and its ineffable strangeness, enhanced by the fact that it represents an almost complete departure from the carefully crafted realism of Rohmer's other films. As Australian critic G.C. Crisp has described this realism, 'The cinema is a privileged art form because it most faithfully transcribes the beauty of the real world ... Any distortion of this, any attempt by man to improve on [God's handiwork], is indicative of arrogance and verges on the sacrilegious.'

Though this might seem to make *Perceval* a betrayal of Rohmer's aesthetic, his medieval musical – which actually feels at times like a studio-shot Western, complete with artificial sky – cogently illustrates his stated conviction as a critic that a true preservation of the past ultimately produces a kind of modernity. (Working against the grain of anything that might be regarded as quaint or old-fashioned in the film is the immediacy of the violence and the utter lack of sentimentality.) When asked how he reconciled his realist aesthetic with this film, Rohmer responded by recalling André Bazin's

defence of Carl Dreyer's *La Passion de Jeanne d'Arc* (*see pages 48–49*) as a realist work: that at least the dirt in that film was real. Here, where there doesn't appear to be any dirt at all – and where the film's settings often seem to resemble the artificial greens on miniature golf courses – it still might be argued that it is actually the 12th century that emerges as real. And the merit of this realism is that it brings something otherwise dead and forgotten to life – not because Rohmer's imagination is especially rich but because he can see no alternative to his literalism, even if it makes some viewers laugh in disbelief.

One striking example of this literalism is the fact that Rohmer's fidelity to the text compels him to include narrative descriptions as well as dialogue in the sung passages. The film opens with musicians and singers who also manufacture bird sounds, and members of this entourage periodically follow the characters around, making further comments. Among those followed are actors Rohmer would memorably use again, including André Dussollier (*Le beau mariage*, 1981; *A Good Marriage*) and, making their debuts, Arielle Dombasle (*Pauline à la plage*, 1983; *Pauline at the Beach*) and Pascal Ogier (*Les Nuits de la pleine lune*, 1984; *Full Moon in Paris*).

Director
Eric Rohmer

Writers
Eric Rohmer, from the novel by Chrétien de Troyes

Producers
Margaret Ménégoz and Barbet Schroeder

Cinematographer
Néstor Almendros

Production companies
Bayerischer Rundfunk, France 3 Cinéma, Les Films du Losange, Südwestfunk

Cast
Fabrice Luchini
André Dussollier
Marc Eyrand
Gérard Falconetti
Arielle Dombasle
Clémentine Amouroux
Michel Etcheverry

Other films
★ *La Collectionneuse* (1966)
★ *My Night with Maud* (1969)
★ *Claire's Knee* (1970)
★ *Le Beau mariage* (1981)
★ *Pauline à la plage* (1983)
★ *Les Nuits de la pleine lune* (1984)
★ *Le Rayon vert* (1986)
★ *Conte de printemps* (1990)
★ *Conte d'hiver* (1992)

A knight in an abstract medieval forest.

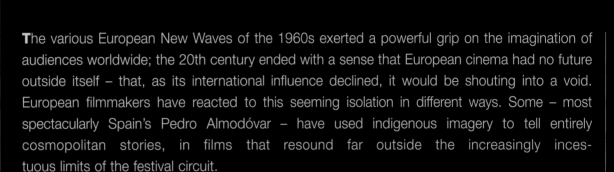

CHAPTER SEVEN

Europe: A New Fin de siècle
Jonathan Romney

7

The various European New Waves of the 1960s exerted a powerful grip on the imagination of audiences worldwide; the 20th century ended with a sense that European cinema had no future outside itself – that, as its international influence declined, it would be shouting into a void. European filmmakers have reacted to this seeming isolation in different ways. Some – most spectacularly Spain's Pedro Almodóvar – have used indigenous imagery to tell entirely cosmopolitan stories, in films that resound far outside the increasingly incestuous limits of the festival circuit.

Other filmmakers use a sense of isolation and impending defeat as a rationale for a whole world-view. It is partly for this reason that I have made what may seem a frivolous choice, selecting two out of 15 films from Portugal's limited output; but there is something distinctive about a cinema that speaks from the geographic edge of Europe, as if it were speaking from the edge of cinema itself.

I make no apology for favouring a certain outsider aesthetic in my list. Rather than opt for the much-loved or for unmitigated success, I have tended to be drawn to films that push a certain idea to its limit, if not to the brink of failure. *Tierra*, for example, is about as strange as a commercial film can be these days without its director irrevocably alienating viewers and financiers.

In fact, the current sense of risk-taking among European filmmakers suggests vigorous if embattled health. French cinema in the 1980s had settled into a glamorous academicism with the so-called *cinéma du look* represented by Jean-Jacques Beineix, Luc Besson and Leos Carax. But, more recently, France has been reinventing the realist low-budget aesthetic of the New Wave, in the process asking pointed questions about political realities: about race, sex and history. The most recent French film in my 15 is by Claire Denis, but for polemical intensity, Catherine Breillat's meta-porn essay *Romance* (1999) could be in there, or *Seul contre tous* (*I Stand Alone*, 1998), Gaspar Noé's unashamedly

grim reworking of Martin Scorsese's *Taxi Driver* (1976). And Europe is still asking many of the key questions about cinema's changing nature. In his 1989 documentary *Notebook on Cities and Clothes*, Wim Wenders asked what it would mean if directors turned to low-cost digital technology. Many of his questions have already been answered: digital video is becoming a new standard, and anyone using celluloid in future will need to do so for a good reason. Whatever the flaws of the digital work made under the aegis of the Danish-based Dogme group, it obliges celluloid to show its hand, to declare its aesthetic intentions.

Video's immediacy may signify the end of mastery – the fall of the auteur who, like Angelopoulos, Tarkovsky and Kieślowski, represents the popular image of director as high priest. That would leave the field open to makers of fragments and wry, provisional commentaries. Others might include João César Monteiro and Ari Kaurismäki; Italy's Nanni Moretti or the Georgian director Otar Iosseliani. Meanwhile, a certain Tarkovskyan mysticism of the sublime image still prevails, but on the absolute margins, in such seldom-celebrated filmmakers as Hungary's Bela Tarr and Lithuania's Sharunas Bartas. It may be that in future there will be no position for European filmmakers to speak from except the margins. And with the mainstream looking increasingly debilitated and formulaic, that may well prove the most exciting place to be.

213

The Enigma of Kaspar Hauser
Jeder für sich und Gott gegen alle

Werner Herzog *1974*

Director, producer and writer
Werner Herzog

Werner Herzog was one of the key figures of New German Cinema in the late 1960s and 1970s, and although his influence has somewhat waned, he has continued to be active as an idiosyncratic documentarist. His achievements have been rather eclipsed by the myth that he has energetically promoted of himself as an intrepid traveller and Promethean mystic, and by the anecdotes of his antagonistic *folie à deux* with the late mercurial actor Klaus Kinski (star of Herzog's *Aguirre, Wrath of God*, 1972, and *Fitzcarraldo*, 1982, among others).

Much of Herzog's work is fuelled less by cinephile obsessions than by the German Romantic tradition, notably in *The Enigma of Kaspar Hauser*: the original German title translates as 'every man for himself and God against all'. The film is based on the true story of a young man who appeared in a square in Nuremberg in 1828 with no grasp of language and, apparently, no past. Quickly learning German, the youth, who signed himself Kaspar Hauser, claimed to have spent his life imprisoned in a cellar with no human contact; a rumour spread that he was heir to the royal house of Baden. Kaspar became a much discussed social figure before being attacked twice by unknown assailants, the second time fatally.

The case became a prominent myth in the 19th century and has continued to inspire modern treatments, a recent example being Peter Sehr's film *Kaspar Hauser* (1993). In Herzog's version, his master stroke was to find a modern Kaspar in the shape of Bruno S., a Berlin street musician who had spent much of his own life in institutions. Herzog was accused of exploiting Bruno, but the film gives the performer a very ample stage to be himself; his distinctive staccato speech and halting body language dominate the film with their own rhythms, just as they dominate another Herzog film that echoes Bruno's own story, 1977's *Stroszek*. In some ways, the film offers a quite conventional critique of society's treatment of outsiders – for example, Kaspar's recruit-ment to a circus freak show. There is something similarly familiar in the theme of 'natural' wisdom versus blinkered rationalism. One of the most memorable scenes features Kaspar's wonderfully blunt refutation of a philosophy professor's logic, as he effortlessly cuts through the mystificatory riddle designed to show the difficulty of telling falsehoods from truth.

But the film transcends its more obvious elements, partly through Bruno's presence, partly in its stylistic execution, which constantly undercuts the evocation of 19th-century German pastoral. With photographer Jörg Schmidt-Reitwein's landscapes recalling the transcendental paintings of Caspar David Friedrich, the film's ostensible realism is repeatedly invaded by glimpses of the unconscious, in dream scenes of the Caucasus and in Kaspar's vision of a holy mountain (the film is not without a certain hippie mysticism).

The film's intellectual grist lies in its inquiry into the relationship between identity and language. François Truffaut's *L'Enfant sauvage* (*The Wild Child*, 1969), based on another 18th-century 'wild child' story, ended with the triumph of science and manners; Herzog's pessimistic vision questions not only rationalism and decorum but the very notion of the soul. The first word Kaspar learns in society is '*leer*' – 'empty' – and Herzog leaves us wondering what it means to look within, when the knowable, visible world is already one of illusions, paradoxes and shimmering chimeras.

Cinematographers
Jörg Schmidt-Reitwein
and Klaus Wyborny

Production companies
Cine International, Werner
Herzog Filmproduktion
and Zweites Deutsches
Fernsehen

Cast
Bruno S.
Walter Ladengast
Brigitte Mira
Willy Semmelrogge
Gloria Dör
Volker Prechtel
Hans Musäus
Clemens Scheitz

Other films
★ *Signs of Life* (1968)
★ *Even Dwarves Started Small* (1970)
★ *Aguirre, Wrath of God* (1972)
★ *Stroszek* (1977)
★ *Fitzcarraldo* (1982)

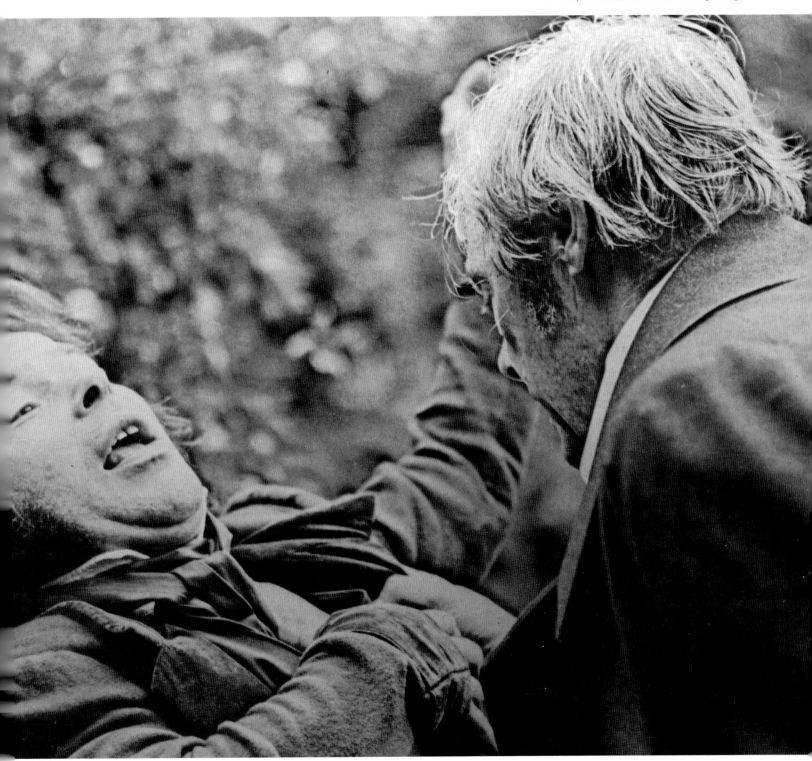

*Bruno S. (left), Herzog's real-life vagrant, as
Kaspar Hauser, with Walter Ladengast, right.*

O Thiassos
The Travelling Players

Theo Angelopoulos *1975*

Director
Theo Angelopoulos

The Greek director and screenwriter Theo Angelopoulos is one of the cinema's great landscape artists, and what often strikes us in his films are those moments when landscape freezes into a vast dramatic panorama: the Balkan no-man's-lands of *Ulysses' Gaze* (*To Vlemma Tou Odyssea*, 1995), or the frontier fence in *Eternity and a Day* (*Mia Eoniotita Ke Mia Mera*, 1998), with its human figures hanging on the wire for dear life.

But Angelopoulos is also a filmmaker of motion, who makes films about travel – on trains, cars, buses, on foot and above all in the imagination. Claiming Welles and Mizoguchi as primary influences, Angelopoulos is known – together with his long-time cameraman Yorgos Arvanitis – as a specialist of the long, flowing, precisely choreographed take. *The Travelling Players* is a prime example of this, a four-hour film containing only 80 shots. In the most distinctive of these, the camera and the actors move in such a way that time and space seem to turn inside out, to achieve a Möbius-strip elasticity.

Angelopoulos's subject is Greece, not the one known to tourists but a wintry one, located in a Balkan landscape and bounded both by its classical and modern past and by geographical borders. Angelopoulos had been a critic on a socialist newspaper and he claimed that the right-wing Colonels' junta that ruled Greece from 1967 to 1974 provided his subject and made him want to understand the historic roots of dictatorship. He made *The Travelling Players* more or less surreptitiously, passing the film off to the authorities as a reworking of the Orestes myth, set in the time of the German occupation. This is accurate up to a point. A travelling theatre troupe moves around Greece between 1939 and 1952, attempting to perform a 19th-century popular play, *Golfo the Shepherdess*. But they are always interrupted by history, from the German occupation through the Civil War to the rise of the Papagos government. The troupe also reinvents characters from Aeschylus's *Oresteia*: Aegisthus is a Nazi collaborator, Orestes a communist partisan, and Agamemnon the troupe's betrayed leader.

This is a film not so much about characters as about a family of archetypes, even of ghosts (the troupe, its dead members brought back to life, make a phantasmal reappearance in Angelopoulos' 1988 production *Landscape in the Mist – Topio Stin Omichli*). Time and space share something of this uncertain quality: a single shot can drift seamlessly from one period to another, and the film begins with the players standing together in 1952 and ends with an almost identical grouping in 1939. A characteristic shot tends to have a band of figures walking through a town and emerging, as the camera tracks through the streets, in a different year, perhaps crossing the path of another, larger body of people.

Angelopoulos is a masterful director of crowd movements, equally fluent at orchestrating wedding processions, political demonstrations or multitudes with umbrellas (see his 1995 film *Ulysses' Gaze*). His films suggest a theory of history as *parade* – not in the derogatory 'heritage' sense of a pageant, but as an endless procession, at once funeral cortege and political demonstration, continually crossing its own tracks, changing its direction, changing its ideological colours. In this extraordinary film, movement itself becomes a formidably acute and supple tool for historical analysis.

Producer
Giorgis Samiotis

Cinematographer
Yorgos Arvanitis

Editor
Takis Davlopoulos

Music
Loukianos Kilaidonis

Production designer
Mikes Karapiperis

Cast
Eva Kotamanidou
Aliki Georgoulis
Statos Pachis
Maria Vassilion
Petros Zarkadis

Other films
★ *Alexander the Great* (1980)
★ *The Beekeeper* (1986)
★ *Landscape in the Mist* (1988)
★ *Ulysses' Gaze* (1995)
★ *Eternity and a Day* (1998)

The players on an uncharacteristically wintry Greek beach, hands raised as they confront the troops.

Stalker Andrei Tarkovsky *1979*

Director
Andrei Tarkovsky

Writers
Arkady and Boris Strugatsky

Andrei Tarkovsky, who died in 1986, is widely considered a spiritual filmmaker, and often attacked as such. Georgian director Otar Iosseliani said of him, 'It is somewhat ill-bred to be always emphasizing how religious you are – it is like boasting that your father is a marquis.' The cult that once regarded Tarkovsky's films as a repository of ineffable insight has somewhat receded, making it easier now to admire his work for its language of fragmentation and discontinuity, one that mobilizes the fluidity of dream in all its resonance and seriousness.

Tarkovsky's most formally experimental film is certainly his autobiographical *Mirror* (*Zerkalo*, 1974), which is the one that deals most directly with the realities of Soviet life. But his most durable blueprint for the cinematic imagination may be *Stalker*, ostensibly an adaptation by Arkady Strugatsky and Boris Strugatsky of their science-fiction novel *Roadside Picnic* (1975), which appeared after his other science-fiction film, *Solaris* (1972). *Stalker* is exploratory in every sense – a venture in topographical cinema. In an unspecified future, a meteorite has created 'the miracle of miracles', the Zone, into which a haunted, specially qualified 'stalker' guides two disillusioned men, a writer and a scientist. The Zone, which offers particular rewards and particular perils (tailored to the recipient), obeys its own laws which seem to make the fabric of space and matter shift randomly.

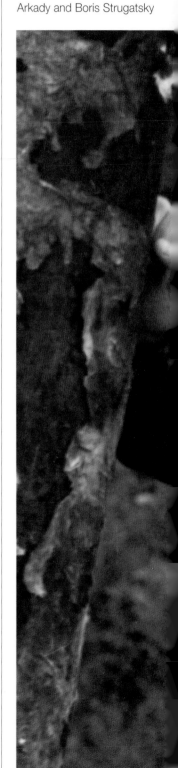

But the Zone is a dislocated space within a world that is already fragmenting. The outside world, filmed in black-and-white, is a militarized region of checkpoints and freight yards, patrolled by police: to all appearances a classic dystopian image of the Soviet Union. But the pastoral inner haven of the Zone – shot in a faded, chemical shade of blue-green – is just as unstable. It is a product of montage, a virtual geography created by editing together different, apparently incompatible spaces: a waterlogged chamber leads to one filled with sand dunes. The *mise en scène* is something between adventure playground and gallery installation art. The way Tarkovsky privileges the labyrinth of imaginative space over the straight line of narrative has its recent echoes in the work of the Hungarian filmmaker Bela Tarr, particularly *Satantango* (1994).

Stalker's universe is, above all, porous: water flows everywhere, just as the dream state floods into the solid world (and cinema into the consciousness of the viewer). Even the extraordinary sound design is prone to a kind of seepage: the distant sound of passing trains and music pervades a sleepers' room in the first scene; the wheezy rattle of the travellers' railway cart blurs into abstract rhythmic electronica.

Stalker can be read as political parable – it is, after all, the story of a man who claims, 'I am in prison everywhere.' A field of abandoned tanks swamped by vegetation seems a clear presage of the fall of power. But, overall, *Stalker* works by allusion rather than by clearly signalled meaning. Its monumental elements are eclipsed by small miracles, so that the film's most resounding event is the entirely enigmatic movement of a glass on a table. The film should be taken less as a discursive proposition than as poetry: Tarkovsky's father, Arseny, quoted in the film, was a prominent lyric poet, but the autonomous fluidity of *Stalker*'s world is closer to the mystical, dream-like universe of Rimbaud. One character talks of being plagued by intangible thoughts 'like jellyfish in the sun' – which gives an idea of how meaning operates in this haunting, supremely hallucinatory work.

Producer
Aleksandra Demidova

Cinematographer
Aleksandr Knyazhinsky

Production companies
Mosfilm, Zweites Deutsches
Fernsehen

Music
Eduard Artemyev

Cast
Aleksandr Kaidanovsky
Alissa Freindlikh
Anatoli Solonitsyn
Nikolai Grinko
Natasha Abramova

Other films
★ *Solaris* (1972)
★ *Mirror* (1974)
★ *Nostalgia* (1983)

The Stalker (Aleksandr Kaidanovsky), leading
others on a grimy pilgrimage.

Passion

Jean-Luc Godard *1982*

Director, writer and editor
Jean-Luc Godard

After his absence from the commercial cinema during the 1970s, Jean-Luc Godard returned in the 1980s with a series of films that seemed primarily to espouse the traditional production values of art cinema. They engaged with the high-art canon (painting, literature, classical music) in order to bring new scrutiny to bear on the tension between art and the economic structures underlying its production.

An ostentatiously and uncharacteristically beautiful work, *Passion*, like Fellini's *8½* (1963) or Godard's own *Le Mépris* (*Contempt*, 1963), is a film about making a film, or rather, not making a film. It is hard to tell exactly what kind of film Polish director Jerzy is shooting: we only know that it appears to have no story and that it features a series of *tableau vivant* recreations of paintings by Goya, Delacroix, El Greco and other great masters.

Narratively, visually and sonically, the film is a sort of cacophony. There are too many characters for us to be sure who is who, and one narrative strand violently interrupts another; a single shot carries too much visual information; and silence or classical music is suddenly disrupted by the violent blaring of car horns.

The film's key theme is light itself, which appears in several forms: daylight, studio lighting, the cheap lighting of hotel rooms, and the sublime lighting of the old masters. We become acutely aware of the way in which lighting can transform the dimensions and meaning of an image. But Godard demonstrates that money too illuminates images: producers pay for studio lights, patrons commission works of art. *Passion* is largely about the comparable but very different production of images in painting and film.

Anyone can point a camera at the sky, as Godard does in his opening shot; to paint the sky involves an entirely different level of skill. However, to produce a painterly film image involves something more: money, and the skills of a director of photography (here, Raoul Coutard, working with Godard for the first time in 15 years).

How much more difficult, then, it must be to recreate a Delacroix painting – to capture the play on fabrics, and to get the extras (in Jerzy's case, workers recruited from a local factory) to hold their positions, especially when they have not been paid properly. What ostensibly appears to be an abstruse debate about aesthetics opens up a host of economic questions: Jerzy, the artist, seems more exploitative than the factory owner.

Passion is also very much a comedy, an extremely unruly one in which order can collapse at any moment – a punch-up breaks out in a car park, Delacroix horsemen ride aimlessly around the studio, Jerzy tussles *mano a mano* with an angel. Godard's later films went deeper and deeper into this stark juxtaposition and chaos, to the limits of intelligibility (such as 1993's *Hélas pour moi*). But *Passion* is a self-mocking masterpiece, at once the consummate art film (the ultimate bourgeois luxury consumable, you might say) and its self-corrosive opposite.

220

Producer
Alain Sarde

Cinematographer
Raoul Coutard

Production companies
Film et Vidéo Companie,
Films A2, JLG, SSR, Sara
Film and Sonimage

Production designers
Jean Baue and
Serge Marzolff

Cast
Isabelle Huppert
Hanna Schygulla
Jerzy Radziwilowicz
Michel Piccoli
Laszló Szábó

Other films
★ *A Bout de souffle* (1960)
★ *Les Carabiniers* (1963)
★ *Le Mépris* (1963)
★ *Pierrot le fou* (1963)
★ *Bande à part* (1964)
★ *Weekend* (1967)
★ *Tout va bien* (1972)
★ *Sauve qui peut* (1980)

One of the tableau vivant *reconstructions that are characteristic of the film.*

Les Trois couronnes du matelot
Three Crowns of the Sailor

Raúl Ruiz *1983*

You can imagine Raúl Ruiz inventing the figure of an impossibly prolific filmmaker travelling the world, accumulating enigmatic fragments of film so fast that no viewer or critic can see them all. And, effectively, Ruiz has created himself. His bizarre career ranges from 1960s Chile, where he made ostensibly political films such as an adaptation of Kafka's *The Penal Colony (La Colonia Penal,* 1970); to France in the 1970s, as an exile from Pinochet, where he established himself as a fabricator of surreal puzzle-films; and into the late 1990s, when he improbably infiltrated the art-house mainstream with a version of Proust's *Time Regained (Le Temps retrouvé,* 1999).

His reconciliation with commercial filmmaking has in no way diminished the strangeness of this joker, scholar and mystic whose aesthetic is grounded in minor American B-movies, a fascination with medieval theology and voracious literary tastes.

Ruiz's oeuvre is so vast that it is hard to choose any one of his films – which admittedly range from mesmerizing to barely watchable. But he was most intensely active in France in the early 1980s, and it is possible to imagine cloning an entire canon of Ruiz films from any one of the densely imaginative works of this period. *Three Crowns of the Sailor* shows Ruiz's imagination at his most mythic: it is a B-movie ghost story and his version of the Ancient Mariner, Flying Dutchman and Odysseus stories all rolled into one. A student kills his tutor and then listens to a sailor's narrative in exchange for passage on his ship. It transpires that the sailor was the only living man on board this ship of ghosts.

The voyage is a frame for a disjointed series of episodes, set in such locations as Singapore, Tangiers, Dakar and Valparaíso – although really this disorientating odyssey takes place nowhere, and in a nowhere of the mind at that. A succession of hallucinatory images indulges Ruiz's taste for visual gimcrackery – cut-price trickery made very evident, displaying a stage conjurer's aesthetic of making something out of nothing. Ruiz owes a lot to Welles above all, especially in the scenes where a dance hall becomes a chamber of mirrors. Grotesque imagery (worms emerging from sailors' chests) proves to be wordplay-based (in French, *vers* are both worms and verses). Lurid images detach themselves from the narrative to become autonomous in their strangeness, just as bodybuilder Lisa Lyon, playing a woman with only one orifice, gradually peels off and tosses aside different parts of her body. The apparently random associations have a coherent shape underlying them: the story is of an exchange, a transaction where a narrative is bartered at the buyer's peril.

With Ruiz's work, we feel we are dipping both into a library of dream images and into the entire repertoire of film, art and literature. *Three Crowns* occupies a special place in his work in that it formulates that experience as a form of travel without clear direction, and potentially without limits. And just as the student's fate is irrevocably changed by the sailor's story, something similar happens to the viewer of Ruiz's film – sign up for this voyage and you will never see cinema in quite the same way again.

Director
Raúl Ruiz

Producers
Jean Lefaux, Maya Feuillette and José-Luis Vasconcelos

Writers
Raúl Ruiz, François Ede and Emilio de Solar

Cinematographer
Sacha Vierny

Editors
Janine Verneau and Valeria Sarmiento

Music
Jorge Arriagada

Cast
Jean-Bernard Guillard
Philippe Deplanche
Nadège Clair
Lisa Lyon
Jean Badin
Claude Derepp

Other films
★ *The Penal Colony* (1969)
★ *The Hypothesis of the Stolen Painting* (1978)
★ *City of Pirates* (1983)
★ *Three Lives and Only One Death* (1995)
★ *Time Regained* (1999)

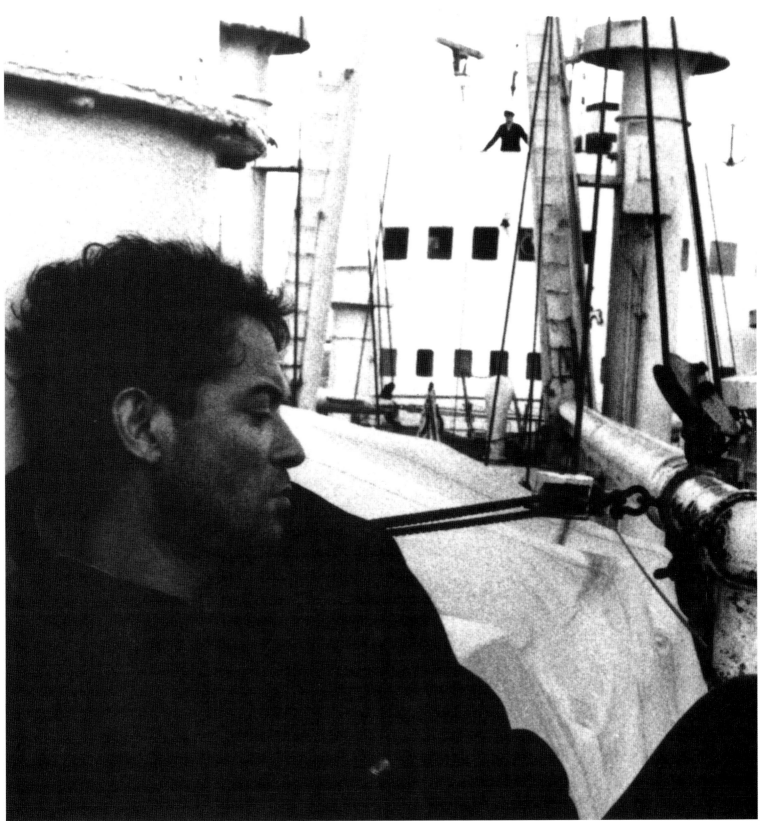

Jean-Bernard Guiilard as the sailor offering a
narrative aboard the ghost ship.

Le Rayon vert
The Green Ray

Eric Rohmer *1986*

Director
Eric Rohmer

It begins with a quotation from Rimbaud: 'Ah! That the time might come when hearts succumb', but *The Green Ray* is less about falling in love than the expectation of falling in love. And in his films, Rohmer repeatedly throws out the challenge to the audience that he can make us fall for his characters, rebarbative though they often are. That is why his work is such a subjective matter: we either warm to his characters (sometimes seemingly indistinguishable from the people who play them), or we don't. If we do, the payoff is unexpectedly satisfying, given the seemingly banal nature of the stories.

One of the original New Wave directors and a critic even before his days at *Cahiers du cinéma*, Rohmer has consistently worked on a smaller scale than his peers (only Jacques Rivette has shared his commitment to low-tech, low-budget methods) and has tended to explore film through thematic series: 'Moral Tales' (1963–72), 'Comedies and Proverbs' (1980–87) and 'Four Seasons' (1989–98).

One of the 'Comedies and Proverbs', *The Green Ray* is about Delphine, a Parisian secretary whose summer comes to a standstill when her holiday plans fall through. Friends rally round and she even goes away with them, but she keeps coming home to sulk. Delphine is, in fact, remarkably irritating company – an airhead who can hold forth inarticulately about her vegetarianism, explaining that a lettuce feels like a friend. Moody and insipid, she seems more lettuce than human, but green is her lucky colour, and she eventually has her amorous epiphany by the sea, watching the 'green ray', the sunset effect noted in a story by Jules Verne.

The brilliance of *The Green Ray*, one of Rohmer's seemingly less structured films, is in the way it balances chance and control. Control is emphasized when Delphine finds those objects (a playing card, a poster) that, she is convinced, signal her destiny, all announced by an ominous violin theme (the film's only touch of directorial rhetoric). Against this is a sense of serendipity, a quasi-documentary effect that makes us feel we are watching real life happen to real people. The cast is credited with creating the dialogue, and while some characters appear to be themselves (a retired taxi-driver, a ski-shop assistant), others are recognizably actors from other Rohmer films. For much of the time, the piece feels less like narrative than a fictional survey of French holiday choices and dating habits: one memorable scene captures the meaningless multilingual babble of flirting tourists.

The Green Ray is rare among Rohmer films, which often involve groups or couples, in that it features a single character unable to attach herself to anyone; romantic intrigue is absent until the last possible moment. Marie Rivière's performance is all the more remarkable in that, paradoxically, the more insubstantial Delphine seems, the more riveting her presence; by the end, she proves she has as much right to our interest as any conventional heroine. Like so many Rohmer films, *The Green Ray* asks the question, 'What makes people interesting?' and answers, 'Never what you expect.'

Producer
Margaret Ménégoz

Writers
Eric Rohmer and
Marie Rivière

Cinematographer
Sophie Maintigneux

Music
Jean-Louis Valéro

Editor
Maria-Luisa Garcia

Production company
Les Films du Losange

Cast
Marie Rivière
Vincent Gauthier
Carita

Other films
★ *La Collectionneuse* (1966)
★ *My Night with Maud* (1969)
★ *Claire's Knee* (1970)
★ *Perceval le Gallois* (1979)
★ *Le Beau mariage* (1981)
★ *Pauline à la plage* (1983)
★ *Les Nuits de la pleine lune* (1984)

Marie Rivière (right) as the 'remarkably irritating' Delphine, with a prospective partner (Vincent Gauthier).

Recollections of the Yellow House
Recordacões da Casa Amarela

João César Monteiro *1989*

The Portuguese director–actor João César Monteiro is a marginal figure by any standards, but it is a position he cultivates and clearly relishes. His wayward approach to filmmaking, exercised since the early 1970s, often seems calculated to test even his admirers' patience: *The Hips of J. W.* (*Le Bassin de J. W.,* 1997) combines a Strindberg performance, a filmed script-reading and a rudimentary plot about a polar expedition in search of John Wayne.

But Monteiro at his best is quite unique – a mixture of dry philosophical fancy, visual comedy *à la* Jacques Tati and corrosive satire of the Portuguese bourgeoisie. Invariably playing his own lead, Monteiro has developed a unique style of self-portraiture, under the mask of a charmingly abject alter ego. João de Deus (literally, 'John of God', but also the name of a Portuguese poet) is an absolute outsider: a lecher, down-at-heel dandy and a self-styled 'left-wing intellectual'. Never quite the same character twice, he features in a trilogy, the second and third episodes being *God's Comedy* (*A Comedia de Deus*, 1995), in which he is an ice-cream vendor and fetishistic cataloguer of pubic hair, and *God's Wedding* (*As Bodas de Deus*, 1999), in which he is conveniently handed all the wealth of the world.

The first film in the trilogy, *Recollections of the Yellow House*, is the most complete and the most lyrical. A panorama of Lisbon lowlife, it is imbued with the melancholy of that city's literature, exemplified by protean poet Fernando de Pessoa. Here, João de Deus is a lodger in a boarding house – literally yellow, although in Portuguese 'yellow house' also means lunatic asylum – who is driven mad by thwarted desire and the inconveniences of genteel poverty. He is at war with his landlady, besotted with her police-cadet daughter and plagued by a combination of blisters, headaches and pubic lice. Few director–actors have portrayed themselves in such uncomplimentary colours, nor given their obsessions such alarmingly free rein. João de Deus is a misanthropist and misogynist, not to mention an intellectual snob, but Monteiro asks us to take him as we find him. The main vehicle for Monteiro's humour is his extraordinary physique, lugubrious goatish features topping a scrawny body that we can believe is subject to the worst indignities. In one of the film's pithiest gags, we hear a crunch as de Deus sits on ice to cool his piles.

Yet Monteiro's lofty, distracted demeanour gives him a Hulotesque comic dignity, and he can also pull off more traditional Chaplinesque mockery, ludicrously strutting in uniform and monocle as de Deus impersonates a cavalry officer. Monteiro's humour runs from post-Salazar anti-militarism to straight scatology, from the haughtily highbrow (a joke about the 19th-century German poet Hölderlin of all things) to a striptease act involving a crocodile and a giant tube of toothpaste – which, of course, we never see. This slow, solemn shaggy-dog comedy ends with de Deus's surreal metamorphosis into a Nosferatu-like phantom, who rises ghoulishly out of the Lisbon gutters before dissolving into thin air.

In both outlook and persona, Monteiro and his work defy description – although you could think of them as a hybrid of Beckett, Céline and Groucho Marx. Monteiro has the mark of a geniune trouble-maker, and everyone should see at least one Monteiro film, ideally this one, if only as proof that European cinema can still accommodate such a dissident oddball.

Director and writer
João César Monteiro

Producers
Joaquin Pinto and
João Pedro Bénard

Cinematographer
José António Loureiro

Production company
Invicta Film

Cast
João César Monteiro
Manuela de Freitas
Sabina Sacchi
Inês de Medeiros
Teresa Calado

Other films
★ *A Flor do Mar* (1986)
★ *A Comedia de Deus* (1995)
★ *The Hips of J. W.* (1997)
★ *As Bodas de Deus* (1999)

Director–actor João César Monteiro as the disease-ridden misanthrope at the centre of the film.

Nao, ou A Vã Gloria de Mandar
No, or the Vainglory of Command

Mañoel de Oliveira *1990*

Director and writer
Mañoel de Oliveira

If Portugal is a forgotten country in European cinema, Mañoel de Oliveira is an undiscovered continent in his own right. He started making films in 1931, at the end of the silent era, after a career as a racing driver, and continues today, in his early 90s, to make roughly a film a year, each one entirely unpredictable. (His impressive productivity may well be compensation for two lost decades, the 1940s and 1950s, when he was out of favour with the Salazar dictatorship.)

Oliveira's extremely diverse oeuvre is unified by a certain moral seriousness, a scholarly fascination with political and literary history and an extraordinary playfulness, even when he seems to be at his most minimal and severe. His autobiographical travel-ogue essay *Journey to the Beginning of the World* (*Viagem ao Principio do Mundo,* 1997) – one of the most genuinely Proustian of films – has Marcello Mastroianni impersonating Oliveira while the director himself discreetly steps in and out of shot as Mastroianni's chauffeur.

Many Oliveira films leave you astounded, if only because their unashamed theatricality seems to exist in a world equally detached from the commercial screen and the art-house. One of the most remarkable is *No, or the Vainglory of Command*, partly because it is so magnificently unapologetic about Oliveira's key preoccupation, one which might seem entirely marginal to world cinema – his own nation's past. *No* is something like a Brechtian history lesson. In a Portuguese colony in Africa, a group of soldiers – in camp and on the back of a truck – discuss the nature of colonialism and war, and one of them narrates episodes in Portugal's history. Each scene is effectively in a different style, but all are equally theatrical: the death of the Lusitanian chieftain Viriatus is half Hollywood biblical epic, half department-store window display; the battle of Alcaçar-Quibir recalls Olivier's *Henry V*; and most extraordinary of all, the voyage of Vasco da Gama, as recounted in Camoëns' epic poem *The Lusiads*, is treated as full-blown operatic kitsch, complete with cupids and goddesses in swan-drawn carriages.

No is not only an extraordinary stylistic exercise, it is also an illustration of war as cultural spectacle and as pantomime. What holds the film together is the austere tone, against which the sometimes absurd visuals are played out. The tone, in fact, is something like that of modern opera, and you could imagine *No* orchestrated by a John Adams or a Gavin Bryars.

All these different styles can co-exist in a single film as illustrations (you might almost say story-book illustrations) of a single topic: the question of war and the way that history and cultural imagination have glorified it. These episodes sketch out a narrative of disaster and ignominy in Portuguese history. Catastrophe finally surfaces in the modern day too, as the 20th-century soldiers experience battle. The last scenes in the field hospital echo another language altogether – the hard illustrative simplicity of silent cinema. And the final irony underlines the futility – the soldier who has introduced all these events dies on the very day of the revolution against Salazar, 25 April 1974.

Producer
Paulo Branco

Cinematographer
Elso Roque

Production companies
Gemini Fllms, Madragoa
Filmes, Radiotelevisão
Portugesa, SGGC and
Tornasol Films

Music
Alejandro Masso

Cast
Luis Miguel Cintra
Diogo Dória
Miguel Guilherme
Luís Lucas
Carlos Gomes
António S. Lopes

Other films
★ *Douro, Faina Fluvial* (1931)
★ *Aniki-Bobó* (1942)
★ *The Satin Slipper* (1985)
★ *Vale Abraão* (1993)
★ *Journey to the Beginning of the World* (1997)
★ *La Lettre* (1999)

War as cultural spectacle and as pantomime: the battle of Alcaçar-Quibir as envisaged by Oliveira.

Europa
Lars von Trier *1991*

No-one could have guessed that the 20th century would end with Denmark taking a central place on the world cinema map. A film culture starved of polemic turned eagerly to the Dogme 95 manifesto, in which four Danish filmmakers, including Lars von Trier, called for a no-frills cinema governed by rules banning traditional cinematic artifice.

This led to a form of filmmaking more playful and provocative than its apparently hard-realist ethos would suggest. For von Trier himself, however, Dogme's 'Vow of Chastity' might be seen as a guilt reaction against the mannerist excesses of his early work. *Element of Crime* (1984) was the first flowering of his deeply eccentric internationalism – an English-language Borgesian thriller in shades of jaundice yellow.

Von Trier's militant cinephilia reached boiling point in his third feature, the baroquely nightmarish *Europa*. With dialogue in English and German, the story is set in Germany in 1945, a night-bound wasteland haunted by a Nazi partisan group, the Werewolves. The idealistic Leopold arrives from America, intending to help Germany's recovery by working as a sleeping-car attendant for the Zentropa railway company. The company is run by the deeply compromised Hartmann family. Leopold marries the vampish Katharina Hartmann and is pressurized into planting a bomb on the train, on the very night that – to farcical effect – he is to take an attendant's exam.

Europa's Germany is in fact another of von Trier's imaginary landscapes, like the Scottish island of *Breaking the Waves* (1996) or the America of his musical *Dancer in the Dark* (2000). It is a cinephile's country, peopled by the cast of other films – Sukowa and Kier (von Trier's *acteur-fétiche*) are former Fassbinder actors, while Eddie Constantine carries his own nocturnal connotations from Godard's *Alphaville* (*see pages 196–197*). This is a world made entirely by cinema's technologies of dream – and von Trier, who once described himself as a cinematic 'masturbator', here achieves orgasmic intensity. *Europa* uses three cinematographers (including Henning Bendtsen, who worked with Danish cinema's austere patriarch Carl Theodor Dreyer), back projection, huge captions, extreme contrasts of scale and 'impossible' space-bending tracking shots; it mixes inky monochrome with faded tint-like colour, often in the same shot. Deep focus creates impressions of vastness – an inferno-like railway shed, swarming crowds, snowfall in a roofless cathedral at night – contrasted with claustrophobia-inducing tightness, above all, in the closing underwater sequences.

There is not just flamboyance but megalomania here, as if von Trier had set out to compete with the Fritz Lang of the 1920s. He also seems determined to take literally Orson Welles' notorious description of a film studio as the best train set a boy could have. But von Trier also wryly undercuts his own mastery – Max von Sydow's hypnotist-narrator effectively dares us to stay awake and resist the dream.

The pyrotechnics dress a hollow narrative that at once mythologizes and trivializes the highly charged theme of rail transport in 1940s Germany – a sudden sighting of Holocaust survivors seems like glib sensationalism. Von Trier may have seen *Europa* as a dead end, but we can only regret that he never pursued this strangely anachronistic path of visionary excess. The film's only real legacy was that von Trier used the name Zentropa for his production company, which became one of the most powerful in northern Europe.

Director
Lars von Trier

Writers
Lars von Trier and
Niels Vørsel

Producers
Peter Aalbaek Jensen and
Bo Christiensen

Cinematographers
Henning Bendtsen, Edward
Klosinki and Jean-Paul
Meurisse

Production companies
Det Danske Filminstitut,
Gérard Mital Productions,
Institut Suisse du Film,
Nordisk Film + TV, PCC
Productions, Svenska
Filminstitut and WMG Film

Cast
Jean-Marc Barr
Barbara Sukowa
Udo Kier
Ernst-Hugo Järegård
Erik Mark
Jørgen Reenberg
Henning Jensen

Other films
★ *Element of Crime* (1984)
★ *Epidemic* (1988)
★ *Breaking the Waves* (1996)
★ *The Idiots* (1998)
★ *Dancer in the Dark* (2000)

Jean-Marc Barr in a scene illustrating the film's extreme juxtapositions of scale.

El Sol del Membrillo
The Quince Tree Sun

Victor Erice *1991*

Director
Victor Erice

Victor Erice's contemplative hybrid of documentary, fiction and philosophical essay has the simplest plot imaginable: man paints tree. In the autumn of 1990, Madrid painter Antonio López sets out to paint a quince tree in his garden. His insistence on precision causes him to transform the object of his scrutiny, surrounding it with a panoply of painterly aids: he hangs a plumb line to give him the vertical, fixes a thread for the horizontal, marks the quinces and leaves with dabs of paint so as to keep track of the tree's movements with time. He even drives nails into the ground to mark the position he must stand in for a fixed viewpoint: López seems the prisoner of his own exacting procedures.

López's methods have more affinity with filmmaking than with most contemporary painting, and Erice's film examines the parallels between the two art forms, especially in their relation to time. López's venture seems doomed if not futile – halfway through, he abandons his painting and settles for a drawing instead. The project highlights a traditional problem of art theory: how can a painting represent the organic world when that world changes faster than the painter can paint – when quinces shrivel and fall almost as fast as paint dries? López's progress is measured against time: world events are heard on the radio news, a group of Polish builders work on López's house and various visitors drop in to interrupt. The painter Enrique Gran reminisces about his and López's shared past, and speculates on the need to work faster with age, to catch up with lost time. But is it wiser to produce more work or, as López does, to work more intensely on a single demanding project?

The question is pertinent to Erice's own career. One of the least prolific of prominent European directors, the former film critic has made only three features, the first two being *The Spirit of the Beehive* (*El Espîritu de la Colmena*, 1973), a highly acclaimed dream-like evocation of childhood after the Spanish Civil War; and the ostensibly more conventional family drama *El Sur* (*The South*, 1983). Erice clearly shares López's perfectionism and aversion to compromise; the 137-minute film expanded much like López's painting, having started as a television short. *The Quince Tree Sun* becomes a self-reflexive essay on Erice's own artistic preoccupations; dispelling the documentary illusion, his camera appears at the end.

López's methods remind us that the film's seemingly detached observation is in reality more complex and hard-won: what appears to be documentary is highly staged and scrupulously framed. A clue to the film's ambivalent position towards its subject is the fact that López's wife María Moreno – herself a painter, seen pursuing her own work throughout – was also the film's executive producer.

Erice's inquiry into perception and artistic performance is always inflected by the resounding question of mortality. The open-ended conclusion implies renewal – by spring, last year's quinces are rotten on the ground while new ones are budding, which means that López can start his work all over again. In the meantime, at the beginning of the new millennium, we are still waiting for Erice's next move.

Writers
Victor Erice and
Antonio López

Producers
Carmen Martínez and
Maria Moreno

Cinematographers
Javier Aguirresarobe and
Angel Luis Fernández

Production company
Maria Moreno PC

Music
Pascal Gaigne

Cast
Antonio López
Enrique Gran
Maria Moreno
José Carretero

Other films
★ *The Spirit of the Beehive* (1973)
★ *El Sur* (1983)

*Antonio López studies the quince tree that
becomes the subject of his painting.*

Trois couleurs: rouge
Three Colours: Red

Krzysztof Kieślowski *1994*

Director
Krzysztof Kieślowski

Writers
Krzysztof Kieślowski and
Krzysztof Piesiewicz

Producers
Yvon Crenn and
Martin Karmitz

Cinematographer
Piotr Sobocinski

Production companies
CAB Productions, France 3
Cinéma, Le Studio Canal+,
MKZ Productions, Tor
Production and Télévision
Suisse–Romande

Cast
Irène Jacob
Jean-Louis Trintignant
Frédérique Feder
Jean-Pierre Lorit
Samuel le Bihan
Juliette Binoche
Julie Delpy

Other films
★ *Camera Buff* (1979)
★ *Blind Chance* (1981)
★ *No End* (1984)
★ *Dekalog* (1988)
★ *A Short Film About Killing*
(1988)
★ *The Double Life of
Véronique* (1991)
★ *Three Colours: Blue*
(1993)
★ *Three Colours: White*
(1994)

In Cannes in 1994, when *Three Colours: Red* was passed over for the Palme d'Or in favour of Tarantino's *Pulp Fiction* (*see pages 142–143*), it seemed like a symbolic victory for American pop culture and a downturn in the fortunes of European art film. That may have been a panic judgement, however; besides, Tarantino's and Kieślowski's rhetorics are not really that far apart. Both *Pulp Fiction* and the *Three Colours* trilogy (1993–94, the first two films being *Blue* and *White*) are tripartite narratives that intersect in unexpected ways, obliging viewers to form their own conclusions about chance, destiny and authorial string-pulling.

Furthermore, both *Pulp Fiction* and *Red* are crammed with attention-catching tricks. Consider the opening sequence of *Red*: the camera follows a phone call down the wires from England, through the telephone system, right underneath the Channel, to the engaged signal in Switzerland and back to source. If this is not a meta-fictional flourish outdoing Tarantino at his flashiest, nothing is.

Kieślowski is renowned both as a realist (he frequently confessed his adulation of Ken Loach) and a moralist, picking at ethical questions with entomological finesse in his *Dekalog* series (1988). But *The Double Life of Véronique* (*La Double vie de Véronique*, 1991) showed him to be a skilled contriver of baroque narratives that wove around parallel events and possibilities, as had 1981's *Blind Chance* (*Przypadek*), with three alternative destinies branching off from the same moment. *Red* makes its preoccupations explicit through an imperfectly omniscient deity figure, the embittered judge eavesdropping on the world by radio.

This is the closing chapter of a trilogy at face value based on the colours of the French flag and the themes of liberty, equality and fraternity. But *Red* suggests that the colour coding is as much an arbitrary starting point as a thematic necessity. *Red* is obsessively foregrounded; in other words, the universe is scoured of any other colour that would detract from the pattern. This is not any kind of real world, but a hermetic zone constructed entirely for the purpose of the demonstration.

We might feel sceptical at Kieślowski's ruthlessness in handling all the strands of his tale, so that they lead to the judge's redemption and also to Valentine's encounter (or near-encounter) with Auguste, who might be her dream partner. Kieślowski gives us a gratifying but entirely implausible convergence of the trilogy's main narratives in the setting of a cross-Channel ferry disaster. It may not be that implausible, however, if we read the story backwards, as *Blind Chance* in reverse, various pasts forking out from a single ending.

'I feel something important is happening around me', says Valentine at one point, and perhaps Kieślowski asks too much in expecting us to believe that the world's fate should revolve around Irène Jacob's luminous innocent. But *Red* does convince us with its sheer confidence – if not as a comprehensive existential statement then as a feat of self-reflexive fictional mastery. Kieślowski, who died of a heart attack in 1996, left behind a reputation as Europe's last high-minded mystic, but I have chosen *Red* because it suggests something else – an exceptionally playful manipulator of narratives and ideas, and a creator of hauntingly resonant (and sometimes brazenly significant) images.

Irène Jacob (right) in a composition that highlights Kieślowski's 'obsessive foregrounding' of the eponymous colour.

Latcho Drom Tony Gatlif *1993*

Director and writer
Tony Gatlif

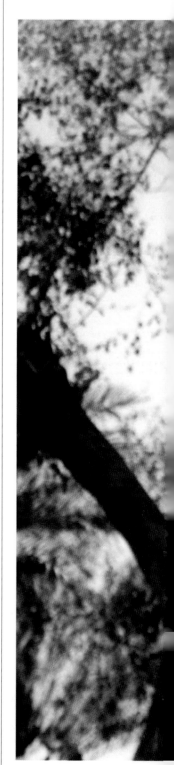

The term 'world cinema', once used as a synonym for the art-house repertoire, is not much used these days; but *Latcho Drom* in itself embodies a world cinema of a different sort, parallel to that fluid marketing category known as 'world music'. Not only is French-based, Algerian-born Gypsy filmmaker Tony Gatlif genuinely a citizen of world cinema, he is also the only prominent practitioner (so far) of Gypsy cinema.

A former actor, Gatlif made his name with *Les Princes* in 1983 and became most prominent with 1997's Romanian-set *Gadjo Dilo* (*The Crazy Stranger*). But his most ambitious work is the category-defying *Latcho Drom*, filmed in several countries, with an almost entirely Gypsy cast, and with song replacing dialogue. Ostensibly a European film, it is really one that, as Jonathan Rosenbaum put it, 'has no nationality at all'. It has no fixed genre either, but is at once musical, documentary, travelogue, ethnographic essay and manifesto for a freer cinema and a freer life.

An impressionistic picture of the migrations of the Gypsy peoples and their music through history and geography, *Latcho Drom* is constructed as a series of musical sequences, beginning with a wedding party in Rajasthan and ending with a hillside lament in Spain. It has no characters but countless briefly encountered members of rural or urban crowds; the central protagonist is the protean Gypsy nation itself. The film is conceived as a single staggered journey from east to west: the revellers in Rajasthan appear to evolve into Egyptian villagers, into a family on a ferry to Istanbul, then into a band waiting for a train in Hungary. The Rajasthan sequence, lit by fires burning in tree trunks, is presented like a recollection of an Edenic past. But from then on we understand that, however buoyant the music, it is always a response to grief and exclusion. An old woman walks across a snowy landscape in Slovakia, singing about the Gypsy victims of the Holocaust. The Romanian band Taraf de Haïdouks sing about Ceausescu's crimes. For every musical utopia there is a cataclysm – the climactic flamenco sequence is followed by a sequence of evictions. The film ends with a woman singing on a Spanish hillside, overlooking an urban landscape as barren as, but less hospitable than, the Asian deserts where we began.

Throughout this panorama of diversity, Gatlif is also seeking a unity in the Gypsy diaspora. His film can be seen as a history lesson, a sketch of a tradition that is so misunderstood because it is so diverse and because it stands outside the historical mainstream. It could be argued that *Latcho Drom* is romantic and impressionistic, that it offers no commentary or analysis of the Gypsies' persecution, simply presenting their culture as an ever-changing eternal spirit. Yet for a film that barely deals in the spoken word, *Latcho Drom* conveys a very concrete sense of historical reality. The fact that the film exists at all, flouting genres and frontiers, is of no small political importance. Its title means 'safe journey', and this is, you could say, the ultimate road movie.

Producer
Michèle Ray-Gavras

Cinematographer
Eric Guichard

Editor
Nicole Berckmans

Art director
Denis Mercier

Other films
★ *Les Princes* (1983)
★ *Pleure pas My Love* (1989)
★ *Mondo* (1996)
★ *Gadjo Dilo* (1997)
★ *Vengo* (2000)

'The central protagonist is the protean Gypsy nation itself': two of Gatlif's young actors.

Take Care of Your Scarf, Tatjana
Pidä Huivista Kiinni, Tatjana

Aki Kaurismäki *1994*

Director, producer and editor
Aki Kaurismäki

The career of Finland's Aki Kaurismäki sometimes seems like a poker-faced joke not to be taken seriously, least of all by the director himself. At first sight, his films divide into two registers: facetious comedies, like his features with the extravagantly quiffed novelty band Leningrad Cowboys, and doleful vignettes of proletarian gloom, such as *The Match Factory Girl* (*Tulitikkutehtaan Tytto*, 1990), which, if misread, resemble self-parodic Scandinavian glumness. In fact, Kaurismäki's career has been a dazzlingly sure-footed balancing act between seemingly incompatible tones, and his most daring work miraculously reconciles the two.

As well as being (together with filmmaker brother Mika) an entrepreneur, distributor and convivial host at Lapland's annual Midnight Sun Festival, Kaurismäki is a passionate cinephile, perhaps as much as any filmmaker since the New Wave. His work shows his commitment to the European art tradition as well as to the Hollywood B-movie, together with his passion for cheap vintage rock 'n' roll (and, more recently, for Finland's impeccably stately tango).

Despite his image as a pessimist, Kaurismäki has developed his own ambivalent form of feel-good cinema, notably in *Drifting Clouds* (*Kauas Pilvet Karkaavat*, 1996), a semi-realist narrative about an unemployed couple who open their own restaurant (imagine what an emotional blow-out a British or American director would have made of that, and compare Kaurismäki's straight-faced restraint). But his most distinctive film is the 1960s-set *Take Care of Your Scarf, Tatjana* – at once road picture, buddy movie and rocking nostalgia fantasy, a kind of *Finnish Graffiti*.

Heroes Reino and Valto are a skinny car mechanic and a hulking tailor who take to the road with a soundtrack of Finnish garage rock, and fuelled by their respective addictions, vodka and coffee. En route, they pick up two young Soviet women bound for Tallinn, and conspicuously fail – initially at least – to form any rapport with them. By the time we reach the tenderly comic payoff – involving an outrageous fake ending – Kaurismäki has made us feel real fondness for these shambling, dreaming buffoons.

Considering how little is said, the film is remarkably eloquent about Finnish–Soviet relations, men's incapacity to express emotions, the European fixation with American pop culture and the difficulties of being a rocker with a 'ruin' of a wallet – as one of the film's running jokes puts it. Several of Kaurismäki's regular repertory players appear, notably the willowy, whey-faced Kati Outinen (star of Kaurismäki's *The Match Factory Girl*, 1990) as Tatjana and the late Matti Pellonpää, a sorrowful comic player with a uniquely twitchy drowned-rat demeanour.

The film's distinctively strange tone comes from its placing ludicrous sitcom-style characters in the most artfully photographed settings: idyllic open landscapes by day, cheap hotel rooms and desolate retro bars by night, shot by Timo Salminen with the chiaroscuro of 1950s *film noir*. Kaurismäki may be the consummate post-modern nostalgist, but he is a very compassionate one, who wants to coax us towards real love for his characters. Against all the odds, *Tatjana* lifts the spirits wonderfully – and, thanks to revivalist garage bands the Regals and the Renegades, it rocks too. The English print also features surely the most eloquent subtitle in cinema (although what the original Finnish means heaven knows) – 'Move your ass, said Johnny Cash.'

FILM: THE CRITICS' CHOICE *Europe: A New Fin de siècle*

Writers
Aki Kaurismäki and
Sakke Järvenpää

Cinematographer
Timo Salminen

Production company
Pandora Film Sputnik

Music
Veikko Tuomi

Cast
Kati Outinen
Matti Pellonpää
Kirsi Tykkläinen
Mato Valtonen
Elina Salo

Other films
★ *Ariel* (1988)
★ *Leningrad Cowboys go America* (1989)
★ *The Match Factory Girl* (1990)
★ *I Hired a Contract Killer* (1990)
★ *Drifting Clouds* (1996)

Kirsi Tykkläinen, Matti Pellonpää, Mato Valtonen and Kati Outinen (left to right) as the comic foursome.

Tierra
Earth

Julio Medem *1995*

It remains a mystery that Julio Medem is not yet a major cult star of European cinema. As much as anyone else in contemporary film, Medem has pursued his own preoccupations and developed a vision that relates to the real world yet is radically detached from it. It may be that entirely fabulist cinema is unfashionable in the art sector, although Medem can more than hold his own with, say, David Lynch. Another problem may be a persistent machismo that cannot always be taken with a pinch of salt.

A former film critic, Medem is very much a Basque director despite working in Spanish. His first film *Vacas* (*Cows*, 1992) explored cultural and dynastic myths through a magic-realist perspective; *The Red Squirrel* (*La Ardilla Roja*, 1993), a trick-box of fragmented narrative, featured some wry joking about pop-video recycling of folkloric imagery; Lovers of the Arctic Circle (*Los Amantes del Circulo Polar*, 1999) took his taste for coincidence to a geometrical extreme.

Medem specializes in the narrative equivalent of optical illusion – in temporal dislocations, wild coincidence and mathematical symmetry taken to an extreme. His most extravagant film is his third, the genre-defying *Tierra*, which could be described as a science-fiction rural romance with elements of the Western (unless, of course, it is a wholly imagined study of dysfunctional psychology). Its hero is half-dead, half-alive or alternatively a radically split personality, who arrives – apparently from space – in an unidentified red landscape on a crop-dusting mission to eradicate woodlice.

Set in a non-place that is not recognizably Basque (although some of the names in the film are), *Tierra* pushes its symbols and parallelisms to a parodic limit. Not only is the hero apparently an angel, he is actually called Angel; his seemingly predestined romantic partner is called Angela, but then so is her daughter; and there is more than one man called Angel in this story. Angel is schematically caught between the 'angelic' blonde woman and the 'demonic' red-headed sexpot Mari; but the stability of this arrangement is quickly turned on its head. (For Spanish audiences, the casting also plays with the reassuring familiarity of the innocent-looking Emma Suárez as Angela, a repertory regular in Medem's first three films, along with Carmelo Gómez and Nancho Novo.)

The visual style of *Tierra* is entirely unique, even viewed alongside Medem's other work. It is dominated by the contrast of red earth and blue sky, its landscape as oppressively artificial as the industrial setting of Antonioni's *The Red Desert* (*Il Deserto Rosso*, 1964). The world's dimensions are destabilized by violent changes of scale: the film begins in the stratosphere and then scales down alarmingly to a woodlouse seen in extreme close-up.

The set-pieces are extravagant: a line of white-suited fumigators, resembling astronauts, turns the film into sci-fi. Elsewhere, visual effects explode realism entirely: Angel's split persona allows him to be in two places at once, or to appear twice, as hero and alter ego, in a single shot.

Medem always risks overplaying his hand and having the whole edifice topple down on itself; he finally seems all the more lawless because he binds himself in with metaphors, systems and symmetries and forces himself to break out of them. *Tierra* lives up to its central paradox – here is a film at once earthbound and genuinely extraterrestrial.

Director and writer
Julio Medem

Producer
Lola Pérez

Cinematographer
Javier Aguirresarobe

Editor
Ivan Aledo

Music
Alberto Iglesias

Production companies
Lola Films, Sociedad General de Television and Sogetel

Cast
Carmelo Gómez
Emma Suárez
Nancho Novo
Silke
Karra Elejalde

Other films
★ *Vacas* (1992)
★ *The Red Squirrel* (1993)
★ *Lovers of the Arctic Circle* (1998)

241

Beau Travail Claire Denis *1999*

Director
Claire Denis

Claire Denis' eighth feature was released just in time for critics on both sides of the Atlantic to acclaim it as the last great film of the 20th century. Since her first feature *Chocolat* (1988), inspired by her childhood in Africa, Denis has been one of the most intelligent, adventurous and under-rated of French directors. A former assistant to Wim Wenders, Jacques Rivette, Jim Jarmusch and others, Denis has consistently returned in her own films to investigations of sex, race and the French post-colonial legacy; *Beau Travail* is at once a concrete and a daringly abstract interpretation of these themes.

Set in the present day, in a French Foreign Legion outpost in Djibouti, *Beau Travail* is inspired by Herman Melville's story *Billy Budd* (published posthumously in 1924), about a sailor martyred for the jealousy he arouses in his superior officer. Denis' version belongs to the officer, here renamed Galoup; it begins with him exiled in Marseille, recounting the events that led to his being drummed out of the Legion. His tragedy really is a fall from Eden; bleak as the Djibouti camp is, it is where he belongs. Acting as a fondly fierce watchdog to his men, he serves a distant, fatigued commander, Bruno Forestier, played by Michel Subor, who was a character of the same name in Jean-Luc Godard's *Le Petit soldat* (1960). The minute ritual of Foreign Legion discipline is a key motif.

On one level, Galoup's lost idyll seems straightforwardly homoerotic – a spartan utopia in which muscular, shaven-headed young men execute elegantly brutal manoeuvres under the sun. In these sequences, the narrative fractures into abstract dance (Denis worked closely with a choreographer, Bernardo Montet). On another level, the legionnaires' world is aggressively heterosexual; in a nightclub, they engage in wary flirtation with African women dancing to Islamic-influenced disco. But they are as much separated from the women by their maleness as they are from Africa by their colonial position. Arguably, the film's predominant theme is military authority and the mixture of solitude and servitude that it entails. The minute ritual of discipline is a key motif: no film ever showed ironing performed with such punctiliousness.

Rather than tell a linear story, Denis opts for a poetic structure, presenting a succession of discrete moments and images – a salt-bleached ram's skull, a burst of blood in green water – for us to connect into an overall pattern. Photographer Agnès Godard has a flawless eye for the placement of bodies in the desert landscape, and Denis matches her images with an eclectic choice of music, using extracts from Benhamin Britten's opera *Billy Budd,* as well as assorted dance tracks, Legion chants, and even a Neil Young number.

The actors are used for their sculptural presence: Grégoire Colin's recruit isolated against a blue sky, Subor's languid basilisk features seemingly calcified by legion life. Galoup is played by Denis Lavant, the commandingly weather-beaten lead of Leos Carax's first three features. Here older and craggier, with the tortured troglodyte physique of an Egon Schiele portrait, Lavant has a galvanizing energy. He stores up his tensions as if in an emotional battery, then releases them in the final scene, dancing a convulsive solo as if shaking the demons out of his body. Set to a rivetingly brainless piece of Euro-disco, this moment is one of the marvels of recent cinema.

242

Writers
Claire Denis and
Jean-Paul Fargeau

Producers
Jerome Minet and
Patrick Grandperret

Cinematographer
Agnès Godard

Editor
Nelly Quettier

Production companies
La Sept-Arte, SM Films
and Tanaïs

Cast
Denis Lavant
Michel Subor

Grégoire Colin
Marta Jafesse Kassa
Richard Courcet

Other films
★ *Chocolat* (1988)
★ *S'en fout la mort* (1990)
★ *J'ai pas sommeil* (1993)
★ *US Go Home* (1994)
★ *Nénette et Boni* (1996)

'A spartan utopia in which muscular, shaven-headed young men execute elegantly brutal manoeuvres under the sun.'

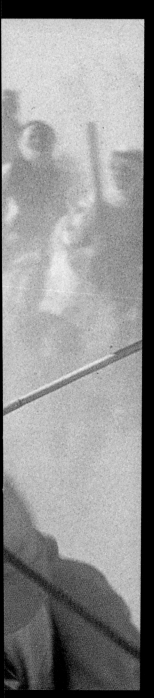

CHAPTER EIGHT

British Cinema
Peter Wollen

British cinema suffers disproportionately from the scourge of American competition. Its film-goers, actors and actresses speak the same language as those of the United States, and the British market has been dominated by American films from its earliest years. Hollywood not only enjoyed much greater resources than the British industry could ever hope for, but talent, especially writers and directors, was attracted to California, thereby draining the energy away from Britain. Hollywood cinema already dominated during the 1920s, when leading British filmmakers – including Alfred Hitchcock – began their careers working for American studios based in London.

American hegemony was first challenged by the success of Alexander Korda's *The Private Life of Henry VIII* (1933), but Korda proved unable to repeat his triumph. Hollywood simply appropriated the formula and made its own film of *The Private Lives of Elizabeth and Essex* (1939). Between 1935 and 1940, following Korda's success, Hollywood made two Shakespeare films, two Dickens films, plus versions of *Wuthering Heights*, *Vanity Fair*, *Treasure Island*, *The Barretts of Wimpole Street*, *The Adventures of Sherlock Holmes*, *Tom Brown's Schooldays*, *Peter Ibbetson* and four Kipling stories (*Wee Willie Winkie*, *Captains Courageous*, *Gunga Din* and *The Light That Failed*). These were the glory years of the Hollywood Cricket Club, when Aubrey Smith, film actor and team captain, was able to send Dr Watson (Nigel Bruce) and Dr Frankenstein (Boris Karloff, né Pratt) out to bat on the playing fields of Los Angeles.

The Britishness of British film was re-established during the war years, when the industry was called upon to sustain morale and unite the nation. At first, this produced a documentary-driven ideology of 'realism' rather than 'tinsel', in the words of producer Michael Balcon, but eventually a new romanticism carried the day, contrary to the supposed instincts of British film-goers. Filmmakers like David Lean, Michael

Powell and Carol Reed dominated post-war British cinema with melodramas like *Brief Encounter* (1945), Technicolor tours de force like *The Red Shoes* (1948) and sinister *films noir* like *The Third Man* (1949). During this golden period, British cinema was both promoted and protected by the post-war Labour government, but relentless competitive pressure from the the Americans eventually suppressed the British initiative.

Despite the farcical nature of their storylines, the Ealing comedies of the 1950s adopted a realistic style and were set in a realistic milieu. In some ways they prefigured the rise of the Angry Young Men, committed filmmakers whose careers began with a documentary revival and were eventually overtaken by the impact of the European New Wave and sixties Pop Art. Films by Joseph Losey and Richard Lester, influenced by the new cinema of Bergman, Godard and Antonioni, laid the foundation for films like *Performance* (1970) and, eventually, the belated appearance in the 1980s of a British 'art cinema', spearheaded by Peter Greenaway and Derek Jarman – two very different filmmakers, who had in common backgrounds as painters. The notable films of the late 20th century played to the British film industry's strengths in independent and niche filmmaking, and looking to the future, it should further develop these strengths.

The Private Life of Henry VIII

Alexander Korda *1933*

Alexander Korda's *The Private Life of Henry VIII* was a breakthrough for British cinema, establishing for the first time that a British film could enjoy both critical and commercial success in the United States. Its producer–director, Alexander Korda, had begun his film career in Hungary, but after being forced to flee the country in 1919, he worked in Vienna and Berlin, making a series of films starring his first wife, Maria. In 1927 he was invited to Hollywood, where he made the first of three 'Private Life' films. Tired of Los Angeles after only three years, he returned to Europe, first to France and then to England, where he established himself as a director, a producer and the creator of Pinewood Studios.

There are several versions of how Korda came up with the idea of a film about Henry VIII. According to one legend, he was inspired by hearing a cab driver singing the old music-hall song, 'I'm 'enry the Eighth, I Am, I Am'. Some say Korda had a brainstorm when Charles Laughton told him that he was hoping to play the lead role in Shakespeare's *Henry VIII* at the Old Vic in London, or when Laughton's agent spotted a statuette of Henry VIII in Korda's office and commented on its likeness to Laughton. Alternatively it is possible that Korda dreamed up the idea because he wanted to work with Laughton and realized that he could enrol Laughton's wife, Elsa Lanchester, as a go-between, offering her a part as Anne of Cleves and enlisting her to persuade Laughton he should agree to make the film.

Henry VIII is a biopic and, like Korda's other biopics about royalty, it is basically about sex. It falls into the same category as the romantic comedies he had made with his wife Maria as star – *The Private Life of Helen of Troy* (1927), for instance. Laughton's Henry is far from the typical biopic hero, who offers us a moral example, pursues meritorious goals, overcomes obstacles, meets challenges and wins our well-deserved respect. Rather, he is a larger-than-life anti-hero, in turn buffoonish, pathetic, ill-tempered and charming, entertaining and appalling us, while our emotional sympathies go to the parade of doomed wives. Yet this portrait of Henry displays a childish enthusiasm and charm, which somehow persuades us not only to like him, but even to forgive his excesses.

Laughton, as always, took his part extremely seriously. He based his characterization on Holbein's famous portrait of Henry VIII, from which, as Elsa Lanchester noted, 'he created a character of almost Rabelaisian mirth, with giant strokes and a boldness that would jolt the audience out of their seats.' He also read about Henry voraciously and spent hours walking around the old Tudor palace at Hampton Court, getting his mind 'accustomed to the square, squat architecture of the rooms and the cloisters. I think it was from the architecture of the house and the rooms that I got my idea of Henry' – an idea that captivated audiences and gave British film a new international standing.

Director
Alexander Korda

Writers
Arthur Wimperis
and Lajos Biro

Producers
Alexander Korda and
Ludovico Toeplitz

Cinematographers
Georges Périnal and
Osmond Borradaile

Production company
London Film Productions

Cast
Charles Laughton
Binnie Barnes
Robert Donat
Elsa Lanchester
Merle Oberon
Wendy Barrie

Other films
★ *Marius* (1931)
★ *The Private Life of Don Juan* (1934)
★ *Rembrandt* (1936)
★ *That Hamilton Woman* (1941)
★ *An Ideal Husband* (1947)

Academy Awards
Winner of Best Actor Oscar (Charles Laughton) and nominated for Best Picture, 1934

The 39 Steps

Alfred Hitchcock *1935*

Alfred Hitchcock was undoubtedly Britain's most outstanding director, operating in the British industry from 1919, when he went to work for Famous Players Lasky (later to become Paramount) after they opened a studio in London. He made more than 20 films in the UK before leaving for Los Angeles in 1940. Even then he frequently came back to work in London, directing the penultimate film of his career, *Frenzy*, in the city in 1971. In the United States his films retained many traces of his British origins, drawn, as they often were, from British plays, stories or novels: *Rebecca* (1940), *Suspicion* (1941), *The Paradine Case* (1947), *Rope* (1948), *Under Capricorn* (1949), *Stage Fright* (1950), *Dial M for Murder* (1953), *The Trouble With Harry* (1955), *The Man Who Knew Too Much* (1955), *The Birds* (1963), *Marnie* (1964), *Topaz* (1969) and *Frenzy* (1972) were either made in the UK or transposed from a British to an American context.

Among the films that Hitchcock made before he left Britain for Hollywood, *The 39 Steps* stands out as by far the most significant and influential. Among other things, it provided the definitive model for a series of suspenseful chase films which culminated in *North By Northwest* (1959). As a young man, Hitchcock had read the famous novel of the same name by the Scottish author John Buchan and, in 1935, he decided to develop Buchan's old-style adventure story into a screenplay, working alongside Charles Bennett, a playwright whom he had known for some years. Bennett, however, was somewhat less impressed by Buchan's novel than Hitchcock was, and was determined to show that he could improve upon the original. 'I thought the Buchan novel was terrible', Bennett said, 'but it had possibilities – the double chase, for example.'

Although most of the characters are constantly on the move throughout the film, it manages to present a tight narrative structure. The timeframe is scheduled to last just four full days, but during this short period Hitchcock playfully expands and contracts our sense of time through his masterful use of devices such as suspense, mystery and shock. Suspense is generated by the audience's foreknowledge of impending threats, of which the protagonist in the film may be unaware. Shock and surprise are caused by a sudden intrusion of the unexpected, an event or a release of information that had hitherto been held back. Mystery derives from the uncertainty as to why things happened or what might happen next. Hitchcock consciously structured his films with these principles of mind.

The perverse and erotic subtext of the film – which sees Hannay literally handcuffed to Pamela, a woman who has previously rebuffed him – is treated superficially as a source of humorous incidents and interactions, but it also carries a symbolic and fetishistic charge. At the same time, as in other Hitchcock films, the hero constantly changes his identity or, at least, his apparent identity, in a cascade of theatrical contrivance. On the first day he poses as a milkman, on the second day as a motor mechanic, on the third day as a Salvation Army marcher, politician and wanted murderer, and on the fourth day, as an eloping newly-wed – Mr Henry Hopkinson of the Hollyhocks, Hammersmith. In these ways, Hitchcock established the blueprint he followed for the remainder of his career, a carefully calibrated mixture of thriller, romance and comedy.

Director
Alfred Hitchcock

Writers
Charles Bennett, Ian Hay and Alma Reville, from the novel by John Buchan

Producer
Michael Balcon

Cinematographer
Bernard Knowles

Editor
Derek Twist

Production companies
Gaumont International, Gaumont-British Picture Corporation

Cast
Robert Donat
Madeleine Carroll
Godfrey Tearle
Lucie Mannheim
Peggy Ashcroft
John Laurie

Other films
★ *The Lady Vanishes* (1938)
★ *Rebecca* (1940)
★ *Notorious* (1946)
★ *Strangers on a Train* (1951)
★ *Dial M for Murder* (1954)
★ *Rear Window* (1954)
★ *Vertigo* (1958)
★ *North by Northwest* (1959)
★ *Psycho* (1960)
★ *The Birds* (1963)
★ *Marnie* (1964)

Madeleine Carroll and Robert Donat, handcuffed together in a typically Hitchcockian plot device.

Brief Encounter

David Lean *1945*

Director
David Lean

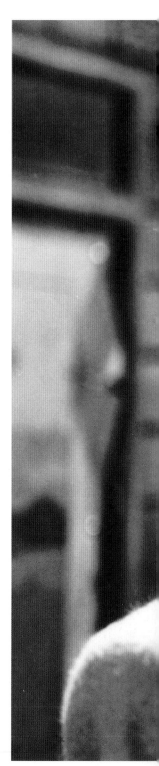

Brief Encounter was the fourth of a series of films directed by David Lean in the early 1940s, all made in collaboration with Noël Coward. The same producer and editor also worked on all four films. Thus the team that made *Brief Encounter* was a tightly knit group with considerable experience of working together. Lean began his career as a runner-cum-teaboy in 1926, graduating to camera assistant and then to editor, before he finally established himself as director through the partnership with Coward. In 1945, Coward advised Lean to give up his dream of making a film about Mary, Queen of Scots, pointing out that he had no experience in costume drama – 'Stick to the contemporary scene. Stick to what you know. Don't be foolish. Here, I'll tell you what, I've got this sketch, have a go at that. I'll write you a script very quickly.'

The sketch in question, *Still Life*, had been written by Coward as a play with just five short scenes, all set in the refreshment room at Milford Junction Station. The film tells the same story of the secret love affair of a middle-class couple, both of them married, but it opens the action out so that their romance takes place, furtively and in flashback, in a series of different locations – the Kardomah Cafe, the Palladium Cinema, a boating lake in Milford's town park. The turning-point comes when Alec borrows a friend's flat for a tryst with Laura, only for the romantic interlude to be interrupted by the owner's unexpected return. Panic-stricken, Laura flees and roams the streets filled with guilt and horror. 'I walked away – trying to look casual – knowing that he was watching me. I felt like a criminal.' In this abyss of shame was a fear of scandal and arrest and a coded metaphor, perhaps, for homosexual love. Soon afterwards, realizing the romance is finished, Alec leaves for Johannesburg and Laura returns to a forgiving husband.

Laura Jesson's voice-over, spoken by Celia Johnson, performs the function of linking the separate scenes into a coherent narrative, but it also gives us access to Laura's own emotional response to events – her happiness and despair, hope and remorse. In effect, Johnson plays three characters: suburban wife and mother; woman in love, full of hope and romantic excitement, but subject to terrible tremors of guilt and shame; and introspective historian, analysing the story of her own romance, coming to terms with it and reflecting upon it with the benefit of hindsight. If the film has a happy ending, it is because of her ability to carry through this painful process of self-analysis. A more romantic interpretation of the film would view the ending as a defeat, as she relapsed into the humdrum life from which she was temporarily released by her passionate, yet chaste, love affair. Back home with her family, her voice sounds dead. She is stuck in middle England, trapped in a brilliantly yet painfully evoked middle-class culture.

Writers
Noël Coward, David Lean
and Anthony Havelock Allan

Producer
Noël Coward

Cinematographer
Robert Krasker

Production company
Cineguild

Cast
Celia Johnson
Trevor Howard
Stanley Holloway
Joyce Carey
Cyril Raymond
Valentine Dyall

Other films
★ *Great Expectations* (1946)
★ *Hobson's Choice* (1954)
★ *Bridge on the River Kwai* (1957)
★ *Lawrence of Arabia* (1962)
★ *Doctor Zhivago* (1965)
★ *Ryan's Daughter* (1970)
★ *A Passage to India* (1984)

Celia Johnson and Trevor Howard as the buttoned-up lovers in this portrait of a thoroughly English affair.

They Made Me A Fugitive

Alberto Cavalcanti *1947*

At the end of World War II, a series of films were made in Britain which have since been called 'British *noir*' or the 'spiv cycle'. This cycle reflected a mutation in the crime film in response to changing patterns of crime that emerged during the war. Controls, rationing and rising prices led to the growth of a black market, operated by a new class of criminals known as 'spivs'. The spiv symbolized a flashy flaunting of authority and petty regulations, attractive as the war ended and people tired of self-denial and wartime restrictions. *They Made Me A Fugitive* was, I believe, the best of the spiv pictures. Like the others, it stripped the glamour from the world of crime and black-marketeering, but it also had a suspenseful man-on-the-run theme. The film's hero, Morgan, played by Trevor Howard, is a black-marketeer framed for the murder of a policeman by his boss, Narcissus, known as Narcy, and sent to jail on Dartmoor. Narcy is a sadistic racketeer whose headquarters are in an East End funeral parlour. Villainy is treated with dark humour: black-market goods (cigarettes, whisky, New Zealand lamb) are transported in coffins accompanied by mourners in full regalia. The name Narcy, of course, suggests 'nasty', 'nark', 'narcotics' – and Narcy indeed has a line in what he calls 'sherbet'.

Eventually Morgan escapes but is framed for yet another murder, this time by a blind woman who befriended him and gave him a change of clothes, before she killed her abusive husband and blamed it on Morgan, whom she dressed in the dead man's suit. Now he is hunted both by the police and by Narcy, who needs to eliminate him to save his own skin. Thus in this film there are two spiv characters – the vicious Narcy and the vulnerable Morgan, an escapee from the underworld, wrongfully accused and hunted, a man who realized too late that Narcy was not just supplying black-market goods but was the kingpin of a ruthless gang. In the end, the man on the run wins out when, after a spectacular fight in the rain on the roof of the gang's headquarters, Narcy falls to his death in the street below.

Cavalcanti himself was a fascinating director. Brazilian by birth, he first attracted attention while living in Paris and working as a set designer. He went on to make the highly regarded avant-garde film, *Rien que les heures* (1926). In the 1930s he moved to London where he played a leading role in the British documentary movement, as a production supervisor and filmmaker, before moving into the commercial cinema in the 1940s and directing a series of successful feature films, culminating with *Nicholas Nickleby* (1947). Eventually he returned to his native Brazil to pursue a further career in cinema and television. Cavalcanti had a significant impact on filmmaking in three countries – France, Britain and Brazil – but *They Made Me A Fugitive* was the best of many extraordinary films.

Director
Alberto Cavalcanti

Writer
Noel Langley

Producers
Nat A. Bronstein and
James A. Carter

Cinematographer
Otto Heller

Music
Marius-François Gaillard

Cast
Trevor Howard
Sally Gray
Griffith Jones
René Ray
Mary Merrall

Other films
★ *Rien que les heures* (1926)
★ *Nicholas Nickleby* (1947)

Trevor Howard, the honourable spiv, and Sally Gray in a prime piece of British noir.

The Red Shoes

Michael Powell and Emeric Pressburger *1948*

The Red Shoes, in this critic's opinion, is the best film ever made in the UK. It took many years, however, for the project to be realized. Emeric Pressburger wrote his first version of the script in 1937, but the film was not made until 1948, by which time Powell and Pressburger were at the peak of their careers. *The Red Shoes* could almost be characterized as a backstage musical, but it is much, much more than that. It is a tragic love story. It is a demonstration of how colour – specifically Technicolor – could be used artistically in the cinema, as the cinematographer became an artist, a partner with the designer in creating a work of amazing beauty. It realizes Michael Powell's dream of the 'composed' film, the synthesis in one work of many different arts: a film in which screenplay, camerawork, design, musical score, choreography and performance are equal partners in a single creative projective.

The screenplay is based on a story by Danish fabulist Hans Christian Andersen about the fatal power of art – the tale of a dancer who cannot stop dancing once the dancing shoes are upon her feet. *The Red Shoes* presents a ballet within a film, framed by the story of the dancer's life, as her passion leads inexorably towards her death. Finally, as if mesmerized, she dances off the stage, down a spiral staircase, across an esplanade and then, in a final leap, rises high into the air and falls to a self-inflicted death on the railway track below. It is one of the most melodramatic sequences in the history of film, the tragic conclusion of a fateful conflict between love and marriage on the one hand, and the magnetic power of dance and art on the other. True art, Michael Powell has maintained, is something worth dying for, and in *The Red Shoes* this romantic claim is fully illustrated, without compromise or hedging.

The Red Shoes is a work of great technical complexity. Powell himself stressed the importance not only of Moira Shearer's performance as dancer, but also of the ways in which the rhythm and emotion of the dance were enhanced by co-operation between the choreographer Massine, the designer Hein Heckroth, and the cinematographer Jack Cardiff. Each were concerned with the timing, rhythm and choreography of the moving camera, which becomes Shearer's partner in the dance. Heckroth story-boarded the film and worked with Massine to transform his sketches into choreographed sequences; Powell and Pressburger assembled what must be the most extraordinary creative team ever brought together in a studio. Their film is inspired by Diaghilev's Ballet Russe, and reflects the tyrannical hold Diaghilev exerted over his greatest dancer, Nijinsky. In *The Red Shoes*, Anton Walbrook gives a mesmerizing performance as Lermontov, the film's Diaghilev, and the dances are choreographed by Massine, Diaghilev's collaborator and successor. These outstanding talents were brought together by the vision of Michael Powell and Emeric Pressburger to create an unforgettable film masterwork.

Directors, writers and producers
Michael Powell and Emeric Pressburger

Cinematographer
Jack Cardiff

Production designer
Hein Heckroth

Production companies
Independent Producers, J. Arthur Rank Films and The Archers

Cast
Moira Shearer
Anton Walbrook
Marius Goring
Leonid Massine
Albert Basserman`

Other films
★ *The Life and Death of Colonel Blimp* (1943)
★ *A Canterbury Tale* (1944)
★ *Black Narcissus* (1947)
★ *Peeping Tom* (1960)
★ *A Matter of Life and Death* (1968)

Academy Awards
Oscars for Art Direction, Set Decoration and Music; nominated for Best Picture, Best Screenplay and Editing, 1949.

The Third Man

Carol Reed *1949*

Director and producer
Carol Reed

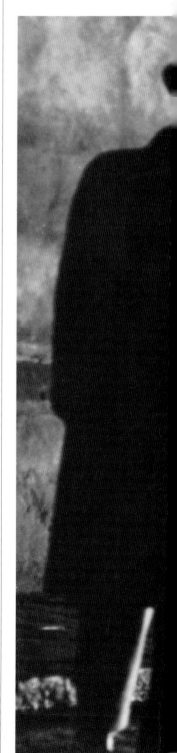

The original idea for *The Third Man* came from the producer Alexander Korda. In 1947 he handed the project to the British novelist Graham Greene, in whose hands it became a black-market story. Yet everything to do with *The Third Man* seems to point unavoidably towards the world of espionage. Greene himself was a spy during the war, working under the legendary double agent Kim Philby; and it was in Vienna (the setting for the film), a world in which you could trust nobody, that Philby himself acquired his first taste of clandestine political activity. Even the hero Holly Martins, played by Joseph Cotten, may not be trusted; he betrays his oldest and dearest friend, Harry Lime, a black-marketeer operating out of the Russian zone.

After World War II, Vienna ceased to be a cultural centre and became a frontier city – an 'invisible' frontier between East and West, as Korda suggested, but one that became more visible each day as the rubble of war was cleared away and the geopolitical lines began to harden. Greene and Reed were fascinated by the metaphoric power of the sewers, the network of underground tunnels that provided a way to avoid the frontier and to cross, unobserved, from one zone to another. The killing of Harry Lime signals an end to this fantasy of a permeable border. The frontier is closed.

In an economy that suffered from endless shortages and in which money was virtually worthless, black-marketeers provided a necessary service. Even penicillin was traded, as *The Third Man* shows heart-wrenchingly. Faulty penicillin was Lime's business, children his victims. Yet, as played by Orson Welles, the black-marketeer wins our sympathy, even when we know that he is a cynic and a monster. In *The Third Man* the monster is on the run, while his loyal friend betrays him and shoots him dead. We sympathize with the pursued monster while the pursuer, Holly Martins, is left to regret his actions, alone and unwanted, abandoned by the woman he loves and unable to stomach his treachery – treachery not to his country, but to his friend. Austria is not really anybody's country, and your friend is not really your friend.

Reed made one decision early – there would be no Strauss, no waltzes in his film. Old Vienna, the Vienna that imagined itself to be at the centre of Europe, was gone for good. Reed's Vienna is a crooked city, shot with tilted angles, in which the cobbled streets are wet and glistening: a city in which a few beams of light cut through deep darkness. Reed, a director who respected the script, envisaged Vienna as Greene did – a no-man's-land; a city on the edge in which the old values are in ruins; a city without much future, in which death beckons.

256

Writer
Graham Greene

Cinematographer
Robert Krasker

Music
Anton Karas

Production company
London Film

Cast
Joseph Cotten
Orson Welles
Alida Valli
Trevor Howard
Bernard Lee
Paul Höbiger
Ernst Deutsch
Wilfrid Hyde-White

Other films
★ *Bank Holiday* (1938)
★ *Odd Man Out* (1947)
★ *The Fallen Idol* (1948)
★ *Outcast of the Islands* (1951)

Academy Awards
Oscar for Cinematography, 1951

Holly Martins (played by Joseph Cotten, left) catches a glimpse of his quarry and old friend Harry Lime (Orson Welles) as he flees through the streets of Vienna.

The Lavender Hill Mob

Charles Crichton *1951*

Director
Charles Crichton

Ealing Studios specialized in comedies and *The Lavender Hill Mob* is one of the best – a droll, light-hearted film in which a fortune in gold bars is stolen from the Bank of England and exported in the form of tourist souvenirs. A sardonic portrait of suburban life as much as a heist film, it presents a gang of thieves, each of whom is an eccentric or misfit, unsuited to a life of crime. Our bowler-hatted hero, Mr Holland, played by Alec Guinness, is a punctual man: a fusser and worrier, whose job at the bank involves supervising bullion delivery. It has never crossed his mind that this humdrum task might open the door to a life of crime until he meets a lodger at the Balmoral Private Hotel, Lavender Hill (a London suburb). Mr Pendlebury's trade consists of selling souvenirs; as he brightly puts it, 'I'm in the "present from" trade'. His particular line of business involves casting miniature Eiffel Tower paperweights from lead. The new acquaintances reach the conclusion that their two trades – bullion delivery and souvenir casting – might be made to interlock, since gold could be shaped into Eiffel Towers as readily as lead. Who would ever suspect?

The unlikely bank robbers still need partners, men with experience of crime. Somehow they manage to lure two desperadoes from the local greyhound track and persuade them to join the plot. The story unfolds with unfaltering logic as the unlikely gang executes the nefarious plan and manages to transport the gold to France in the form of Eiffel Towers. The stage is set for an increasingly chaotic and hilarious unwinding of their scheme, triggered by a madcap race down the Eiffel Tower's exterior staircase. More chases follow, and a cascade of mishaps, until eventually the gang members are apprehended; but not before Mr Holland has managed to outwit the police and make a getaway to Rio de Janeiro – only to be tracked down and publicly arrested, to his embarrassment.

The Lavender Hill Mob was released in 1951, the year of the Festival of Britain; it fits well into the world of eccentricity and aspiration described by the Festival's Lion and Unicorn Pavilion. This was director Charles Crichton's ninth film for Ealing Studios, although it was only his third comedy (in 1988 he returned to direct another internationally successful comedy, *A Fish Called Wanda*). The script was by T. B. E. Clarke, whose credits include *Hue And Cry* (1947), *Passport To Pimlico* (1949) and *The Titfield Thunderbolt* (1952). Clarke is often seen as the mainstay of Ealing, a man whose role at the studio rendered him more important than most of its directors. In *The Lavender Hill Mob* he reworked an earlier script, *Pool of London* (1950), in which another robbery goes wrong, ending – unlike the milder scenario of *The Lavender Hill Mob* – in real violence. The latter's lasting appeal comes from the fact that neither robbery nor bowler-hatted mastermind can be taken too seriously, given the unfailing amateurism of his accident-prone gang.

258

Writer
T. B. E. Clarke

Producer
Michael Balcon

Cinematographer
Douglas Slocombe

Production companies
Ealing Studios, Rank
Organisation

Cast
Alec Guinness
Stanley Holloway
Sid James
Alfie Bass
Marjorie Fielding
John Gregson
Clive Morton
Robert Shaw
Audrey Hepburn

Other films
★ *Hue and Cry* (1947)
★ *The Titfield Thunderbolt* (1952)
★ *A Fish Called Wanda* (1988)

Academy Awards
Oscar for Best Screenplay; nominated
for Best Actor (Alec Guinness), 1953

*Mr Pendlebury (Stanley Holloway, left) and Mr
Holland (Alec Guinness, centre) watch as gold
bullion is miraculously transformed into tacky
souvenirs before their eyes.*

The Servant Joseph Losey 1963

After working in New York theatre and as a director in Hollywood, Joseph Losey moved to the UK in 1953 as a refugee from McCarthyism. By the early 1960s he had established himself as one of the UK's leading filmmakers, with films such as *Blind Date* (1959), *The Criminal* (1960) and *Eve* (1962). Losey had been interested in Robin Maugham's novella *The Servant* since 1954, when he lent his copy to Dirk Bogarde. In 1961 he heard that another director had acquired the screen rights and commissioned a screenplay from the playwright Harold Pinter. Losey admired Pinter's work and had already been in touch with him to propose a collaboration. Later that year, he was delighted to learn that the rival project had fallen through and that Bogarde, who had read Pinter's script, was excited by it, observing that Pinter wrote with 'the precision of a master jeweller'. Losey set to work annotating Pinter's original script, persuading him to refashion it so that it would fit better with Losey's own reading of the characters.

The film entered production in 1963 with Bogarde playing the role of the unctuous manservant, Barrett, who ingratiatingly subjugates his employer, Tony – an idle young toff played by James Fox – and destroys him psychologically. Sarah Miles is Sarah, the flirtatious maid who acts as the instrument of Barrett's sinister plans. Barrett claims that she is his sister; but when caught in bed with her he changes his story and claims she is his fiancée, noting that Tony has no moral right to complain, given that she had seduced him too. All this takes place in front of Tony's own upper-class fiancée, Susan (played by Wendy Craig), who flees the house, thereby consolidating Barrett's dominion. Eventually, through a series of cruel games, Barrett acquires total ascendancy over his master, reducing him to a drunken wreck and conducting orgies in the master bedroom. The film ends with Susan's horrified departure, having blundered in during one of Barrett's parties, while Barrett locks the door behind her and a drunken Tony crawls up the stairs to curl up in a corner on the landing.

The film is an unrelenting satire of a class-ridden society, approached in an unusual way. It caricatures Susan's family in traditional style, presenting them as waxwork figures of a brain-dead aristocracy; but it deals with Tony even more viciously, relishing his gradual degradation as he becomes increasingly unfit to make any decisions of his own and is ruthlessly manipulated by Barrett, who takes command of the household. *The Servant* is a sardonic allegory of the class dynamics of English society, in which we are coolly presented with two unappetizing alternatives: ineffectual aristocrat and servile Svengali.

Director
Joseph Losey

Writer
Harold Pinter

Producers
Joseph Losey and
Norman Priggen

Cinematographer
Douglas Slocombe

Music
John Dankworth

Production Design
Richard MacDonald

Production companies
Elstree Studios and
Springbok Productions

Cast
Dirk Bogarde
James Fox
Wendy Craig
Sarah Miles
Catherine Lacey
Patrick Magee
Harold Pinter

Other films
★ *The Prowler* (1950)
★ *Eve* (1962)
★ *The Damned* (1963)
★ *Accident* (1967)
★ *Secret Ceremony* (1968)
★ *The Go-Between* (1971)

Dirk Bogarde (left) as the sinister servant, and James Fox as the ineffectual master.

A Hard Day's Night

Richard Lester *1964*

Director
Richard Lester

Writer
Alun Owen

By 1963 the world was gripped by Beatlemania; *A Hard Day's Night* began filming in early March 1964. The producer, Walter Shenson, hired Richard Lester, a young director with whom he had previously worked, and who had also directed a pop musical (*It's Trad, Dad*) in 1962. Lester was an American who came to London to pursue a career in British television – one of the main targets for satire in *A Hard Day's Night*. The Beatles were happy with Shenson's choice because Lester had previously worked with the comedy troupe The Goons, whose own brand of eccentric humour the mop-heads loved and learned from. In fact, Lester filmed the Goons' madcap short, *The Running, Jumping and Standing Still Film*, to which due homage is paid in *A Hard Day's Night*. Shenson also hired Alun Owen, a writer from Merseyside who had gone through a tough apprenticeship in television, where he had worked on the pilot for the *Dick Lester Show*. Shenson sent Owen off to Dublin to hang out with the Beatles, who were performing there.

A Hard Day's Night was shot in London; it was begun only six days after the Beatles returned from their triumphant US tour and was completed within eight weeks. Most of the songs were already written, and the Beatles began recording them at Abbey Road studios two days after their return from tour; the title song, commissioned by Shenson, was composed later. The film's title words were first uttered by Ringo Starr, and the song's lyrics were written by John Lennon in just one evening, for a recording session the next day. The whole shoot was unusually hectic, since the Beatles had many other commitments and were shuttling back and forth between Abbey Road, the film set, awards ceremonies, television studios and, in John Lennon's case, literary luncheons. Yet the frantic, chaotic pace of the shoot actually worked to the film's advantage, as it developed its own Keystone Kops rhythm. Its strength comes from its mix of documentary realism, crazy comedy and celebrity close-ups – plus, of course, its string of Beatles hits. Decades later, the amazing energy and impromptu creativity of the group still captivate us.

A Hard Day's Night redefined the concept of the musical film, dominated for decades by the Hollywood model; it owes more to the French New Wave and specifically films like Godard's *A Bout de souffle* (1959), with its real-life street scenes, wild stretches of improvisation and shamelessly absurdist gags. At times, it is almost as if we have entered a parallel world in which everyone behaves unpredictably: a world of hysteria and paranoia, as seething crowds fight their way ever closer to the Fab Four and television executives wring their hands as mayhem descends upon their carefully controlled schedules and procedures. The film is drenched in what we might call innocent sexuality, although the innocence is systematically undermined by flagrant innuendo and terrifying fans; a tunnel of love crossed with a roller-coaster ride.

Producer
Walter Shenson

Cinematographer
Gilbert Taylor

Production companies
Proscenium Films and
United Artists

Cast
The Beatles
Wilfrid Brambell
Norman Rossington
John Junkin
Victor Spinetti
Anna Quayle
Lionel Blair
Brian Epstein

Other films
★ *The Knack* (1965)
★ *Help!* (1965)
★ *How I Won the War* (1967)
★ *Petulia* (1968)
★ *The Three Musketeers* (1973)

Academy Awards
Nominated for Best Music and
Best Screenplay, 1965

*The Beatles in performance, demonstrating
their classic 'mop-top' mode.*

Performance

Donald Cammell and Nicolas Roeg *1970*

Directors
Nicolas Roeg and
Donald Cammell

Performance is the definitive 1960s film, fearlessly portraying sex, violence, drugs, beauty and style. As Marianne Faithfull said, 'It preserves a whole era under glass,' uniting the decadent remnants of the Chelsea Set with the newly fashionable world of London's criminal fraternity. The creator, Donald Cammell, had previously co-written the script of *Duffy* (1968) and, as a result, had become friendly with actor James Fox and established a relationship with the producer Sandy Lieberson. Lieberson was now interested in making a film in the tradition of Antonioni's *Blow Up* (1966), with a story set in the new 'swinging' social world that brought rock stars together with aristocrats. Lieberson encouraged Cammell to write a new script for him, which could then be offered to Marlon Brando and Mick Jagger.

The script Cammell produced combined a crime thriller with the new youth culture; a world of drugs and rock 'n' roll, exemplified by the 'Chelsea Set' that gathered around Christopher Gibbs (a dandy who had made the pilgrimage to Morocco, whence he returned with Arab robes and slippers and quantities of hashish). The Chelsea Set had their very own informant within the world of the infamous gangsters the Krays – David Litvinoff, an old Etonian fascinated with the gangster milieu, who served as a link to the underworld figures who both tutored Fox and appeared as gangsters in the film.

As Cammell's script evolved it was shown to Fox and Jagger, both of whom were known to Cammell. Just as the film was set to go into production, anxieties about Cammell's inexperience were finally allayed when he himself suggested that Nic Roeg should be brought on to the team in the role of cinematographer, a title that Lieberson insisted should be upgraded to co-director because of Cammell's inexperience in direction and Roeg's track record as a professional. The themes, concepts, behavioural patterns and basic imagery of the film come from Cammell's vision, but the professionalism of its execution comes from Roeg. In fact, *Performance* could be seen as a kind of home movie, in which everybody knew each other and enacted aspects of their own lives and characters, but which was given professional status by Roeg's involvement as co-director. Even the gangsters in the film are basically playing themselves, or at least a stylized version of themselves. The only one forced to play a role was James Fox, portraying a gangster on the run, pursued and eventually murdered for breaking the rules of his profession – a role in which he was guided by the underworld figures to whom Litvinoff introduced him. The result was an extraordinary film, combining a fascination with violence and death, Chelsea dandyism, polymorphous sexuality, the literary influence of Jorge Luis Borges and William Burroughs, and the hippie milieu of music, drugs and sex.

264

Writer
Donald Cammell

Producer
Sandy Lieberson

Cinematographer
Nicolas Roeg

Production companies
Goodtimes Enterprises

Cast
James Fox
Mick Jagger
Anita Pallenberg
Michèle Breton
Ann Sidney
Johnny Shannon
Anthony Valentine

Other films: Cammell
★ *Demon Seed* (1977)
★ *White of the Eye* (1986)

Other films: Roeg
★ *Walkabout* (1971)
★ *Don't Look Now* (1973)
★ *The Man Who Fell to Earth* (1976)
★ *Bad Timing* (1980)

Michèle Breton (far left), Anita Pallenberg and Mick Jagger share a quiet moment in the bath.

The Draughtsman's Contract

Peter Greenaway *1982*

Director and writer
Peter Greenaway

From the mid-1960s to the end of the 1970s Peter Greenaway established himself as an experimental filmmaker with his short, formally precise films, whose subject matter reflected a private mythological world he had created. This world had its own cast of characters, led by Tulse Luper, and revolved around a recurring series of obsessions – death, numbers, lists, systems of classification, the alphabet, coincidences and journeys. *Dear Phone* (1977), *Vertical Features Remake* (1978) and *The Falls* (1980) all feature an imaginary character named Cissie Colpitts; the male characters in *Dear Phone* all bear the initials H. C. and have wives called Zelda. From 1978 onwards Greenaway's films were financed by the British Film Institute, and in the 1980s he was encouraged by Peter Sainsbury, head of the Institute's Production Board, to embark on a full-length feature film. The result was *The Draughtsman's Contract*, a work retaining many of the features of Greenaway's early films, but with a plot, characters, dialogue and production values of a different order.

The Draughtsman's Contract is set in August 1694, during the English reign of William of Orange. The action takes place in the house and formal garden of the rich, land-owning Herbert family. They have decided that their child, Augustus, should have a drawing teacher and have hired a Mr Neville for this task. The film is structured around Mr Neville's drawings of their country house, commissioned by Mr Herbert's daughter, Mrs Tallman. Mr Neville suggests that pleasure would be a more important inducement to him than monetary payment. Pleasure, it turns out, should be taken to mean sexual pleasure. With the aid of a perspective glass Mr Neville sets about making the drawings, 12 in all, to be produced on 12 consecutive days. He has made it a contractual obligation that he should control exactly what he draws on each day. For instance, he may demand that no windows should be opened or closed, no carriages should intrude, no smoke should billow from the chimneys. For one drawing, wet sheets must be hung out to dry. For another, Mr Tallman's clothes must be approved by the draughtsman, who also requires him to puff out his cheeks. At the same time, the draughtsman cannot help noticing unanticipated things appearing illicitly in his perspective glass. He suspects that some plot is afoot, to culminate perhaps in the murder of Mr Herbert. He becomes the inadvertent witness of a complex conspiracy, involving a struggle over marriage agreements and the control of property.

The surprising tale of *The Draughtsman's Contract* has many similarities to the traditional English country-house murder, in the tradition of Agatha Christie or Dorothy Sayers; yet it is a structural film in the avant-garde tradition, as well as an erotic tale and a perverse meditation on the role of art in society. It is the portrait of an ambiguous England, beneath whose façade of peace, respectability and order lies a seething cauldron of murder, libertinism and conspiracy.

Producer
David Payne

Cinematographer
Curtis Clark

Production design
Bob Ringwood

Production companies
BFI and Channel 4 Films

Cast
Anthony Higgins
Janet Suzman
Anne Louise Lambert
Neil Cunningham
Hugh Fraser
Dave Hill
David Grant

Other films
★ *The Belly of an Architect* (1987)
★ *Drowning By Numbers* (1988)
★ *The Cook, The Thief, His Wife and Her Lover* (1989)
★ *Prospero's Books* (1991)
★ *The Pillow Book* (1996)

The draughtsman (Anthony Higgins) with his equipment outside the Tallman home.

Brazil

Terry Gilliam *1985*

Terry Gilliam's early years were spent in Minnesota, in the northwest United States. He treasures fond memories of old comic strips, Walt Disney's *Snow White* (1937) and, especially, television comedies, many of which bordered on surrealism, always a reference point for Gilliam – 'the moment when you make that leap and nothing is just what it seems'. Eventually Gilliam's family left Minnesota for Los Angeles, where he attended Occidental College and worked on the campus humour magazine, inspired by *Help!*, the successor to *Mad* magazine. When his education was completed he left for New York where, to his surprise and satisfaction, he was actually hired as an editor of *Help!*. Gilliam eventually ended up in the UK in 1967, and soon found animation work in television with the help of John Cleese, whom he had encountered while Cleese was in New York on a Cambridge Footlights tour.

In due course, Gilliam's animation work became a crucial feature of the seminal television comedy *Monty Python's Flying Circus*, and this success led to the leap into film. In 1974 he co-directed the first Python film, *Monty Python and the Holy Grail*, followed by solo direction of *Jabberwocky* (1977) and *Time Bandits* (1981), and involvement in the screenplays and animation sequences of other Python films directed by Terry Jones.

Brazil, made in 1985, was the first film Gilliam directed completely outside the Python umbrella. Over the years he had assembled a thick pile of notes and ideas for a film that was pulled into shape as a script in collaboration with playwright Tom Stoppard – although it was a third writer, Charles MacKeown, who completed the final version to Gilliam's satisfaction. In many ways, however, the extraordinary futuristic sets are as important as the script. Gilliam and his art directors created an imaginary city which, in his own words, is located somewhere 'on the Los Angeles/Belfast border', a dream vision of the psychotic totalitarian city of the future.

Brazil can be seen as the model for a group of films released over the following five years – such as *Batman* (1989) and *Dick Tracy* (1990) – which were highly stylized and rooted in cartoon art. *Brazil* stands out from the others because it mixes futurism with what we might call 'retro-primitivism', combining a Cold War, Orwellian vision of bureaucracy with flights of much weirder dystopian fantasy, in which the society depicted is dependent for almost everything on pipes and mysterious tubes, and its buildings are like demented versions of the Beaubourg in Paris. Elements of contemporary reality – terrorist bombs in central London, elaborate face-lifts and dental work – are meshed with visions of torture, a world of rebellious freedom fighters, and tough-girl truck-drivers, free spirits who are the ultimate objects of desire. A landmark film that opened the door to a new era of absurdist science fantasy with a dark side, typified by later Jeunet and Caro films such as *Delicatessen* (1990) and *The City of Lost Children* (1995), *Brazil* stands out as a surreal tragicomedy of terrifying frustrations and liberating visions.

Director
Terry Gilliam

Writers
Terry Gilliam, Tom Stoppard and Charles McKeown

Producer
Arnon Milchan

Cinematographer
Roger Pratt

Production design
Norman Garwood

Production companies
Embassy International Pictures, Universal Pictures

Cast
Jonathan Pryce
Robert De Niro
Katherine Helmond
Ian Holm
Bob Hoskins
Michael Palin
Ian Richardson

Other films
★ *Time Bandits* (1981)
★ *The Adventures of Baron Munchausen* (1988)
★ *The Fisher King* (1991)
★ *Twelve Monkeys* (1995)
★ *Fear and Loathing in Las Vegas* (1998)

Academy Awards
Nominated for Best Art Direction and Best Screenplay, 1986

Billy the Kid and the Green Baize Vampire

Alan Clarke *1985*

Few people are familiar with Clarke's work, least of all with *Billy The Kid and the Green Baize Vampire* – arguably his best film, although it is also his quirkiest and weirdest. Clarke was born in Liverpool in 1935 and moved to Canada when he was 21, eventually settling down to take courses in television arts at college in Toronto. After graduating he returned to the UK and found a floor job at the BBC, while staging Beckett and Genet in the evenings after work. It was a stage production – *Macbeth* at the Questors Theatre – that won him the chance to direct for television, and in 1977 he established his reputation with the television version of *Scum*, a wrenching portrait of life in a borstal which the BBC declined to broadcast. As originally intended, he remade *Scum* as a film, which opened in cinemas in 1979. Six years passed – time that was spent back with the BBC directing David Bowie in Bertolt Brecht's *Baal* and making *Contact*, which was shot in Northern Ireland with infra-red night-vision lenses – until the chance came to make *Billy The Kid*.

This strangest of strange films is a Brechtian musical in the tradition of *The Threepenny Opera*, but is set in the world of snooker, portraying an epic encounter between an older player (modelled on the rather sinister-looking, real-life Welsh snooker champion Ray Reardon), and a younger player (based on the fresh-faced English snooker prodigy Jimmy White). The script and lyrics were by Trevor Preston, and the music was by George Fenton. Clarke was a fan of the classic British punk band The Clash, and through the music and the style, his film somehow combines Brecht's surrealism with punk. The snooker match mutates into a dream-like ritual, carrying us back to the eerie expressionism of *Nosferatu (see pages 34–35)* and *The Cabinet of Dr Caligari (see pages 32–33)*. Clarke typically follows his characters with hand-held camera sequences, but in the snooker scenes the movements are slow and deliberate, and the camera becomes frozen in its place. The musical numbers, however, are shot in extremely long takes, in brazen defiance of the quick-cutting conventions of modern music video. For many, the weirdness of the film proved too much. But it is precisely its quality of wild eccentricity that makes it great.

Director
Alan Clarke

Writer
Trevor Preston

Producer
Simon Mallin

Cinematographer
Clive Tickner

Production companies
Incorporated Television Company, Zenith Productions

Cast
Phil Daniels
Alun Armstrong
Bruce Payne
Louise Gold

Other films
★ *Scum* (1979)
★ *Rita, Sue and Bob Too* (1986)
★ *Christine* (1987)
★ *Elephant* (1989)

Alun Armstrong, playing the Green Baize
Vampire, rises to face another frame.

271

Blue

Derek Jarman *1993*

Director and writer
Derek Jarman

Producers
James Mackay
and Takashi Asai

Music
Simon Fisher Turner

Production company
Basilisk Communications

Voices
Nigel Terry
John Quentin
Derek Jarman
Tilda Swinton

Other films
★ *Jubilee* (1977)
★ *The Tempest* (1979)
★ *Caravaggio* (1986)
★ *The Last of England*
  (1987)
★ *The Garden* (1990)
★ *Edward II* (1991)
★ *Wittgenstein* (1993)
★ *Glitterbug* (1994)

Blue opened at the Camden Parkway cinema in London in August 1993 and was broadcast on the UK's Channel 4 network the following month, with a simultaneous broadcast of the soundtrack on BBC Radio 3. A few months later Jarman was dead from complications derived from AIDS. *Blue* is an autobiographical film that deals directly with the director's blindness and his awareness of impending death. At the same time, it is a companion to his book *Chroma*, a meditation on colour that was published posthumously in 1994; much of the text of *Blue* reappears in *Chroma*. The film itself consists, for its entire length, of the on-screen projection of a rectangle of pure blue light, with the filmmaker reading his voice-over and music composed by his collaborator Simon Turner.

In 1987, after the success of his film *Caravaggio* (1986), Jarman had floated the idea of making a film about the painter Yves Klein, whose work he had long admired. In particular he was fascinated by Klein's use of International Klein Blue, a pigment that Klein had invented, patented and used in a series of monochrome blue works. Three years later Jarman finally made some pilot reels of lab-generated blue film, in the hope of raising money for *Blueprint* or *Bliss*, as the project was then known. The critic Michael O'Pray remembers him 'falling over with glee at the thought of offering up just a blue colour field – he was always cheered up by the thought of shocking his potential backers.' Shocked or not, backers were found and in 1991 Jarman, now suffering from AIDS-related blindness, wrote the autobiographical text that brought Klein Blue together with his experience of blindness; the eye-drops that he took as part of his treatment produced the experience of a blue colour field. Monochrome painting, in itself, was nothing new but a monochrome film, with no other imagery and no change of hue, was something else.

Jarman insisted on film's 'presentness'. In an earlier Jarman film, *Jubilee* (1978), one character takes as her motto: 'Don't dream it. Be it.' Another, who lives in an empty and entirely black room, announces: 'Painting's extinct, it's just a habit. I started when I was eight, copying dinosaurs from a picture book. It was prophetic.' Jarman's loss of faith in painting and sculpture was to lead eventually to his loss of faith in film, an endless stream of images produced by an industry dedicated only to entertainment, celebrity and marketing. It was the involvement of painting with the art market that disenchanted him, yet the film media proved even worse. Faced with death, Jarman no longer had any interest in 'commodity and worldly success'. Yet, speaking about *Blue*, Jarman observed, 'I always said I would end up painting again. And I suppose in a sense that's what I'm doing.' His wrenchingly personal film celebrates a symbolic blue, associated both with impending death and with life re-experienced as memory: 'Blue of my heart. Blue of my dreams. Slow blue love of delphinium days.'

Topsy Turvy

Mike Leigh *1999*

It came as a great surprise when Mike Leigh embarked on a musical. He had achieved success with improvised plays and films notorious for their acidity: wrenching portrayals of misfits and families struggling with divisive dilemmas, portraits of the odd corners of life that moved you to tears or triggered embarrassed laughter. A period piece about the making of Gilbert and Sullivan's light opera *The Mikado* (1885) seemed disconcertingly out of character. Yet when it was released it was an undoubted triumph, as acute and pointed in its depiction of characters faced with difficult moral issues and complex emotional problems as any of his previous work, but also brazenly entertaining in its re-creation of the late Victorian age.

Leigh had been taken to the opera in Manchester as a young boy, when the D'Oyly Carte productions of Gilbert and Sullivan were still touring. He listened to the records, memorized the words and hummed the melodies; it was part of the family ritual. 'To this day, I remain a closet Savoyard,' he revealed in 1993. 'I play Gilbert and Sullivan records when I am on the rowing machine at home.' Now he is out of the closet. By 1997, news of his US$20 million project was doing the rounds. 'Let's say it won't be a remake of the 1953 biopic', he said. 'I'm attracted to the idea of getting out there and subverting the period movie, the costume drama. But I thought it was about time I did a proper movie. Just for the hell of it.' In 1999 he explained that 'after several decades devoted to making hard-edged films about contemporary life, all an unlikely contrast with the succulent Sullivan I was still whistling joyously around the house, I decided it was time to turn the uncompromising lens on Gilbert and Sullivan themselves – and *Topsy Turvy* is the result'.

The key word here is 'uncompromising'. *Topsy Turvy* gives us the stage performances and the songs, but also the crises and heartaches, the patient struggles and emotional outbursts, the problems at home with the family, and the problems of drunkenness and drugs backstage. Sullivan turns out to be something of a libertine, enjoying his erotic romps, while also feeling that his commitment to Gilbert and the D'Oyly Carte has cost him the chance of greatness as a serious composer. Gilbert, while trapped in his own dysfunctional family, continues to churn out wit and merriment; he is a workaholic whose commitment to topsy-turvydom precludes any meaningful social life outside the theatre. Yet, in the end, they submit to Carte's blandishments and produce another opera, based on an idea brought to Gilbert by his long-suffering wife, who drags him to the new exhibition of Japanese arts. The result is *The Mikado*, which became their greatest triumph – but it is a victory achieved only after the cast rebels against Gilbert's harsh dismissal of one of their number. The film owes its success to Mike Leigh's script, Carl Davis's musical adaptation, great art direction and, most importantly of all, some wonderful performances by actors and actresses who gleefully seized their extraordinary opportunity.

Director and writer
Mike Leigh

Producer
Simon Channing-Williams

Cinematographer
Dick Pope

Editor
Robin Sales

Music
Carl Davies

Production companies
Goldwyn Films, Newmarket Capital Group, The Greenlight Fund and Third Man Productions

Cast
Jim Broadbent
Allan Corduner
Timothy Spall
Lesley Manville

Other films
★ *High Hopes* (1988)
★ *Life Is Sweet* (1990)
★ *Naked* (1993)
★ *Secrets and Lies* (1996)

Academy Awards
Oscars for Costume Design and Make-Up; nominated for Art Direction, Set Decoration and Best Screenplay, 2000

Three little maids ... a still illustrating the riotously colourful sets and costumes that marked a departure from Leigh's more familiar utilitarian style.

MAIN: *Satyajit Ray's* Pather Panchali *(India, 1955).*

FAR LEFT: *Zhang Yimou's* Raise the Red Lantern *(China/Hong Kong, 1991).*

MIDDLE LEFT: *King Hu's* A Touch of Zen *(Taiwan, 1969–71).*

LEFT: *Akira Kurosawa's* Seven Samurai *(Japan, 1954).*

International Cinema
Tony Rayns

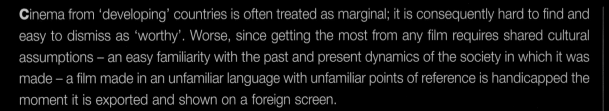

Cinema from 'developing' countries is often treated as marginal; it is consequently hard to find and easy to dismiss as 'worthy'. Worse, since getting the most from any film requires shared cultural assumptions – an easy familiarity with the past and present dynamics of the society in which it was made – a film made in an unfamiliar language with unfamiliar points of reference is handicapped the moment it is exported and shown on a foreign screen.

Historically, only two genres from the rest of the world have made real inroads into the North American and European mass markets: martial arts films (mostly kung-fu and 'heroic bloodshed' films from Hong Kong) and animated fantasy (mostly from Japan). A wider range of titles has reached smaller niche markets through art-house distribution and political and student-movement screenings. However, the idea that rest-of-the-world films might offer valid alternatives to Hollywood and mainstream western cinema dates back to the 1920s, when it was voiced in small-circulation magazines. It took the growth of independent art-house circuits in the post-war decades to bring the alternatives to their potential audiences. The elements that proved likeliest to appeal to western sophisticates were exoticism (a tradition stretching from Kurosawa's *Seven Samurai* (1954) and King Hu's *A Touch of Zen* (1969–71) to Zhang Yimou's *Raise the Red Lantern* (1991) and beyond) and liberal humanism (Satyajit Ray's *Apu Trilogy*, inaugurated with *Pather Panchali* (1955); latterly Iranian movies about children).

No film intended for commercial release is conceived in a creative vacuum. Global cinema has always been marked, for better or worse, by Hollywood; this influence can take the form of admiration, emulation or aggressive hostility. And many film-makers anxious to do something different have located inspiration in earlier non-Hollywood movements. Pioneers such as Satyajit Ray found it in the work of Jean Renoir and some of his French contemporaries. The Italian 'neo-realist' movement of the post-war years was more widely influential, especially in developing countries. Some of these roots are explored on the following pages.

My selection of 15 titles from Asia, Africa and Latin America on the following pages has an unapologetic bias towards East Asia. In part this is because it seems about time to make some amends for past neglect. Asia has several of the oldest continuously operating film industries in the world and most film-producing countries in the region could boast of outstanding achievements well before the years of the Pacific War. And yet the western world became aware of Japanese and Indian cinema only in the 1950s, of Chinese and Filipino cinema in the 1980s, and it is only now beginning to catch up with what is happening in Korean cinema. The other reason for the bias is purely subjective: I think these films are more interesting and achieved than rival contenders for the 15 slots. In fact most of them strike me as being among cinema's finest achievements.

Little Toys

Xiao Wanyi

Sun Yu, *China 1933*

Director and writer
Sun Yu

Producer
Luo Mingyou

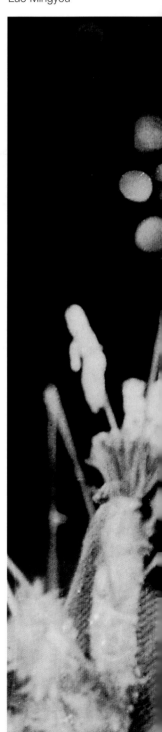

Sun Yu (1900–1990) was the only pioneering writer-director in the nascent Shanghai film industry who studied in the United States. The son of a historian, he went to write a doctoral thesis on the poet Li Po, but then joined film technique classes at Columbia University and sat in on David Belasco's acting classes. He began making films soon after he returned to China, aligning himself with much of the left's agenda but not joining the underground communist group that was infiltrating the film industry. Overtly influenced by Hollywood – especially the films that Josef von Sternberg made with Marlene Dietrich in the early 1930s – but fiercely patriotic in content, his work is often seen as a test case in discussions of cultural specifics in national film styles.

Little Toys is perhaps the finest of the series of melodramas he made for the Lianhua Company (United Photoplay Service, one of the two major production companies) between 1930 and 1937, when Shanghai fell to the Japanese. Many of the films starred Sun's homegrown 'Dietrich', Li Lili, but here she has a supporting role alongside the legendary Ruan Lingyu, unknown outside China at the time but now widely recognized as one of the greatest film actresses of the 1930s. (Ruan, then 23, was driven to suicide by articles in the tabloid press only two years later.)

The film follows the fragmenting Ye family, buffeted by wars and economic hardships, as it tries to relocate its cottage toy-making industry from a village on the shore of Lake Tai to a shantytown in the suburbs of Shanghai. The action spans the years 1921 (when the village is trampled in a clash between local warlords) to 1932 (when Shanghai is first shelled by Japanese warships). The plotting has orthodox melodramatic twists: the impossible love of a young intellectual for a married woman; the loss of one child to kidnappers and another to a Japanese shell; the death of a weak but decent husband; a woman driven mad by war who ironically fails to recognize the son who was snatched from her years earlier. Rather than wallowing in tears, however, Sun transmutes pathos into anger and underpins the whole with a remarkably sophisticated discourse on the politics and semantics of toys.

The film's quasi-documentary footage of the design, manufacture and sale of toys yields the three polarities which provide its deep structure: first, hand-crafting versus mechanised production; second, domestic production versus imports; third, war toys versus war itself. The first two express the film's economic critique and make it synonymous with its agit-prop thrust: its call for patriotic resistance to the invading Japanese. The third gives the film its most subversive strand: the dream-like images of war suggest that the destructive weapons – the cannons and tanks – are equivalent to war toys, which implies that the two must be taken equally seriously. The lyrical visuals, vivid performances and complex subtext make *Little Toys* a genre classic.

Cinematographer
Zhou Ke

Art director
Fang Peilin

Cast
Ruan Lingyu
Li Lili
Yuan Congmei
Luo Peng

Other films
★ *Wild Rose* (Ye Meigui, 1932)
★ *Daybreak* (Tianming, 1933)
★ *The Highway* (Da Lu, 1934)
★ *The Story of Wu Xun* (Wu Xun Chuan, 1950)
★ *Folk Tales of Lu Ban* (Lu Ban de Chuanshuo, 1958)

Ruan Lingyu (left) is now recognized as one of the greatest film actors of the 1930s.

Humanity and Paper Balloons
Ningen Kamifusen

Yamanaka Sadao, *Japan 1937*

Made when he was aged 28, in collaboration with the covertly left-wing theatre troupe Zenshin-za, Yamanaka Sadao's last film is strikingly different from other historical dramas of its period. The main characters and incidents are taken from a 19th-century *kabuki* play (Kawatake Mokuami's *Kamiyui Shinza/Shinza the Barber*, 1873), but Yamanaka and his writer Mimura reworked them into something more like a variation on Maxim Gorky's *The Lower Depths*, with the setting transposed to an Edo slum. As militarism pervaded almost every aspect of Japanese life in the 1930s, it became all but mandatory for filmmakers to imbue *jidai-geki* (period dramas) with affirmations of heroism and *bushido* (martial spirit). Yamanaka deliberately went in the opposite direction. His film insists that life in feudal Japan was nasty, brutish and short for everyone on the lower rungs of the social ladder.

Deeply pessimistic in its implications, the film traces patterns of disappointment, frustration and defeat across the blighted lives of two neighbours in a run-down alley. One is the *ronin* (masterless samurai) Matajuro, who spends his days looking for work while his wife, Otaki, sits at home making cheap paper balloons for festivals; Matajuro has a claim on the patronage of Mori, a local official, but Mori is unwilling to acknowledge his indebtedness to the *ronin*'s family. The other is the barber, Shinza, equally penni-less, who one rainy night impulsively kidnaps the daughter of a wealthy merchant; he hides her in Matajuro's home and tries to extort a ransom from her father, only to run foul of his hired thugs. The film, beginning and ending with off-screen suicides, points up the irony in the fact that funerals provide the local community with its only excuses for drinking and merriment.

Yamanaka had worked with the Zenshin-za theatre troupe once before, on the 1935 film *Machi no Irezumi-mono*. This second collaboration yielded both superb ensemble playing and 'modern', naturalistic performances of a kind found in few other 1930s films in Japan or anywhere else. But there is nothing uncinematic about *Humanity and Paper Balloons*. Yamanaka was not a formalist of the kind that his contemporary (and close friend) Ozu Yasujiro became, but his sense of rhythm and visual poetry was no less acute. He used as little movement of the camera as possible, and his fixed-frame compositions often have a considerable depth of field, integrating background and peripheral action. Relationships between the main characters are developed less through dialogue than through the composition of individual images and sparing use of point-of-view shots.

The Zenshin-za troupe survived the war and finally came out as pro-communist in 1950. Yamanaka was not so lucky. He received notice that he was drafted into the army on the day this film premiered; he was sent to fight in Manchuria and died in battle on 17 September 1938, aged 29. He had directed some 22 films (all *jidai-geki*) in a career lasting just six years; all but three of them are currently believed lost.

Director
Yamanaka Sadao

Producer
Takemaya Masanobu

Writer
Mimura Shintaro

Cinematographer
Mimura Akira

Art directors
Kubo Kazuo and
Iwata Sentaro

Production company
Toho

Music
Ota Tadashi

Cast
Kawarazaki Chojuro
Nakamura Kanemon
Suketakaya Sukezo
Yamagishi Shizue

Other films
★ *Tange Sazen and the Pot Worth a Million Ryo* (Hyakuman Ryo No Tsubo, 1935)
★ *Kochiyama Soshun* (1936)

The ronin *Matajuro* and his wife
Otaki, surrounded by the eponymous
paper balloons.

Tale of the Late Chrysanthemums
Zangiku Monogatari

Mizoguchi Kenji, *Japan 1939*

Mizoguchi is generally revered for the best of his later films, *Ugetsu Monogatari* (1953) and *Sansho the Bailiff* (1954), made when it became important to him to equal or surpass the international success of the relative newcomer Kurosawa Akira. But masterly as some of the late work is, it is clear that his creative peak came nearly 20 years earlier. The surviving Mizoguchi films of the late 1930s and early 1940s are potent, intensely felt melodramas focused on the gap between performances and the realities behind them, and they mark the apogee of his daring experiments with film form. Resisting the pressure to make 'national policy' films for the war effort evidently spurred him to his greatest creative heights.

Tale of the Late Chrysanthemums, based on a story by Muramatsu Shofu, was the first of three films about actors; the other two, sadly, are lost. This is a version of the archetypal Mizoguchi subject: the story of a working-class woman sacrificing everything for the sake of a middle-class man. This motif had auto-biographical resonances for the director, since his own education was paid for by his sister's work, and he always infused his films with a proto-feminist pathos; only in the films of the late 1940s, made under the eyes of the US occupation forces, did that pathos explode into anger.

The action covers 1885 to 1890 (Mizoguchi had a predilection for the Meiji Period), five years in which the mediocre *kabuki* actor, Kikunosuke (played by Hanayagi Shotaro), abandons the prestigious stage family who adopted him and relearns his craft on the boards of tumbledown provincial theatres with a penniless repertory company. He is sustained and guided throughout by his wife, Otoku (Mori Kakuko), the former nursemaid who was the only person who dared tell him to his face that his performances were bad. By the time he makes a triumphant return to the *kabuki* stage – playing a female role – she is dying of ill-health and exhaustion. The title is a play on his stage name: *Kiku* (or *-giku*) means 'chrysanthemum'.

Mizoguchi offers a meticulously detailed re-creation of the era, crowded with extras and crammed with authentic period props, spanning extremes of poverty and wealth. More remarkably, around three-quarters of the film is mounted in elaborate sequence shots, entailing complex choreography of movement in front of the camera in synch with the movement of the camera itself. Some sequence shots explore labyrinthine, multi-level spaces, such as the backstage of the *kabuki* theatre; others, such as the seminal conversation between Kikunosuke and Otoku that takes place as they walk home in the small hours, are languorous follow-shots which allow the viewer to 'edit' by looking from one part of the frame to another; still others use the mobile camera to segment domestic interiors. This brilliant experimentation with form is at once a superb consolidation of the film's fictional world and a self-justifying adventure in film artifice. The film is both a tragic, late-feudal love story and an exquisite aesthetic object in its own right.

Director
Mizoguchi Kenji

Producer
Shirai Nobutaro

Writers
Yoda Yakashita and
Kawagachi Matsutaro

Cinematographers
Miki Shigeto and Fuji Yozo

Editor
Kawahigashi Koshi

Art director
Mizutani Hiroshi

Music
Ito Senji and Fukai Shiro

Cast
Hanayagi Shotaro
Mori Kakuko
Takada Kokichi

Other films
★ *The Loyal 47 Ronin* (Genroku Chushingura, 1941)
★ *My Love Has Been Burning* (Waga Koi wa Moenu, 1949)
★ *The Life of O-haru* (Saikaku Ichidai Onna, 1952)
★ *Ugetsu Monogatari* (1953)
★ *Sansho the Bailiff* (Sansho Dayu, 1954)

The unpromising kabuki actor Kikunosuke and his long-suffering wife Otoku.

Spring in a Small Town
Xiao Cheng Zhi Chun

Fei Mu, *China 1948*

Director
Fei Mu

The belated integration of Chinese cinema into world film history has been slow: the achievements of some of the films of the 1930s and 1940s are not yet valued as highly as eventually they will be. *Spring in a Small Town* is a case in point. It was virtually unknown even in Chinese film circles until the negative was restored in the early 1980s; director Fei Mu was neither a Communist Party member nor a fellow traveller, and so the Party servants who compiled the official history of Chinese film in the 1960s routinely vilified him and underestimated his output. However, the film is now accepted as a masterwork, at least in Hong Kong and Taiwan, and its international standing grows with each screening.

It could be bracketed with some contemporary Italian films as an account of post-war *anomie*, but its mood, form and implications are distinctively its own. The Chinese would classify it as a *wenyi pian* (a 'literary film'), meaning in this case a domestic melodrama. It was Fei's first post-war film and he made it for one of the two left-leaning companies that were reactivated in Shanghai after the defeat of Japan. But with the civil war between nationalists and communists continuing, Fei went against the grain of the company's generally upbeat productions and channelled all his ambivalent feelings about China's present and future into the film.

The setting is actually not a small town but an isolated country house; the Chinese title refers to the traditional stone wall which surrounds the grounds, now half-collapsed. (War damage? Or simply years of neglect?) The film centres on an emotional/sexual triangle. The household of four – ailing husband, unfulfilled wife, husband's sister and elderly manservant – receives its first visitor in some time, an old friend of the husband's who was also once the wife's lover. The visitor, Zhang (Li Wei, typically excellent), is scrupulously proper, but eventually finds himself alone with the wife, Yuwen (Wei Wei, a dormant volcano). Both are tentative. She is torn between an Emma Bovary-like desire to escape and her obligations to her sick husband (Shi Yu, the very archetype of the impotent intellectual); Zhang is both thrilled and terrified by the prospect of rekindling their lost romance. He finally leaves without her.

Without mentioning the war, the film crystallizes the mood of defeat-in-victory, consigning the future to the next generation (represented by the young sister) and leaving the main characters to stew in their failures, regrets and cowardice. But thanks to very 'modern' performances that vividly capture their inner lives, the film is entirely caught up in the emotional and psychological problems of the adults. And Fei's lyrical direction, which makes brilliantly innovative use of dissolves within scenes *without* implying the passage of time, succeeds in implicating the viewer in the action. The level of self-reflection is unique in Chinese cinema of the period. The film is less a Chinese parallel to Italian neo-realist films than an anticipation of the mature Antonioni of such films as *La Notte* (1961) and *L'Eclisse (see pages 192–3).*

Producer
Wang Yun

Writer
Li Tianqing

Cinematographer
Li Shengwei

Art director
Chi Ning

Music
Huang Yijun

Cast
Wei Wei
Shi Yu
Li Wei
Zhang Hongmei

Other films
★ *Song of China* (Tianlun, 1935)
★ *Blood on Wolf Mountain* (Langshan Diexue Ji, 1936)
★ *Children of the World* (Shijie Ernü, 1941)

Yuwen (Wei Wei, left) and her ailing husband (Shi Yu).

The Young and the Damned
Los Olvidados

Luis Buñuel, *Mexico 1950*

Director
Luis Buñuel

Producer
Oscar Dancigers

Of the 20 films Buñuel directed in Mexico between 1946 and 1965, *Los Olvidados* – literally 'the forgotten ones' but known as *The Young and the Damned* – is the one closest to social realism. This is very probably the reason it brought the director back to international attention after two decades out of sight; 'neo-realism' was in fashion at the time, and the film's sociological gravity and seemingly free-form structure produced the illusion that Buñuel was, for once, riding a trend. Seen now, though, *Los Olvidados* looks more like a (superior) foreshadowing of *A Clockwork Orange* (1971) than a companion-piece to Vittorio De Sica's *Shoeshine* (1946).

A portentous opening (an earnest narrator compares the problems of juvenile crime in Mexico City with those behind the modern façades of New York, Paris and London) heralds a narrative that is episodic in structure and anecdotal in tone. It centres on two kids from the slums, one of whom dominates, entraps and eventually kills the other. Jaibo is on the run from a reformatory; he enjoys reasserting his leadership of a group of slum kids and deliberately implicates the younger Pedro in his revenge attack on Julian, the boy who got him arrested. From then on, Pedro is helplessly under his thumb. Jaibo seduces Pedro's mother (a single parent who had her son at the age of 14 and has never loved him), causes Pedro to lose his first legitimate job, and steals money entrusted to Pedro by a well-meaning, reform-minded adult. Pedro is finally driven to attack Jaibo, but dies himself in the unequal fight. Soon after, Jaibo is shot dead by a policeman.

These incidents are integrated into a flow of other vignettes, some tangential to the story of the two, others shadowing or counterpointing it. Buñuel said that he wanted to introduce inexplicable, absurdist images into the margins of the film (his example was a glimpse of a symphony orchestra in an unfinished building) but was forbidden to do so by his producer. As it stands, his film is most often remembered for its scenes of pitiless cruelty (street kids tormenting a blind man and a legless beggar) and for the disturbing dream sequence in which Pedro imagines his smiling mother giving him raw meat, only for it to be snatched away by Jaibo.

There is a clear continuity from the early 1930s films that established Buñuel's notoriety (*Un chien andalou*, 1928; *L'âge d'or*, 1930; and the documentary *Las Hurdes*, 1932) to *Los Olvidados*. It is there not only in the recurrence of Buñuel's personal obsessions and fetishes – cripples, feet, milk splashed across naked thighs, chickens – but also in the abolishment of all the moral, ethical and sentimental filters usually deployed when middle-class artists tackle working-class squalor. The film indicts neither the 'bad' kids and their floundering parents nor the social workers and cops who have to deal with them. All of the characters are complex, fallible and messy. Nothing will improve, the film implies, until society sees itself more clearly and rethinks accordingly.

Writers
Luis Buñuel and
Luis Alcoriza

Cinematographer
Gabriel Figueroa

Production company
Ultramar Films

Art director
Edward Fitzgerald

Cast
Alfonso Mejía
Roberto Cobo
Estela Inda

Other films
★ *Un chien andalou* (1928)
★ *L'âge d'or* (1930)
★ *El* (1952)
★ *Viridiana* (1961)
★ *Belle de jour* (1967)
★ *The Discreet Charm of the Bourgeoisie* (1972)
★ *That Obscure Object of Desire* (1977)

'The film is most often remembered for its scenes of pitiless cruelty': the vagrant children torment a legless beggar.

Manila: In the Claws of Neon
Maynila, Sa Mga Kuko Ng Liwang

Lino Brocka, *The Philippines 1975*

The title metaphor, evoking flames and moths, summarizes the theme of Brocka's classic. But it is equally emblematic of 'Third World' cinema as a whole, since it represents the issue at the heart of almost all engaged filmmaking from developing countries: people raised in rural communities who migrate to big cities (the argument runs) will inevitably be confounded by the absence of the values with which they were raised, will find themselves preyed upon and will likely meet sad fates. The ways in which this issue is articulated by individual filmmakers vary from case to case, depending on local economic conditions and the context in which the film is made and shown. Brocka, working for a new independent production company but within a studio system modelled on Hollywood, articulates it as melodrama – but with a sharp, social-realist edge.

His protagonist is the fisherman, Julio (Bembol Roco, later in Peter Weir's *The Year of Living Dangerously,* 1982). He travels from his village to Manila to look for his fiancée, Ligaya, who went to work as a maid in the city but then disappeared. He works as a casual labourer on a dangerous building site and finds solidarity of a sort with his fellow workers, as impoverished and powerless as he is. His later attempts to earn a living include a disastrous day as a prostitute in a gay brothel. Meanwhile, as his new friends and acquaintances die or get into various kinds of trouble, he discovers that Ligaya was sold to a brothel by her employer and subsequently bought as a 'concubine' by a Chinese shopkeeper. His desperation finally drives him to derangement and murder.

This plot was taken from a controversial, recently published novel by Edgardo Reyes, and the film certainly brings the book's serious sociological agenda into the pop-culture arena of cinema. (There is also, of course, an implied political agenda; but both novel and film were produced under the Marcos dictatorship and explicit critiques of the government were impossible.) The film, however, trumps the book in two ways: first, by making the city itself the visual key to the drama – shot on location in Manila's worst slums, it achieves a level of visceral immediacy not possible on the printed page; second, by applying a *mise-en-scène* learned from American *films noirs* of the 1940s and 1950s to a contemporary social-realist melodrama, it gives the plot a new dynamic by allowing it to exceed the conventions of genre – the viewer is given reassuring generic signposts, only to have them snatched away by such scenes as the startlingly frank episode in the gay brothel.

Brocka, a one-time trainee priest who turned to filmmaking after co-founding a theatre group for young people from the slums, used similar strategies in the more serious of his later films. But *Manila* was the first time he found a viable balance between his political anger and his commitment to mass-market filmmaking. The intervening years have done nothing to diminish the film's sincerity or its potency.

Director
Lino Brocka

Producers
Severino Manotok Jr
and Mike de Leon

Writer
Clodualdo 'Doy' del Mundo

Cinematographer
Mike de Leon

Editors
Edgardo Jarlego and
Ike Jarlego Jr

Cast
Rafael 'Bembol' Roco
Hilda Koronel
Mario O'Hara

Other films
★ *Weighed But Found
   Wanting* (Tinimbang ka
   Ngunit Kulang, 1974)
★ *Insiang* (1976)
★ *Jaguar* (1979)
★ *Bayan Ko* (1984)
★ *Fight For Us*
   (Orapronobis, 1989)

Ai No Corrida
In the Realm of the Senses

Oshima Nagisa, *Japan 1976*

Director and writer
Nagisa Oshima

Producer
Anatole Dauman

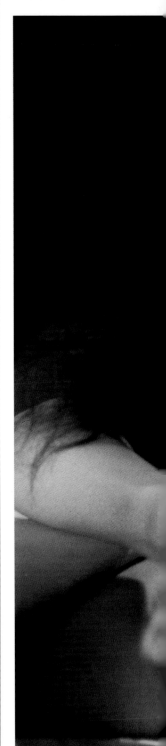

Oshima is unique among major directors in combining high seriousness with a flamboyant interest in sex and crime and a keen sense of the value of publicity. His work always has intellectual rigour, not to mention formal rigour, but more often than not it applies them to material from a pop-culture agenda. *In the Realm of the Senses* reflects both sides of his talent rather precisely. In 1975, Oshima was so disillusioned with Japanese culture and politics that he had stopped working with Japanese producers; he hadn't made a film since 1972. He undertook this project at the suggestion of the French producer Anatole Dauman, and shot material that could not legally be processed or edited in Japan. Part of his intention was to challenge Japan's censorship regime. But he had also been struck by the newly visible rise of hard-core pornography in some western countries and wanted to respond by making a different kind of sexually explicit film.

Typically, he chose to start from fact: a real-life incident that occurred at the height of Japan's militarism in 1936, when he himself was just four years old. A woman named Abe Sada was found wandering the streets with the severed penis of her late lover, Kichizo, in her possession. Tried for her *crime passionel*, she became the 1930s equivalent of a tabloid celebrity, won much public sympathy and was jailed for only six years. In the closing moments of the film, a voice-over (spoken by Oshima himself) reminds us of these facts. But the film proper is less a reconstruction of the actual incident than a vehicle for a set of troublesome questions.

In Oshima's version of the story, Sada works as a maid in the inn run by Kichizo. Rumours of past scandals and nymphomania already cling to her. Kichizo notices and seduces her, ignoring her protests. As soon as they are lovers, they detach themselves from everyday life – he from his family and business, she from her work – and retreat from the militarized society around them into a world of their own. Fuelled by his fantasies of priapic stamina and hers of limitless desire, this world apart admits sexual experimentation and additional partners but constantly foreshadows its own inevitable end in death, the final climax. By presenting the sexual activity explicitly, Oshima obliquely stresses how little can be understood by sight. By showing what is conventionally hidden, he actually exalts the power of the imagination.

Superbly sensual and rapturous, the film reasserts erotic traditions of sex-play, song and *gourmandise* that date back to the pleasure-houses of Edo in the 17th century, poignantly bequeathing them to an uncultured, working-class couple. But questions are always present as an undercurrent: the question of voyeurism (ours and theirs); what it means politically to withdraw from a hated, censorious society; and what is the price of transgression – not forgetting the biggest question of all: where exactly is the line between sex and death?

Cinematographer
Ito Hideo

Production companies
Argos Films and Oshima
Productions

Art director
Toda Jusho

Editor
Uraoka Keiichi

Cast
Matsuda Eiko
Fuji Tatsuya
Nakajima Aoi
Tonoyama Taiji

Other films
★ *Death by Hanging* (Koshikei, 1968)
★ *Diary of a Shinjuku Thief* (Shinjuku Dorobo Nikki, 1968)
★ *Boy* (Shonen, 1969)
★ *The Ceremony* (Gishiki, 1971)
★ *Dear Summer Sister* (Hatsu no Imoto, 1972)
★ *Merry Christmas, Mr Lawrence* (Senjo no Merry
Christmas, 1983)
★ *Gohatto* (1999)

*Matsuda Eiko (left) and Fuji Tatsuya as the
lovers; this scene shows the moment of death.*

Mandala

Im Kwontaek, *South Korea 1981*

Director
Im Kwontaek

The year 1981 was a difficult one in South Korea. Memories of the Kwangju Massacre in the spring of 1980 were still alive, and Chun Doohwan's authoritarian new government was provoking increasingly desperate and violent protests from the pro-democracy movement. Even if Im Kwontaek (with some 75 features already to his credit) had wanted to comment directly on this situation, strict censorship would have made it impossible. But *Mandala* nonetheless seems to represent a response to the wretched state of the nation. It is there not only in details, such as the appearance of military checkpoints or the protagonists' pointed failure to contribute money to a political candidate's campaign, but also in the philosophical debate that underpins the entire film.

The frame of reference is Buddhist. The opening montage shows the 'winter meditation' rituals in a mountain temple; it establishes the Buddhist orthodoxy of training, asceticism, discipline and, of course, meditation. But the rest of the film plays out on the country roads and city streets of Korea, counterpointing the experiences and memories of two very different monks. Pobun (Ahn Songki) is a recent graduate from university whose decision to become a monk entailed breaking with the girlfriend he once nearly raped. Jisan (Chun Musong) is a 'degenerate' monk who seeks – and apparently finds – aspects of Buddha in meat, liquor and sex. The two men meet when Pobun intercedes to rescue Jisan from the military (he is being held for travelling without proper ID), and the film chronicles the two periods of time they spend together.

Western viewers will find echoes of Hermann Hesse's novel *Narziss and Goldmund* (1930) in the contrast between the two men. Pobun is nervous, inhibited, terrified by sex and fundamentally conservative. Jisan, a traditional 'renegade monk' figure, is all too conscious of the suffering, poverty and injustice in the society around him; his answer is to dirty his hands, to seek 'oneness' with others through sex, to find Buddha on the material plane. He carries suicide pills ('my express ticket to the other world') and carves an unsmiling Buddha as his protest against the world's cruelties. His behaviour constantly appals Pobun, provoking unwelcome reflections on his own reasons for turning his back on society. But Pobun cannot escape the disturbing conviction that Jisan is closer to enlightenment than anyone he has ever met. The film's elegiac ending suggests that this is one more illusion which Pobun will have to leave behind.

The film was based on a recent, controversial novel by ex-monk Kim Songdong. Im Kwontaek wanted to film it as soon as he read it, despite knowing little about Buddhism, and fought to persuade the company to let him do so. The film marked a turning-point for him, a shift from commercial assignments to more personal projects, latterly often dealing with Korea's vanishing traditions. *Mandala* contains none of Im's later experiments with form, but its skill in framing Buddhist debates within a real and immediate social context fully anticipates his mature style.

Producer
Park Jongchan

Writers
Lee Sanghyon and
Song Kilhan

Cinematographer
Jong Ilsong

Production company
Hwa-Chun Trading

Art director
Kim Yoojoon

Cast
Chun Musong
Ahn Songki
Pang Hee

Other films
★ *Gilsodum* (1985)
★ *Surrogate Mother* (Sibaji, 1987)
★ *Come, Come, Come Upward* (Aje Aje Bara-Aje, 1989)
★ *Sopyonje* (1993)
★ *Festival* (Chukje, 1996)
★ *Chunhyang* (2000)

*The getting of wisdom: Chun Musong, left,
and Ahn Songki playing the 'degenerate' monk and
the novice.*

Yol

Serif Gören, *Turkey/Switzerland 1982*

To label *Yol* as a Swiss production – and to identify Serif Gören as its director – is technically accurate but entirely misleading. The film was conceived and written by Yilmaz Güney (a dissident imprisoned in Turkey at the time), shot on Turkish locations according to his instructions by his assistant Gören, and edited and post-produced by Güney himself in Paris after he escaped from jail and fled the country. There is no doubt that it is a deeply Turkish film, or that Güney was its actual creator. It was to be his penultimate film; he died of cancer soon after making *The Wall* in 1983.

Yilmaz Güney was a singular figure. Once Turkey's most popular movie star, a cross between a matinée idol and an action hero, he turned director with a self-imposed mission to drag Turkish cinema into a modern arena by dealing with all the troublesome issues routinely excluded from Turkey's mainstream culture. His filmmaking ran the gamut from neo-realist dramas shot in monochrome to Pasolini-like social parables with a philosophical/political edge; much of it deliberately baited the country's successive military coup leaders and their censors, and he was imprisoned several times . *Yol* (literally, 'The Road') was the third film he masterminded from jail during his last period of incarceration.

The film's clear ambition is to be taken as a ruinous 'state of the nation' address. Five prisoners from an island jail are given a week's parole, and the film crosscuts among their grim and tragic experiences to build a comprehensive picture of a society riven with prejudice, sexism, economic hardship and barely contained violence. (Güney's initial plan was to follow 11 prisoners; the film was scaled down during production.) One of the five is no sooner released than he is re-arrested for losing his parole permit. The other four travel to different parts of Turkey, two seeking reunions with their wives, one wanting to spend time with his fiancée, and the fourth, a Kurd, simply hoping to see his family. Most of them make appalling discoveries: one finds his wife literally shackled by her family (punishment for having turned to prostitution to support herself); another is shot dead by his brother-in-law while trying to run away with his wife. But the only one able to translate his anger into action is the Kurd, who finds his village under siege from the Turkish army and his brother killed in action; he breaks his parole and rides off to join the resistance.

The most surprising thing about *Yol* is its non-reliance on dialogue to make its points. It is an overwhelmingly visual film that renders everything from its perception of the problems of dating or finding a private space for marital sex in an Islamic culture to its sense of the many ways women are oppressed, in images so elemental that they have an almost expressionist power. Even in jail, Güney thought in images – as if he felt that words could never be enough. His film argued for revolutionary change with superb visual rhetoric.

Director
Serif Gören

Producers
Edi Hubschmid and
K. L. Puldi

Writer and editor
Yilmaz Güney

Cinematographer
Erdogan Engin

Production company
Güney Film/Cactus Film

Cast
Tarik Akan
Halil Ergün
Serif Sezer

Other films (Güney)
★ *Hope* (Umut, 1970)
★ *Elegy* (Agit, 1971)
★ *The Friend* (Arlcadzs, 1974)
★ *Anxiety* (Endize, 1974)
★ *The Wall* (Le mur, 1983)

*Officers check identification papers as the
prisoners leave on parole.*

295

Horse Thief
Daoma Zei

Tian Zhuangzhuang, *China 1986*

Director
Tian Zhuangzhuang

Seen by more people abroad than inside China (where it was effectively shelved), Tian Zhuangzhuang's remarkable film is nonetheless one of the defining works of modern Chinese cinema. Tian, the son of two well-known actors, made it in oblique reflection of his own teenage experiences in the Cultural Revolution, when he was exiled from Beijing to 'learn from the people'. The film (his third as sole director) owes its existence to a short-lived policy of producing innovative films at the Xi'an Film Studio in western China, and it reflects the moment – ten years after the death of Mao – when Chinese society was beginning its convulsive transition from Stalinist communism to free-market capitalism 'with Chinese characteristics'.

A film about individual choices and morality, *Horse Thief* centres on a Tibetan man named Norbu who supports his wife and young son by stealing horses and robbing Muslim travellers at knifepoint. He prays regularly and attends major festivals in the Buddhist calendar; he also donates a large part of his ill-gotten gains to the temple to buy blessings for his family. But, despite his piety and generosity, the community expels him for his crimes. After settling his family in a tent on a mountain plateau, he continues his life as before; soon after, his son falls ill and dies. Ultimately, poverty and the need to provide for a new baby force him to take the lowest of jobs: pelted with stones, he carries a totem intended to exorcise an anthrax epidemic. Finally, all that remains of Norbu is an abandoned dagger and a bloodstain in the snow.

Tian tells this timeless story in fragmentary episodes punctuated by fades to black. There is nothing remotely unrealistic about the depiction of Norbu's domestic life or community, but the absence of conventional exposition and the elliptical storytelling (at one point we realise that two years have passed between scenes) generate a clear sense that Tian's aim is more than ethnographic. This sense is redoubled by the scenes showing Buddhist ceremonies, documentary images given a psychedelic intensity by the use of multiple superimpositions and by Qu Xiaosong's other-worldly score. The film begins and ends with scenes of sky burials (the dead laid out on sacred platforms to be consumed by carrion birds), not only underlining Norbu's inevitable fate but also respecting the ancient Buddhist doctrine of cyclical return.

At the time it was made, the film's sincere curiosity about Tibetan culture and rituals could be seen as questioning China's claim to Tibet, just as its dreamlike qualities amounted to a riposte to the preceding 37 years of didactic, Maoist propaganda film-making. The authorities insisted on adding an opening caption setting the film in 1923, decades before the People's Liberation Army marched into Tibet. But the film's underlying thrust is censor-proof. By showing a man at once enslaved by his religion and flouting every tenet of its morality, it raises fundamental questions about belief systems – questions as relevant to political ideologies as to religious faiths.

Executive producer
Wu Tianming

Line producer
Li Changqing

Writer
Zhuang Rui

Cinematographer
Hou Yong and Zhao Fei

Production company
Xi'an Film Studio

Editor
Li Jingzhong

Cast
Tseshang Rigzin
Dan Jiji
Jayang Jamco
Gaoba Daiba

Other films
★ *On the Hunting Ground* (Liechang Zhasa, 1985)
★ *Li Lianying, the Imperial Eunuch* (Da Taijian Li
Lianying, 1991)
★ *The Blue Kite* (Lan Fengzheng, 1993)

*Buddhist piety of a thief: Tseshang
Rigzin as Norbu.*

Yeelen
Souleymane Cissé, *Mali 1987*

Director, producer and writer
Souleymane Cissé

Souleymane Cissé (also known by the African spelling of his name, Sisé) is one of the handful of directors who brought a credible, black-African cinema into being in the last quarter of the 20th century. Born in Mali and trained (under Mark Donskoi) at the VGIK film school in Moscow, he began directing documentaries for Mali State Information Services in 1970 and began a parallel career as an independent filmmaker the following year. Material and financial problems prevent him from working prolifically; there are gaps of years between his feature projects. But each film is different in form and theme from the others, and each one counts.

Yeelen – which translates as 'the light', or 'brightness' – uses elements from Bambara mythology to tell an allegorical story about individual and collective coming of age. Allegorical, since the central figures are plainly ciphers for their genders, generations and tribal origins, and the telling involves both ancient teachings and homespun magic. But at the same time strangely naturalistic. The time-frame is not specified. It could be an old, old story, or it could be happening right now.

A father, Soma, is hunting down his son, Nianankoro. Soma is armed with a cloth-wrapped wooden rod, used to trace and punish thieves, traitors and perjurers, which seems anomalously heavy judging by the way it makes its bearers stagger and trip. Nianankoro is protected by a jewel given to him by his mother, who advises him to take it to his blind uncle Djigui, Soma's twin. Journeying across country, without even realising it, Nianankoro immerses himself in the *komo*, the secret knowledge of inner and outer worlds that represents the highest wisdom of his people; he also effects a rapprochement with the Bambaras' traditional enemies, the Peuls, and marries their king's youngest wife, the 'barren' Attu, who is soon pregnant with his son.

Finally reaching Djigui, Nianankoro and his wife purify their bodies in a sacred waterfall and listen to the seer's prophecies of calamity and coming change. When Soma arrives, Djigui denounces him for abuse of power and corruption. The final confrontation of father and son, each with a magic totem, results in an explosion of white light that obliterates both of them. Afterwards Nianankoro's young son digs two giant, luminescent eggs from the desert sands and carries them off with his mother.

There are visual clues that one of Cissé's starting points could have been a reaction against Pasolini's *Oedipus Rex* (1967), filmed in neo-primitive anthropological terms on North African locations. However, Cissé's allegory has no Oedipal implications, or indeed any psycho-sexual dimension. Its naturalistic feel springs from the non-professional performances and from its sensitivity to human interactions; its meaning springs from the way it co-opts cultural specifics, memories, superstitions and tribal lore into the service of an urgent call for renewal, expressed as a timeless fable. Far from being hermetic, it reaches out to embrace the widest possible references and implications. But it is irreducibly African, palpably physical and extraordinarily beautiful.

Cinematographer
Jean-Noël Ferragut and
Jean-Michel Humeau

Production company
Les Films Cissé

Music
Michel Portal and Salif Keita

Cast
Issiaka Kané
Aoua Sangare
Niamanto Sanogo

Other films
★ *Den Muso* (1975)
★ *Baara* (1978)
★ *Finyé* (The Wind, 1982)
★ *Waati* (1995)

*Nianankoro's son discovering two huge,
luminescent white eggs in the desert sands.*

Close-Up
Namayeh Nazdik

Abbas Kiarostami, *Iran 1989*

Director, writer and editor
Abbas Kiarostami

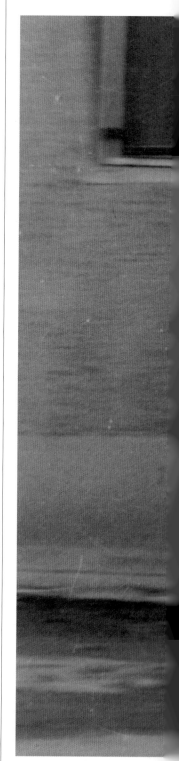

Kiarostami's astonishing body of work, begun in 1970 when he co-founded Kanoon (The Institute for the Intellectual Development of Children and Young Adults), came to international attention only in the late 1980s. Some of this delay reflected the demonization of Iran as a hard-line Islamic theocracy, but the modest scale and unassertive tone of Kiarostami's films made them unlikely to break through walls of prejudice. Happily, coming to Kiarostami when he had already made nearly 20 shorts and features had the side-effect of revealing him to be the fully-functioning master of a film idiom that he had made his own.

Close-Up exemplifies his methods, although its urban setting and its incorporation of both real and fake documentary sequences place it slightly outside the main current of his work. Its starting point was a news report about an unemployed man, Hossain Sabzian, arrested for impersonating the film director Mohsen Makhmalbaf; he had been welcomed into the Tehran home of the middle-class Ahankhah family, who hoped that they and their house would appear in one of 'his' films. Kiarostami gets permission from the judge to film Sabzian's trial, and wins agreement from all concerned (including the journalist who exposed the impostor) that they will re-enact for his camera the events that brought Sabzian to court. The film crosscuts between authentic documentary (Kiarostami calling on the jailed Sabzian and the judge, the trial itself) and reconstruction (necessarily, filmed after Sabzian's release). It ends with a fake-documentary sequence showing Sabzian meeting the real Mohsen Makhmalbaf and going with him to visit the Ahankhahs.

Kiarostami cites the neo-realist cinema of the late 1940s as a point of inspiration, but he and his films remain admirably detached from debates about cinematic 'realism' that occupy the minds of film theorists. For him, the ontology of the film image is simply not an issue: the image is one 'reality' among many others, incapable of encompassing or even registering the spectrum of individual experiences and perceptions. Clearly it matters to him that his films – through the casting of non-professional actors and the integration of non-fiction elements – refer to recognizable realities. But he is no more interested in crude social observation than he is in telling neatly constructed stories. His films raise issues, potentially relevant to every viewer, and provide enough space in the editing to leave ample room for thought and reflection.

To know that Sabzian really did pose as his hero Makhmalbaf adds piquancy to the film, but is not really the point. *Close-Up* is about achieving a sense of dignity and self-esteem, an issue that concerns everyone on screen, from the jobbing journalist to the Ahankhah's pompous younger son, from the impostor to the taxi driver. Kiarostami suggests that everyone 'plays a role', implying that Sabzian simply took the process one step further than most. It is a bracingly egalitarian vision, which goes as far beyond the platitudes of humanism as it flies above the bombast of conventional drama.

300

FILM: THE CRITICS' CHOICE *International Cinema*

Executive producer
Ali Reza Zarrin

Line producer
Hassan Agha-Karimi

Cinematographer
Ali Reza Zarrin-Dast

Production company
Kanoon Institute

Cast
Hossain Sabzian
Abolfazi Ahankhah
Mohsen Makhmalbaf

Other films
★ *The Traveller* (Mossafer, 1974)
★ *Where Is the House of My Friend?* (Khaneh-Je Doost Kojast, 1988)

★ *And Life Goes On* (Zendegi Va Digar Hich, 1992)
★ *Through the Olive Trees* (Zir-e Darakhtan-e Zeyton, 1994)
★ *A Taste of Cherry* (Ta'm e Guilass, 1997)
★ *The Wind Will Carry Us* (1999)

The real Mohsen Makhmalbaf (left) takes Hossain Sabzian to visit the family he tricked.

Boiling Point
3–4x Jugatsu

Kitano Takeshi, *Japan 1990*

Director and writer
Kitano Takeshi

Although it gave Kitano his second director credit, *Boiling Point* has all the hallmarks of a film by a debut director determined to get every idea he has ever had about film, life, death and baseball up there on the screen. Kitano (aka 'Beat' Takeshi, Japan's most popular comedian and television personality) began directing the year before, when he took over his own starring vehicle, *Violent Cop* (1989), from its intended director. But he clearly saw *Boiling Point* as a more personal project; it is from his own script and he gave himself only a supporting role, the better to concentrate on giving the film its structure and tone. The result is erratic, but its ingenuousness perfectly channels most of Kitano's idiosyncrasies, from his innovative editing syntax and use of off-screen space to his unorthodox attitudes to masculinity and teamwork. His subsequent films, such as *Sonatine* (1993) and *Hana-Bi* (1997), are more mature but cannot recapture the raw aesthetic excitement of these beginnings.

As always, Kitano focuses on characters excluded from Japan's 'economic miracle'. His protagonist, Masaki (Ono Masahiko), is a hopeless loser: no education (he is slow on the uptake); no prospects (he works part-time as a petrol-station attendant); no baseball skills (which implies a deficient sense of his place in Japanese society). The entire film is framed by near-black shots of him, sitting in the gloom of a toilet cabin while The Eagles, the amateur baseball team in which he is the weakest link, struggle to avoid another humiliating defeat on the adjacent pitch. These framing shots define the rest of the film as Masaki's daydream. He imagines getting his employer and friends into trouble by standing up to a *yakuza* bully on the garage forecourt, flying to Okinawa with his equally clueless friend Kazuo to buy a gun, spending a wide-eyed day in the company of a crazy gangster, and returning to Tokyo to crash a stolen oil-tanker into the *yakuza* headquarters. In his mind, this suicide gives meaning and shape to a lifetime of underachievement.

Kitano's own extended cameo as Uehara, the Okinawan gangster who commands self-sacrificing loyalty from his friend Tamagi despite expecting him to sever a finger, submit to sodomy and so on, is a creation in the league of French writer Alfred Jarry's Ubu Roi: a lord of misrule, the embodiment of the disorderly underside of orderly Japan. The entire film supports the character with an anarchic vision of a society in which disasters (predictable or otherwise) lurk around every corner – or rather, given Kitano's predilection for long-held, frontal reaction shots, just outside the boundaries of the frame. As a controlled, music-free account of violence, crime and immorality on the verge of erupting through society's placid surfaces, the film is remarkable enough. What makes it phenomenal is Kitano's completely instinctive reinvention of the grammar and syntax of narrative filmmaking, unique in the popular cinema of the 1990s. He was not yet crediting himself as editor, but his ideas were already here bursting to find form.

302

FILM: THE CRITICS' CHOICE International Cinema

FILM: THE CRITICS' CHOICE *International Cinema*

Executive producer
Okuyama Kazuyoshi

Producers
Nabeshima Hisao, Mori
Masayuki and Yoshida Takio

Cinematographer
Yanagijima Katsumi

Art director
Sasaki Osamu

Cast
Ono Masahiko
Iizuka 'Dankan' Minoru
'Beat' Takeshi

Other films
★ *Violent Cop* (1989)
★ *A Scene at the Sea* (Ano
  Natsu, Ichiban Shizukana
  Umi, 1992)

★ *Sonatine* (1993)
★ *Getting Any?* (Minna
  Yatteruka, 1994)
★ *Kids' Return* (1996)
★ *Fireworks* (Hana-Bi, 1997)
★ *Kikujiro* (Kikujiro no Netsu,
  1999)
★ *Brother* (2000)

Torashiki Katsuo as Tamagi, an Okinawan gangster's loyal but long-suffering sidekick.

The Day a Pig Fell into the Well
Dwaeji-ga Umulae Pajinnal

Hong Sang-Soo, *South Korea 1996*

The creative surge in Korean filmmaking in the 1990s sprang, obviously, from the country's political and social changes: the arrival of non-military governments after the long campaign for democracy; over-rapid economic development; the shift from Confucian orthodoxies to a new cosmopolitanism; the deregulation of the film industry and the relaxation of censorship. All Korean films of the period indirectly reflected these changes; however, few of those which directly addressed the state of the nation transcended the urge to grandstand. Hong Sang-Soo's phenomenal debut feature was one of the few.

Belying its title, *The Day a Pig Fell into the Well* is entirely urban in setting and sensibility. It tracks four main characters – two women, two men – across a few weeks in and around Seoul, (South Korea's capital city). The lives of the four characters are interconnected, but the film is divided into four 'chapters', each centred on only one of them: the failed novelist, Hyosup, despised by his peers but loved by both women; the water-purifier executive, Tongwoo, who catches a venereal disease from a prostitute on a business trip; the box-office girl and dubbing artist, Minjae, who spends all her free time and most of her money supporting Hyosup; and Tongwoo's wife, Pokyong, on the verge of divorcing so that she can be with Hyosup. The network of dependencies that links the characters is revealed only gradually, as they appear in each others' chapters; the film has no strong narrative thrust, and what keeps the viewer engrossed is the sense that pieces are inexorably falling into place.

Hong (a graduate of the Art Institute of Chicago) started from a characteristically original idea: he assigned one character each to four different writers, asking them to script an itinerary and set of events for that character, and then welded the four resulting scenarios together to give the film its structure. The actors also made substantial contributions, since 90 per cent of the dialogue was improvised. The film was shot entirely on location and almost entirely with available light. All of these strategies suggest that Hong was aiming for some kind of social realism, and the film certainly captures mundane routines and day-to-day setbacks with precision and wry wit. But the film can equally be seen as a revolt against the conventions of 'realism'. Its artful framing and editing, an interpolated dream sequence and the fact that two of its main characters meet un-expected, violent deaths all militate against reading it as a 'slice of life'.

As the metaphorical title suggests, larger inferences are in order. Hong certainly sets out to get the sociological details right, but he is more interested in pinpointing what happens mentally when the generation raised in the activist 1980s finds itself falling into premature middle age in the materialist 1990s. His piercingly original approach sees through quotidian banalities to what Freud dubbed the psychopathology of everyday life.

Director
Hong Sang-Soo

Executive producer
Lee Hosung

Producer
Lee Wooseok

Writers
Hong Sang-Soo, Chung Daesung, Yeo Haeyoung, Kim Alah and Seo Shinhae

Cinematographer
Cho Eunsook

Cast
Kim Uisung
Lee Eungkyung
Park Jinsung
Cho Eunsook

Other films (Güney)
★ *The Power of Kangwon Province* (Kangwon-do iu Him, 1998)
★ *Virgin Stripped Bare by her Bachelors* (Oh! Soojung, 2000)

A dramatic image from this Korean classic.

Happy Together
Chunguang Zhaxie

Wong Kar-Wai, *Hong Kong 1997*

Director, producer and writer
Wong Kar-Wai

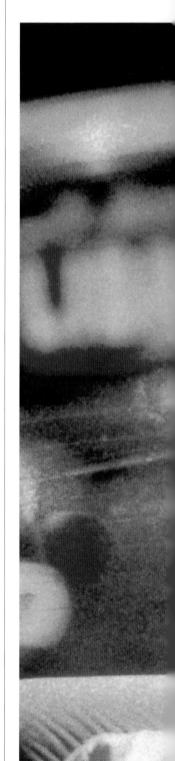

The line most often repeated in *Happy Together* is 'Let's start over'. It is the watchword of Ho Po-Wing (Leslie Cheung), a good-time boy from Hong Kong travelling through Argentina with his more introverted boyfriend Lai Yiu-Fai (Tony Leung); he uses the line to effect a reconciliation whenever the tensions between them reach breaking point. But it could equally be a watchword for Wong Kar-Wai himself, whose approach to filmmaking is less improvisatory than aleatory.

Starting out with a few key elements (a story idea, lead actors, a setting, a piece of music), Wong develops and writes his films during the shooting, allowing the material already shot to help determine the direction of the rest. There is always that risk that the process will become unwieldly and drawn out; *Happy Together*, inspired by the writings of Argentine novelist Manuel Puig and planned as a two-month shoot in Latin America, eventually took five months – including a coda set in Taipei, added at the last minute. But the result here is a perfect match of method and theme. Like its central couple, the film's narrative keeps starting over, searching through patterns of repetition and variation for that elusive new beginning.

The narrative core is slim. The fraught romance comes to an end; Ho teases Lai by coming back for tender loving care when he gets into trouble, but Lai steels himself to earn enough for his passage home. Before leaving, he fulfils an ambition by visiting the huge Iguaçu Falls on the Brazilian border, and he drifts into a non-sexual friendship with a Taiwanese backpacker (Chang Chen), which, subjectively at least, seems to give him the new start he needs. Slim it may be, but this minimal storyline is enough to give Wong the leeway for a dizzying account of one man's struggle to find himself. The mortifications that Lai bears so stoically, from emotional breakdown to work in an abattoir, are preludes to a reawakening of sorts, signalled by the coda, in which he visits the food stall run by the backpacker's family, steals a photo of the boy, and takes a trip on Taipei's new automated elevated railway – a driverless ride through the night in fast motion.

Wong, a former screenwriter who has been one of the world's most popular art-house directors since he made *Chungking Express* in 1994, says that he went to Argentina to get as far away as possible from Hong Kong in the run-up to the territory's reversion to Chinese sovereignty in 1997. Once there, he found himself making a film about 'identity' – precisely the issue most on the minds of the people of Hong Kong at the time. But the film carries its symbolic inferences lightly. Its mixture of kinetic energy and unvoiced feelings, tangos and secrets, manages to be absolutely true to the situation it describes and at the same time representative of all struggles to assert the Self, with and without the presence of The Other. Far more visual than verbal, the film explains nothing. Wong trusts his images to say enough.

Cinematographer
Christopher Doyle

Editors
William Chang and
Wong Ming-Lam

Production companies
Jet Tone Productions

Music
Danny Chung

Art director
William Chang

Cast
Leslie Chung
Tony Leung
Chang Chen

Other films
★ *As Tears Go By* (Wongjiao Kamen, 1988)
★ *Days of Being Wild* (A-Fei Zheychuan, 1990)
★ *Ashes of Time* (Dongxie Xidu, 1994)
★ *Chungking Express* (Chongqing Senlin, 1994)
★ *Fallen Angels* (Duolo Tianshi, 1996)
★ *In the Mood for Love* (Huayang Nianhua, 2000)

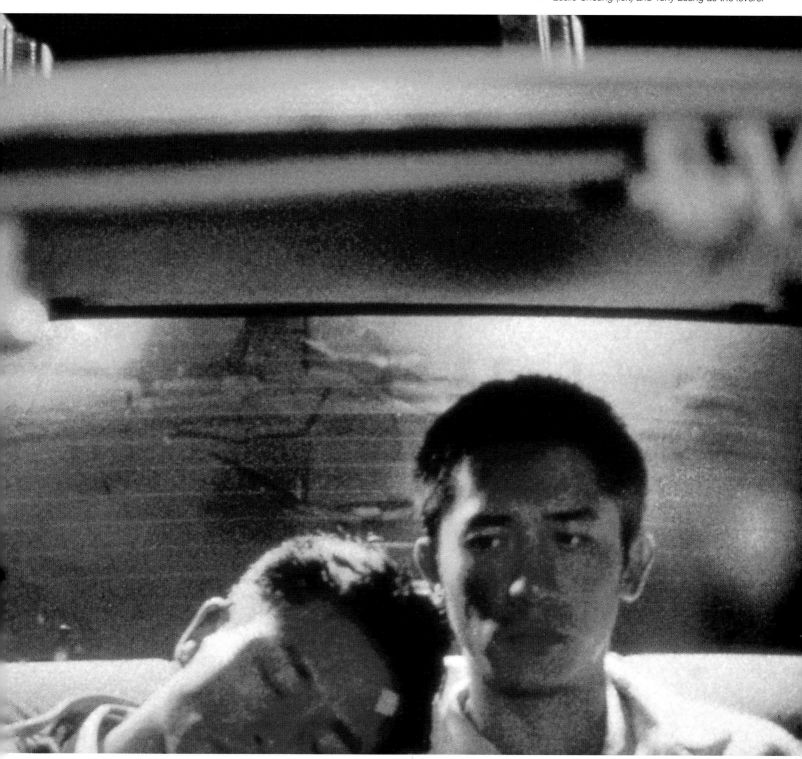

Leslie Cheung (left) and Tony Leung as the lovers.

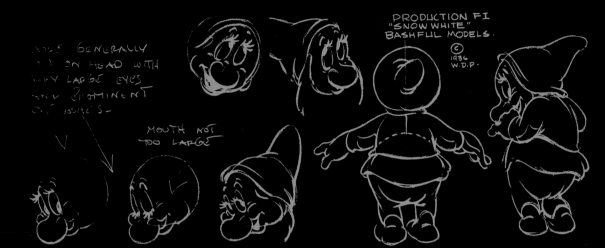

MAIN: *A finished frame from Disney's* Snow White and the Seven Dwarfs *(1937);* LEFT: *'Bashful', from* Snow White and the Seven Dwarfs.

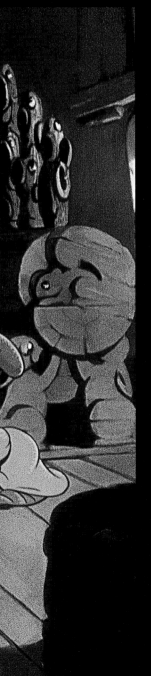

The Art of the Impossible

Paul Wells

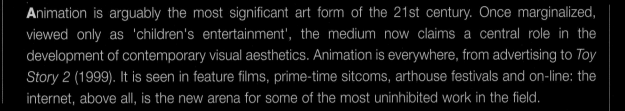

Animation is arguably the most significant art form of the 21st century. Once marginalized, viewed only as 'children's entertainment', the medium now claims a central role in the development of contemporary visual aesthetics. Animation is everywhere, from advertising to *Toy Story 2* (1999). It is seen in feature films, prime-time sitcoms, arthouse festivals and on-line: the internet, above all, is the new arena for some of the most uninhibited work in the field.

In early cinema, animation – creating movies frame-by-frame, using drawings, puppets or inanimate objects – was inseparable from moving-image novelties such as 'trick' films employing stop-motion. It was pioneering newspaper comic-strip artists-cum-vaudevillians like Winsor McCay who ensured that graphic narrative forms translated into distinctive 'cartoon' films. McCay's *Little Nemo* (1910) represents both the rise of the unique vocabulary of the 'cartoon' and the translation of modernist art into popular forms. The technique was painstaking; with 24 frames per second, even a short demanded hundreds of drawings.

Elsewhere, Emile Cohl's *Fantasmagorie* (1908), Arnaldo Ginna's *A Chord of Colour* (1910) and Ladislaw Starewich's *The Cameraman's Revenge* (1911; Starewich is also known as Wladislaw Starewicz) initiated traditions of their own: Cohl concerned with the free play of the graphic line; Ginna painting directly on to film; Starewich creating persuasive stop-motion three-dimensional narratives. These European innovators anticipated the experimental work of later key figures such as Oskar Fischinger (*Composition in Blue*, 1937), George Pal (*Sky Pirates*, 1938) and Alexandre Alexeïeff (*The Nose*, 1963).

However, from the landmark *Steamboat Willie* (1928), featuring Mickey Mouse, through the first Technicolor cartoon, *Flowers and Trees* (1932), to the ground-breaking full-length feature, *Snow White and the Seven Dwarfs* (1937), it was Walt Disney who successfully managed to combine technological innovation with artistic excellence to create an anima-

tion industry. The classic works that followed, *Pinocchio* (1940) and *Fantasia* (1940), defined the form, perfecting a state-of-the-art 'hyper-realist' style of caricatural design and authentic movement.

The comic bravura of Tex Avery (*Red Hot Riding Hood*, 1943) and Chuck Jones (*What's Opera, Doc?*, 1957) at Warner Brothers and the surreal intensity of the Fleischer brothers' *Betty Boop* shorts brought adult maturity to the cartoon. Politically charged European traditions – puppet animation from Czechoslovakia such as Jiri Trnka's *The Hand* (1965), graphic minimalism from the Zagreb Studio in Yugoslavia, for example Dusan Vukotic's *Ersatz* (1961), and folk-orientated dreamworks from the former Soviet Union in the style of Andrei Khrzhanovsky's *The Grey Bearded Lion* (1994) – extended the form. And the National Film Board of Canada (who sponsored, for example, Richard Condie's *The Big Snit*, 1985) and the Shanghai Studio in China (behind Hu Jinquing's *Snipe Clam Grapple*, 1984) combine indigenous concerns and artistic traditions in new works.

Modern Disney classics, like the computer-generated *Dinosaur* (2000), vie with Japanese *animé* (*Ghost in the Shell*, 1995, and *Princess Honomoko*, 1999), British animation by Nick Park (*Chicken Run*, 2000), Joanna Quinn (*Britannia*, 1997) and Barry Purves (*Gilbert and Sullivan*, 1998), and television cartoons, exemplified by *The Simpsons*, *South Park* and *Starship Troopers*. Revising categories, challenging boundaries, illustrating the world afresh, animation – the art of the impossible – continues to amaze and astound.

The Cameraman's Revenge
Miest Kinooperatora

Ladislaw Starewich *1911*

Director, writer, cinematographer and production designer
Ladislaw Starewich

Ladislaw Starewich was born in Moscow in 1882. A childhood interest in entomology was satisfied in adult life when he became Director of the Natural History Museum at Kovno and was also reflected in two early films he made featuring animated insects, *The Grasshopper and the Ant* (1911) and *The Cameraman's Revenge* (1911). Starewich originally made natural history shorts to explore aspects of insect behaviour, but the inevitable deaths of live insects under hot studio lights led him to animate models. The persuasiveness of the animation, coupled with an early example of paranoia about the capabilities of Eastern Europe, led *The Times* to report that the insects were alive and trained by Russian scientists!

Influenced by *The Animated Matches*, a 1908 film by the pioneering French animator Emile Cohl, Starewich joined up with the Khanzonkow Film Production Company in 1911. He ultimately specialized in three-dimensional work, which allowed him to play out the modernity of early cinematic technique through the narrative and thematic ambiguities of the traditional fairytale. Starewich's use of insects gives the material a Kafkaesque tone, playing on the 'otherness' of insect forms to suggest the possibility of human perversity and desire.

Starewich saw in insects and animals characteristics that could be projected onto the human condition – the reverse of the process of anthropomorphization which underpins much animation. *The Cameraman's Revenge* foregrounds our intrinsic perception of the insect as the signifier of 'inhuman' properties; here is an unsentimental world characterized by the brutal indifference and claustrophobia characteristic of the fairytale. Sal sends the Fly to spy on Bill, her husband, who is recorded on camera with his mistress. Sal also enjoys an affair with Clarence, a flamboyant artist. But Bill discovers Sal's dalliance, breaking a portrait painted by Clarence over her head. He too is undone, however, when the Fly, also a cinema projectionist, shows the film of Bill's betrayal to a public audience. A melodramatic masterpiece of love, deception and betrayal, the piece is considerably enhanced by its cinematic reflexivity, readily acknowledging the voyeuristic and intrusive capabilities of film itself.

Starewich's approach began a tradition in stop-motion animation which in the Hollywood context became absorbed into special-effects work, best illustrated by Willis O'Brien in *King Kong* (1933, *see pages 56–57*), George Pal's short 'Puppetoons' and his feature *Tom Thumb* (1958), Ray Harryhausen's *Jason and the Argonauts* (1963), and the contemporary blockbusters made by George Lucas' Industrial Light and Magic, most notably *Star Wars* (1977, *see pages 112–113*). Henry Selick's *The Nightmare Before Christmas* (1992) and *James and the Giant Peach* (1995) signalled a resurgence in stop-motion animation as a distinct style in feature-length filmmaking and included direct tributes to Starewich's films. Starewich's influence can also be traced in animated insects from Jiminy Cricket in Disney's *Pinocchio* (1940, *see pages 318–319*), the Fleischer brothers' *Mr Bug Goes to Town* (1941), Lotte Reiniger's *The Grasshopper and the Ant* (1954), Pixar's *A Bug's Life* (1997), and the television cartoon *Pokémon* (1999), based on the children's toys and, interestingly, also inspired by creator Satoshi Tajiri's love of insects.

310

Production company
Khanzonkow

Other films
- ★ *The Grasshopper and the Ant* (1911)
- ★ *Terrible Revenge* (1913)
- ★ *Voice of the Nightingale* (1923)
- ★ *Love in Black and White* (1928)
- ★ *The Tale of the Fox* (1930)

The flamboyant artist Clarence paints a self-portrait to give to Sal, his mistress.

Gertie the Dinosaur Winsor McCay *1914*

Warner Brothers' master animator, Chuck Jones, once remarked that 'the two most important people in animation are Winsor McCay and Walt Disney, and I'm not sure which should go first'. A New York comic-strip virtuoso, McCay established the iconography and technical methodology for full animation in *Little Nemo* (1910), a fluid adaptation of his own strip.

The first example of McCay's stated intention to use animation to depict physical objects and phenomena in ways that could not be achieved in another medium, *Nemo*'s dream-narrative, with its fluid meta-morphoses, was soon followed by *How a Mosquito Operates* (1912). An early example of the horror genre, this features 'personality' animation in the form of the mosquito who draws blood from a sleeping man, only to later explode through overindulgence!

From 1906, McCay toured as a 'lightning sketch' artist in vaudeville. These performers drew rapid chalk sketches on blackboards to illustrate jokes and routines in the show, the drawing process itself producing amusement as recognition dawned, and McCay became an accomplished entertainer. He combined his filmmaking and performance practices by incorporating his film *Gertie the Dinosaur* (1914) into his stage act. McCay's extraordinary draughtsmanship, based on the working process of drawing two 'extreme' poses for his characters and 'in-betweening' the movement from one to the other, rather than drawing in the 'direct' fashion of moving from one image to the next, revolutionized animation: he was effectively working less with the graphic codes encouraged by the unpredictability of immediate visual improvisation and more with 'realist' conventions of preconceived action.

McCay sought to bring plausibility to his 'fantastic' forms so that they would transcend their status as animation. This approach suited the American Histor-ical Society, which had approached McCay in 1912 to consider a 'dinosaur' film. The film opened on 8 February 1914 at the Palace Theater, Chicago, and amazed audiences, who could not work out how the illusion had been achieved. This was partly because *Gertie the Dinosaur* was the first example of an 'inter-active' cartoon, where McCay appeared to be giving instructions to Gertie – the first identifiably 'female' cartoon character -- throwing a pumpkin to her, and finally, entering the image himself, being carried away by her. McCay's fluid illustration is enhanced by the attention he gave to the ways in which Gertie's size and weight would affect the environment, and the way he informed the rhythm and timing of her movements with 'thought' processes and emotive actions. A cliff gives way when Gertie consumes an entire lake; rocks slip and earth moves; a mammoth is playfully hurled into the far distance. Even Gertie's breathing is clear. Such detail emphasized Gertie's 'reality' in the eyes of an astonished audience.

Gertie's legacy is profound. From Willis O'Brien's *The Lost World* (1925) to Disney's *Dinosaur* (2000), pre-history has been reanimated. More importantly, the caricaturial conviction in Gertie's personality informs character animation into the contemporary era. No more appropriate tribute came than Dick Huemer's re-enactment of McCay's vaudeville act in the television series *Disneyland* in an episode called 'The Art of the Animated Drawing' (1955). McCay once presciently suggested that 'artists working hand in hand with science will evolve a new school of art that will revolutionize the whole field'.

Director, writer, producer and animator
Winsor McCay

Tracer
John A. Fitzsimmons

Production company
McCay

Cast
George McManus
Thomas A. Durgan
Roy L. McCardell
Winsor McCay
Tom Powers

Other films
★ *Little Nemo* (1910)
★ *How a Mosquito Operates* (1912)

Gertie the dinosaur gets an opportunity to display her 'personality' as she throws a minor tantrum.

Betty Boop's Snow White

Dave Fleischer *1933*

The Fleischer brothers – Max, Dave, Joe and Lou – fascinated by 'cartoons', 'science' and 'mechanics', created the rotoscope (which facilitated the frame-by-frame copying of filmed live-action movement onto transparent animation cels), made the hour-long *Einstein's Theory of Relativity* (1923), the *Song Car Tune* singalong cartoons (1924–27), which used live accompaniment and a 'bouncing ball' to follow the lyrics, and the half-animated, half-live-action *Out of the Inkwell* series featuring Ko-Ko the clown, all before the end of the 1930s.

The Fleischers' five-minute version of *Snow White*, made four years before Walt Disney's groundbreaking feature, was animated virtually single-handed by Roland 'Doc' Crandall in six months and is more faithful to the spirit of the Grimms' fairytale and to 'cartoon' as a unique vocabulary of expression.

Miscasting the 'child-whore' Betty Boop as the virginal, much-harassed Snow White eroticizes an arbitrary and surreal narrative, loosely based on the central tension between the wicked Queen and Betty about 'who is the fairest in the land'. The 'plot' becomes a series of seemingly unrelated or non-motivated events, illustrating the Fleischers' subversive use of metamorphosis as a barometer of the fragile, taken-for-granted stabilities of the modern world. The Queen's face turns into a frying pan with two fried eggs; a ghost entwines into a 25-cent piece and a bottle; a skeleton is literally pulled from within a dragon's body. This improvised, non-linear yet persuasively evocative approach enhances the mature themes and ambiguities of the fairytale.

Betty Boop first featured as a dog in *Dizzy Dishes* (1930), was named 'Betty' in *Betty Co-ed* (1931), and was fully humanized in *Any Rags* (1932). Her designer, Grim Natwick, refined her into a 'Jewish American Princess' in *Minnie the Moocher* (1932), gaining a reputation for animating adolescent girls and the job of animating Disney's Snow White. Betty provokes a sexual predatoriness in the objects around her, which are drawn with the adult knowingness and sceptical wit that coloured urban experience. The cartoon plays out its 'underground' credentials further in embracing the earthy, transgressive, quasi-dionysian qualities associated by many white Americans with black culture in the 1930s. Lou Fleischer visited Harlem's Cotton Club to see Cab Calloway and selected three songs for use in Fleischer cartoons. *Snow White* features a version of 'St James Infirmary Blues' and the rotoscoped body of Calloway himself as a ghost traversing an underworld of gambling dens and charnel houses. These cartoons were shown in the weeks before Calloway was due to play in a particular town and served as promotional vehicles, long anticipating the contemporary music-video.

Part provocative, part paranoid, these images define the milieu of 'adult' culture at Paramount Studios which challenged, endured but finally fell in the wake of the censorious Hays Code (or the Motion Picture Production Code, which in 1930 enshrined moral standards and limits), the murder of director William Desmond Taylor, the Fatty Arbuckle sex scandals, and the reining-in of major Paramount stars Mae West and Marlene Dietrich. *Betty Boop's Snow White* remains an important reminder of Betty at her 'purest' and Fleischer animation at its freest, before the inevitable onset of creative and commercial conservatism that implicitly paid homage to Disney's style, status and success.

Director and writer
Dave Fleischer

Producer
Max Fleischer

Animator
Roland 'Doc' Crandall

Designer
Grim Natwick

Production companies
Fleischer Studios

Cast
May Questel

Other films
★ *Out of the Inkwell* (1915)
★ *Einstein's Theory of Relativity* (1923)
★ *Song Car-Tune* (1924–27)
★ *Minnie the Moocher* (1932)

INKWELL

Papageno
Lotte Reiniger *1934*

Director, writer and producer
Lotte Reiniger

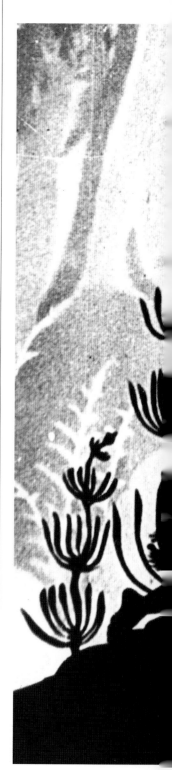

Lotte Reiniger, born in 1899, made more than 50 animated films, principally engaged with the fable, fairytale and folk idioms. Her prodigious and influential output has made her one of the most significant figures in animation and has particularly encouraged women to embrace the auteurist potential intrinsic to the form and to explore a specifically 'feminine aesthetic'. Reiniger's work has also influenced Michael Ocelot (*Three Inventors*, 1980).

The German Expressionist film director Paul Wegener in a 1916 lecture entitled 'The Artistic Possibilities of Cinema' noted, 'I can imagine a cinema which would use nothing but moving surfaces, against which there would impinge events that would still participate in the natural world but transcend the lines and volumes of the natural.' Although Wegener thought that this goal might be achieved using three-dimensional marionette animation, Reiniger, inspired by his vision, saw such possibilities in silhouette animation, recalling the ancient Chinese shadow plays.

Reiniger began her career at Max Reinhardt's acting studio, where she drew silhouettes of actors, published in 1917, which anticipate the hand-cut titles she made for Wegener's *The Pied Piper of Hamelin* (1918). Recommended to the Institute of Cultural Research, which was directed by Hans Cürlis, Reiniger became more fully involved in experimental animation, collaborating with Carl Koch (later her husband), Berthold Bartosch (with whom she had made shorts on geographical subjects) and Walter Ruttmann. Together they made the 'One-Thousand-and-One Nights' tale, *The Adventures of Prince Achmed* (1923), a film which uniquely defined the delicacy and beauty of cut-out silhouette, stop-motion animation, marking out an unsurpassed craft-based technique as Reiniger's signature style. She made scissors as viable a tool as the pencil and created figures and environments of such lyrical intensity that she redefined the two-dimensional graphic space.

In fully exploring the limits of her technique, Reiniger drew attention to the importance of the relationship between character design and individual movements. Papageno is a bird catcher, inspired by the character in Mozart's *The Magic Flute* (*Die Zauberflöte*), and in a spirit of camouflage and of empathy with the birds, his figure is designed to look like a bird, his head covered in extravagant plumage. Without colour, the qualities of shape, form and motion become particularly significant, and it is the light-footedness of the character's movements that underpins the narrative requirement that he must silently and carefully pursue the birds, as well as the technical and aesthetic need to embody lightness and lyricism – both within the *mise en scène,* and in relation to the score, which is made up of music from Mozart's opera. Reiniger's figure, who carries a net and a small cage, thus becomes a character informed by a dance-like mobility and romantic gesture rather than by intimidation or threat. The emphasis is placed on the theatricality of the work and the free play of 'moving surfaces' rather than on the issues that might arise from a story of hunter and hunted. For Reiniger, the aesthetic imperative of the film, its intrinsic 'task', is to translate 'musical value' into 'screen-space value'; and in achieving this she denies the work a relationship to its historical context and prioritizes a dream-like abstraction which heightens her credentials as a leading modernist artist in the field. Sound counterpoints image, heightening the idiom.

Music
Taken from Mozart's *The Magic Flute* (*Die Zauberflöte*)

Other films
★ *The Adventures of Prince Achmed* (1923)
★ *The Grasshopper and the Ant* (1954)
★ *The Frog Prince* (1961)

The unthreatening lyricism of the bird catcher's movement makes him an intrinsic part of the animated and natural world.

Pinocchio
Hamilton Luske and Ben Sharpsteen *1940*

Writing in the *Spectator* in 1940, the filmmaker and critic Basil Wright described *Pinocchio* as 'absolutely real but also absolutely fantastic', pinpointing the ambiguity in a film which is both a bleak morality tale – at once thematically and graphically 'dark' – and a picaresque adventure of bravura and ingenuity. Based on Carlo Collodi's didactic fable of 1881, the film transforms the delinquency of Pinocchio and the cruel anarchy of childhood into a rites-of-passage story of innocence, redemption and American heroism – albeit one populated by Dickensian grotesques.

Ironically, this approach emphasizes the arbitrary brutality of the 'real' world inhabited by Pinocchio and, arguably, undermines the moral clarity of the story. Such complexity, coupled with the aesthetic advances made since *Snow White and the Seven Dwarfs*, was embraced by critics but resulted in an initial box-office failure. The $2.6 million outlay seemed unlikely to be recouped, particularly as the European market had been shut down by the outbreak of the Second World War, but subsequent re-releases bolstered *Pinocchio*'s reputation and ensured that the film ran into profit.

Pinocchio represents the defining moment in the evolution of Disney's style, which was predicated partly on 'realist' authenticity and partly on caricaturial innovation. Designers Gustaf Tenggren and Albert Hurter created Alpine scenery, based on the area around Rothenburg in Bavaria, which separated the story from its Italian roots and allowed the transformation of Pinocchio's character from an unruly *commedia dell'arte* clown to, incongruously, an American folk-innocent, replete with cowlick and (in a nod to the context) Tyrolean garb. Pinocchio is accompanied by Jiminy Cricket, a wholly Americanized little green carpetbagger, who speaks like the 18th-century American statesman Benjamin Franklin and plays the ambivalent role of Pinocchio's conscience. In the book, Jiminy Cricket is crushed on the hearth early in the story and appears in infrequent scenes of ghostly admonition; in the film he is Disney's ideological voice. These adjustments sought to make the emotional journey in the story appealing, and Pinocchio, the 'wooden' puppet whose nose grows when he lies, sympathetic and comic. However, the 'boyishness' of the character throughout the film arguably undermines Pinocchio's final transition from puppet to boy.

The film's greatest achievements, however, are Hamilton Luske's sensitive direction of live-action movement that was then used as rotoscoped animation; Bob Jones's three-dimensional models of key interiors – Geppetto's boat, the whale skeleton, the birdcage prison, Stromboli's caravan – which were used as templates for detailed design; Bill Tytla's striking animation of the muscular energy of Stromboli; Oscar Fischinger's 'wand-sparkle' for the Blue Fairy; and Woolie Reitherman's extraordinary animation of Monstro the whale, in which the scale, weight and impact of the creature match the verisimilitude of its oceanic world. The involvement of such talented technicians and artists contributed to the trend in animation towards the cinematic conventions of the 'real' and the fullest emotive exploitation of the *mise en scène* while demonstrating and celebrating the freedoms of self-conscious artifice. This aesthetic contradiction still underpins the orthodoxies of feature animation today, but has rarely been achieved with such graphic detail and emotional intensity.

Directors
Hamilton Luske
and Ben Sharpsteen

Producer
Walt Disney

Writers
Aurelius Battaglia, William Cottrell, Otto Englander and others, based on the original novel by Carlo Collodi

Music
Leigh Harline, Paul J. Smith and Ned Washington

Production companies
Walt Disney Productions

Cast
Don Brodie
Walter Catlett
Frankie Darro

Other films: Luske
★ *Lady and the Tramp* (1955)
★ *101 Dalmatians* (1961)

Other films: Sharpsteen
★ *Dumbo* (1941)

Academy Awards
Oscars for Best Original Score and Best Song ('When You Wish Upon A Star'), 1941

Jiminy Cricket, Pinocchio's 'conscience figure', watches in alarm as his charge lies himself into branching out.

Blitzwolf Tex Avery 1942

While Chuck Jones' lyricism and literariness and Bob Clampett's surrealism and musicality may lay claim to extending the parameters of the cartoon form (Clampett being best known for the now notorious *Coal Black and de Sebben Dwarfs*, 1943), it is Tex Avery's work which best represents a marked reconfiguration of the animated short. Avery's emphasis on the centrality of 'the gag', the self-reflexive nature of 'cartoonalness' (the recognition of the cartoon's own frames of reference and its independence from the material world), his engagement with adult themes, and the redefinition of the kinetic and aural conditions of the cartoon, challenged the Disney aesthetic which, by the early 1940s, had already come to define the medium.

Avery's cartoons at Warner Brothers' 'Termite Terrace' studio and at MGM included characters speaking directly to the audience; his gags exposed the conventions of film practice, while his representation of sex, sexuality, power-relations and status-conflicts was innovative and daring. His anti-Disney stance is exemplified, for example, in *Screwball Squirrel* (1944): a cutesy rabbit extolling the virtues of all his forest friends is gently coerced behind a tree by the cartoon's eponymous hero and is clattered with a baseball bat!

Blitzwolf (1942) was Avery's first cartoon for MGM after he left Warner Bros. It represents his distinctive contribution to the war effort. Parodying Disney's *Three Little Pigs* (1933), Avery portrays Sergeant Pork in the brick-built house as the United States at its most prepared – the house here being the repository of endlessly extending missile launchers – and the other pigs as America at its most naive and, by implication, most Disneyesque. These pigs respect the Non-Aggression Pact signed by 'Adolf Wolf, Colossal Stinker', who promises 'With your freedom, I will not tinker', but this undertaking is soon seen as worthless as the wolf himself makes a melodramatic entrance in his tank, which has written on it 'Der Fewer (Der Better)'. He speaks to the audience – 'Go on, hiss, who cares?' – and gets a tomato in the face. He tip-toes and goose-steps and uses 'Der Mechanized Huffer und Puffer' to blow away the straw house to the strains of 'Dixie', revealing a sign with 'Gone with the Wind' written on it. The camera then moves to another sign saying 'Corny gag, isn't it?' Indeed.

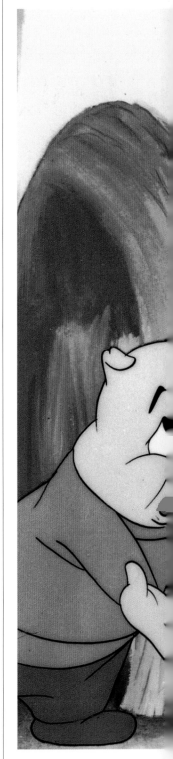

The wolf – who in later films like *Red Hot Riding Hood* (1943) becomes Avery's symbol for the unfettered libido – is here merely an unmitigated transgressor and carrier of Avery's love for the literal joke, the visual pun and incongruous slapstick. His tank is opened with a can-opener and then fractures into smaller tin cans; his missiles are rendered impotent when they gaze at the beautiful girls in *Esquire* magazine. Other typically phallic Avery gags include a drooping American gun-turret revived into an erection by Vitamin B_1. The wolf bombs the pigs in a 'Stinka-Bomber P-U', calls for 'Dr Kildare' on his descent from his blown-up aircraft, and finally lands in hell. Such Avery-style propaganda lost out in the Oscar stakes to Disney's more fear-inducing *Der Fuehrer's Face* (1942), but his influence on the frenetic pace and bug-eyed slapstick of Hanna-Barbera's *Tom and Jerry* series (which first appeared in the 1930s) is immediately evident, and his contribution to the prominence of the cartoon as a comic art form pronounced.

Original story
Rich Hogan

Animators
Preston Blair, Ray Abrams,
Irven Spence and Ed Love

Music
Scott Bradley

Production company
MGM

Other films
★ *Red Hot Riding Hood*
  (1943)
★ *Screwball Squirrel* (1944)

Sergeant Pork pleads with Adolf Wolf outside one of a succession of houses.

La Poulette grise
The Young Grey Hen

Norman McLaren *1947*

Director, animator, writer and producer
Norman McLaren

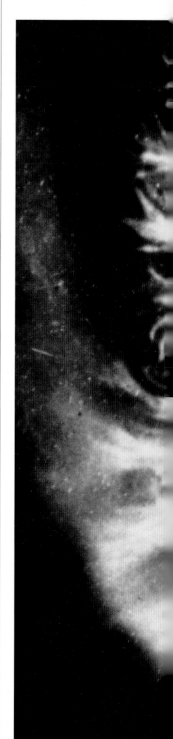

Norman McLaren studied at the Glasgow School of Art in 1933 before concentrating on a career in experimental filmmaking. Combining interests in modernist art, technical innovation and social empowerment, McLaren made his first film, *Hell Unlimited* (1934), as a pacifist statement, critical of particular forms of nationalism. Although his socialist sensibility always underpinned his career, as in films like *V for Victory* (1941) and *Neighbours* (1952) and his work for UNESCO in India and China, educating local artists about visual communication to promote preventative medicine, such political leanings were soon subsumed by McLaren's aesthetic imperatives.

His work for the Post Office in Britain (with the left-wing documentarist John Grierson) and later at the National Film Board of Canada embraced abstraction and promoted avant-garde animation. McLaren's non-objective, non-linear work aimed to define its own terms and conditions and seldom referred to things outside itself. However, such work – arguably a method by which unconscious processes are made concrete – became subject to psychoanalytical interpretation, and one example, *Love on the Wing* (1938), was deemed 'too erotic and too Freudian' by the British Minister of Posts.

McLaren's synthesis of sound and vision always engages the viewer, and in *La Poulette Grise*, for example, this combination succeeds in creating change within the image *as* a narrative event. Rather surprisingly, some animation critics have suggested that this degree of comprehensibility compromises the work and so renders it insufficiently 'modernist', but McLaren's art rises above such criticism by virtue of its ambition to explore new relationships between the arts as well as the potential of the animation medium itself. *Begone Dull Care* (1949), influenced by Len Lye who made the experimental *Rainbow Dance* (1936), and created by painting directly on to film, was hailed by Picasso as 'Finally, something new!'; *Pas de Deux* (1967) successfully explored the intrinsic relationship between animation and dance, simultaneously exploiting the camera for different effects; while *Synchrony* (1971) literally animated the soundtrack on the film itself.

McLaren's key interest lay in what could be achieved within the frame itself, and in the literal and technical space that lies between creating one frame and creating the next. In the late 1940s, he was exploring the *process* of painting, seeking to simplify, clarify and record successive 'canvases'. This is most explicit in *La Poulette grise*, which is in effect a second-by-second evolution of a single 5.5 x 7.3 metre (18 x 24 foot) chalk and pastel landscape. Each frame, improvised during shooting rather than pre-storyboarded, advanced lyrical metamorphoses, heightening the relationship between the abstract and the mimetic, the interplay between light and dark, and the contrast between organic mutability and an endless travelling forward in time and space. These effects in turn prompt realizations about nature and nurture, birth and regeneration (expressed playfully here in the metaphor of the chicken and the egg), the integration of life forms, and the influence of cosmic forces. Accompanied by popular songs sung by Anna Malenfant and the music of Maurice Blackburn, the piece works as an unconscious illustration of a higher plane of human existence, expressed with child-like freedom.

322

Production company
Office nationale du film du
Canada

Music
Anna Malenfant and
Maurice Blackburn

Other films
★ *Hell Unlimited* (1934)
★ *V for Victory* (1941)
★ *Neighbours* (1952)
★ *Pas de Deux* (1967)
★ *Synchrony* (1971)

McLaren uses the everyday strangeness of a creature – in this case a chicken – to explore abstract and figurative patterns.

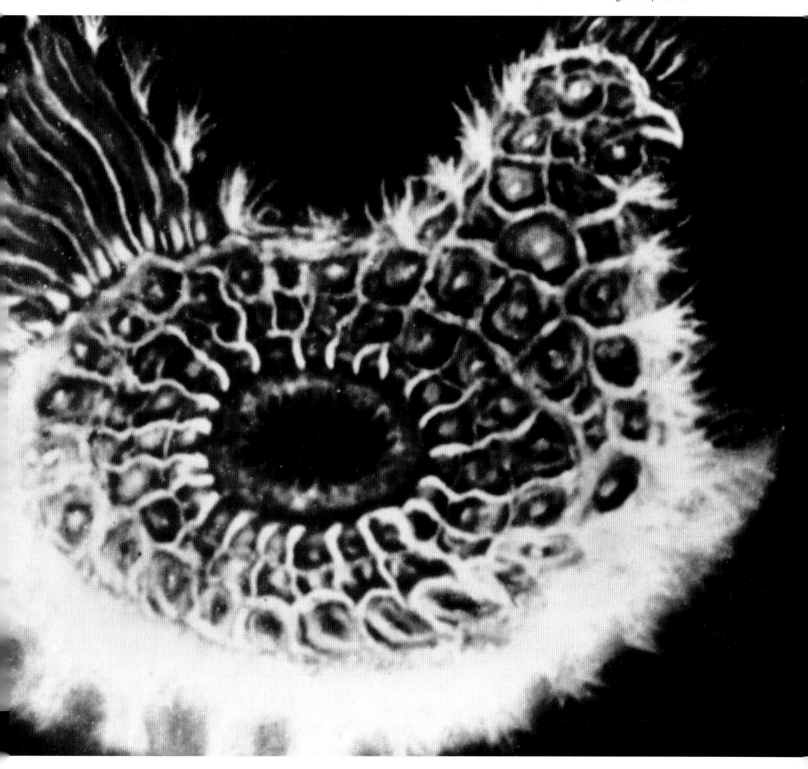

What's Opera, Doc? Chuck Jones *1957*

Director
Chuck Jones

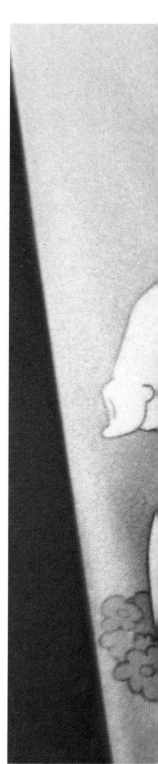

Chuck Jones' 1957 masterpiece *What's Opera, Doc?* has the honour of being the first animated short to be selected for the National Archives in the United States. This achievement is not merely testimony to its quality as a cartoon but to the way it embraces classical art works in a popular form. Jones compresses the 14 hours of Richard Wagner's *Der Ring des Nibelungen* cycle into six minutes, along the way redefining the parameters of the cartoon by using 104 camera 'edits' – the usual average being around 60 – in which the animated *mise en scène* changes from one point of view to another for different purposes and effects.

Further, aesthetic innovation occurs throughout the film in Maurice Noble's unusual abstract designs, which underpin the emotional aspects of each scene and also successfully bring to the foreground the intentions of the character action, whether in regard to the storm-dwarfed Teutonic knight Elmer Fudd, or the cross-dressed romantic bravura of Bugs Bunny as 'Brunhilda'.

Jones, who was the most literate, conceptually-minded and articulate of the Warner Bros directors – he was a devotee of Mark Twain, G. K. Chesterton, George Santayana and Sergei Eisenstein, among others – conceived the cartoon as a project that was to last seven weeks instead of the more typical five weeks that were usually allotted to such short films. Sandwiched between two *Roadrunner* cartoons, which were made in just four weeks each, Jones managed to insert *What's Opera, Doc?* into the conventional schedules, while keeping the project a secret from studio production chief Eddie Selzer, who Jones feared would object to the film. The intrinsic risk taken by the cartoon was that it was not driven by jokes but by the incongruity that arises from the juxtaposition of cartoon personality and the intensity and highbrow nature of the music, which was orchestrated and played with integrity and seriousness by the Burbank Symphony Orchestra rather than in the anticipated usual 'comic' manner. The laughs would emerge from the recognition that Elmer was *not* a mighty warrior; that Bugs, when told that 'she' was 'wuvvwy' (Fuddian for 'lovely'), would sing 'Yes, I know it, I can't help it'; that the theme of 'Ride of the Valkyries' would thereafter be remembered for Elmer singing 'Kill the wabbit! Kill the wabbit!'; that Bugs' rectangular stallion would prance nimbly and self-consciously like a dancing sofa; and that the tragic denouement of the opera would be respected in the mock-death of Bugs, who notes, 'What did you expect in an opera, a happy ending?'

From the vast shadow of Elmer, animated by Abe Levitow, which opens the cartoon and respectfully recalls the Chernabog devil animated by Bill Tytla in the 'Night on Bald Mountain' sequence of *Fantasia* (1940), to the balletic sequence featuring Bugs and Elmer, which is based on the modernist dance configurations of Tatiana Riabouchinska and David Lachine of the Ballet Russe de Monte Carlo, *What's Opera, Doc?* is self-consciously *about* 'art' as it is executed through the cartoonal vocabulary. Jones' 500 key drawings – again 200 more than usual – and 1500 unused roughs recall both Degas *and* Disney; and the film itself is ultimately a playful engagement with the remoteness of mythology and the universality of classical and popular themes. Mark Twain once remarked, 'Wagner's music is better than it sounds'; in Jones' cartoon, it looks good too.

324

Writer
Michael Maltese, based
on the opera by Richard
Wagner

Editor
Tony Brown

Production company
Warner Brothers

Animators
Abe Levitow, Ken Harris
and Richard Thompson

Cast
Mel Blanc
Arthur C. Bryan

Other films
★ *The Dover Boys* (1942)
★ *Fresh Airedale* (1945)
★ *Fast and Furry-ous* (1949)
★ *Duck Dodgers and the 24½ Century* (1953)
★ *Duck Amuck* (1953)

The irrepressible Bugs and his 'dancing sofa'.

Tale of Tales
Skazka Skazok

Yuri Norstein *1979*

Yuri Norstein's 26-minute *Tale of Tales* was voted as the greatest animated film of all time by a panel of animation specialists at the Los Angeles Olympic Arts Festival in 1984. It remains an artwork of extraordinary substance, and an exemplary example of the ways in which animation can facilitate the expression of states of consciousness, memory and folk experience. The personal symbolism employed by Norstein, who is Russian, transcends the work's intrinsically private, autobiographical origins and prompts recognition of the deep processes by which humankind thinks, feels, knows and comes to terms with its experiences.

Tale of Tales represents a profound understanding of 'time', using the particular process of animation to control its flow and reveal its effect on the perception of place, and, as the title of the film implies, there is a strong recognition of the role of time within the act of storytelling.

Norstein's technique and style may be seen to be completely in tune with both his narrative and thematic concerns. He understands the act of memory to be an act of creativity, and the transmutations that are made possible by the animated form thus become the embodiment of an emerging thought or emotion. The memory of a childhood lullaby – 'Sleep, sleep or the grey wolf cub will take you away into the woods' – mixes with the recollection of a baby suckling, a lost Eden under snowfall, and a summer picnic populated by half-imagined figures. Scenes of pastoral idyll and peasant culture are combined with the impact of industrial change. Seasonal change similarly underpins some significant moments of personal recollection and revelation; and transient fragments of time sustain themselves as the evidence of 'pastness' and history. At various point in the film, this mélange accrues into a potent confluence of the poetic and the prosaic, the private and the public, and the past and the present. This coming together is exemplified by a dance sequence in which couples tango beneath the light of a single lamp; but with the onset of war they are parted from each other, as the husbands transform into soldiers, drifting with supernatural somnambulance to their inevitable deaths. The sudden extraction of the men from their joyful dancing leaves a sense of absence and loss – the atmosphere made a physical, tactile presence by Norstein's inherently painterly command over the *plasticity*, motion and timing of his unfolding narrative. Idea and image combine as visualization.

Choosing the multiple levels of Eastern aesthetic traditions rather than the vanishing-point perspective of Western art, Norstein facilitates the production of multiple reflections upon a core feeling. At the level of specific detail, this may be about creating what Norstein describes as a 'field of gravity' around a gesture or image, for example, an apple glistening with raindrops; while, at a more textually complex level, it could involve communicating the import of Chekhovian dramatic intensity, the strains from Bach's *Well-Tempered Clavier* or Mozart's Piano Concerto No. 5, or the folk idioms of Pushkin and Tolstoy. Most notably, though, Norstein's art is about the fundamentals of light, literally drawing the subject out of darkness and portraying it with the luminosity of a Rembrandt portrait and the simple poignancy of a children's book illustration. Simply, Norstein uses animation to fully express and represent the essence of cinema itself.

Director
Yuri Norstein

Other films
★ *The Battle of the Kerzhenets* (1971)
★ *The Heron and the Crane* (1974)
★ *Hedgehog in the Fog* (1975)

326

FILM: THE CRITICS' CHOICE *The Art of the Impossible*

Crac! Frédéric Back *1980*

Frédéric Back's exquisite Oscar-winning short *Crac!*, charting the changing culture of French Québec, portrays a simple story in which a woodcutter's home-crafted rocking chair, made on the occasion of his wedding, becomes a metaphor for movement and stasis, ruin and repair. The tale also embodies both a nostalgia for the skilled artisan and the realities of modern uniformity. Animated in vivid, hand-drawn images, the film works as a series of personal impressions, memories and insights, celebrating indigenous cultures and lamenting their demise.

The 'crac' of the title represents the sound that is made by the felling of the tree. The tree is then used to make the rocking chair, an ornate, somewhat anthropomorphized domestic object, which carries a symbolic function as a resistance to both industrialization and the damaging environmental consequences of modernization. The craftsman's children are shown using the rocking chair in the course of their games, reinventing the chair as a train, a ship at sea, a knight's steed and a car. The chair metamorphoses from one to the other, at once illustrating the innocence of invention and the consequences of change.

The German-born Back studied art in Paris and Rennes under the tutelage of Méheut, a consummate painter of marine life, and moved to Montreal after the war. Upon joining the graphic arts department of the Canadian Broadcasting Corporation in the early 1950s, his work involved conducting research into stained-glass window design. Later, he joined the animation unit that was working with Hubert Tison. Back's films, particularly *La Création des oiseaux* (1973), *Illusion* (1974), *Tartata* (1977) and *Tout rien* (1978), all exhibit a deep empathy with the natural world and a fear of the consequences that arise from its exploitation and abuse. The beauty of his depiction of birds, mammals and the environment is captured in the simplicity and radiance of his graphic technique, which often recalls the spectral effects of stained glass. In *Crac!*, he particularly emphasizes the spontaneity of line and expressionist shading to capture the energy at the heart of the French-Canadian communities he represents, not merely recalling the fine-art influences of Degas and Monet, but the work of local painters Horatio Walker and Cornelius Krieghoff, who recorded the landscape of Québec and the life of its people.

Crac! carefully traces the transition that occurs between this powerful sense of community and tradition, and the alienation and abstraction that is endemic in the modern world. The people in Québec embrace folklore and mythology, the value of art, and the shared exuberant experience of dancing and ice-skating. This is not only the tactile, emotive *joie de vivre* of the community; it is also the underpinning spiritual motivation behind Back's work. His rocking chair survives repair, rejection and renewal, finally coming to rest in a museum of modern art, ironically *not* as a museum piece but in good working order, the pride and joy of the security guard who mends it to sit on during the night shift. Back satirizes the elitism of modern art when a young girl blows and pops a gum 'bubble' which echoes the shape of a 'bubble' in a modern painting. As night falls, the chair imbues the environment with the spirit of a more authentic social and aesthetic past, recalling images and sounds of folk music and dancing presented earlier in the film.

Director, writer and producer
Frédéric Back

Co-producer
Hubert Tison

Music
Normand Roger

Camera operators
Claude Lapiere and
Jean Robillard

Other films
★ *La Création des oiseaux* (1973)
★ *Illusion* (1974)
★ *Tartata* (1977)
★ *Tout rien* (1978)
★ *The Mighty River* (1993)

Academy Awards
Winner of Best Short Film and Best Animated Film in 1982

One of the scenes of the community dancing and singing, based on the director's experience of French Québec's culture.

Dimensions of Dialogue
Moznosti Dialogu

Jan Svankmajer *1982*

Jan Svankmajer, born in 1934, trained in applied arts and drama in Prague and began making animated films to engage with what he describes as 'militant surrealism' – a politically motivated approach to making the 'real' imaginary and the imaginary 'real'. Svankmajer is careful not to make his statement entirely abstract, preferring to redefine the representation of human figures and to reclaim the latent histories and memories with which objects, he believes, are imbued.

Svankmajer's work has taken place against a backdrop of constant ideological change: from democracy to Nazism, reconstruction to Stalinism; from the 'normalization' of Soviet oppression in 1968 to the end of the Cold War, to the separation of the Czech and Slovak republics. Consequently, Svankmajer's films have often invited scrutiny by the authorities, and a number of his works, including *Dimensions of Dialogue*, were previously banned in Czechoslovakia.

The film, a virtuoso tripartite anti-Stalinist tract, embraces all Svankmajer's concerns: confrontation and the breakdown of the material world; the tension between 'reality' and modes of play, symbolism and association; and the arbitrary matter-of-factness of dream as a type of black humour. These issues are played out through representations of the body in transition, under threat or as a mechanism.

The first section, 'Exhaustive Discussion', is based on the work of the 16th-century Mannerist painter Arcimboldo, best known for his grotesque arrangement of objects into human forms, and deploys three heads in profile, respectively composed of metallic objects, fruit and vegetables and office stationery. Each, in turn, devours another, masticating and pulping the materials before disgorging them into an increasingly corrupted version of the original head. At one level, this is a symbolic interaction between industrialism, nature and bureaucracy; at another, it is a sensuous redefinition of the acts of consumption, colonization and change. The section ends with clay heads disgorging new clay heads, seemingly ad infinitum; an insistence upon the invocation of animism even at the moment of utter dissolution.

'Passionate Discussion', part two, features a man and woman, at first represented with realist verisimilitude. However, their immediate descent into love-making is played out as a protean mass of clay, signifying the mutability, transcendent pleasure and impersonality of intercourse, before the figures, again realistic, return to their sense of separateness. A piece of clay remains – a baby, an unresolved tension, a provocation? – that leads the couple to brutally and literally tear each other apart. Here is the influence of the social and public seen in the destructiveness of the personal and private.

The final section, 'Factual Dialogue', sees Svankmajer conclude his satire on the effects of Stalinist oppression with a metaphor about the Cold War and the commodity culture. Two heads circle, disgorging material goods – toothpaste and brush, shoes and shoelaces, pencil and pencil-sharpener, bread and butter – which echo, complement but ultimately clash with and destroy each other. With this, the redundancy of autocratic political economies and the deep-rooted suspicion between conflicting ideologies are represented in a challenging and complex way. Svankmajer's radical agitprop methods use a form of 'total animation', where all the materials used are aesthetically manipulated, signifying the director's political and artistic intervention.

Director, writer and production designer
Jan Svankmajer

Cinematographer
Vladimir Malík

Production company
Krátk Film Praha

Music
Jan Klusák

Editor
Helena Lebdusková

Animator
Vlasta Pospísilová

Other films
★ *Punch and Judy* (1966)
★ *Jabberwocky* (1971)
★ *Down to the Cellar* (1982)
★ *Virile Games* (1988)
★ *Food* (1992)
★ *Faust* (1994)
★ *Conspirators of Pleasure* (1997)

Svankmajer's perfect clay figure before it descends into the material representation of sensuality and brutalism.

Laputa, The Flying Island
Tenku No Shiro Rapyuta

Hayao Miyazaki *1986*

Director, writer and designer
Hayao Miyazaki

Producer
Isao Takahata

Music
Jo Hisaishi

Production companies
Studio Ghibli

Writer, designer and director Hayao Miyazaki is arguably the leading creator of feature-length *animé*, taking his place alongside Ozu, Kurosawa and Mizoguchi as one of Japan's greatest filmmakers. His work, a spiritual engagement with the pursuit of human values, largely played out through the innate innocence of children but in the shadow of the bombings of Hiroshima and Nagasaki, invokes the power of nature and the supernatural as proof of continuity and progress.

Japanese *animé*, so often informed by dystopic, violent, technologically advanced but also spiritually redundant worlds, exemplified in Katsuhiro Otomo's *Akira* (1988) and Mamoro Oshii's *Ghost in the Shell* (1995), has become part of the nation's enduring 'apocalyptic imagination' in postwar art. Miyazaki's work, however, reaches further back to a range of influences: to the tradition of 14th-century 'Garden Art', to the colourful work of the late-18th-, early-19th-century 'Floating World' printmakers Utamaro and Hokusai, to the aesthetics of modernist Japanese live-action cinema and to the hyper-realist effects of 'golden age' Disney. With this vocabulary, he challenges the dominant aesthetic and thematic preoccupations of Japanese animation.

Miyazaki effectively reverses or redefines many of the assumptions of Japanese science-fiction *animé*. In *Laputa, The Flying Island*, he creates a historically indeterminate world. A rain-washed late 19th-century terrain, based on mining towns in Wales and overflown by Jules Verne-style airships, it also hints at postwar technologies, the industrial revolution mixing freely with an imagined machine age that is driven by magic as well as by mechanism. The anticipated parallel world, which in dystopic *animé* is often populated by vengeful demons, is here represented as an idyllic flying island, a lost Eden of organic plenitude and advanced technology. Even the robot who tends the island, styled after the Fleischer Brothers' 1941 episode of the *Mechanical Monsters*, is gentle and sensitive; a far-cry from the hi-tech war machines of much *animé*. The idyll is rooted in a nostalgia for high-minded spiritual values and contemplation, and it is in this setting that Miyazaki's customary moments of transcendent epiphany take place, when Sheeta, a young girl in possession of a levitation stone from which the island is composed, and Pazu, her boy companion, innocently engage in adolescent sexual awakening and begin the process towards adult maturity.

Miyazaki's preoccupation with 'flight' is readily evidenced in Sheeta's angelic levitation, confirmation of a naturalized spiritual capacity in Miyazaki's heroines that male figures can only aspire to in their flying contraptions. Throughout the film, air-pirates and official military bodies vie to capture Sheeta, often engaging in air battles which are state-of-the-art animation sequences, but their efforts, it is implied, are always doomed in the light of the magical 'invisible force' that protects Sheeta, made up of what Miyazaki describes as 'man's imaginings'. From birds, to angels, kite-flyers, helicopters, giant aircraft and mythical flying islands, Miyazaki's skies are the stuff of creativity and dreams. This is grounded, however, in the parallel imagery of trees, which, in Miyazaki's view, are 'the basis for all living creatures' and often subvert the iconic imagery of the atomic mushroom cloud, operating as proof of organic and spiritual survival. Miyazaki's humanist vision insists upon progress, but on human terms and conditions.

The Wrong Trousers Nick Park *1993*

Nick Park has rapidly established himself as a master animator, winning Oscars for *Creature Comforts* (1989), *The Wrong Trousers* (1993) and *A Close Shave* (1995). In 1999, he was also named as one of the five greatest animators of all time in a poll conducted among industry professionals, along with Norman McLaren, Jan Svankmajer, Oscar Fischinger and Yuri Norstein. Park has perfected the art of clay animation, allying extraordinary technique to subtleties of character comedy and social observation, while combining the aesthetic credibility of European animated art cinema with the benign parochialism of early British children's television animation.

Such children's animation is exemplified by Oliver Postgate's highly influential *The Clangers*, *Ivor the Engine* and *Bagpuss* of the 1960s and 1970s, all depicting self-contained, romantic, artisan-inspired worlds. But Park's nostalgic embrace of these gentle communities, with their paternalistic goodwill and respect for homemade contraptions, harks further back, to George Orwell's wartime view of England as 'a nation of stamp-collectors, pigeon-fanciers, amateur carpenters, coupon-snippers, darts-players, [and] crossword-puzzle fans'.

Park's most impressive contribution to the world of animation is the creation of two enduring characters: Wallace, a Lancastrian inventor, and his dog, the silent Gromit, who have become iconic figures worldwide on a par with Hollywood's cartoon stars. Ironically, this success directly relates to the couple's intrinsic 'Britishness'. As Park himself notes of *The Wrong Trousers*, 'where else could you get eccentric surrealities (sic) like automated trousers and villainous penguins – it could only come from Britain'. Park believes that quintessential 'Britishness' is 'something understated, ordinary, yet quirky', and shows in the gestural details and behavioural foibles of Wallace and Gromit. Like their formative influences – characters from British comics the *Beano* and the *Dandy* (most notably Desperate Dan, the cowboy incongruously living in a bungalow in Dundee), Laurel and Hardy, and British comic actors George Formby and Robb Wilton – Wallace and Gromit create humour which arises from innocently and unselfconsciously inhabiting their own world, while failing fully to embrace its terms and conditions. The tension between Wallace's well-meaning ineptitude and Gromit's canine loyalty and intelligence is both amusing and understandable, provoking sympathy and identification in audiences of all ages. It illustrates the generosity in human relationships, but also the follies common to us all.

The characters' qualities fully inform *The Wrong Trousers*, in which Wallace's mechanized dog-walking trousers are stolen by a villainous penguin for use in a cunningly planned jewellery heist. Gromit, temporarily usurped in Wallace's affections, saves the day, apprehending the penguin in the film's tour de force finale, a spectacular Hollywood train chase which takes place in a Wigan living room. It is based on the chariot race in *Ben-Hur* (1959), and Park uses the whole cinematic vocabulary to capture what he describes as the 'thrill of the movement'. Referencing Hitchcockian suspense sequences, John Ford Westerns, *The Third Man* (1949, *see pages 256 –257*) and *film noir* motifs, he emphasizes the ironic mix of epic allusion and domestic banality. His wit and economy demonstrate how the innocence of animation can be used for highly sophisticated purposes.

Director
Nick Park

Writers
Nick Park and Bob Baker

Producer
Christopher Moll

Production company
Aardman Animation

Music
Julian Nott

Editor
Helen Garrard

Art director
Yvonne Fox

Cast
Peter Sallis

Other films
★ *Creature Comforts* (1989)
★ *A Grand Day Out* (1992)
★ *A Close Shave* (1995)
★ *Chicken Run* (2000)

Academy Awards
Winner of Best Animated Short Film, 1994

Wallace, much to Gromit's amazement,
is over-run by his motorized trousers
(thankfully not available at gentlemen's
outfitters everywhere).

Toy Story John Lasseter *1995*

Director
John Lasseter

Walt Disney Pictures' *Toy Story* would claim its place in animation history by virtue of the fact that it is the first fully computer-generated feature film. Yet, while it is certainly a technical masterpiece, its credentials ironically reside in its traditional approach to storytelling and character-building. The 'toys-coming-to-life' motif in animation goes back as far as J. Stuart Blackton's *The Humpty Dumpty Circus* (1898) and proved particularly appropriate for director John Lasseter's ground-breaking venture because toys present an ideal vehicle for the full exploitation of the intrinsic capabilities of CGI (computer generated imagery).

CGI is characterized by several features, which include geometric precision, a 'plastic', glossy aesthetic, the use of 'infinite' depth, and the highly convincing sense of a 360°, three-dimensional space in which motion can take place. The toy characters and the ways in which they use their environment epitomize the dynamics of CGI so persuasively that form and content become inseparable, and the viewer is left to be impressed not so much by technique as by the tale.

Woody, the pull-string cowboy, who is patterned after the popular 1950s television Westerns and marionette shows, is usurped in the affections of his owner, Andy, by Buzz Lightyear, the gadget-laden electronic astronaut, who also impresses the rest of the playroom toys previously in thrall to Woody's benign but unchallenged leadership. Uncharacteristically, Woody tries to dispose of Buzz, who is accidentally ejected from the playroom, prompting a picaresque 'buddy' movie in which Woody saves Buzz, befriends him, discovers his own heroic qualities, and thwarts the film's sadistic villain, Sid, Andy's neighbour who destroys and rebuilds his toys as monstrous hybrids.

Woody and Buzz represent the well-worn tension between the past and the future; between frontier nostalgia and brave new worlds; and between playroom and 'Playstation'. In addition (and on a more adult level), they embody the crisis that social critics have observed in modern masculinity and even the fear of sociocultural obsolescence within late capitalist market economies. The film elegantly engages with the idea that contemporary life is characterized by a fear of the loss of personal identity and social purpose, that recognition and value are measured only in commodity terms, and that love and friendship are the only unifying principles which overcome the threat of alienation. The fact that such mature and complex themes are handled with good humour and poignancy is testament to the integration of Disneyesque sentiment and emotion with Warner Bros-style irony. This is epitomized in Randy Newman's bittersweet songs, particularly the ballad 'I Will Go Sailing No More', sung when Buzz, who throughout the film has sustained its main comic conceit by believing he actually *is* Buzz Lightyear, attempts to fly, only to crash to the floor in full recognition that he is just a toy.

In a post-lapsarian, material world, Woody and Buzz prove, however, that there is such a thing as 'falling with style'. Though they cannot really fly, they *can* embrace their complex feelings of aspiration, petty jealousy, loneliness, rejection, respect and deep affection, and represent for children, and to 'children' of all ages, just what it is to be an adult. As Buzz ought to say, 'To affinity ... and beyond!'

Producers
Bonnie Arnold and Ralph
Guggenheim

Writers
Joss Whelan, Joel Cohen,
Andrew Stanton and Alec
Sokolow

Music
Randy Newman

Production companies
Walt Disney Pictures/Pixar
Animation Studios

Cast
Tom Hanks
Tim Allen
Don Rickles
Jim Varney
John Ratzenburger

Other films
★ *Tin Toy* (1988)
★ *Geri's Game* (1997)
★ *A Bug's Life* (1998)
★ *Toy Story 2* (1999)

Academy Awards
Nominations for Best Music
and Best Screenplay, 1996

Woody, the pull-string cowboy, and Buzz Lightyear, the electronic astronaut, battle it out on the domestic frontier.

Pleasures of War Ruth Lingford *1999*

Director
Ruth Lingford

Since the early 1980s, the rise of animation courses in British universities and colleges and the investment from television's Channel 4 in the commissioning and broadcasting of new independent work have prompted the emergence of highly talented female animators. The Leeds Animation Collective (*Out to Lunch*, 1989), Joanna Quinn (*Girls Night Out*, 1986), Candy Guard (*Fatty Issues*, 1990), Erica Russell (*Triangle*, 1994), Marjut Rimmenen (*The Stain*, 1991) and Ruth Lingford (*Death and the Mother*, 1996) have created a distinctively 'feminine aesthetic' which has challenged dominant orthodoxies not merely in British animation but in the form per se.

This fresh approach has been achieved, first, by using the craft-orientation and auteurist scope in animation to reconfigure the practice of filmmaking itself, and, second, by redefining aspects of representation, particularly in regard to the depiction of the body and issues about gender politics and social identity.

Lingford's progress, like that of her contemporaries, is characterized by a willingness to extend the parameters of the form while expressing private and complex emotions that have often been withheld from public articulation. She goes beyond the conventional limits of representation and uses the dream-logic of animation to redefine issues concerning sexuality, desire and violence in an often provocative way. This forces the audience to address its sense 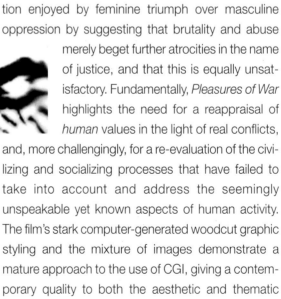 of responsibility and culpability. *Pleasures of War* deliberately engages with the relationship between sex and power within the context of the abuses of war. Co-devised with the radical Christian writer Sara Maitland, and based on a contemporary retelling of the Judith and Holofernes story from the Apocrypha, the film uses the story of Judith's seduction and decapitation of her warring oppressor, the barbarous soldier Holofernes, in order to address the ambivalence and contradictions surrounding warfare.

While the original story stops short of suggesting that Judith used sex to undermine and oppose her antagonist, the film depicts the ritualization of her sexual manipulation of Holofernes as an aspect of the libidinous imperatives underpinning the act of waging war. The eroticization of brutality and indifference also gains a lyrical yet troubling frisson from its juxtaposition with live-action newsreel footage and Holocaust imagery, itself a warning against the fetishization and consensual, sanitizing selectivity of images of war in film and television.

The film also refutes the idea of the easy satisfaction enjoyed by feminine triumph over masculine oppression by suggesting that brutality and abuse merely beget further atrocities in the name of justice, and that this is equally unsatisfactory. Fundamentally, *Pleasures of War* highlights the need for a reappraisal of *human* values in the light of real conflicts, and, more challengingly, for a re-evaluation of the civilizing and socializing processes that have failed to take into account and address the seemingly unspeakable yet known aspects of human activity. The film's stark computer-generated woodcut graphic styling and the mixture of images demonstrate a mature approach to the use of CGI, giving a contemporary quality to both the aesthetic and thematic agendas of the piece. However, Lingford's embrace of new technologies is simply a means of expressing repressed or suppressed ideas in a radicalized form, reflecting a strong belief that animation can achieve contentious but contemplative artwork.

Writer
Sara Maitland

Producer
Dick Arnall

Additional animation
Ron McRae

Editor
Jo Ann Kaplan

Music
Andy Cowton

Visual effects
Caroline Parsons

Other films
★ *Death and the Mother* (1996)

'The eroticization of brutality': an image from Lingford's feminist film.

Glossary

A

Agitprop: (Abbreviated from the Russian words *agitatsiya-propaganda*.) A means whereby the masses could be educated in political principles and correct ideas. This term was used extensively in post-revolutionary Russia to promote the Bolshevik cause, in films that were known as *agitki*.

Anthropomorphism: The tendency in animation to endow creatures with human attributes, abilities and qualities. This can redefine or merely draw attention to characteristics that are taken for granted in live-action representations of human beings.

Art-house film: A film that has commonly acknowledged artistic merit. Such films may be either low-budget, made primarily for the art-house market, or commercial films that also appeal to this audience.

Auteur theory: (Literally, 'author' theory.) A critique of film that places the emphasis on the work of the director. It originated in France in the 1950s, as an ideology known as *la politique des auteurs* (literally, 'the policy of authors'), and views the director as the sole or primary artistic driving force in the making of a film. A film is examined, therefore, as a work of art with a sole author, as one piece in a director's 'canon' of works. This led to a backlash as each 'canon' was studied without taking into account the circumstances surrounding each film, and without reference to any collaborative effort with writers, producers, actors, etc.

B

Backlighting: The placing of lighting behind and often slightly above the subject in order to highlight the edges and so add depth, by separating the subject from the background.

Back-projection: (Also, rear-projection.) A technique whereby live action is filmed in front of a screen onto which background action is projected. This is very often used for dialogue scenes within moving vehicles.

Best boy: The chief assistant to the gaffer *(see below)*, or the second in charge of the lighting team.

C

Cartoonalness: The recognition of the cartoon's own frames of reference and association. This includes the ways in which the cartoon signals its difference from live-action cinema (i.e. the capacity for imagery to demonstrate a re-determination of the physical laws and concrete principles of the material world and facilitate expression that could not be achieved in any other medium).

Celluloid: The base on which light-sensitive emulsion is coated, thus producing film. Also sometimes used as an adjective relating to an aspect of the cinema (e.g. 'the celluloid hero').

Chiaroscuro: (Literally, 'bright-dark'.) The effect of light and shade or of variety and contrast; originally a fine-art term.

Cinéma du look: (Roughly, 'the image is the message'.) A style, sometimes referred to as 'post-modern' *(see below)*, that emerged in the 1980s in the work of the directors Jean-Jacques Beineix, Luc Besson and Leos Carax. It was influenced by the aesthetics of advertisements and rock videos.

CinemaScope: The anamorphic wide-screen process, named after the first commercially successful process developed for 20th Century Fox in the early 1950s. In this process the optical system uses different magnifications in the horizontal and the vertical to fill the screen.

Cinématographe: The moving-picture machine with which early films were both shot and projected, patented by the Lumière brothers in 1895.

Cinematography: The process by which an image is captured either electronically or on film stock by means of visual recording devices.

Cinéma verité: (Literally, 'cinema truth'.) A style of documentary film-making in which members of the crew participate in the action of the film and no direction is given to the participants – neither actors nor crew. This term is now often widely used to describe the trend of hand-held camera techniques.

Composition: The arrangement of the different elements – lighting, colours and shapes – in a frame, just as in a painting. The term may also be applied to movement within a shot which creates the illusion of a third dimension.

Computer-generated imagery (CGI): Images produced by means of computer technology and used on their own, or more generally in combination with filmed images, to create special effects (such as the dinosaurs in *Jurassic Park*).

Cross-cutting: A technique whereby one action is interspersed with another, thus combining the two sequences. This is often used as a means of creating suspense, or as a way of allowing the audience to draw comparisons between the two narratives.

Cutting: Creating a transition in camera angle or placement, time or location, by splicing together two strips of film. A 'cut' can also refer to a complete edited version of a film (e.g. 'rough cut').

D

Deep focus: A cinematography technique with great depth of field, in which foreground, middle-ground and background images can be held in focus. This contrasts with the more traditional style of shallow focus, where only one plane is in focus and the rest is blurred.

Digital editing: Editing part of a film by digitizing one or more frames and changing them electronically, or combining them with other digitized images. The modified frame is then printed.

Director: The person who guides the actors, camera shots, lighting and sound. Directors tend to have artistic control over each scene in the film. To this end they may also cast, write and edit the film.

Dolly shot: A shot in which the perspective of the subject and background is changed by moving the camera towards and away from the subject along special tracks, often in a small, hydraulically powered truck known as a dolly.

E

Editing: Collating pictures and sound into coherent sequences by joining together strips of exposed film and mixing and adding soundtracks (see below). In video editing this is achieved by entering frame numbers into a computer.

Epic: A film with a large dramatic scope or one that needs a costly production (often set in biblical times or the ancient world and dealing with heroism).

Expressionist: The cinematic style that expresses emotions through material means. Such films are usually characterized by dark visual images and the heavy use of shadows to convey a morbid feel.

F

Fast film: Film that is ideal for using in natural light conditions or dark sets, due to its high sensitivity to light.

Film noir: (Literally, 'black film'.) A style of film (often applied to crime movies) that usually focuses on seedy urban life and is distinguished by a pessimistic or cynical tone and expressionist visuals. Such films are generally populated with brooding anti-heroes, duplicitous *femmes fatales*, downbeat detectives and corruption.

Flashback: A scene or shot that interrupts the chronological linearity of a film by depicting events that occurred in the past, usually events occurring prior to the action of the film.

Flashforward: A scene or shot that interrupts the chronology of a film to show future events.

Frame: An individual image which, when juxtaposed in a sequence with all of the other frames in the movie, provides the moving action of the film.

G

Gaffer: The chief electrician on a production, who is assisted by the best boy (see above) and works on the lighting under the direction of the cinematographer.

Genre: A particular type of film characterized by either milieu, narrative or mood. For example, western, thriller or romantic comedy.

Gothic: A style of film usually associated with horror films. However, gothic films emphasize the supernatural rather than violence.

K

Kinetoscope: A moving picture camera patented by Thomas Alva Edison in 1891 to create a peep-show for the paying public. Kinetoscopes were placed in peep-show parlours, hotels and department stores throughout the United Kingdom from 1894, and the term was used generically to mean a movie camera.

L

Leitmotif: A recurring theme associated with a particular person, idea, milieu or action.

Lightning sketch: Rapid chalk sketches drawn by music-hall and vaudevillian performers on blackboards to illustrate jokes, routines, etc. They were first translated onto film as records of the performance but were soon animated frame-by-frame in their own right. The physical performance of drawing was highly conducive to recognition of what the animated form might distinctively represent.

Long shot: A shot that is taken some distance away from the subject. It generally shows subjects in their entirety, together with some of their environment.

M

Magic lantern: A precursor of the cinema. The magic lantern device consisted of candles placed behind coloured lenses that projected images onto a screen.

Metamorphosis: The ability of a figure, object, shape or form to relinquish its seemingly fixed properties and mutate into an alternative model. This transformation is literally enacted within the animated film and acts as a model by which the process of change becomes part of the narrative of the film. A form starts as one thing and ends up as something different.

Method acting: A style of acting expounded by Konstantine Stanislavsky (1863–1938) and popularised in the US by Lee Strasberg and Stella Adler, practised by actors to bring about more realistic performances. The actors use personal experiences and emotions as a basis for their portrayals.

Mise-en-scène: (Literally, 'that which is put into the scene'.) The sum of everything, both technical and non-technical, which makes the scene look and feel the way that it does.

Monochrome: (Literally, 'of one colour'). A film shot in black and white or, occasionally, one that is shot in shades of one colour.

Montage: An editing style, usually rapid in effect, that is particularly associated with Soviet revolutionary filmmakers such as Sergei Eisenstein and Vsevelod Pudovkin, who developed various theories of montage.

N

Neo-realism: An influential movement of the late 1940s and 1950s that started in Italy. Neo-realism used non-professional actors, and locations rather than studios. The exponents also tended to make movies about contemporary social and political issues, with an emphasis on the plight of the poor and needy.

New German Cinema: A movement started in Germany in the mid-1960s and at its peak in the 1970s. It often criticized society, touching on contemporary issues such as racial prejudice, bourgeois decadence and political inertia or, in Werner Herzog's work, on eccentrics driven to extreme or destructive behaviour by their obsessions.

New Wave: An English translation of the French term *nouvelle vague (see below)*. It has been applied since the early 1960s to any new movement in a national cinema (e.g. in Czechoslovakia), as well as to many fields other than film, including journalism, music and criticism.

Nouvelle vague: (Literally, 'new wave'.) A journalistic term used to describe the development of a new style of cinema in 1958–9 when Jean-Luc Godard, Claude Chabrol, François Truffaut and others (mainly critics associated with the magazine *Cahiers du cinéma*) set themselves up as directors who espoused the principles of auteur cinema *(see above)* and the 'personal' approach. Their films made considerable reference to other cinematic and literary works, ignored or transformed many standard cinematographic practices and made extensive use of location shooting.

O

Orthochromatic stock (Literally, 'correct colour' stock). A type of black and white film that is sensitive to blues and greens but not to reds. Its speed enabled a degree of deep focus *(see above)* to be achieved.

P

Peep-show: A small film or exhibition of pictures seen through a magnifying lens or hole set into a box.

Plasticity: The capacity for an animated film to demonstrate the malleability or protean quality of the material forms being used by the film itself. Renowned Russian filmmaker and theorist Sergei Eisenstein called this 'plasmaticness' and defined it as 'a rejection of once-and-forever allotted form, freedom from ossification, the ability to assume any form'.

Post-modern: A term used generally to describe the return to traditional materials in reaction to a style deemed 'modernist'.

Producer: The person who arranges the financing and logistics of a film, but may also be responsible for aspects ranging from its inception to its distribution.

Production design: The design of the overall appareance of a film, from the set and costumes to external locations and sometimes continuity sketches.

R

Road movie: A primarily American genre that generally has the protagonist(s) travelling the highways of the continent, sometimes in a rather aimless attempt to understand the country's values and problems. It has been much imitated in Europe and arises in some degree from the picareque novel.

Rotoscope: The frame-by-frame copying of filmed live-action movement onto transparent animation cels. It is used to solve animation problems involving difficult perspective changes or human characters.

S

Sequence shot: A shot that forms part of an autonomous series making up a single action. Such shots are usually linked, either temporally or thematically (for example, a chase sequence).

Silent era: The period stretching roughly from 1895 to 1927 when most films were shot without sound, although they were often accompanied by a live spoken commentary, piano improvisations, an orchestra or sound effects. *The Jazz Singer* in 1927 was the first 'talkie' feature.

Sleeper: A film that takes a while to make a good return on the initial monetary investment, but that is eventually highly successful – either as a cult movie or in financial terms.

Soundstage: An extensive area where sets can be built, usually located in a studio. Greater control is thereby given to the filmmaker over matters such as lighting, sound, climate, etc.

Soundtrack: A narrow band of film on which the sound element is recorded: its music, dialogue or sound effects.

Sovcolor: A colour reversal film, based on Agfacolor, which was used in the Soviet Union in the period following 1950, the USSR having seized Agfacolor's factory during the Second World War.

Spaghetti western: A low-budget Italian-made western of the type that came to the fore during the 1960s. Clint Eastwood became an international star in such films, the most renowned of which were Sergio Leone's *A Fistful of Dollars* and *The Good, The Bad and The Ugly*.

Special effects: Images (often of a fantastical nature) that are created by technical means, whether mechanical, photographic or computerized.

Still: One of the three static images: a frame still – a blown-up image of a frame from a finished film; a production still – an image taken from a film while shooting is still in progress; and a standard publicity shot of an actor or scene.

Stop-motion: An animation technique that involves shooting one frame at a time, using three-dimensional figures, models or puppets, to photograph minute changes in their positions from frame to frame. It is also known as stop-frame motion and stop-motion animation.

Storyboard: A series of sketches, often rather like a comic strip, of the various shots in a complex scene or of the key moments in the action of an entire film. It is often used for animated films.

Surrealism: A widespread movement in the arts, which predominated in France in the 1920s and spread to painting, poetry, theatre and cinema. Its principal exponent was André Breton. The photographic nature of film lent itself to the experimentation, absurd juxtapositions and dream-like logic that were characteristics of Surrealism.

T

Technicolor: The trade name of the most famous colour film process, first developed in the mid-1910s by the Technicolor Motion Picture Corporation. The process was adapted and expanded in four different versions during the 1930s and 1940s, using first a single reel of film, then two sets, then a three-strip system and finally just a single stock, but was largely superseded in the 1950s by Eastman Color. The word Technicolor has come to be used by many as a generic term for rich, vibrant colours.

Total animation: In some animated films only specific elements of the *mise-en-scène (see above)* are actually animated, but in other films all aspects of the material within the frame are subject to frame-by-frame manipulation, and this represents 'total' animation.

Tracking shot: A term used to describe a smooth dolly shot *(see above)* in which the camera is moved towards and away from, or alongside, a subject.

Two-shot: A shot featuring just two people, often framed from the chest up – a staple device of Hollywood productions, often referred to in Europe as the 'American shot'. It is generally employed to show the characters in conversation.

W

Widescreen: A production technique based on film running horizontally through the camera. Panavision and VistaVision used this system, as did the Todd-AO process, which was used in *Oklahoma!* in 1955 and *Around the World in Eighty Days* the following year.

Index

A

3-4x Jugatsu (1932) 302–3
The 39 Steps (1935) 248–9
Abel, Alfred 44–5
Abramova, Natasha 218–19
Agee, Arthur 140–1
Agee, Arthur 'Bo' 140–1
Agee, Sheila 140–1
Ahankhah, Abdolfazl 300–1
Ahankhah, Manoochehr 300–1
Ahankhah, Mehrdad 300–1
Ai No Corrida (1976) 290–1
Aiello, Danny 130–1
Aimée, Anouk 174–5
Akan, Tarik 294–5
Albert, Julius 200–1
Albertazz, Giorgio 190–1
Alexandrov Grigori 36–7
Aliens (1986) 126–7
Allen, Mary 28–9
Allen, Tim 336–7
Allen, Woody 110–11
Alphaville (1965) 196–7
Alpi, Domenico 194–5
Altman, Robert 106–7
Amouroux, Clémantine 210–11
Anatomy of a Murder (1959) 82–3
Anderson, Jeff 138–9
André, Victor 24–5
Andreyev, Boris 178–9
Angelopoulus, Theo 216–17
Aniki-Bobó (1942) 160–1
Annichiarico, Uito 164–5
Annie Hall (1977) 110–11
Anspach, Susan 96–7
Antonioni, Michelangelo 192–3
Antonov, Nikolai 36–7

Aoi, Nakajima 290–1
Aoki, Tomio 50–1
Aquistapace, Jean 162–3
Arashi, Tokusaburro 282–3
Arletty 166–7
Armstrong, Alun 270–1
Armstrong, Robert 56–7
Arquette, Rosanna 142–3
Artaud, Antonin 48–9
Ashcroft, Peggy 248–9
Ashes and Diamonds (1958) 182–3
Ashikawa, Makato 302–3
Asti, Adriana 194–5
Astor, Mary 70–1
Audran, Stéphane 188–9
Avery, Tex 320–1
The Awful Truth (1937) 58–9
Ayme, Jean 30–1
Aznavour, Charles 186–7

B

Back, Frédéric 328–9
Backer, Brian 120–1
Badin, Jean 222–3
Bagabaldo, Juling 288–9
Balázsovits, Lajos 206–7
Bálint, András 206–7
Balint, Eszter 124–5
Baranovskaya, Vera 46–7
Barbaud, Pierre 190–1
Barilli, Francesco 194–5
Barker, Lex 174–5
Barnes, Binnie 246–7
Barnet, Boris 158–9
Barr, Jean-Marc 230–1
Barrault, Jean-Louis 166–7
Barrie, Wendy 246–7

Barrymore, Lionel 72–3
Barsky, Vladimir 36–7
Bass, Alfie 258–9
Basserman, Albert 254–5
The Battleship Potemkin (1925) 36–7
The Beatles 262–3
Beatty, Ned 106–7
Beatty, Warren 92–3
Beau Travail (1999) 242–3
Before the Revolution (1964) 194–5
Being John Malkovich (1999) 116–17
Bellamy, Ralph 58–9, 64–5
Bennett, Billie 40–1
Berger, Nicole 186–7
Bergman, Henry 38–9
Berkeley, Xander 144–5
Bernon, Bleuette 24–5
Bertin, Françoise 190–1
Berto, Juliet 208–9
Bertolucci, Bernardo 194–5
Betti, Laura 202–3
Betty Boop's Snow White (1933) 314–15
Biehn, Michaell 126–7
Billy the Kid and the Green Baize Vampire (1985) 270–1
Binoche, Juliette 234–5
The Birth of a Nation (1915) 28–9
Black, Karen 96–7, 106–7
Blair, Lionel 262–3
Blanc, Mel 324–5
Blind Venus (1943) 162–3
Blitzwolf (1942) 320–1
Blue (1993) 272–3
Blue Velvet (1986) 128–9

Bob le flambeur (1956) 170–1
Bogarde, Dirk 260–1
Bogart, Humphrey 74–5
Bogdanovich, Peter 98–9
Boiling Point (1932) 302–3
Bonge, Wilson 40–1
Bonnie and Clyde (1967) 92–3
Borgnine, Ernest 94–5
Borgström, Hilda 26–7
Bottoms, Timothy 98–9
Botz, Gustav 34–5
Boulanger, Daniel 186–7
Boyer, Charles 168–9
Brambell, Wilfrid 262–3
Brando, Marlon 100–1
Brasseur, Pierre 166–7
Brazil (1985) 268–9
Bremer, Lucille 70–1
Bressart, Felix 62–3
Bresson, Robert 172–3
Breton, Michèle 264–5
Bridges, Jeff 98–9
Brief Encounter (1945) 250–1
Brignone, Lilly 192–3
Brill, Steven 132–3
Broadbent, Jim 274–5
Brocka, Lino 288–9
Brodie, Don 318–19
Bronenosets 'Potemkin' (1925) 36–7
Bruckman, Clyde 42–3
Bryan, Arthur C. 324–5
Buckley, Jim 204–5
Buñuel, Luis 176–7, 286–7
Burgess, Julie 144–5
Burnett, Charles 116–17
Bürös, Gyöngyi 206–7
Burr, Raymond 76–7

Burstyn, Ellen 98–9

Buscemi, Steve 142–3

Bush, Billy 'Green' 96–7

By the Bluest of Seas (1936) 158–9

C

Caan, James 100–1

The Cabinet of Dr Caligari (1920) 32–3

Cabot, Bruce 56–7

Calado, Teresa 226–7

Calvo, José 176–7

The Cameraman's Revenge (1911) 310–11

Cameron, James 116–17, 126–7

Cammell, Donald 264–5

Capra, Frank 72–3

Carey, Joyce 250–1

Carita 224–5

Carlson, Les 122–3

Carné, Marcel 166–7

Carradine, Keith 106–7

Carretero, José 232–3

Carroll, Madeleine 248–9

Casarès, Maria 166–7

Caselli, Chiara 134–5

Cates, Phoebe 120–1

Catlett, Walter 318–19

Cauchy, Daniel 170–1

Cavalcanti, Alberto 252–3

Cavendar, Glen 42–3

Cazale, John 114–15

Céline et Julie vont en bateau (1974) 208–9

Cerhova, Jitká 200–1

Cerval, Claude 170–1

Cesková, Marie 200–1

Chabrol, Claude 188–9

Chakiris, George 198–9

Chaoming, Cui 284–5

Chaplin, Charles 38–9

Chaplin, Geraldine 106–7

Chen, Chang 306–7

Chiu-Wai, Tony Leung 306–7

Chojuro, Kawarazaki 280–1

Christiakov, A. P. 46–7

Chronicle of a Summer (1961) 184–5

Chronique d'un été (1961) 184–5

Chung, Leslie 306–7

Chunguang Zhaxie (1997) 306–7

Chuvelov, Ivan 46–7

Chuvelyov, V. 46–7

Chytilová, Vera 200–1

Cimino, Michael 114–15

Cintra, Luis Miguel 228–9

Cissé, Souleymane 298–9

Citizen Kane (1941) 66–7

Clair, Nadège 222–3

Clarke, Alan 270–1

Clerks (1984) 138–9

Close-Up (1989) 300–1

Cobb, Lee J. 80–1

Cobo, Roberto 286–7

Colin, Grégoire 242–3

Colman, Ronald 40–1

Comingore, Dorothy 66–7

Congmei, Yuan 278–9

Constantine, Eddie 196–7

Cooper, Gary 54–5, 80–1

Cooper, Merian C. 56–7

Cooper, Miriam 28–9

Coppola, Francis Ford 100–1

Corduner, Allan 274–5

Corey, Isabelle 170–1

Corey, Wendell 76–7

Cotten, Joseph 66–7

Cotton, Joseph 256–7

Courcet, Richard 242–3

Cowper-Cowper, Mrs 40–1

Crac! (1980) 328–9

Craig, Wendy 260–1

Crichton, Charles 258–9

Cronenberg, David 122–3

Cruise, Tom 146–7

Crux, Andrès José 202–3

Cumming, Alan 146–7

Cunningham, Neil 266–7

Cuny, Alain 174–5

Curtis, Jackie 204–5

Curtis, Ken 140–1

Cybulski, Zbigniew 182–3

D

Dagover, Lili 32–3

Daiba, Gaoba 296–7

Daijiga Umule Pajinnal (1996) 304–5

Daisies (1966) 200–1

Dale, Grover 198–9

Daniels, Phil 270–1

Daoma Zei (1986) 296–7

Darrieux, Danièle 168–9, 198–9

Darro, Frankie 318–19

Das Cabinet des Dr Caligari (1920) 32–3

Daumery, Carrie 40–1

Davalos, Dick 78–9

David, Feliciano 160–1

David, Mario 188–9

Davis, Geena 136–7

Davis, Ossie 130–1

Davoli, Ninetto 202–3

Davor, Alexsei 46–7

The Day a Pig Fell into the Well (1996) 304–5

de Freitas, Manuela 226–7

de Havilland, Olivia 60–1

de Medeiros, Inês 226–7

De Niro, Robert 102–3, 114–15, 118–19, 268–9

de Sica, Vittorio 168–9

Dean, James 78–9

Debucourt, Jean 168–9

Dee, Ruby 130–1

The Deer Hunter (1978) 114–15

Delahaye, Michel 196–7

Delannoy, Henri 24–5

Delon, Alain 192–3

Delpy, Julie 234–5

Delubac, Jaqueline 156–7

Demy, Jaques 198–9

Deneuve, Catherine 198–9

Denis, Claire 242–3

Depierre 25

Deplanche, Phillippe 222–3

Dereau, Rosine 156–7

Derepp, Claude 222–3

Dern, Laura 128–9

Deutsch, Ernst 256–7

Dickerson, George 128–9

Dietrich, Marlene 54–5

Dimensions of Dialogue (1982) 330–1

Do The Right Thing (1989) 130–1

Dodson, Betty 204–5

La Dolce Vita (1960) 174–5

Doller, Mikhail 46–7

Dombasle, Arielle 210–11

Donat, Robert 246–7, 248–9

Dör, Gloria 214–15

Doria, Diogo 228–9

Dorleac, Francoise 198–9

Drahota, Andrea 206–7

The Draughtsman's Contract (1982) 266–7

Dravic, Milena 204–5

Dreyer, Carl Theodor 48–9, 152–3

Dreyfuss, Richard 104–5

Dubois, Marie 186–7

Duchesne, Roger 156–7, 170–1

Dunaway, Faye 92–3

Dunbar, Helen 40–1

Dunne, Irene 58–9

Duran, Michael 154–5

Durgan, Thomas A. 312–13

Duryea, Dan 68–9

Dussollier, André 210–11

Duvall, Robert 100–1

Duvall, Shelley 106–7, 110–11

Dvorsky, Peter 122–3

Dyall, Valentine 250–1

d'Yd, Jean 48–9

E

Earth (1995) 240–1

East of Eden (1955) 78–9

Eastwood, Clint 108–9, 116–17

The Eclipse (1962) 192–3

Edson, Richard 124–5

Eisenstein, Sergei 36–7

Ekberg, Anita 174–5

El Sol del Membrillo (1991) 232–3

Elejalde, Karra 240–1

Elko, Matsuda 290–1

The Enchanted Desna (1970) 178–9

The End of St Petersburg (1927) 46–7

The Enigma of Kaspar Hauser (1974) 214–15

Epstein, Brian 262–3

Ergün, Halil 294–5

Erice, Victor 232–3

Esmond, Carl 68–9

Esposito, Giancarlo 130–1

Etcheverry, Michel 210–11

Eungkyung, Lee 304–5

Eunsook, Cho 304–5

Europa (1991) 230–1

Eyes Wide Shut (1999) 146–7

Eyrand, Marc 210–11

F

Fabrizi, Aldo 164–5

Falconetti, Gérard 210–11

Falconetti, Renée 48–9

Farasmand, Hossain 300–1

Farley, Jim 42–3

Fast Times at Ridgemont High (1982) 120–1

Feder, Frédérique 234–5

Feher, Friedrich 32–3

Feist, Henry 164–5

Fellini, Federico 174–5

Fernandes, Nascimento 160–1

Feuillade, Louis 30–1

Field, Todd 146–7

Fielding, Marjorie 258–9

Fisher, Carrie 112–13

Five Easy Pieces (1970) 96–7

Flagg, Fannie 96–7

Flamant, George 162–3

Fleischer, Dave 314–15

Fleming, Victor 60–1

Ford, Harrison 112–13

Fox, James 260–1, 264–5

Frankenheimer, John 90–1

Fraser, Hugh 266–7

Freindlikh, Alissa 218–19

Friedman, Peter 144–5

Fröhlich, Gustav 44–5

Fuentes, Alma Delia 286–7

Fuji, Hiroko 290–1

Fuji Tatsuya 290–1

Furneaux, Yvonne 174–5

G

Gable, Clark 60–1

Gallagher, Peter 132–3

Gamboa-Mendoza, Lily 288–9

Gance, Abel 162–3

Garcia-Ville, Luce 190–1

Garland, Judy 70–1

Garrot, André 170–1

Gates, Emma 140–1

Gates, William 140–1

Gatlif, Tony 236–7

Gaumont, Léon 30–1

Gauthier, Vincent 224–5

Gazzara, Ben 82–3

The General (1927) 42–3

George, Chief Dan 108–9

George, Heinrich 44–5

Georgoulis, Aliki 216–17

Gertie the Dinosaur (1914) 312–13

Ghigliotti, Marilyn 138–9

Gilliam, Terry 268–9

Girotti, Massimo 202–3

Gish, Lillian 28–9

Gleason, Jackie 88–9

Glenn, Scott 106–7

Godard, Jean-Luc 196–7, 220–1

The Godfather (1972) 100–1

Godfrey, Nancy 204–5

Gold, Louise 270–1

The Gold Rush (1925) 38–9

Goldblum, Jeff 106–7

Gomes, Carlos 228–9

Gómez, Carmelo 240–1

Gomorov, Mikhail 36–7

Goncharov, Vladimir 178–9

Gone With the Wind (1939) 60–1

Gören, Serif 294–5

Goring, Marius 254–5

Grahame, Gloria 74–5

Gran, Enrique 232–3

Granach, Alexander 34–5

Grant, Cary 58–9, 64–5

Grant, David 266–7

Gray, Lorraine 104–5

Gray, Sally 252–3

Green, Marika 172–3

The Green Ray (1986) 224–5

Greenaway, Peter 266–7

Gregson, John 258–9

Grey, Philippe 162–3

Griffith, D. W. 28–9

Grinko, Nikolai 218–19

Grüngers, Gustaf 150–1

Guilherme, Miguel 228–9

Guillard, Jean-Bernard 222–3

Guinness, Alec 112–13, 258–9

Guisol, Henri 162–3

Guitry, Sacha 156–7

Güney, Yilmaz 294–5

H

Hackman, Gene 92–3

Hale, Georgia 38–9

Hamil, Mark 112–13

Hamilton, Murray 104–5

Hanks, Tom 336–7

Happy Together (1997) 306–7

A Hard Day's Night (1964)
   262–3

Harris, Julie 78–9

Harry, Deborah 122–3

Harvey, Laurence 90–1

Harvey, Rodney 134–5

Hawks, Howard 64–5

Hayden, Sterling 100–1

Haynes, Todd 144–5

Heckerling, Amy 120–1

Hee, Pang 292–3

Helm, Brigitte 44–5

Helmond, Katherine 268–9

Henn, Carrie 126–7

Henriksen, Lance 126–7

Hepburn, Audrey 258–9

Herrand, Marcel 166–7

Herrmann, Fernand 30–1

Herzog, Werner 214–15

Hieronimko, Jan 152–3

Higgins, Anthony 266–7

Hill, David 266–7

His Girl Friday (1940) 64–5

Hitchcock, Alfred 76–7, 86–7,
   248–9

Höbiger, Paul 256–7

Holden, William 94–5

Holloway, Stanley 250–1, 258–9

Holm, Ian 268–9

Hongmei, Zhang 284–5

Hoop Dreams (1994) 140–1

Hopper, Dennis 128–9

Horse Thief (1986) 296–7

Hoskins, Bob 268–9

Howard, Leslie 60–1

Howard, Trevor 250–1, 252–3,
   256–7

Hu, King 276–7

Hui, Pang 292–3

Humanity and Paper Balloons
   (1937) 280–1

Huppert, Isabelle 220–1

The Hustler (1961) 88–9

Hyde-White, Wilfred 256–7

I

I Was Born, But ... (1932) 50–1

Igawa, Hisashi 302–3

Iguchi, Takahito 302–3

Iizuka, Minoru 302–3

In a Lonely Place (1950) 74–5

In the Realm of the Senses
   (1976) 290–1

Inda, Estela 286–7

Ingeborg Holm (1913) 26–7

Ishida, Yuriko 302–3

It's a Wonderful Life (1946) 72–3

Ivana, Karbanova 200–1

J

Jackson, Samuel L. 142–3

Jacob, Irène 234–5

Jagger, Mick 264–5

Jambrina, Francisco 286–7

Jamco, Jayang 296–7

James, Sid 258–9

James, Steve 140–1

Jancsó, Miklós 206–7

Järegård, Ernst-Hugo 230–1

Jarman, Derek 272–3

Jarmusch, Jim 124–5

Jason Leigh, Jennifer 120–1

Jaws (1975) 104–5

*Jeder für sich und Gott gegen
   alle* (1974) 214–15

Jensen, Henning 230–1

Jiji, Dan 296–7

Jinsung, Park 304–5

Joano, Clitilde 188–9

Johnson, Ben 94–5, 98–9

Johnson, Celia 250–1

Jones, Chuck 324–5

Jones, Griffith 252–3

Jonze, Spike 116–17

3–4x Jugatsu (1932) 302–3

Junkin, John 262–3

K

Kaidanovsky, Aleksandr 218–19

Kakuko, Mori 282–3

Kane, Carol 110–11

Kané, Issiaka 298–9

Kanemon, Nakamura 280–1

Kar-Wai, Wong 306–7

Karina, Anna 196–7

Kassa, Marta Jafesse 242–3

Kassagi 172–3

Kaurismäki, Aki 238–9

Kazan, Elia 78–9

Keaton, Buster 42–3

Keaton, Diane 100–1, 110–11

Keaton, Jim 42–3

Keitel, Harvey 102–3, 136–7,
   142–3

Kelly, Gene 198–9

Kelly, Grace 76–7

Ki-Jong-Su 292–3

Kiarostami, Abbas 300–1

Kidman, Nicole 146–7

Kier, Udo 134–5, 230–1

Kieślowski, Krysztof 234–5

King Kong (1933) 56–7

Kiriyenko, Zinaida 178–9

Kitano, Takeshi 302–3

Klein-Rogge, Rudolph 44–5

Klusák, Jan 200–1

Kobiela, Bogumil 182–3

Kojufita, Seiichi 50–1

Kokichi, Takada 282–3

Koloper, Jagoda 204–5

Konyets Sankt-Peterburga (1927)
   46–7

Korda, Alexander 246–7

Koronel, Hilda 288–9

Kotamanidou, Eva 216–17

Koudria, Georges 154–5

Krauss, Werner 32–3

Kryuchkov, Nikolai 158–9

Krzyzewska, Ewa 182–3

Kubrick, Stanley 146–7

Kumarov, Sergei 46–7

Kupferberg, Tuli 204–5

Kurosawa, Akira 276–7

Kuzmina, Yelena 158–9

Kwon-Taek, Im 292–3

L

Labourier, Dominique 208–9

Lacey, Catherine 260–1

Ladengast, Walter 214–15

Lady Windermere's Fan
   (1925) 40–1

Lafont, Bernadette 188–9

Lambert, Anne Louise 266–7

Lanchester, Elsa 246–7

Landgut, Inge 150–1

Lang, Fritz 44–5, 68–9, 150–1

Lange, Hope 128–9

L'Année dernière à Marienbad (1961) 190–1

Lansbury, Angela 90–1

Laputa, The Flying Island (1986) 332–3

L'Arrivee d'un train en gare de La Ciotat (1895) 23

Lassalle, Martin 172–3

Lasseter, John 336–7

The Last Picture Show (1971) 98–9

Last Year in Marienbad (1961) 190–1

Latcho Drom (1993) 236–7

Laudry, Gerard 162–3

Laughton, Charles 246–7

Laurie, John 248–9

Laurie, Piper 88–9

Lavant, Denis 242–3

The Lavender Hill Mob (1951) 258–9

Lazano, Margarita 176–7

le Bihan, Samuel 234–5

Le Marchand, Lucienne 162–3

Le Rayon vert (1986) 224–5

Leachman, Cloris 98–9

Lean, David 250–1

L'Eclisse (1962) 192–3

Lecomte, Géo 162–3

Lee, Bernard 256–7

Lee, Spike 130–1

Leigh, Janet 86–7, 90–1

Leigh, Jennifer Jason 120–1

Leigh, Mike 274–5

Leigh, Vivien 60–1

Les Bonnes Femmes (1960) 188–9

Les Demoiselles de Rochefort (1967) 198–9

Les Enfants du paradis (1945) 166–7

Les Trois couronnes du matelot (1983) 222–3

Les Vampires (1915-16) 30–1

Lester, Richard 262–3

Leung, Tony 306–7

Lévesque, Marcel 30–1

Lewis, Ralph 28–9

Leymarie, Pierre 172–3

Lili, Li 278–9

Lindgren, Aron 26–7

Lingford, Ruth 338–9

Lingyu, Ruan 278–9

Linhölm, Erik 26–7

Little Toys (1933) 278–9

Locke, Sandra 108–9

London, Julie 80–1

Loos, Theodore 44–5, 150–1

Lopes, António S. 228–9

López, Antonio 232–3

Lorit, Jean-Pierre 234–5

Lorre, Peter 150–1

Los Olvidados (1950) 286–7

Losey, Joseph 260–1

Lovejoy, Frank 74–5

Lubitsch, Ernst 40–1, 62–3

Lucas, George 112–13

Lucas, Luís 228–9

Luchini, Fabrice 210–11

Lumière, Auguste 22

Lumière, Louis 22–3

Lurie, John 124–5

Luske, Hamilton 318–19

Lynch, David 128–9

Lyon, Lisa 222–3

Lytell, Bert 40–1

M

M (1931) 150–1

McAvoy, May 40–1

McCardell, Roy L. 312–13

McCary, Leo 58–9

McCay, Winsor 312–13

McDaniel, Hattie 60–1

MacDonald, Christopher 136–7

MacDowell, Andie 132–3

Mack, Marion 42–3

McKinney, Bill 108–9

MacLachlan, Kyle 128–9

McLaren, Norman 322–3

McManus, George 312–13

Madame de (1953) 168–9

Madaras, József 206–7

Madsen, Michael 136–7

Magee, Patrick 260–1

Maghenzani, Giuseppe 194–5

Magnani, Anna 164–5

Makavejev, Dusan 204–5

Makhmalbaf, Mohsen 300–1

Man of the West (1958) 80–1

The Manchurian Candidate (1962) 90–1

Mandala (1981) 292–3

Mandel, Rena 152–3

Mangano, Silvana 202–3

Manila: In the Claws of Neon (1975) 288–9

Mann, Anthony 80–1

Mannheim, Lucie 248–9

Mansard, Claude 186–7

Manville, Lesley 274–5

Mark, Erik 230–1

Marsh, Mae 28–9

Masahiko, Ono 320–3

Massey, Raymond 78–9

Massine, Leonid 254–5

Mastroianni, Marcello 174–5

Mathé, Edouard 30–1

Matos, Fernanda 160–1

Matsuda, Eiko 290–1

Mayhew, Peter 112–13

Maynila, Sa Mga Kuko Ng Liwang (1975) 288–9

Mean Streets (1973) 102–3

Medem, Julio 240–1

Meet Me in St Louis (1944) 70–1

Még Kér a Nép (1971) 206–7

Mejia, Alfonso 286–7

Méliès, Georges 24–5

Melville, Jean-Pierre 170–1

Menjou, Adolph 54–5

Merrall, Mary 252–3

Metropolis (1927) 44–5

Mewes, Jason 138–9

Michi, Maria 164–5

Midgette, Allen 194–5

Miest Kinooperatora (1911) 310–11

Miles, Sarah 260–1

Miles, Vera 86–7

Milland, Ray 68–9

Miller, Seton I. 68–9

The Ministry of Fear (1944) 68–9

Minnelli, Vincente 70–1

Minoru, Iizuka 'Dankan' 302–3

Mira, Brigitte 214–15

Miyazaki, Hayao 332–3

Mizo, Kenji 282–3

Modot, Gaston 166–7

Monteiro, João César 226–7

Moo-Song, Chun 292–3

Moore, Julianne 144–5

Morandini, Morando 194–5

Moreno, Marguerite 156–7

Moreno, Maria 232–3

Morgan, Frank 62–3

Mori, Kakuko 282–3

Moriarty, Cathy 118–19

Morin, Edgar 184–5

Morocco (1930) 54–5

Morton, Clive 258–9

Mother (1926) 46–7

Moznosti Dialogu (1982) 330–1

Mu, Fei 284–5

Murnau, F. W. 34–5

Murphy, Michael 106–7

Murray, Tom 38–9

Musäus, Hans 214–15

Musidora 30–1

Musong, Chun 292–3

My Own Private Idaho (1991) 134–5

N

Nakajima, Aoi 290–1

Namayeh Nazdik (1989) 300–1

Nao, ou a vã gloria de mandar (1990) 228–9

Napierkowska, Stacia 30–1

Nashville (1975) 106–7

Newman, Paul 88–9

Nicholson, Jack 96–7

The Night of the Crossroads (1932) 154–5

Ninchi, Annibale 174–5

Ningen Kamifusen (1937) 280–1

No, or the Vainglory of Command (1990) 228–9

Noël, Magali 174–5

Norman, Susan 144–5

Norris, Dean 144–5

Norstein, Yuri 326–7

Nosferatu, A Symphony of Horror (1922) 34–5

Novo, Nancho 240–1

La Nuit du carrefour (1932) 154–5

Nunn, Bill 130–1

O

O Thiassos (1975) 216–17

Oates, Warren 94–5

Oberon, Merle 246–7

Obolensky, V. 46–7

O'Brian, Margaret 70–1

O'Brien, Edmond 94–5

O'Connell, Arthur 80–1

Ogier, Bulle 208–9

O'Halloran, Brian 138–9

O'Hara, Mario 288–9

Oliveira, Mañoel de 160–1, 228–9

Ono, Masahiko 302–3

Ophüls, Max 168–9

Oshima, Nagisa 290–1

Ou samovo sinevo moria (1936) 158–9

Outinen, Kati 238–9

The Outlaw Josey Wales (1976) 108–9

Ozu, Yasujiro 50–1

P

Pachis, Statos 216–17

Pacino, Al 100–1

Pagliero, Marcello 164–5

Palin, Michael 268–9

Pallenberg, Anita 264–5

Palma, Antonio 160–1

Pather Panchali (1955) 276–7

Papageno (1934) 316–17

Park, Nick 334–5

Parsons, Estelle 92–3

Pasolini, Pier Paulo 202–3

Passion (1982) 220–1

La Passion de Jeanne d'Arc (1928) 48–9

Pawlikowski, Adam 182–3

Paxton, Bill 126–7

Payne, Bruce 270–1

Peckinpah, Sam 94–5

Pedro, Armando 160–1

Pélégri, Jean 172–3

Pellonpää, Matti 238–9

Peng, Luo 278–9

Penn, Arthur 92–3

Penn, Sean 120–1

Perceval (1979) 210–11

Perez, Rosie 130–1

Performance (1970) 264–5

Perkins, Anthony 86–7

Pesci, Joe 118–19

Phoenix, River 134–5

Piccoli, Michel 220–1

Pickpocket (1959) 172–3

Pidä Huivista Kiinni, Tatjana (1994) 238–9

Pierson, Jane 154–5

Pinal, Silvia 176–7

Pinocchio (1940) 318–19

Pinter, Harold 260–1

Pisier, Marie-France 208–9

Pitoeff, Sacha 190–1

Pitt, Brad 136–7

Pleasures of War (1999) 338–9

Pollack, Sydney 146–7

Pollard, Michael J. 92–3

Popiól i Diament (1958) 182–3

La Poulette grise (1947) 322–3

Powell, Michael 254–5

Powers, Tom 312–13

Prechtel, Volker 214–15

Preminger, Otto 82–3

Pressburger, Emeric 254–5

Prima della rivoluzione (1964) 194–5

The Private Life of Henry VIII (1933) 246–7

Proval, David 102–3

Prowse, David 112–13

Pryce, Jonathan 268–9

Psycho (1960) 86–7

Pudovkin, Vsevelod 46–7

Pulp Fiction (1994) 142–3

Q

Quayle, Anna 262–3

Quentin, John 272–3

Questel, May 314–15

The Quince Tree Sun (1991) 232–3

R

Rabal, Francisco 176–7, 192–3

Rabal, Teresa 176–7

Radmilovic, Zoran 204–5

Radziwilowicz, Jerzy 220–1

Rafelson, Bob 96–7

Raging Bull (1980) 118–19

Raise the Red Lantern (1991) 276–7

Rasp, Fritz 44–5

Ratzenburger, John 336–7

Ray, Nicholas 74–5

Ray, René 252–3

Ray, Satyajit 276–7

Raymond, Cyril 250–1

Rear Window (1954) 76–7

Recollections of the Yellow House (1989) 226–7

Recordacões de Cas Amarela (1989) 226–7

Red Psalm (1971) 206–7

The Red Shoes (1948) 254–5

Reed, Carol 256–7

Reed, Donna 72–3

Reenberg, Jørgen 230–1

Reeves, Keanu 134–5

Reichert, William 134–5

Reinhold, Judge 120–1

Reiniger, Lotte 316–17

Reiser, Paul 126–7

Remick, Lee 82–3

Rémy, Albert 186–7

Renoir, Jean 154–5

Renoir, Pierre 154–5, 166–7

Resnais, Alain 190–1

Rey, Fernando 176–7

Reynolds, Marjorie 68–9

Rich, Irene 40–1

Richardson, Ian 268–9

Richardson, Marie 146–7

Richert, William 134–5

Rickles, Don 336–7

Rigzin, Tseshang 296–7

Ritter, Thelma 76–7

Rivette, Jacques 208–9

Rivière, Marie 224–5

Roberts, Tony 110–11

Robinson, Amy 102–3

Roco, Rafael 'Bembol' 288–9

Roeg, Nicolas 264–5

Rohmer, Eric 210–11, 224–5

Roma, città aperta (1945) 164–5

Romance, Viviane 162–3

La Roman d'un tricheur (1936) 156–7

Romanus, Richard 102–3

Rome, Open City (1945) 164–5

Rosen, Danny 124–5

Rossellini, Isabella 128–9

Rossellini, Roberto 164–5

Rossen, Robert 88–9

Rossington, Norman 262–3

Roth, Tim 142–3

Rouch, Jean 184–5

Ruiz, Raúl 222–3

Russell, Rosalind 64–5

Russo, James 134–5

Ryan, Robert 94–5

S

S., Bruno 214–15

Sabzian, Hossain 300–1

Sacchi, Sabina 226–7

Sadao, Yamanaka 280–1

[Safe] (1995) 144–5

Sahamoto, Takeshi 50–1

Saint-Simon, Lucille 188–9

Saito, Tatsuo 50–1

Sallis, Peter 334–5

Salo, Elina 238–9

Salon, Louis 166–7

Salvador, Lou Jr 288–9

Samojlov, Yevgeno 178–9

Sampson, Will 108–9

San Giacomo, Laura 132–3

Sanchez, Jaime 94–5

Sangare, Aoua 298–9

Sang-Soo, Hong 304–5

Sanogo, Niamanto 298–9

Santesso, Walter 174–5

Santos, Antonio 160–1

Sarandon, Susan 136–7

Sateyeva, Lyalya 158–9

Savage, John 114–15

Scal, Dolly 172–3

Scheider, Roy 104–5

Scheitz, Clemens 214–15

Schildkraut, Joseph 62–3

Schmitz, Sybille 152–3

Schnell, G. H. 34–5

Schoedsack, Ernest B. 56–7

Schreck, Max 34–5

Schröder, Greta 34–5

Schroeder, Barbet 208–9

Schultz, Maurice 48–9, 152–3

Schygulla, Hanna 220–1

Scorsese, Martin 102–3, 118–19

Scott, George C. 82–3, 88–9

Scott, Ridley 136–7

Sedmikrásky (1966) 200–1

Seigner, Louis 192–3

Semmelrogge, Willy 214–15

Seri, Meika 290–1

The Servant (1963) 260–1

Seven Samurai (1954) 276–7

sex, lies and videotape (1989) 132–3

Sezen, Serif 294–5

Seyrig, Delphine 190–1

Shannon, Johnny 264–5

Sharpsteen, Ben 318–19

Shaw, Robert 104–5, 258–9

Shaw, Vinessa 146–7

Shearer, Moira 254–5

Shepherd, Cybill 98–9

Sherbedgia, Rade 146–7

Shizue, Yamagishi 280–1

Shoot the Pianist (1960) 186–7

The Shop Around the Corner (1940) 62–3

Shotaro, Hanayagi 282–3

Sidney, Ann 264–5

Silke 240–1

Silva, Henry 90–1

Silva, Horacio 160–1

Silvain, Eugene 48–9

Simon, Michel 48–9

Simon, Paul 110–11

Sinatra, Frank 90–1

Sisé, Solomani 298–9

Sjöström, Victor 26–7

Skazka Skazok (1979) 326–7

Sloane, Everett 66–7

Smith, Charles 42–3

Smith, Kevin 138–9

Smits, Sonja 122–3

Soaves, Antonio 160–1

Soderbergh, Steven 132–3

Solnteseva, Vera 178–9

Solonitsyn, Anatoli 218–19

Songki, Ahn 292–3

Spader, James 132–3

Spall, Timothy 274–5

Spielberg, Steven 104–5

Spinetti, Victor 262–3

Spoonauer, Lisa 138–9

Spring in a Small Town (1948) 284–5

Stalker (1979) 218–19

Stamp, Terence 202–3

Stranger Than Paradise (1984) 124–5

Star Wars (1977) 112–13

Starewich, Ladislaw 310–11

Stark, Cecilia 124–5

Stein, Franz 150–1

Stewart, James 62–3, 72–3, 76–7, 82–3

Stockwell, Dean 128–9

The Story of a Cheat (1936) 156–7

Streep, Meryl 114–15

Suárez, Emma 240–1

Subor, Michel 242–3

Sugawara, Hideo 50–1

Sukezo, Suketakaya 280–1

Sukowa, Barbara 230–1

Sullivan, Margaret 62–3

Suzman, Janet 266–7

Svankmajer, Jan 330–1

Svanshenko, Semyon 158–9

Sverdlin, Lev 158–9

Swain, Mack 38–9

Swinton, Tilda 272–3

Szábó, Laszló 196–7, 220–1

T

Taiji, Tonoyama 290–1

Takeshi, 'Beat' 302–3

Take Care of Your Scarf, Tatjana (1994) 238–9

Tale of the Late Chrysanthemums (1939) 282–3

Tale of Tales (1979) 326–7

Tamiroff, Akim 196–7

Tarantino, Quentin 142–3

Tarkovsky, Andrei 218–19

Tatsuya, Fuji 290–1

Tearle, Godfrey 248–9

Teorema (1968) 202–3

Terminator 2 (1991) 116–17

Terry, Nigel 272–3

Thelma and Louise (1991) 136–7

Theorem (1968) 202–3

They Made Me A Fugitive (1947) 252–3

The Third Man (1949) 256–7

Three Colours: Red (1994) 234–5

Three Crowns of the Sailor (1983) 222–3

Thurman, Uma 142–3

Tierra (1995) 240–1

Tirez sur le pianiste (1960) 186–7

To Sleep with Anger (1990) 116–17

Tomlinson, Lily 106–7

Tonoyama, Taiji 290–1

Topsy Turvy (1999) 274–5

A Touch of Zen (1969–71) 276–7

Toy Story (1995) 336–7

The Travelling Players (1975) 216–17

Travers, Henry 72–3

Travolta, John 142–3

Trintignant, Jean-Louis 234–5

A Trip to the Moon (1902) 24–5

Trois couleurs: rouge (1994) 234–5

Troupe, Tom 134–5

Truffaut, François 186–7

Turturro, John 130–1

Twardowski, Hans Heinz von 32–3

Tykkläinen, Kirsi 238–9

U

Uisung, Kim 304–5

Unforgiven (1992) 116–17

Une Voyage dans la lune (1902) 24–5

V

Valentine, Anthony 264–5

Vali, Aida 256–7

Valtonen, Mato 238–9

Vampyr (1932) 152–3

Van Fleet, Jo 78–9

Van Sant, Gus 134–5

Varney, Jim 336–7

Vassilion, Maria 216–17

Vautier, Elmire 156–7

Vawter, Ron 132–3

Veidt, Conrad 32–3

La Venus aveugle (1943) 162–3

Vernon, Howard 170–1, 196–7

Vernon, John 108–9

Videodrome (1982) 122–3

Vincent, Frank 118–19

Viridiana (1961) 176–7

Vitoldi, Beatrice 36–7

Vitti, Monica 192–3

von Sternberg, Josef 54–5

von Trier, Lars 230–1

Vroom, Frederick 42–3

W

Wajda, Andrzej 182–3

Walbrook, Anton 254–5

Walken, Cristopher 114–15

Walston, Ray 120–1

Walthall, Henry B. 28–9

Wangenheim, Gustav von 34–5

Weaver, Sigourney 126–7

Wei, Li 284–5

Wei, Wei 284–5

Welles, Orson 66–7, 256–7

Wernicke, Otto 150–1

West, Juliet 152–3

What's Opera, Doc? (1957) 324–5

Wiazemsky, Anne 202–3

Widmann, Ellen 150–1

Wiene, Robert 32–3

The Wild Bunch (1969) 94–5

Wilder, Gene 92–3

Willis, Bruce 142–3

Winfried, Winna 154–5

Woods, James 122–3

WR – Mysteries of the Organism (1971) 204–5

Wray, Fay 56–7

The Wrong Trousers (1993) 334–5

X

Xiao Cheng Zhi Chun (1948) 284–5

Xiao Wanyi (1933) 278–9

Y

Yeelen (1987) 298–9

Yimou, Zhang 276–7

Yol (1982) 294–5

Yoshikawa, Mitsuko 50–1

The Young and the Damned (1950) 286–7

The Young Girls of Rochefort (1967) 198–9

The Young Grey Hen (1947) 322–3

Yu, Shi 284–5

Yu, Sun 278–9

Z

Zabriskie, Grace 134–5

Zacharovannaya Desna 178–9

Zangiku Monogatari (1939) 282–3

Zarkadis, Petros 216–17

Zastrzezynski, Waclaw 182–3

Zhuangzhuang, Tian 296–7

Zinny, Victoria 176–7

Acknowledgements

Every effort has been made to trace copyright holders and obtain permission for the use of images. The publishers apologise for any omissions and would be pleased to make any necessary changes at subsequent printings.

Images reproduced courtesy of the The Kobal Collection and the production companies named in the individual film credits.

Additionally :
pps:12 © Disney Enterprises, Inc., 26–27 BFI, 46–47 and 50 David Boardwell, 52tl © Warner Bros., courtesy of © John Wayne Estate, 52tr Paramount, 52–53b © Warner Bros., 56–57 RKO © Warner Bros., 62–63 MGM/©Warner Bros., 66–67 RKO/© Warner Bros., 70–71 MGM/© Warner Bros., 72–73 MGM/RKO, 77 BFI, 84tl Mirisch/United Artists, 84bl Faces Music, 84–85 Warhol Films, 92–93 Tatira Miller © Warner Bros., 94–95 Warner Sevenarts/© Warner Bros, 108–109 Malpaso © Warner Bros., 115 EMI/Universal, 116tl Universal, 116tm MK2/CED/France 3/CAB/TOR/Canal, 116tr © Warner Bros., 118–119 United Artists, 137 Della/MGM/Pathe © Warner Bros., 146–147 © Warner Bros., 148tl Sashamassur, 148tr Cady/Discina, 148b Mosfilm, 158–159 and 160 BFI, 169 Franco London/Indus Film, 175 Riama/Pathe-Gray/Astor-AIP, photograph © Pierluigi Praturlon/Reporters Associati s.r.l, Rome, 176–177 Unici-S.A.-Filma 59- Gustavo, 178–179 BFI, 180tl ComptonTelki/Royal, 180tm Argos, 180tr Cino del Duca/PCE/Lyre, 180b Compton Telki, 190 Terra/Tamara/Cormoran, 204 Conoisseur Films, 212tl Danish Film Inst., Nordic Film and TV, 212tr Triumph Films/Columbia-Gaumont, 212b El Deseo/CIBY 2000, 220–221 and 222 Les Films du Losange, 227 BFI, 236 K.G. Films, Paris, 237–238 BFI, 242 Artificial Eye, 244tl Selznick/United Artists, 244tm Polygram/Channel 4/Working Title, 244tr Figment/Noel Gay/Channel 4, 244b Columbia, 253 Shipman Gloria Alliance © Warner Bros., 264–265 Goodtimes ©Warner Bros., 276tl + m Tony Rayns, 276tr TOHO, 276–277 BFI, 278–279 and 281 and 284–285 and 289 and 290–291 Tony Rayns, 292 BFI, 296–297 Tony Rayns, 298–299 and 300–301 BFI, 302–303 Artifical Eye, 305 Tony Rayns, 308t and b © Disney Enterprises,I nc, 310 and 316–317 BFI, 318–319 © Disney Enterprises, Inc, 320–321© Tex Avery/Blitzwolf © 1942 Turner Entertainment Co., A Time Warner Company. All Rights Reserved., 322–323 BFI, 324–325 © Chuck Jones Enterprises Inc./What's Opera Doc? Looney Tunes characters, names and all related indicia are the trademark of Warner Bros. © 2001. All Rights Reserved. 326–327 BFI, 329 © 1986 Societie Radio/Canada, 331 and 332 BFI, 335 © Aardman/W&G Ltd 1989, 336–337 © Disney Enterprises, Inc., 338–339 © Finetake Productions for Channel 4 and the Arts Council of England

Thanks to all at the Kobal Collection for expert advice and assistance.